Dual Allegiance

Dual Allegiance

Freud as a Modern Jew

MOSHE GRESSER

STATE UNIVERSITY OF NEW YORK PRESS

Published by
State University of New York Press, Albany

Printed in the United States of America

For information, address the State University of New York Press,
State University Plaza, Albany, NY 12246

Production by Bernadine Dawes • Marketing by Dana Yanulavich

Cover photo by Max Halberstadt, courtesy of W. E. Freud
by arrangement with Mark Paterson & Associates

Library of Congress Cataloging-in-Publication Data

Gresser, Moshe, 1951–
Dual allegiance : Freud as a modern Jew / Moshe Gresser.
p. cm.
Includes bibliographical references and index.
ISBN 0-7914-1811-1. — ISBN 0-7914-1812-X (pbk.)
1. Freud, Sigmund, 1856–1939—Religion. 2. Judaism and psychoanalysis. 3. Freud, Sigmund, 1856–1939—Correspondence. I. Title.
BF109.F74G74 1994 93-11648
CIP

1 2 3 4 5 6 7 8 9 10

For my Parents, who taught me,

and

For Ruth,

Maayan,

Tamar,

Yocheved,

and Rachel,

with hopes for the future

Table of Contents

Preface

At many points in the years I have worked on this book, people have asked me—indeed, I have asked myself—why I was writing it. The question could be either curious in a friendly sort of way, and sympathetic to the subject matter, or hostile and challenging, seeking a justification. The friendly ones seemed to assume that enough had already been written on the subject of Freud's Jewish identity—Freud was a Jew; so what? The unfriendly ones seemed to assume that the less said about such a self-hating Jew (if he really *were* a Jew, they hinted), the better. Both sorts of questions shared a common irritant: what's the point of all this? A fair question.

But there was another reaction too, one that I shared, and one that I suspect lay at the heart of my puzzled amusement at the questions, namely, eager and engaged interest (its own justification), which appeared as a kind of light in some people's faces when I mentioned my topic. I knew instinctively that the real motive for my book was related to this reaction, but I also knew that I would have to wait for an articulation of its basis.

The answers I gave initially to the questions always seemed to leave me unsatisfied, either because they were too practical—namely, that the project had been a strategy for getting out of graduate school, after ten years, and publishing it in revised form would be a kind of "closure" on that period of my life—or because somehow they didn't touch the wellspring of my interest—for example, that Freud was much more Jewish than most people realized and there was a need to correct the false image.

In fact, the reason Freud's Jewish identity engaged me so only became clear as I reflected in Jerusalem on the nature of modern Jewish identity, something given to and yet withheld from most Jews today. For it seems to me that authentic modern Jewish identity consists in a kind of positive dual allegiance, a balancing point between Jewishness (in all its forms) and general humanity (in both its political and cultural senses). I was attracted to and held by Freud's image and identity as a Jew because I sensed without even realizing it that Freud was one of the first of a new breed, the modern Jew, whose unwitting descendant I was. And it seems to me now that this descent—which is of course cultural and widespread, a function of changing social and intellectual conditions—triggered my interest, as well as that of others. That is, who I am as a Jew is bound up somehow with who Freud was as a Jew, at least in outline if not in substance. Freud's chthonic or genetic Jewishness—that is, its nonnegotiable depth—in tandem with his thoroughly modern attitude—his psychological and developmental historicity—captured my attention because I recognized its authenticity as my own hope for the realization of an infrastructure, the crystal lattice of an identity that could only take shape in the future, as I learned more. Writing the book thus became a dual search for Jewish identity, both Freud's and my own. It is my hope that reading it can encourage a personal participation in a similar shared search, whether Jewish or not.

I do not apologize for confessing so personal a motivation, since even so fine and objective a scholar as Yosef Yerushalmi in his brilliant book, *Freud's Moses: Judaism Terminable and Interminable*, finds it appropriate to conclude with a chapter addressed to Freud himself, utilizing a confessional mode and speaking as a Jew to a fellow Jew, to articulate some of his most insightful conclusions. And as he implies about the Jewishness of psychoanalysis, this particularity is what gives access to the human universals we seek: *Judaeus sum, nihil humani a me alienum puto.*[1]

I suspect that an unconscious perception of Freud as a structural paradigm for the modern Jew also triggered the hostile questions I encountered, for one recognizes a competitor. In the modern environment of free choice with regard to Jewish identity (its voluntarism), Freud's example, one freed from halachic demands while affirming a deep loyalty to the Jewish people, threatens traditional Jewish identity with a newfound autonomy. The good news is that like Freud's, that autonomy can be brought into deeper relation with the Jewish tradition in such a way that both the individual and the tradition of Jewish learning can be enriched. For Freud's "deliberately Jewish" last book, *Moses and Monotheism*, can be characterized as such in part because it is an attempt *l'shem shamayim*—for the sake of the pure truth—to probe the origins of antisemitism[2] and the nature of Jewish identity. It is in dialogue with Jewish tradition, and it seeks to add to it and even correct it. In this way, Freud is a brother Jew, and his life is a familial and familiar conversation with all of us. Freud's example is so human precisely because he is so Jewish, and it is so Jewish because he is so human.

Acknowledgments

Permission to print selected materials is gratefully acknowledged from the following sources:

Selected excerpts from *Letters of Sigmund Freud,* edited by Ernst L. Freud, © 1960 by Sigmund Freud Copyrights Ltd. Copyright Renewed. Reprinted by permission of Basic Books, a division of HarperCollins Publishers, Inc.

Selected excerpts from Mannheim, Ralph, and Hull, R. F. C., *The Correspondence between Sigmund Freud and C. G. Jung.* Copyright © by Princeton University Press. Reprinted by permission of Princeton University Press.

Freud's letter of 26 February 1930 to Chaim Koffler. Copyright © 1973, reprinted by permission of A. W. Freud et al., by arrangement with Mark Paterson & Associates.

Selection from Graf, Max, "Reminiscences of Professor Sigmund Freud," Vol. II, 1942, pp. 465–476. Reprinted by permission of *the Psychoanalytic Quarterly.*

Selection reprinted from *Jokes and Their Relation to the Unconscious* by Sigmund Freud, translated and edited by James Strachey, with the permission of W. W. Norton and Company, Inc. Copyright © by James Strachey, renewed 1980 by Alix Strachey. For U.K rights, reprinted by permission of Routledge and Kegan Paul.

Selection from Bergman, Martin S., "Moses and the Evolution of Freud's Jewish Identity," in M. Ostow, ed., *Judaism and Psychoanalysis* (1982), reprinted by permission of the author.

Selections from Rainey, Reuben M., *AAR Dissertation Series,* No. 7, "Freud as a Student of Religion: Perspectives on the Background and Development of his Thought." Reprinted by permission of Scholars Press © 1975.

Selections from Yerushalmi, Yosef, *Freud's Moses: Judaism Terminable and Interminable* (1991) Yale University Press. Reprinted by permission of Yale University Press, Copyright © 1991.

Selection from *Jewish Heritage Reader,* published by Taplinger Publishing Company, Lily Edelman, Editor. Reprinted by permission. Copyright © by B'nai B'rith Adult Jewish Education.

Selection from Meitlis, Jacob, "The Last Days of Sigmund Freud," in *The Jewish Frontier,* September 1951. Reprinted by permission.

Selections from Mendes-Flohr, Paul, *A Land of Two Rivers. The German-Jewish Vision of a New Babylon,* forthcoming from Yale University Press. By permission of the author.

Selections from Gay, Peter, *Freud: A Life for Our Time,* (1988) © W. W. Norton and Co. Reprinted by permission.

1

Introduction

This book, a study of Sigmund Freud's correspondence as it relates to his Jewish identity, presents evidence for and argues in support of two claims. First, Freud's Jewish identity, far from being a single homogenous reality, in fact develops in three stages—early (to 1907), middle (1907–23), and late (1923–39).[1] These periods are reflexes of one another, and they affect the presentation and content of Freud's psychoanalytic work. The late period in particular recapitulates the contents and patterns of the early period, after Freud passes through the maturational crucible of the "recessive" middle period.

Secondly, Freud's Jewish identity is built upon a dual allegiance, namely, to *Judentum* (Jewish ethnicity and a Freudian version of Judaism) and *Humanität*, German Enlightenment humanism and its liberal values. Freud affirms both his particularity as a Jew and his rightful participation in a vision of universal humanity. In this dual allegiance he is, I suggest, a model for *modern* Jewish identity, whose authenticity depends upon a commitment to such dual allegiance. Furthermore, such duality characterizes all responsible human identity in the modern period (that is, ours), in which all must affirm particular cultural and familial roots while simultaneously acknowledging the claim of the larger, global culture that has emerged as a consequence of mass communications, political evolution, and the catastrophic events of our century. Thus, this work is related not only to Jewish Studies, but also to the humanities.

The book will examine Sigmund Freud's correspondence between the years 1872 and 1939 (the year of his death), and on this basis describe the development of his Jewish identity, using his own words to elicit the images that expressed and shaped his development. Because Freud related to his Jewishness differently in different periods of his life, his

Jewish identity must be seen in chronological context in order to understand clearly both what he meant by what he said about it and how it was related to his work in founding, developing, and promoting psychoanalysis. Letters that provide such insight will be selected and interpreted in detail in the context of three major periods—early, middle, and late—that correspond to those into which Samuel Jaffe (University of Chicago) divides the development of Freud's psychoanalytic corpus.[2] Freud's personal and professional lives nurture and define one another in his life, and although my focus will be on Freud's correspondence, his psychoanalytic writings will be introduced at appropriate points to complement and complete the picture of his Jewish self-understanding drawn from the correspondence at a particular point in time.

Chapter 1 will introduce the topic and state the book's argument. Chapters 2, 3, and 4 will interpret Freud's correspondence in biographical and cultural context, each chapter focusing on one period in Freud's development—early (1872–1906), middle (1907–22), or late (1923–39). Chapter 2 will also include a discussion of Freud's Jewish and humanist educations to give a sense of the cultural resources in his youth from which he drew. A closing chapter will turn to a discussion of Freud's Jewish identity as a model for the dual allegiance of *modern* identity, both Jewish and human, and its implications for humanistic multicultural education.

Freud's last book, *Moses and Monotheism*, will receive special attention, on the assumption that it is Freud's mature statement of what his Jewish identity meant to him. It is then that Freud really comes to terms with the depths of his Jewish allegiance in spite of all rational considerations. Confronted with this inalienable and unavoidable depth, his own approaching death, and the political and social challenge to the value of Jewish life (i.e., the Nazis), he is driven to forge the bridge that is *Moses and Monotheism*. As Maryse Choisy writes, *Moses and Monotheism* is "Freud's deathbed confession. In it are engraved the secret hieroglyphics of the total Freud."[3] A developmental picture of the evolution of Freud's Jewish identity, based on his correspondence, can provide a key to help decipher these "hieroglyphics." That understanding, in turn, may help us as moderns to shape our own lives in a more effective way, as we search for alternatives to the "melting pot." Thus this book is a historical study of a particular Jewish identity that seeks to be of use also to contemporary thinking about modern identity and cultural in general. How can particular identity and culture best be preserved and developed in a pluralistic, free, and open society under conditions of universal citizenship, assimilation or acculturation, and secularization, in order that the resources of that particular culture can make a contribution to a larger human community made up of many such particular cultures? The question attempts to grapple with the multicultural nature of our common future in the modern world. It may be that Freud's own proud combination can offer us guidance, at least in a formal sense, in confronting this difficult question.

The Division of Freud's Psychoanalytic Corpus in Relation to His Jewish Identity

Reference has been made to Samuel Jaffe's division of Freud's psychoanalytic corpus into three periods as a framework for examining Freud's Jewish identity based on his correspondence, so a brief exposition will be helpful at this point. Jaffe sees the first period of Freud's development of psychoanalysis (1895–1906) as devoted to the development of the tools of psychoanalytic interpretation. Psychological "texts," such as the dream, symptom, witticism, and parapraxis, are analyzed for the insights they provide into the contents and workings of the human mind, especially its unconscious depths. In this way, Freud developed his techniques of interpretation. In such works as *The Interpretation of Dreams* (1900), *The Psychopathology of Everyday Life* (1901), and *Wit and Its Relation to the Unconscious* (1905), Freud explored these human phenomena and developed concepts and methods for interpreting them in order to found his science (*Wissenschaft*) of psychoanalysis. During this period, he is also actively involved in the Vienna B'nai B'rith, after the death of his father, and the consolidation of his Jewish identity parallels the consolidation of psychoanalysis as a "knowledge-craft" on its own terms.

The second period (1907–23) saw the application of these interpretive tools to larger psychoanalytic problems, such as case history and metapsychology. In this period, Freud wrote about the "Rat Man" (1909),[4] "Little Hans" (1909),[5] the "Wolf Man" (1918),[6] and the Schreber case (1911),[7] demonstrating the usefulness of his method for understanding neurosis and working for a cure. But he also began to develop the deeper theoretical infrastructure of psychoanalysis and its method, even revising his picture of the mind, as in *The Ego and the Id* (1923), and moving beyond his own earlier formulations into bold speculations about the nature of the human psyche, as in *Beyond the Pleasure Principle* (1920). During this period, too, Freud's Jewish identity receded behind the advance of a universal psychoanalytic science. Secure in his Jewishness, Freud subordinated it to larger concerns.

The third period (1923–39) involved Freud in more general problems of human culture, with special attention, significantly, to religion.

Such works as *The Future of an Illusion* (1927), *Civilization and Its Discontents* (1930), *New Introductory Lectures* (1933), and *Moses and Monotheism* (1939), indicate that Freud had moved on to consider the wider implications of his discoveries, and that he considered them profound. *Totem and Taboo,* published in 1913–14, anticipates this period in its subject matter, but the book is probably best understood as part of the split in the psychoanalytic movement, Freud making clear his difference from Jung and the Gentile Swiss in response to their "heresy." It may therefore be considered a first intellectual catalyst, whose gestation culminates in Freud's return to Jewish roots. His discovery of his cancer in 1923 was the major personal, existential catalyst for this return, I suggest, when the prospect of his own death and the rise of Nazism lead him to reconsider what it all means. It is natural therefore that this period culminates in a major exploration of what a Jew is, as he tells Arnold Zweig, "how the Jew has come to acquire the character he has." Freud's answer is *Moses and Monotheism.*

These three periods actually follow Freud's own descriptions in his *Autobiography* (1925). With reference to the time Jaffe designates as the third period, in particular, Freud writes in a 1935 supplement to this work,

> Threads which in the course of my development had become intertangled have now begun to separate; interests which I had acquired in the later part of my life have receded, while the older and original ones have become prominent once more.[8]

He speaks of having entered a "phase of regressive development,"[9] having "returned to the cultural problems which had fascinated me long before, when I was a youth scarcely old enough for thinking."[10] He refers to the beginning of this interest "at the climax of my psycho-analytic work," when he wrote *Totem and Taboo* "in order to investigate the origins of religion and morality," and he says that this work was carried a stage further in *The Future of an Illusion* and *Civilization and Its Discontents. Moses and Monotheism* had not been published yet, but Freud refers to his new formula for religion, contained nowhere else, that he says does "better justice to it," namely, that the truth of religion is not a "material" (*reale*) truth but a historical one.[11]

Thus Freud himself supports the idea that the key to his later interests is to be found in his early life. Freud is speaking in his *Autobiography* about his professional work, but I will take his title seriously and extend the insight to his personal "work" as well (they are interconnected), namely, the development of his Jewish identity.

This periodization also explains Freud's focus on religion in the late period, when he becomes concerned again with his Jewish identity. By 1907, according to Jaffe, Freud had vindicated as a "text" all the elements of Jewish identity vilified in antisemitic propaganda, *except* religion: the dream, *Witz* or the joke, the slip, the symptom, neurosis, and sexuality. Each was shown to give meaningful and universal access to humanity, to truth about the mind, even to *Humanität*, in the recognition of psychological kinship. Rather than being meaningless nonsense and elements of Jewish shame, these phenomena, treated like texts to be carefully interpreted, were shown to be meaningful and so valuable, even to non-Jews.

All except religion. In his 1907 article, "Obsessive Acts and Religious Practices,"[12] Freud thinks of religion as consisting in practices and rites, rather than belief or experience. Thus, even though he may have been thinking of the ceremonial practices of Viennese Catholicism, his conception of religion could equally apply to Judaism, with its emphasis on deed over creed or inner experience. So instead of vindicating Jewish religion (certainly an antisemitic target), by implication he condemns it as an obsessive, neurotic ceremonial, devoid of positive meaning in itself, and furthermore, as unhealthy and infantile. When it comes to Jewish religion, Freud seems to agree with the antisemites.

Therefore, when faced with death after 1923, Freud must return to vindicate Jewish religion. True, he does not vindicate Jewish ritual or its theism. But he finds that religion contains if not a "material" truth, at least a historical one. And when Freud applies this formula to Judaism (from whose history he seems to have derived it, when he was writing *Moses and Monotheism*), he finds that the historical truth of Judaism shows that it is the bearer of the finest flower of mankind, namely, the psychological capacity for instinctual renunciation. Furthermore, this capacity is responsible for the progress of all spirituality in Western civilization. In this way, Freud reproduces his creative reaction to antisemitism from the early period, namely, a pattern of vindication, of the rescue of the Jewish people from its maligners.

An Exposition of the Argument

Before turning to the correspondence, it will be helpful to present an overview and discussion of the argument for the periodic development of Freud's Jewish identity. The argument for Freud's dual allegiance will be present throughout the book. Given that the "early" period extends to 1906, through fifty years of Freud's life, it is important to observe that the early period includes a periodicity of its own, covering as it does Freud's childhood, adolescence, and early manhood. Furthermore, Freud's lifetime periodicity recapitulates the one embedded in the early period.

The Early Period, to 1906

On the basis of the obvious pride Freud felt throughout his life in being Jewish (in spite of flourishing antisemitism in his environment),[13] it makes psychological sense to assume an original positive Jewish identification in Freud's childhood, conveyed by his parents and family. Robert Wistrich observes that Freud's personality was formed

> in an East European Jewish home and then nurtured in the semi-proletarian Leopoldstadt district of Vienna to which Freud's parents had moved in 1859 from his birthplace in Pribor (Freiberg), Moravia.[14]

Freud's mother, Amalia, who "had never been fully acculturated" and had "retained the language [i.e., Yiddish], manners, and beliefs of her native [Galician] environment,"[15] was the center of this family. Given Freud's closeness to her, she was probably the root of both his ethnic Jewish pride and the "dark emotional powers" (*dunkele Gefühlsmächte*) that Freud confessed to his B'nai B'rith brethren were at the heart of his irresistible attraction to Jews and Judaism.[16] Martin Freud described her as "emotional and untamed, full of life and vitality."[17] "She had a hunger for life and an indomitable spirit."[18]

Freud's own strength had its roots in his relation to his mother,[19] who called him "my golden Sigi." A genogram of Freud's family system shows that he was very close or fused with his mother (and his daughter Anna) and *distant* from his father.[20] Michael Molnar reports that "Freud's sense of obligation to his mother was seen by those around him as one of the fundamental traits of his character."[21] Franz Kobler suggests that Amalia's *Gefühlsleben* represented the remainder of her religious inheritance,[22] for according to Martin, "Amalia ignored Jewish feasts."[23] If Kobler is right, then Freud would have associated such life-affirming feeling with Jewish identity even in the absence of religious practice.

On the other hand, Freud's early Jewishness has a positive root in Judaism too, contrary to what is usually thought. Freud's childhood home has sometimes been described as an "enlightened" one from which religious practice was largely absent,[24] and the fact that Jakob and Amalia were married in Vienna by the liberal Chief Rabbi of Vienna, Isaac Noah Mannheimer, who was associated with the Reform movement, has been taken as evidence of an allegiance to Reform Judaism. However, Emanuel Rice has pointed out that conditions in Vienna at the time of their marriage (1855) were such that Mannheimer was the only person in Vienna empowered by the Austrian government to perform Jewish marriages, so that the Freuds' choice probably reflects their desire to have their children considered legitimate, rather than being evidence of their being Reform and/or assimilated Jews.[25] Rice argues instead that "a continued, though somewhat weakened, Orthodoxy may well have been the true situation for the Freud family."[26]

As will become clear from the correspondence, the major Jewish holidays were indeed celebrated in the Freud household while Freud was growing up, though the family was only "moderately pious," and therefore probably lax in terms of daily ritual practice. Freud's earliest Jewish education was at home with his father, when the two studied together using the German-Hebrew Philippsohn Bible. The use of this Bible indicates that intellectually Freud was free from the strictures of fundamentalist Orthodoxy and was taught an openness to modern developments. It is clear from later developments that this early Jewish learning was a positive experience, a deep root of Freud's Jewish identification to which he returns at the end of his life when seeking the essential nature of Jewish character. Therefore, although Jewish religion was practiced weakly in the Freud home, accompanied by Amalia's vitality and Jakob's learning (which as will be seen, was not inconsiderable), it too probably made a positive contribution to Freud's early Jewish identity. This positive sense of Jewishness is part of Freud's inheritance from his parents' Eastern European background, a subconscious knowledge of the goodness of being Jewish that is worth fighting for, in spite of all its hardships and faults. In any event, because the family's daily ritual observance was probably lax, Freud was able to assimilate into German society as he grew up in the 1860s, without the impediment of religious difference that Judaism's rituals underscore, and supported by a healthy pride in his Jewish heritage as a source of life and practical wisdom.

Thus I assume an original developmental positive coherence in Freud's Jewish identity, a naïve sense of the goodness and wholeness of being Jewish. This positive Jewish identity was learned in the home, in Freud's informal Jewish education at the hands of his mother and father, and later in school, from his teacher of Jewish religion, Samuel Hammerschlag, and from his mentor and collaborator, Josef Breuer.

As he grew older however, and entered the *Gymnasium,* Freud would have been taught the humanist, German Enlightenment ethic of *Bildung*, namely, the "self-cultivation of one's intellectual and moral faculties through a study of literature and philosophy, and the refinement of one's aesthetic sensibilities through the arts and music."[27] Such an education would have prepared him to relinquish his attachment to Jewish tradition, considered to be "ill-suited to the cognitive and axiological requirements of the modern world,"[28] in order to make possible his "citizenship in the new era—a tolerant and humane era—envisioned by the Enlightenment."[29] As Paul Mendes-Flohr points out, there existed an inner affinity between Judaism and the concept of *Bildung*,[30] so this allegiance need not have been in conflict with Freud's Jewishness, and insofar as Jakob Freud shared this humanistic ideal, it was probably not a conflict for him. Nevertheless, as will be seen, Freud's adolescence was indeed marked by a rejection of Jewish religious tradition and its practice in favor of an "enlightened" *Weltanschauung*.

This combined experience—positive *Judentum* in the home and humanistic *Bildung* in the *Gymnasium*—laid the foundation for Freud's dual allegiance in his youth, even though at first the two resources were not balanced. Still, Freud's aggressive self-assertion against antisemitism, both in the early period and throughout his life, is psychologically based not only in his feeling of Jewish self-worth and Jewish pride, in spite of Jewish marginality, but also in his humanist patrimony, and Freud's sense of his legitimate citizenship in a cosmopolitan culture based on the Enlightenment ethic of *Bildung*.[31] Freud retains this dual core to his Jewish identity to the end of his days: the tree grows as the twig is bent.

Born 6 May 1856, Freud grew up in the period of Austrian liberalism (roughly the 1860s). Austrian society seemed to be welcoming the participation and contributions of its Jewish citizens, assuming that they assimilated to the dominant German Enlightenment culture. Freud mentions the enthusiasm and "cheerful hopes" he felt as a Jew for politics during this period, when "every industrious Jewish schoolboy carried a Cabinet Minister's portfolio in his satchel."[32] Furthermore, when Freud was "a boy of eleven or twelve" (1867–68), an itinerant poet declared that he would probably grow up to be a cabinet minister,[33] demonstrating that it was indeed a period when Jews were perceived to be more socially acceptable, or at least upwardly mobile. But on the other hand, Freud could have expected to enter Austrian society confident of acceptance and success only insofar as he would assimilate and become "truly German." Though the ethic of *Bildung* had prepared Freud for this adaptation, it would have introduced a natural ambivalence.

Eissler describes Freud's identity at the end of his adolescence:

> Like a serpent shedding its confining, outgrown integument, the young Freud emerged from his *Matura* in a state of consolidation, and feeling estranged from his past.[34]

Thus, Freud achieved a coherent humanist allegiance and identity in his adolescence, and his Jewish identifications were placed in abeyance, their relationship to this humanist consolidation unclear. So, we can understand the atheism and mockery of religion and of Jewish tradition that we find in Freud's letters to his friends Emil Fluss and Eduard Silberstein in 1870–72, for example, as expressions of this ambivalence and of the need to distance himself from Judaism in order to find his own place in Austrian society. Such distancing represented a period of Jewish recession in the early period of the development of Freud's identity.

An important psychological catalyst for Freud's reassessment of his Jewish identity also occurred during the period of political liberalism, when Freud was "ten or twelve years old" (i.e., 1866–68). At this time he felt deeply disillusioned by the story of his father's passivity in the face of a humiliating antisemitic attack, when a Christian ordered Jakob off the pavement during his "Shabbes" stroll and knocked his *Streimel* into the mud.[35] On the one hand, Jakob's deference in not rebuking the antisemite and instead simply picking up his fur hat made Freud as a boy feel ashamed of his father and of his pusillanimous Judaism. Such embarrassment would have contributed to the feeling of estrangement to which Eissler refers. But on the other hand, Freud's own aggressive or martial response to the story, illustrated in his retelling of the event, is conceived of as a Jewish response, for he relates his association of it with

> the scene in which Hannibal's father, Hamilcar Barca, made his boy swear before the household altar to take vengeance on the Romans.[36]

In this juxtaposition of the action of the "Semitic" Hannibal's father, the young Freud forges through his response a primary characteristic of his own Jewish identity. He is, as his son Martin characterizes him, a "fighting Jew."[37] Perhaps the fact that Freud's Jewishness emerges most strongly in *defiance*, as Peter Gay observes,[38] is a legacy of this memory. However, as Wistrich says, Freud's Jewish allegiance cannot be reduced simply to "a kind of defiance."[39] It is richer in content than this reflex.

In any event, the personal authenticity and depth of Freud's aggressive Jewish response are shown by his associations in *The Interpretation of Dreams* that follow the report of this memory. If the sequence of Freud's memories and associations is arranged chronologically, the development of Freud's personality is clear. Freud says that his response to his father's story was "a transference of an already formed emotional relation onto a new object."[40] At age three, Freud fought with his nephew John (probably not for the only time), who was older by a year. "I hit him 'cause he hit me,"[41] he replied to his father. So we see that this reaction to attack, this vigorous self-defense even against stronger opponents, was learned early at home, in relation to family members, with Jews. Jewish self-defense comes naturally and un-self-consciously to Freud because it is rooted so deeply in his past.

These struggles helped implant a "martial ideal" in the younger boy's psyche. This emotional tendency led to his boyhood identification with "Jewish" soldiers, such as Massena and Hannibal. Freud tells us that as a boy he stuck identifying labels onto the backs of his wooden soldiers representing Napoleon's marshals. He identified personally with the marshal Massena, whose birthday he believed he shared, and he gave this marshal what he assumed was his Jewish name, Manasseh. That Freud attached his self-assertion to Jewish figures points to the naturalness of his Jewish identity: the vehicles of self-assertion and self-defense are Jewish, like the self. Thus Freud's early image of Jews, or at least of himself as a Jew, is that they fight, they stand up for themselves. We can understand therefore his distress and conflict at hearing of his father's "unheroic," that is, passive and deferential, conduct when his Chassidic *Streimel* was knocked into the mud by a Christian antisemite. With this background, his "martial" response seems only natural.

Freud fantasizes an oath of vengeance in response to his father's story. How could his own vengeance be carried out? Freud tells us that this event in his youth contained a power that was "still being shown in all these emotions and dreams"[42] so many years later. So when he tells us that his youthful identification with Hannibal and his longing for entering Rome symbolized "the conflict between the tenacity [*Zähigkeit*] of Jewry and the organization of the Catholic Church,"[43] may we not understand the "other passionate wishes" that he says the wish to go to Rome symbolized to include the fulfillment of the oath of vengeance, for example, by Freud's being appointed to a professorship?[44]

Freud describes his appointment in a letter to Fliess by saying, "One must look somewhere for one's salvation, and I chose the title as my savior."[45] Such language probably indicates Freud's assimilation, rather than a hidden attraction to Catholicism, as Vitz hypothesizes.[46] Given Freud's association of the Catholic church and antisemitism, Freud's professorial success can be seen as the overcoming of this adversary and the fulfillment of his fantasied oath to his father.

The prediction that Freud would grow up to be a cabinet minister (which Freud connects with his ambitiousness) and the experience of being told of his father's humiliation while holding his hand (and Freud's associated oath of vengeance) occurred roughly around the same time, during the era of Austrian liberalism. Freud's father told his humiliating story to show him "how much better things were now than they had been" in Jakob's younger days in Freiberg. Shortly before the prediction of the boy's political success, Jakob had brought home portraits of the "bourgeois ministry"—"these middle class professional men" (like Freud himself)—and, Freud tells us, "we had illuminated the house in their honor," for "there had even been some Jews among them." The family celebration must have made quite an impression on the Jewish boy, since lighting candles or lamps is a religious and festive act in Jewish tradition, marking special occasions. For Freud's Eastern European parents to have acted in this manner would have conveyed a strong feeling of Jewish triumph at successful participation in the larger culture, the fruits of Emancipation. It would certainly have given familial legitimation to liberal ideals for the future. Therefore the painful experience of his father's humiliation at just this time (as a child Freud did not perceive the old man's dignity, wisdom, and self-control) naturally produced a desire for revenge in the boy to whom antisemitism seemed such an unjust contrast to the "bourgeois ministry."

So when Freud says, "the events of that period no doubt had some bearing on the fact that up to the time shortly before I entered the University it had been my intention to study Law,"[47] it seems plausible that a ministerial career was to be Freud's chosen path to a just revenge, the full implementation of an enlightened triumph over antisemitism. However, he changed paths and chose a medical career, working in neurological research for many years (first publishing in 1877) before turning to psychology. Therefore I suggest by extension that Freud's ambitions for a professorship in neuropathology are connected with his desire for Jewish revenge for the Christian antisemitic humiliation of his father, and consequently are connected with filial piety. Note that the oath of Hannibal is sworn "before the household altar."[48] When in 1902 Freud finally achieves his "salvation" in the form of the title *Professor Extraordinarius*, after years of perceived antisemitic discrimination (whether real or not),[49] he has also fulfilled his fantasized vow to avenge his father, and in doing so he helps to consolidate his own Jewish identity towards the end of the early period, by making a peace with the past.

As mentioned above, Jaffe argues that Freud creates psychoanalysis by the "vindication" or revaluation of "texts" that were identified by antisemites as typically Jewish, such as the dream, wit, parapraxes, and neuroses such as hysteria and neurasthenia.[50] Freud reinterpreted texts that had been seen as valueless and insignificant in such a way as to show not only that they were meaningful and highly significant on their own terms, but also that they were valuable as an access to a new

Humanität and a new view of man. Freud's rescue of these "Jewish" texts is consistent with his personal response of aggressive Jewish self-defense. As he dreams Theodor Herzl tells him, "Something must be done to save the Jewish people."[51] Psychoanalysis is for Freud at this time that "something," and it will save them by contributing to the creation of a new cultural whole.[52]

But after his *matura*, estranged from and embarrassed by Judaism, Freud went beyond his father's passivity by assimilating to German nationalism when he entered the University of Vienna in the autumn of 1873. It was in that first year that he joined the *Leseverein der deutschen Studenten Weins*, "a radical student society wholly committed to the German nationalist cause."[53] As is often the case in adolescence, Freud was "trying on" identities to see if they fit. How German was he? As he writes in his correspondence and in his *Autobiography*, the rise of antisemitism at the university,[54] including in the *Leseverein*, helped answer this question, for now German *Kultur* had excluded him, betraying its own Enlightenment ideals. Being Jewish seemed to exclude him from equal participation in society.

This conflict continued into the next decade as Freud sought to find a balance, with antisemitism acting as "a catalyst in Freud's growing inner affirmations of Jewish identity during the mid-1880s."[55] In fact, Freud's vigorous self-defenses against antisemitism at that time may have been part of his attempt to resolve his ambivalence. He defended his Jewishness against any implication that it made him inferior.[56] Still, he describes his heart in a letter to Minna Bernays in 1885 as "German provincial."[57] At the same time, in 1882 he can write the "Nathan" letter (see chapter 2), in which his identification with Jewish tradition (even if qualified by humanist allegiances) is clear and proud.

The death of his father (in 1896) and his subsequent self-analysis pushed Freud toward the resolution of this ambivalence. As Dennis Klein shows in his *Jewish Origins of the Psychoanalytic Movement* (1981), Freud's disillusionment with liberal assimilation after the period of antisemitism in the 1880s caused him to withdraw into Jewish self-assertion, but he did not abandon the liberal ideals of his youth. Instead he found for them a Jewish context of social support and personal expression in the Vienna B'nai B'rith. When Freud joined B'nai B'rith on 29 September 1897 (the earliest possible opportunity after his father's death in October 1896), he found that the humanist ideals of his youth could be expressed *through* his Jewish identifications. That is, his particular Jewish identity could be the vehicle for an expression of his commitment to the universal, humanist values of the Enlightenment, and perhaps *Judentum* could even be an instrument for *Bildung*.

Freud's active membership in B'nai B'rith, furthermore, contributed to the formation of a cultural expression for these liberal ideals in the psychoanalytic movement. His "vindication" of "Jewish texts" can be seen as an expression of this Jewish self-assertion in the service of liberal ideals. Finding himself relegated to the margins of society by the collapse of political liberalism and the concomitant rise in antisemitism, Freud responded to the breakdown of the coherent Jewish-humanist identity of his youth by both identifying with the humanism that minimizes Jewish difference and at the same time by proudly asserting his Jewishness as a member of the community of nations (e.g., to Giles de la Tourette in 1886).[58]

Rothman and Isenberg describe three strategies for coping with marginality: assimilation, universalism, and nationalism.[59] They argue that psychoanalysis is Freud's universalistic strategy.[60] I would go further. When Freud discovers his own marginality in adolescence and at the University of Vienna after a youth full of the confident expectation of influential participation in Austrian society, he responds with versions of the latter two strategies. Freud's humanism continues the universalistic agenda of political liberalism, whereas his identification with the Jewish people and with Zionism (though initially with a universalistic emphasis) demonstrates a nationalistic strategy. McGrath points to the complex elements of Jewish tradition, such as Freud's identification with Joseph and with Moses, that Freud was struggling with in his dreams and in his thinking at this time.[61] It is not coincidental that Jewish figures lead Freud to his dual allegiance, because in fact access to the universal is given precisely *through* the particular. Formed *in nuce* here in the early period in B'nai B'rith, this new configuration is the shape of Freud's Jewish identity, namely, the dual allegiance of a Jew committed to liberal humanist ideals.

In August and September of 1901 Freud visits Rome, overcoming a long-standing phobia that Martin Bergmann suggests is related to Freud's guilt at honoring an old enemy of the Jewish people, a symbol of Freud's disloyalty to his Jewish past.[62] Visiting Rome enabled Freud to take steps to acquire for himself in 1902 a prize he had coveted for many years, namely, the title of *Professor Extraordinarius.* In gaining this appointment, Freud repaid a debt of vengeance he felt he owed for the antisemitic insult to his father,[63] and so he cleared himself of filial guilt that could have obstructed his sense of wholeness.

This final resolution consolidated Freud's Jewish identity in a mature and confident Jewish-humanist amalgam at the end of the "early" period, after the death of his father, his active membership in the Vienna B'nai B'rith, and the publishing of the work that would create psychoanalysis. It created the psychological infrastructure for the subordination of Freud's Jewish identity to the "liberal cause" of psychoanalysis and its launching in the larger, Gentile sea in the middle period.

The collapse of political liberalism and the rise of antisemitism in Austria gave impetus during Freud's adolescence to a withdrawal of his Jewish identification with the larger society. However, it is Freud's defiant *response* to this new configuration of personal and social challenge, namely, (1) his B'nai B'rith membership and activity, (2) his pursuit of professional advancement, and (3) the founding of psychoanalysis as a self-conscious movement (i.e., the Psychological Wednesday Society), that gives a confident and coherent shape to Freud's Jewish identity at the end of the early period.

Thus, the early period of Freud's Jewish development moves from naïve identification, through ambivalent questioning and distance, to a proud commitment to a Jewishness that expresses humanitarian ideals through particular Jewish allegiance, defined in both ethnic and intellectual terms. The periodicity of Freud's Jewish development over the course of his lifetime recapitulates this pattern.

Freud's first mature consolidation of his Jewish identity enabled him in the middle period to promote the development and expansion of the psychoanalytic movement so that it became international and worldwide. During the early period, Freud married, fathered six children, experienced the death of his father, and formed a deep friendship with fellow Jewish physician Wilhelm Fliess. He also joined and played an active role in the Vienna B'nai B'rith, even helping to found a new chapter.

The social and personal support for these achievements came from fellow Jews, for Freud felt increasingly isolated from professional and academic society, which was either non-Jewish or whose Jewish character—for example, in the medical profession—he did not perceive as a support. Freud's personal social circle consisted entirely of Jews, from his lawyer to his fellow tarock card players. The roles that his teacher of Jewish religion, Samuel Hammerschlag, his Jewish colleagues Josef Breuer and Wilhelm Fliess, as well as his brethren in B'nai B'rith, played in the formation of Freud's secure Jewish identity were crucial. Thus it is in this early period that Freud is confirmed in his ethnic solidarity with other Jews—*Zusammengehörigkeit*—independently of any adherence to religious belief. Until 1906, when Jung became part of the movement (meeting Freud personally in 1907), all seventeen members of the psychoanalytic movement were Jewish. Furthermore, "the analysts were aware of their Jewishness and frequently maintained a sense of Jewish purpose and solidarity."[64] These Jewish contexts contributed to the clarity of Freud's own Jewish identity as psychoanalysis moved out into the larger culture.

It is worth noting too in this connection the Jewish elements of the series of "Rome dreams"[65] from 1897 (the year following Jakob Freud's death) that Freud in *The Interpretation of Dreams* relates *between* the "bourgeois ministry" memories and that of the walk with his father, because they illustrate not only Freud's feeling of solidarity with other Jews, but also his affection for Jewish jokes, which is another important element of his Jewish identity rooted in the early period. Two of the Rome dreams prominently feature Jewish jokes in which Freud seeks Jewish help from other Jews. As Klein remarks, "The Hannibalian conquest could not be achieved without assistance."[66]

One joke in particular serves to illustrate the "Hannibalian" tenacity Freud identifies as characteristically Jewish. The poor Jew in the joke perseveres in his determination to reach Karlsbad, in spite of being repeatedly thrown off the train, hoping his "constitution" (i.e., his Jewish nature) can endure the trip. In 1908 Freud writes to Karl Abraham, "Do not lose heart! Our ancient Jewish tenacity *[unsere altjüdische Zähigkeit]* will prove itself in the end."[67] Freud's sense of his own tenacious Jewish identity is firmly in place with this remark.

Another joke about "a confused Jew, alone and lost in a strange city, who received the kind of reassurance [in Yiddish] that only a fellow Jew could offer," shows that Freud recognized "how important the element of Jewish solidarity was in his psychological rebellion against antisemitism."[68] Since Freud had recently joined the Vienna B'nai B'rith, Klein interprets these dreams as the fulfillment of Freud's wish for Jewish fellowship.[69] In his quest for satisfaction against "Rome," Freud seeks other Jews to "show him the way."[70]

Freud often shared the pleasure of Jewish jokes with friends, and their wisdom was a consolation at critical times in his life, as will be seen in Freud's correspondence. Theodor Reik observes that

> Jewish wit was an integral part of [Freud's] universe of discourse, woven into the warp and woof of much of his thinking, a reservoir from which he draws at all times to illuminate and explain the most complex and profound of his psychological observations.[71]

Ernst Simon argues that in fact Freud presents in his book on humor, *Wit and Its Relation to the Unconscious* (1905),[72] a "theory of the Jewish soul in miniature."[73] So Freud's use of Jewish wit is not insignificant for understanding the "inner identity, the intimate familiarity of a common psychic structure," that he recognized in common with Jews. As

Bergmann says, Freud's book on *Witz* is that of "a man at home with the Jewish attitude toward life."[74] Furthermore,

> The Jewish joke, the unique creation of the Jews, requires no adherence to Judaism in any organized sense, and can, therefore, become a vehicle for the expression of feelings of solidarity for those who have retained a sense of belonging, without religious or national affiliation.[75]

Freud was just this sort of Jew, though we will have reason to explore the extent of his "religious" and "national" affiliation further. From the Fliess correspondence it is clear that Freud began collecting Jewish jokes for this book shortly after his father's death,[76] and Rcik tells us that "Freud inherited his taste for Jewish wit from his father, Jakob."[77] Telling Jewish jokes may be a way that Freud expresses an identification with his father, and so relevant for understanding the son's Jewish identity.

Significantly, evidence for Freud's early identification with Moses is also clear in *The Interpretation of Dreams:*

> someone led me to the top of a hill and showed me Rome half-shrouded in mist . . . There was more in the content of this dream than I feel prepared to detail; but the theme of "the promised land seen from afar" was obvious in it.[78]

This dream immediately precedes the ones with Jews and Jewish jokes, reinforcing the impression that the image of Moses was associated with Freud's relation to his Jewishness and his fellow Jews. As Klein notes,

> For Jews seeking to articulate a deep sense of ethical purpose [for example, righting an old injustice] and a universal vision [transcending Jewish particularity], Moses, the lawgiver and liberator of the Israelites, could serve as a supreme archetype.[79]

McGrath also points to Freud's identification with the biblical figures of Joseph and Moses in the land of Egypt as role models helping to lead Freud to a satisfying resolution of the question of his Jewish identity in a foreign culture.[80]

Thus even Freud's Moses-identity "crystallized as early as the 1890s," Klein says, that is, in our early period. It was pressed into a transformed service in the middle period; as Freud tells Jung in 1909, "If I am Moses, then you are Joshua and will take possession of the promised land of psychiatry, which I shall only be able to glimpse from afar."[81] Note the recessed Jewish role in the middle period. In the late period of course it emerged fully developed, the basis of Freud's final assessment of Jewish identity. Freud's Jewish identifications in the early period set the stage for his Jewish self-understandings and responses in the middle and late periods: *Die Urzeit gleich die Endzeit.*[82]

Freud's loyalty to his father's memory is also expressed, ironically, in his rebelliousness against his father, to which he admits through his dreams.[83] Freud relates two memories of micturition at an early age (two and seven or eight) in relation to his father, and in connection with his own ambitiousness.[84] Freud's protests against his father's doubts ("'You see I *have* come to something'") and his repeated statement that he had kept his promise to console his father (originally by replacing the bed he had wet) are linked later with the wish to avenge his father, for both reactions (protest/consolation and vow of vengeance) are based on Freud's love for and admiration of his father. The boy seeks his father's approval and admiration even as he himself seeks to admire and approve of his father. In order to fulfill his own ambitiousness, the boy must rebel against his father's authority in his angry prediction ("The boy will amount to nothing"); but in order to fulfill his vow of vengeance, he must also rebel against the authority of his father's passive example. In this way there is a "transference of an already formed emotional relation" onto a new objective. That is, Freud seeks to *win* his father's love in the wake of the micturition scenes by proving his own worth with his success, and thereby being able to console his father. He seeks to *protect* the love he feels for his father in his reaction to the antisemitic attack, by avenging the harm done to his admired image of his father. The old man can remain heroic in the son's eyes only if the dishonor done to his image is avenged.

Interestingly, as David Blatt notices, the second memory Freud has of deliberately urinating in his parents' bedroom at the age of seven or eight coincides with the time when he began to study the Bible with his father,[85] a few years before the *Streimel*-in-the-mud episode. In this light, *Moses and Monotheism* may function as Freud's further settling of accounts with his father, fulfilling his own ambition and showing Jakob that he has indeed come to something. As Freud says, "Happiness is the fulfillment of a childhood wish."

Freud's fulfillment in 1902 of his "debt" to his father completed the consolidation of his Jewish identity around values that he felt were Jewish, or at least were associated with Jews he admired, such as defiance in the name of self-worth, self-defence, solidarity, loyalty to oath, liberalism, humanism, and humor. This achievement paved the way for psychoanalysis to be released from its Jewish moorings to set sail in a larger, Gentile sea. At this point the middle period of the development of Freud's Jewish identity began. As we shall see, the Jewish achievements of the late period will similarly embody Freud's fulfilment of an "oath" or mandate from his father.

Additional psychological support for the dividing line after 1906 may be found in the fact that Freud destroyed his papers in 1907, when he moved his office from the ground floor of Bergasse 19 to the apartment opposite his family's on the second floor, expanding his own home in the process.[86] Freud had literally changed his home base. He had destroyed his papers once before, in 1885, and he wrote to Martha at that time in terms that make it clear that the destruction reflected his sense of a turning point.[87] Thus we may take the second destruction in 1907 as evidence that Freud felt he had again passed through a threshold of some kind that warranted the obliteration of the past, lest it prevent him from maturing, from "thinking himself" all over again, as he put it in 1885. His move to a new "home" reflects this sense of a turning point.

The Middle Period, 1907–22

The middle period, roughly 1907–22, is characterized by the development and expansion of psychoanalysis as a worldwide, pointedly humanistic movement, and therefore Freud the humanist seeks to place his own Jewishness, clearly defined by now in his own mind, in the background, a part of his private life. As he says, psychoanalysis must not become "a Jewish national affair."[88] Even further, as he tells his followers at the Second Psychoanalytical Congress in 1910, Jews must be satisfied with "the modest role of preparing the ground,"[89] allowing Gentiles, like Jung (whom Freud had just made president of the Vienna Psychoanalytic Society), to take the lead in presenting psychoanalysis to the world. That the ambitious Freud can make such a concession as a Jew shows a sense of security in his Jewish identity that is not easily threatened or shaken, an identity not dependent upon external recognition for its sense of worth. This recession of the Jewish character of psychoanalysis is not due to Freud's Jewish self-hatred, but rather to his secure Jewish self-confidence. It is a form of self-transcendence, a reflection of Jewish experience and teaching, and of course astute politics for the times. However, with Jung's defection, this strategy of deference to Gentiles seems to have failed, and like Christian supersessionism in seeing the "Old Testament" as a preparation for the New, it provokes a natural Jewish resentment. As Jewish and Gentile elements in the psychoanalytic movement separate "like oil and water,"[90] Freud reasserts his Jewishness, no longer content to remain in the background.

At the same time, behind the scenes in the middle period, Freud has an important encounter with the figure of Moses that has an impact on the development of his Jewish identity. In 1914 Freud writes an essay which he publishes anonymously, entitled "The *Moses* of Michelangelo."[91] In his interpretation of the statue, Freud creates for himself an image of self-restraint in the face of provocation, an ideal that he characterizes as "the highest mental achievement that is possible in a man."[92] Martin Bergmann argues that this vision forges in Freud a new understanding of his father's self-restraint in response to the antisemitic attack in Freiburg, and a new mature respect.

Bergmann sees "an intrasystemic change within Freud's own superego," in which

> a less destructive father figure is created of Freud. The new Moses who is not violent is a shade closer to Jacob Freud who also conquered his wrath in the fur cap incident.[93]

Bergmann points out that in the context of organized Jewish life, Jakob Freud's behavior was neither undignified nor cowardly, but rather noble and wise, since for the Jew the ability to control his anger was a sign of his spiritual superiority, inner dignity, and even heroism.[94] Freud's "*Moses* of Michelangelo" essay transfers this nobility of spirit to Michelangelo's version of the Hebrew leader, and in so doing Freud makes peace with his father, restoring his ideal. In altering his internal relationship with his father, Freud also opens himself to a new relationship with Jewish tradition.

Mortimer Ostow, responding to Bergmann, transfers this insight to the end of Freud's life:

> Freud finally understood at eighty-two what he had failed to understand at twelve, that is, that his father's behavior had been discreet rather than cowardly, and that when you are in a physically weak position, as the Jews in the Diaspora are, physical defiance is a poor strategy.[95]

Though in his younger days Freud made use of physical defiance, even as a Jew in the Diaspora, Ostow implies that later in life, Freud's recognition of his father's wisdom and true nobility paved the way for Freud himself to value his own Jewishness as mediated by his father. Freud found himself in 1914 in an analogous situation vis-à-vis Jung as his father had vis-à-vis the antisemitic Christian when he was a mature man. It is as though Freud had had his "hat" knocked off by Jung (let the symbolic castration not be missed). By defining his own Jewishness in terms of self-control and self-transcendent dedication, as Freud interprets Michelangelo's "Moses," Freud identifies with his father, and he is able to write *Moses and Monotheism* at the end of his life, extending his view of Moses to include the Jewish people and their history, in order to make himself whole. The development of Freud's Jewish identity is furthered by and yet is also a consequence of his work. Seeing a new Moses leads Sigmund to see a new Jewish Freud, one that will find clearer articulation in the final period. Significantly, Freud acknowledges his authorship of "The *Moses* of Michelangelo" in 1924.

The Late Period, 1923–39

The final period begins on a personal level in 1923, when Freud learns that he has cancer and his own death becomes real before him. This event triggers a return to issues of Jewish identity that parallels the psychoanalytic concern with what Freud calls the "cultural" problems, such as religion, civilization, and life and death. In addition, the resurgence of antisemitism in the 1920s and 1930s acts again as a social catalyst to trigger Freud's Jewish return.

Freud makes many statements in this period about what kind of a Jew he is (for example those to B'nai B'rith in 1926 and 1935), and his own Jewishness is more evident to him. Even his dog, Jofie, is associated in Freud's mind with his Jewishness. As Yosef Yerushalmi points out, the dog's name, pronounced in German "Yofi," sounds just like the Hebrew word meaning "beauty,"[96] and Freud corrects Arnold Zweig's mistake in 1936, to underscore his attachment: not "Zofie," but "Jo as in Jew."[97] Freud takes a growing interest as well in the Zionist movement, formally becoming, at his own request at the age of eighty (in 1936), an honorary member of "Kadimah," the student Zionist society. The late period is thus one in which Freud reasserts his Jewishness in a public way, and as such it results in a greater and more mature clarification and assessment than was possible in the early period, or during the middle period when he was not focused on the problem of his Jewish identity. As an expression of this concern with Jewish identity, and in response to Nazi threats to its survival, the final period culminates in Freud's last book, *Moses and Monotheism*. According to Freud's own description,[98] this work was generated by the problem of Jewish identity, both internal (or self-related) and external (or other-related).

Summary

Freud's correspondence, divided into three parts, will show that his Jewish identity developed over the course of his life in relation to both internal and external forces. Internally, Freud had a need for wholeness in the midst of dual commitments to Jewishness and humanism; externally, antisemitism repeatedly denied value to his life and work. Freud's Jewish identity became a strategy to respond to both these pressures.

His primary Jewish identification was familial and positive, strengthened (as will be shown) by his formal and informal Jewish education at home and at school, and supported by the humanist framework of the *Gymnasium*. This positive Jewish identity was threatened in Freud's youth both by Jakob's passive example in the face of antisemitism and by the collapse of the supportive liberal humanistic sociopolitical context of Austrian life, with its attendant assimilationist expectations. Freud eventually responded to these threats by a defiant affirmation of Jewish worth and a reassertion of liberal values, significantly in a specifically Jewish setting, the B'nai B'rith. This Jewish consolidation had its professional analogue in Freud's founding the psychoanalytic movement, which served *inter alia* as a vehicle for the expression of these Jewish-humanistic values.

Freud's success in becoming *Professor Extraordinarius* in 1902 gave him the degree of inner freedom from his past that he needed to enable him in the middle period to move psychoanalysis beyond its Jewish moorings without threatening the coherence of his own Jewish identity. At the same time, a reencounter with the image of Moses enabled him to develop below the surface a more mature relationship with his father's Jewish identity, and so too later with his own. Freud's psychoanalytic return to the issue of Jewish identity and its redefinition and reassessment at the end of his life in the late period is related both to the shock of his own mortality and to a repetition of early provocation, namely, antisemitic attack, both of which trigger a renewed identification with his father, Jakob, and an attempt to vindicate *Judentum*.

As mentioned above, the periodicity of Freud's Jewish development over the course of his lifetime recapitulates on a larger scale the pattern established in the early period. Thus the early period as a whole corresponds to Freud's early or first identification with Jewishness, expressed in stable form through his B'nai B'rith membership. The middle period corresponds to Freud's rejection of Judaism in his adolescence in favor of the assimilation of German Enlightenment humanism. Finally, the late period involves a resolution of the repressed conflict and resentment introduced by the suppression of Jewish identity in the middle period, but in a higher key, a more mature configuration or coherence than was possible at the close of the early period. At that time, Freud was satisfied with the successful vengeance he had been able to visit upon the "enemies of his people," who represented the antisemite who had attacked his father. The discharge of filial debt freed Freud to accept the liberal Jewish-humanist compromise of the B'nai B'rith and commit himself to it as a Jewish "son of the covenant."

In the late period, Freud needed something more mature than vengeance; he needed to give, to make a Jewish contribution to truth, progress, and reconciliation. He needed not to win another battle, but to make peace. *Moses and Monotheism* represents his best effort, though it is an ambivalent reconciliation. We moderns too need not to win battles against those who are different from us, but rather to build a larger whole with their help. We will see if Freud's example can point us in the right direction.

2

The Early Period

Freud's Jewish and Humanist Educations

Freud's Jewish and humanist educations are an important biographical crucible for his self-understanding, both as a Jew and as a humanist, and so their description as a context for understanding Freud's correspondence will be helpful. In addition, such a description will indicate the reservoir of Jewish knowledge and information that Freud might have drawn upon, even unconsciously, in describing himself as a Jew and in writing *Moses and Monotheism,* his final psychoanalytic self-description.

We know from his own report and from observations by others that the young Freud was an avid reader, and so to some extent he was self-taught. But both Freud's parents played an influential role in his early education. Freud's sister Anna is emphatic on the point, saying in her *Memoirs* (1930), "My mother taught him at home throughout the primary school years,"[1] and reporting elsewhere, "My father taught him privately until he entered high school."[2] Anna insists that Freud did not attend a primary or public school (*Volksschule*) before he attended the *Gymnasium,* but Freud himself in a curriculum vitae statement written in 1885 reports the following:

> I received my first instruction at home, then attended a private primary school. In the autumn of 1865 I entered the *Real- und Obergymnasium* in Leopoldstadt.[3]

So Freud's early educational influences were familial and they were strong (if we may so interpret Anna's slip).

In order to flesh out a sense of what this early home-centered education might have been like for Freud, we turn to his reported recollections. Some interpreters (e.g., Krüll, Vitz) have drawn attention to Freud's earliest memory of religious instruction at the hands of his Catholic Czech nursemaid. Freud tells Fliess that she taught him about God and hell and he in turn gave dramatic expositions before his parents on "how God conducted his affairs."[4] At age three his precociousness must have been delightful. The effect of these teachings is unclear, though when this nursemaid was later dismissed and jailed for theft, the sense of abandonment may have produced an early distrust of Christianity and a dislike for its beliefs and ceremonies.[5] Admittedly, some have seen in this early experience the root of an unconscious *attraction* to Catholicism.[6]

Paul Vitz details Freud's admiration for Christian art (both paintings and sculpture), Christian churches (e.g., Notre Dame in Paris or the Cathedral in Rome), ambivalent Christian literature (e.g., C. F. Meyer), and his attraction to/obsession with Rome over a twenty-year period (1882–1902) during Freud's early maturity.[7] Vitz interprets this involvement in Christian culture during a "midlife crisis" as an attempt to recover his lost Catholic nanny, and he moves from that emotional nostalgia to argue for an unconscious attraction on Freud's part to Christian religion and its themes (rebirth, resurrection, even the Devil) and to conversion.[8] However, Vitz fails to distinguish between the fulfillment of a childhood longing for reunion with his nanny, which Freud may have felt unconsciously in Rome, and his conscious rejection of Christian religion, evidence for which is abundant and serious. Additionally, Freud's humanism enables him to enjoy the human struggle for truth, beauty, and wisdom in Christians (cf. his friendship with Oskar Pfister), without that admiration indicating an attraction to Christianity per se. Similarly, Freud's use of Christian terms like "Easter" or "Pentecost" in place of Jewish ones like "Passover" or "Shavuot" may be more an indication of his educated assimilation to the majority culture than an attraction to Christianity, and though Vitz interprets Freud opening his medical practice on Easter Sunday in 1886 as an expression of "rebirth, a new beginning," related to Easter's theme of resurrection, Jones points out that "to begin work on such a day seems like an act of defiance."[9] The importance of biographical and cultural context in determining the meaning of Freud's words and acts is underscored by this difference of interpretation over the meaning of Christian elements in Freud's life.

With regard to the learning he did with his parents, Freud has given us a glimpse of an early conversation with his mother concerning the veracity of the creation account in Gen. 2:7. The six-year-old doubted whether "we were all made of earth and must therefore return to earth."

His mother rubbed her hands together and thus proved "by the blackish scales of epidermis produced by the friction" that "we were made of earth." Writing in 1899, Freud says that as a boy he was astounded by this demonstration and that he believed his mother, but his later interpretation in his report has revealed his skepticism too: "I acquiesced in the belief which I was later to hear expressed in the words: 'Du bist der Natur einem Tod schuldig.'"[10] The substitution of "Nature" for "God" in Prince Hal's remark to Falstaff in *I Henry IV* (act 5, scene 1), whose basis Trosman locates in "the coming of romanticism at the beginning of the nineteenth century,"[11] reflects Freud's own "religious" substitution as an adult, as its context in the Fliess correspondence also shows,[12] and it implies that his astonishment did not suffice to retain his allegiance to the simple *uninterpreted* meaning of the Scriptures. Rather, Freud believes, their truth must be understood from a humanistic standpoint, in this case best expressed by Shakespeare instead of Moses.

In any event, it is significant that Freud recalls a dispute over the meaning of a text from the Jewish Bible. As he says, "My early familiarity with the Bible story (at a time almost before I had learnt the art of reading) had (as I recognized much later) an enduring effect upon the direction of my interest."[13] From this recollection concerning his mother, it seems that Freud was learning the Bible story at least by age six. The recontextualization of a biblical text by a humanist understanding of its meaning is perhaps the form that this "enduring effect" on the direction of Freud's interest took, for that is his approach to the Bible.

The Bible was also clearly an important part of Jakob Freud's early instruction of his son, as is indicated by the Hebrew inscription the father writes in the family "Philippsohn Bible" when he presented it to Freud on the latter's thirty-fifth birthday[14] in 1891. This Bible was a massive three-volume work with parallel columns of Hebrew and German, whose commentaries and extensive introductory essays were written by Ludwig Philippsohn, a German rabbi active in the Reform movement. It is a work of serious scholarship in the spirit of the *Wissenschaft des Judentums* movement, dealing with topics such as biblical criticism, comparative religion, and the nature of myth.[15] Jakob's words (see below) make it clear that he and Freud made use of this work to study together before Freud entered the private *Volksschule*. The fact that the father writes in Hebrew indicates that the "Holy Language" of the Bible was a link between father and son, even if Freud no longer understood Hebrew at age thirty-five. In any event, as Yerushalmi and others have pointed out, it is plausible to think that Jakob would have written a dedication to his son in a language that he would have expected him to understand, even if he needed a little help along the way.[16] But the Hebrew itself would in any event have triggered the memory of their learning together. Yerushalmi (1991), Ostow (1989), and Rice (1990) have recently published discussions of this inscription, underscoring its importance for an understanding of Freud's Jewish identity and his Jewish education. In the summary that follows, both Jakob's Jewish learning and its effect on Freud's involvement with the Bible—especially as it culminates in *Moses and Monotheism*—become clear. The inscription, in Yerushalmi's literal translation, is as follows:

> Son who is dear to me, Shelomoh.
> In the seventh in the days of the years of your life
> the spirit of the Lord began to move you
> and spoke within you: Go, read in my Book
>   that I have written
> and there will burst open for you the
> wellsprings of understanding, knowledge and wisdom [*haskel*].
> Behold, it is the Book of Books, from which the
>   sages have excavated
> And lawmakers learned knowledge and judgement.
> A vision of the Almighty did you see;
> you heard and strove to do,
>   and you soared on the wings of the Spirit.
> Since then the book has been stored like
> the fragments of the tablets in an ark with me.
> For the day on which your years were filled to
>   five and thirty,
> I have put upon it a cover of new skin
> and have called it: "Spring up, O well, sing ye
>   unto it!" [Num. 21:17]
> And I have presented it to you as a memorial
> and as a reminder of love from your father,
> who loves you with everlasting love.
>
> Jakob son of R. [probably Reb, i.e., Mr.] Shelomoh Freid [*sic*],[17]
> In the capital city Vienna, 29 Nisan [5]651, 6 May [1]891.[18]

This dedication is a testimony both to the important role the Bible played in the relationship between father and son and to the prominent part it played in Jakob's instruction of his gifted Shelomo-Sigismund. The age of "seven" here may be a convention, symbolic of a completed period, a time to begin a new phase, like the biblically based seven-day week, for it is clear that unless a faulty memory misleads us, Freud was already reading the Bible with his mother at least by age six. Traditionally boys begin learning the Bible much earlier, even by age three, when they receive their first haircut.

In any event, the father seems to see this Bible and its "understanding, knowledge and enlightenment [*haskel*]" as a bridge between the tradition of the fathers ("the sages") and the future endeavors of his son, for as Yerushalmi observes, "Jakob Freud's gift to Sigmund on his thirty-fifth birthday meant that he was giving him the Bible for the second time, a parallel to the two sets of the tablets of the Law, the first of which had been shattered by Moses."[19] Just as the second tablets, traditionally understood to have been given on Yom Kippur, meant that the Jews were forgiven their apostasy at the Golden Calf and given a second chance to fulfill their covenant, so too Jakob may be hopefully offering his son a chance and an encouragement to return to the Bible and tradition that were his spiritual beginning. Herein lies, Yerushalmi, Rice, and Ostow suggest, the key to a psychological understanding of Freud's repeated return to images of Moses at crucial points in his life, and especially his return, with *Moses and Monotheism,* to the Bible. If Freud received a mandate from his father, as Krüll insists, Yerushalmi argues that its true basis is to be found here in this Hebrew inscription. In *Moses and Monotheism,* as Ostow says, "Freud obeyed his father's request to 'sing to' the old well that had sprung up anew, the Bible."[20] A closer look at the dedication will give us a picture of Jakob Freud's learning, the profile of "a learned Jewish layman who has a total command of the Pentateuch, of the rest of the Bible at least in the prophetic portions read in the synagogue as haftarot, of the Jewish liturgy."[21] Ostow goes further, claiming that "Jakob Freud is a master of Scripture and of the method of midrashic interpretation."[22]

Significantly, the inscription is written in the tradition of *melitzah.* As Robert Alter explains, *melitzah* was a literary tradition of biblical allusion, by which poets like Yehudah HaLevi and Solomon ibn Gabirol sought to produce "extraordinary resonances by playing their own experience against the recollection of the biblical passages from which they [drew] their language."[23] Jakob is doing the same thing. Based on knowing the Bible virtually by heart, *melitzah* is a way of saying several things at once by associating the original biblical context with the new context of the poem. By disclosing these associations, we gain a deeper insight into Jakob's subliminal and complex message to his son on his thirty-fifth birthday. The very fact that he writes in such a stylized form may be an attempt to illustrate his own *Bildung*, to demonstrate an education that in traditional terms is equal to that Freud received in the *Gymnasium*, and therefore furnish a warrant for a dual allegiance.

Yerushalmi and Ostow note that the dedication is framed by expressions of love from the thirty-first chapter of Jeremiah, which is the *haftara* for the second day of Rosh HaShanah. Jakob's "Son who is dear to me, Shelomoh" alludes to Jer. 31:19, "Truly, Ephraim [Jakob's grandfather's name, incidentally] is a dear son to Me," which also occurs in the "Remembrances" of the Musaf service on Rosh HaShanah. But, Yerushalmi continues, in Jeremiah "Ephraim" represents the Jewish people in exile, the ten lost northern tribes, and the chapter is part of Jeremiah's promise that God will bring them back home again, for "the people who survived the sword found grace in the wilderness" (Jer. 31:2). That is, they will be reconciled to their father (v. 9) who will restore them to their former glory (vv. 4–5): "Again I will build you and you shall be built." These contexts, inferred by *melitzah,* confer a heightened status, authority and dignity on Jakob's loving call for Sigmund's return to and reconciliation with the tradition of his fathers. In symmetry with this salutation, Ostow observes, is Jakob's closing line, "From your father, who loves you with everlasting love" [*ahavat olam*]. The last phrase is drawn from Jer. 31:3, where God confesses, "With an everlasting love I have loved you [Israel]. Therefore I have remained true to you." Jakob's use of Jeremiah's "consolation" to Israel offers reconciliation to Sigmund as well.

Jakob's reference to the Spirit of the Lord stirring within his son at age seven recalls Judg. 13:25, where following the Lord's blessing on Samson "the spirit of the Lord began to stir him in the camp of Dan." Samson, dedicated to God from his mother's womb (Judg. 16:17), will of course go on to defeat the enemies of the Jewish people, the Philistines, avenging his own as well as his people's humiliation. One wonders whether this association is not also woven into Freud's image of his father's charge to him, mingled in his mind with his wishes for revenge against the enemies of his Jewish father.

In any event, in Jakob's dedication, the Spirit commanded Freud to "Go, read"[24] in the Bible ("my Book"). Freud obeyed this command ("you heard and you strove to do"), and it left a deep imprint on his identity ("you soared on the wings of the Spirit" [cf. Ps. 18:11]). "Wellsprings of understanding, knowledge and wisdom" "burst open" for him in this study, Jakob's language recalling both the bursting "wellsprings of the deep" in Gen. 7:11 and the formulation of the fourth blessing of the daily Eighteen Benedictions in the Sephardic rite.[25] The metaphor of water for Torah (literally, "instruction") is of course traditional, but it is developed significantly further by Jakob's use of Num. 21:16–18, which bridges the early period of their learning together and Jakob's present hopes for Freud's return and further endeavors: "Spring up, O well! — Sing ye to it! The well which the princes dug, which the nobles of the people delved, with the sceptre, with their staves."

The aptness of Jakob's use of the biblical material conveys a sense of the skill and quality of his teaching. Ostow even suggests that Jakob has composed an original midrash, or exegetical homily.[26] Num. 21:16–18 refers to a divinely commanded gathering of the people at Be'er (that is, "Well") in order that God may give them water. In response, Israel sang the song whose opening line Jakob uses to name his gift to his son: "Spring up, O well! — Sing ye to it!" Just as God gathered the people at "The Well" in order to give them His Teaching, so too should Freud return to drink from this ancient source in order to find "understanding, knowledge and enlightenment [*haskel*]." Jakob may be expressing a wish that his son not go forth too long without the "water" of the Torah (a traditional caution based on Num. 10:33ff., and institutionalized in the public reading of the Torah in the synagogue at fewer than three-day intervals). But he seems to have had the rest of the song in mind too when he wrote the dedication, for the song continues, "The well that the princes dug / that the nobles of the people delved, with the scepter [*mechoqeq*], with their staves."

Jacob Milgrom points out that in rabbinic tradition, *mechoqeq* is related to "the teaching of the Torah—the teacher being God, who gave the Torah, or Moses, who is the scribe par excellence, or scribes in general. . . . Moses' staff is a branch from Israel's tree of life, the Torah; and Israel . . . continues to be nourished by its waters."[27] Thus, reminding his son of what the *mechoqim*, the "lawmakers," received from this Book of Books and of the "vision of the Almighty" Freud experienced himself,[28] Jakob connects his son to his early experience with the Bible's treasure.

"Since that time," however, Freud had left off studying the Bible. "*Min az*," a rare usage, may refer ironically to the Jews' complaint to Jeremiah of their troubles since the time they left off their idolatrous worship of the "Queen of Heaven" (Jer. 44:18). Jakob may associate Freud's abandonment of Judaism with idolatry at some level, as is traditional. In any event, since then Freud's father has stored the Book they shared in an *aron*—"bookcase" or "Ark" in Hebrew—"like the broken fragments of the Tablets." Yerushalmi details the talmudic source for this midrashic tradition that the pieces of the first tablets, broken by Moses when he saw the rebellion of the Golden Calf, were deposited in the Ark of the Covenant along with the newly hewn second tablets. Interpreting Deut. 10:2, "you shall put them in the ark," to refer to "the first tablets which you broke," R. Yosef in the Babylonian Talmud (Menachot 99a) infers from this as well that "a scholar who has forgotten his learning by reason of his misfortune [i.e., through old age, sickness or trouble, and not willful neglect], must not be treated with disrespect [that is, the broken tablets are holy too]."[29] Yerushalmi asks whether Jakob identified with the scholar who had forgotten his learning, so that this reference may imply a plea for respect from his son. But the broken fragments may also represent the learning they had together when Freud was seven. Jakob could be urging Freud to respect that experience even though he may have forgotten its content. Jakob's act of "retrieving the broken fragments" of the Bible Freud has discarded could represent a controlled response to Freud's anger (which resembles Moses' hurling down the tablets),[30] connecting this image again to Freud's interpretation of the *Moses* of Michelangelo and the valued self-restraint of his father.

Interestingly, the tradition is ambivalent about Moses' breaking the Tablets, as Ernst Simon notes,[31] finding positive meanings in Moses' response (e.g., a desire to protect the Jews) as well as negative ones (e.g., a desire to punish). Avot de Rabbi Natan even records God as praising Moses for his act, and the tradition attributes to Moses the idea of breaking the tablets with the intention of reforming the people and then making new ones.[32] Thus Freud's "breaking of the tablets," that is, his leaving the fold of traditional Judaism, may have received a positive warrant from his father too, perhaps with the idea that Freud would become a new kind of Jew.

Therefore at this propitious time (7 x 5 years), the father covers the Book anew with a *michseh 'ur chadash,* perhaps recalling, Yerushalmi suggests, the "*michseh 'ur tachash* that covered and protected the holiest appurtenances of the Desert Sanctuary when the camp travelled."[33] In Jakob's extended simile to his son, the Bible and their learning together become the well of water that their ancestors dug and drank from. Just as he saw a vision of the Almighty then, now too Freud should return, his father exhorts, to those roots for inspiration and strength. Like covers of a book, study of the Bible should enclose Freud's study of the Enlightenment's humanist texts. In fact, Freud will construct this frame by returning to the Bible at the end of his life.

When Jakob names the newly bound Bible "Spring up" (addressing the well), it is as though he expects the "broken tablets" to be hewn anew; and when his naming continues with the imperative, "Sing ye unto it," Jakob seems to be urging his son to "sing" (or "respond": *anu*) to the nourishing source that inspired his first intellectual (i.e., *geistig*) developments. Jakob blesses a new beginning for his son, as if to say, "Even though you have left Jewish religious life behind, yet still have your work be a song to the Bible of your people that inspired your first beginnings." Jakob makes this dedication "for a reminder of love / from your father, who loves you with everlasting love," implying that their Bible embodies both the Jewish tradition and this love. Thus in the early period, Freud's Jewish identity received a strong paternal warrant for a biblical base. In this context, *Moses and Monotheism* appears as a recapitulation and fulfillment of a mandate "to return to the Bible, to the originally shared values with the father."[34]

Ostow also points to allusions in the inscription that indicate hidden anger Jakob may have felt over his son's defection from Judaism. "A vision of the Almighty [Shaddai]" refers to Num. 24:4, where the prophet of Moab and Midian, Bilaam, characterizes himself as one "who sees the vision of the Almighty [*Shaddai*]." Through this allusion, "Jakob associates his son with the divinely inspired vision of this heathen prophet who intends to curse Israel but remains to bless it."[35] Furthermore, a few lines later, "stored . . . with me" (*kamus . . . imadi)* reproduces Deut. 32:34, in the "Ha'Azinu" song of Moses. Its context is the vengeance God will take upon Israel for its rebellion and apostasy (cf. Deut. 32:15ff): "he forsook God who made him / And lightly esteemed the rock of his salvation / They provoked him to jealousy with strange gods. . . ." As Ostow comments, "It is not difficult to guess why Jakob might have referred to this passage."[36]

On the other hand, Ostow also notes the loving symmetrical frame created by the closing signature, in which Jakob signs himself "Ya'acov, ben Reb Shelomo Freid [*sic*]," reminding his son that he was named after Jakob's father ["Son who is dear to me, Shelomo"] and implying that Jakob loves them both.[37] The inscription suggests in fact that this love is expressed in this Bible and the transmission of its teaching, the bridge to the Jewish life of the fathers. *Moses and Monotheism* would thus unconsciously forge a link with Freud's grandfather, a reconciliation that Jakob alludes to by joining Shelomo-Sigismund to Reb Shelomo Freid.

The Hebrew medium is also part of this message. Jakob's "Gedenkblatt" in the same Bible, recording his father's death and Freud's birth and circumcision, is written in Jakob's hand in both Hebrew and German, so it is clear that the father could have written to his son on this occasion in German, had he wanted to. Therefore Jakob's use of Hebrew itself implies a call from the tradition. Even if Freud no longer understood its semantic content, its symbolic meaning would have been clear to him, expressing a deep connection to his people. As mentioned, the Philippsohn Bible had parallel columns of German and Hebrew. In his 1930 preface to the Hebrew translation of *Totem and Taboo,* Freud indicates how moved he is at seeing his work in the ancient language of his people, in spite of his estrangement from their religion:

> It is an experience of quite a special kind for such an author when a book of his is translated into the Hebrew language and put into the hands of readers for whom that historic idiom is a living tongue.[38]

Freud believes that in spite of his unbelief, what is left to him that is Jewish is still "a very great deal, probably its very essence." With this translation of his psychoanalytic work, the Hebrew language can be a bridge for this essence. As the "Holy Language" in Jewish tradition, Hebrew has always been such an essential bridge. In any event, these traditional meanings suggest that Jakob's choices were not arbitrary, and his use of biblical context bespeaks an intimate familiarity with the biblical text and its story that would have been part of his teaching. Freud's words in this preface indicate that his father's influence was deeply felt.

Jakob's intimacy and familiarity with the Bible were also conveyed to his son, as Ernst Simon points out in his analysis of Freud's reference to 2 Sam. 1:20,[39] when Freud wrote to Fliess of the collapse of his seduction theory. Freud says,

> Of course I shall not tell it in Dan [*sic*], nor speak of it in Ashkelon, in the land of the Philistines, but in your eyes and in my own, I have more the feeling of a victory than a defeat (which surely is not right).[40]

Simon notes that in spite of David's grief at the death of Saul, "yet the declaimer of the elegy recognizes that the Kingdom is now open to him and although anxious to conceal the facts of his predecessor's death from the Philistines [lest they exult], he cannot suppress a note of triumph." "Only someone well acquainted with the Bible could quote so feelingly from it at such a critical hour in his life as did Sigmund Freud,"[41] Simon adds. Yerushalmi notes in connection with Freud's misquote ("Dan" instead of "Gath") the allusion in Jakob's dedication to the Spirit of the Lord stirring Samson in the camp of Dan, and suggests that the slip is an unconscious allusion to Samson, who had his victory, even in defeat.[42] Note also the opposition between the biblical enemies (that is, non-Jews, the "uncircumcised" of 2 Sam. 1:20) and "in your eyes and in my own," that is, between us Jews. The Bible is a matrix or an instrument for his solidarity with Jews. Both this feeling of solidarity and this easy familiarity and intimacy with the "Bible story" are part of the enduring legacy of Freud's Jewish education that began at home with his parents.

On the basis of school records and cultural historical studies of Vienna between 1863 and 1873, when Freud was in school, Reuben Rainey has drawn a plausible picture of the kind of Jewish education (we will turn to the humanist one shortly) Freud was likely to have received, beginning with his entrance into the private *Volksschule* Freud mentions in his curriculum vitae and continuing through his years in the *Gymnasium*. More recently, Emanuel Rice has provided us with the curricula for Jewish religious instruction in primary school, *Gymnasial-*, *Unterrealschul*, and *Oberrealschul*-classes during the time Freud attended school (1862[?]–74).[43] The following is a summary of their research.

Religious education was compulsory in Austrian schools during Freud's time, and this requirement "extended from the first year of the *Volksschule* through the last year of the *Gymnasium*." Rainey mentions the likelihood, which Yerushalmi thinks "plausible," that Freud attended the private *Volksschule* operated by S. Szanto,[44] a liberal journalist whose Reform persuasion Rainey argues "was probably in harmony with the ideas of Freud's father,"[45] suggesting that the Freud household probably followed a moderate form of Reform Judaism. Emanuel Rice's research strongly challenges this conclusion, which has been followed by many, suggesting instead that "a continued, though somewhat weakened, Orthodoxy" was more likely.[46] Rice supports his conclusion by reference to Jakob's

> mastery of the Bible, Talmud and Hebrew language and the religious nature and content of the Hebrew writings themselves; his handling according to the highest Orthodox Jewish tradition, of the Tetragrammaton and the elimination of the number "1" in the writing of the calendar year; Emanuel and Philipp's knowledge of the Hebrew language and their continued affiliation with the Orthodox Jewish community in Manchester, England; the observance of the laws of *Kashruth* (i.e., kosher food and kitchen).[47]

As will become clear, evidence from Freud's correspondence also supports Rice's view of the Jewishness of Freud's home as he was growing up.

In private primary schools such as Szanto's, students received religious instruction for five hours each week (twice that of public schools), the core of whose ten-month curriculum was formed by the study of the Hebrew Bible and selected prayers from the Jewish prayer book, the Siddur. There was no study of the Talmud or its commentaries. The curriculum was designed to bring about a "personal encounter" with the "spirit of Judaism" through a careful analysis of major portions of the Pentateuch and synagogue prayers, the translation from Hebrew being done in class by the teacher. This translation tactic was strategic rather than ideal however; a judicious use of the little time allotted for religious instruction rather than a rejection of the value of Hebrew language study in principle. Contrary to Freud's claim, the study of Hebrew was considered an essential part of the curriculum by his teachers, but since the primary purpose of biblical study was "to confront the students with the 'power and vitality' of their tradition," the teachers could not afford to devote much class time to Hebrew language itself. So it is understandable that Freud forgot it and characterizes himself regretfully in later life as being ignorant of Hebrew.[48] Since Freud tells us that he received the highest grade in his class, his claim of *total* ignorance of Hebrew seems defensive at best, perhaps even expressing an implied transcendence of "primitive" Judaism in favor of "enlightened" German and classical languages, at which Freud excelled. Freud may even have been required to attend brief worship services,[49] because Simon notes that Freud's pronunciation of Hebrew words (or at least his transliteration of them) has been influenced by the Ashkenazi pronunciation of the prayer service.[50] In any event, yearly study of the major prayers of the Siddur and traditional services was included in the curriculum of the *Volksschuleklassen* provided by Rice.[51]

Jakob's enrollment of his son in a Jewish private school may imply a concern that the boy receive a better background in the Jewish tradition than he would have if he had been enrolled in the public schools, where religious instruction was limited to two or three hours per week, but admittedly, Jakob's choice could also have been due to a concern for the general quality of Sigismund's total education, for "the private schools in Austria were generally better than the public ones."[52] Be this as it may, we can see that the curriculum of Freud's primary school education would have strengthened the initial grounding in Bible that he had received from his parents, and his teachers' concern for a personal encounter with the biblical text would appear to have continued his parents' approach. Thus when Freud entered the *Gymnasium* at age nine-and-a-half (a half-year early, and so requiring a special waiver of age limit),[53]he would have come with a reservoir of Jewish knowledge that included an emphasis on the Pentateuch, as is traditional. The absence of any training in Talmud is of course in sharp contrast to Orthodox Jewish tradition.

Freud would have been familiar too with the observance of the major Jewish festivals, for it is clear from Freud's own correspondence and from the reports of family members that Rosh HaShanah, Yom Kippur, Passover, and Purim at least, were "observed in the Freud household as late as 1874, when Freud was in his second year of medical studies."[54] Furthermore, even ten years after Freud had left home, Jakob still made a Passover seder in his home and could recite the Haggadah by heart.[55] These observances would have been part of Freud's familial Jewish education, and their meaningfulness is perhaps indicated by the prominent placement of what must be the family "kiddush cups" on the table in Freud's office displaying part of his collection of antiquities.[56]

Besides a home-based Jewish education, it is also clear that Freud's humanist education, even if self-directed, had his father's support. Anna Bernays tells us of a "family council" session in 1866 at the birth of the youngest son, to discuss with the family what the boy's name should be. Sigismund chose the name Alexander, "basing his selection on Alexander's generosity and prowess as a general," and "he recited the whole story of the Macedonian's triumph in support of his choice."[57] Alexander's other names were Gotthold and Ephraim. The former may be associated with Lessing (at least it holds German associations), but the latter, though it is also Lessing's middle name, is almost certainly a remembrance of Jakob's grandfather, Efraim Freud.[58] Thus Jakob would have named his first son from Amalie after his father and his last son after his grandfather, joining traditional Jewish reverence for family forebears with the humanist and German values associated with the names Alexander Gotthold and Sigismund/Sigmund.[59] Freud's allegiance to the humanist tradition, without the need to forsake his Jewish identity, has a familial, even paternal, root. This amalgam, I would argue, is a part of his education in his "liberal household," as Anna termed it—one that well-prepared Freud to enter the *Gymnasium* and later in life to take an active role in the Vienna B'nai B'rith.

An examination of Freud's education in the *Leopoldstädter Communalgymnasium*, the public secondary school in the Jewish section of Vienna (Leopoldstadt) where the Freud family lived, must proceed on two fronts. The *Gymnasium* must be considered as one of the humanist "wellsprings" of Freud's identity, strengthening and extending the youth's participation in and allegiance to the humanist fruits of the Enlightenment.[60] But at the same time, Freud also studied Jewish religion there with Samuel Hammerschlag, who must also have been his teacher in the *Volksschule*,[61] extending his instruction over a period of eight years. Hammerschlag became a lifelong friend and Jewish father figure to young Sigmund. As Freud told his fiancée,

> He has been touchingly fond of me for years; there is such a secret sympathy between us that we can talk intimately together. He always regards me as his son.[62]

Hammerschlag several times helped Freud out of financial difficulties,[63] and the young man was a frequent visitor in his teacher's home. Freud held the Hammerschlag family in high esteem: "I do not know any better or more humane people, or so free from any ignoble motives."[64] And he named two of his girls after Hammerschlag's daughter and niece (Anna and Sophie, respectively). On his old teacher's death in 1904, Freud wrote an obituary eulogizing the man's spirit and teaching, revealing the strong influence Hammerschlag had on his pupil. Thus although the instruction in religion occupied only two hours of the curriculum per week in the *Gymnasium* (one hour devoted to Bible and one to both history and doctrine), its influence on Freud may have been out of proportion to its small part, due to this personal context. Therefore it will be helpful to examine Hammerschlag's teaching philosophy and curriculum as Rainey has reconstructed it with an eye to its influence on Freud.

As was true of the curriculum in the *Volksschule*, Hammerschlag's curriculum in the *Gymnasium* was built around the study of the Bible. This strategy was designed to develop in the student "a consciousness of the particularity of his faith as well as its universal import."[65] Rainey cites a passage from an essay by Hammerschlag entitled "Das Programm der israel Religionsschule in Wien" which makes his ideal clear:

> [Today] it is understood that progress and humanity can best be achieved through the preservation of the unique spiritual characteristics that ethnic origin, language, or religion have given particular people. The nurture of these abilities is the best way of reaching by divergent paths the common goal of all, which is the attainment of the highest culture and spiritual [*geistig*] knowledge.[66]

Here is a clear philosophical, humanist (though also Jewish)[67] justification for the value of Jewish particularism, namely, its service to the universal. According to Dennis Klein, Hammerschlag's teaching educated Freud to the Jewish role in the struggle for the cultural whole. Freud's teacher of Jewish religion considered humanitarian ideals to be central to Jewish teaching, and he taught that "attention to the whole is the highest task of the group."[68] Such a position would have enabled Freud to pursue humanist aims as a Jew, less fettered by guilt than if the two allegiances were seen as competing and mutually exclusive. Freud went further than his teacher however, and rejected all traces of traditional Judaism, especially its ritual practice. Klein argues that this rejection, especially between the ages of thirteen and eighteen (1869–74), "makes clear Freud's desire to surrender his Jewish heritage to the dominant liberal ideals of human freedom and social rationality."[69] As Rainey observes in relation to Freud's essay on Michelangelo's *Moses*, there is evidence that he suffered some guilt at this "betrayal."[70]

In any event, the spiritual goals and values that Hammerschlag expresses are also Freud's, even if Freud does not follow his teacher's particular means to the goals of "progress" [*Fortschritt*], "humanity" [*Humanität*], and "spiritual knowledge." Freud's section-title in *Moses and Monotheism* comes to mind: "The Progress in Spirituality" [*Fortschritt im Geistigheit*]. More immediate is Freud's obituary for Hammerschlag, in which he reports of his former teacher that "religious instruction seemed to him a way of educating towards humanism" [or "a love of humanity"].[71] Overall, Freud saw his work as an effort towards just such an attainment of humanistic culture for all. As he said in 1909,

> The work of psychoanalysis puts itself at the orders of precisely the highest and most valuable cultural trends, as a better substitute for the unsuccessful repression.[72]

Sterba says that these cultural trends corresponded for Freud to the "humanist values."[73]

Hammerschlag expresses his belief in the value of Jewish particularism (not emphasized by Freud in his obituary) in the same essay mentioned above, when he writes,

> The particular abilities and spiritual possessions which Nature or the course of history has brought to a particular group—whether of a national or a religious character—are powers whose development and perfection enable that people to contribute its share to the general work of the whole.[74]

Hammerschlag's humanist substitute for the traditional "God and His Providence," namely, "Nature or the course of history," is also found in Freud's thought, as noted above. To illustrate Hammerschlag's influence, Freud's substitution of "Nature" for "God" in his quote from Shakespeare can be coupled with Freud's use of "history" as the standard of judgment in his Nathan letter to Martha (see below). Freud's humanism and his commitment to the service of the universal have Jewish backing, both at home and at school.

However, the Judaism that Freud was taught also has what might be called "humanist" backing. Rainey notes that "the 'ideas' of 'religion' and 'morality' were considered by the government authorities to be the 'focal point' of the students' general education."[75] Freud tells his B'nai B'rith "brothers in the faith" that despite his atheism, he was raised with a "respect for the so-called 'ethical' demands of human civilization."[76] The moderate Reform Judaism of men like Adolf Jellinek (1820/21–93), who was Chief Rabbi of Vienna while Freud was growing up, "placed great stress upon the universal relevance of Jewish ethics for the problems of contemporary life." And if, as seems likely, the climate of Freud's own home also emphasized the ethical dimensions of Judaism,[77] even in the form of a "weakened Orthodoxy," then Freud's statement to B'nai B'rith can logically be related to his reception of Hammerschlag's teaching, which also appears to have espoused a Judaism of the moderate Reform position.[78] Hammerschlag "regarded the concepts of 'a free, autonomous personality' and 'innate human rights', two of the fundamental affirmations of the Enlightenment, as firmly rooted in the Jewish prophetic tradition."[79] Therefore we can see why Hammerschlag, like Jellinek, was "fond of drawing links between Jewish tradition and modern European culture." In the obituary, Freud describes his teacher's passionate side as being "happily tempered by the ideal of our German classical period" so that Hammerschlag could make the enthusiasm of young people "flow out beyond the limitations of nationalism or dogma." This "transcendence" is Freud's interpretation of Hammerschlag's teaching, leaving out his emphasis on a full realization of one's particularity as a Jew. But it does fit Freud's description of his own youthful education in the ethical demands of *human* civilization, so Rainey suggests plausibly that Freud may have been thinking of Hammerschlag when he made his statement to B'nai B'rith.

So much for the spirit of Freud's Jewish education in the *Gymnasium*. As we have seen, this education allowed for a Jewish confessional particularism without sacrificing a commitment to a general universal humanist goal. In fact Hammerschlag taught that such particularism could be an instrument to achieve service to the whole. Furthermore, this form of Judaism had the institutional support of the government authorities, who wanted religion and morality to be the focal point of the students' general education. Judaism and humanism were given reciprocal support and legitimation. Such an education would have nourished the development of dual allegiance as a positive commitment. As Robert Wistrich writes,

> Hammerschlag, rather like the preacher Adolf Jellinek, emphasized the progressive humanitarian message of the Old Testament, seeking to combine Jewish group particularism with the universal truths of mankind.[80]

It was this combination that enabled Freud to absorb ideas from the Reform movement while at the same time living in an environment closer to Orthodoxy than has been realized, also absorbing its strong, natural Jewish pride and self-confidence.

But what of the specifically Jewish content of the curriculum? In Rainey's report of Hammerschlag's curriculum, the dual emphasis of Bible study and Jewish history and doctrine are clear. The curriculum's Bible study strengthened Freud's familiarity with the Pentateuch and biblical history, including the death of Saul, a review of Genesis and Exodus, and selections from the Psalms and major prophets. The edition of the Bible employed in Freud's classes was Jacob Auerbach's *Kleine Schul-und-Haus Bibel,* which contained German translations of selected passages with a few clarifying notes. Freud most likely supplemented his study at home by reading the Philippsohn Bible, whose author "argued strongly for the Mosaic authorship of the Pentateuch" and "placed great emphasis on the universality of the message of the prophets."[81] Rainey suggests that it may have been this study which "initiated Freud's ardent, lifelong interest in ancient history and archaeology."[82] Furthermore, he observes that *Moses and Monotheism* probably owes some of its origins to the fact that Freud spent twelve years of his youth in a curriculum of religious instruction that was structured around a thorough study of the Pentateuch, in much of which the figure of Moses plays a dominant role. Freud's Jewish self-understanding was largely informed by a study of the Bible and Jewish history. Thus it makes sense that in his last work, when he comes to address the question What makes a Jew? Freud would attempt a "historical" reconstruction of Moses.[83] Freud has been taught that a Jew is defined by biblical history.

But in addition, Freud was taught Jewish doctrine based on a textbook by Leopold Breuer, Josef's father. Rainey gives us a detailed summary of its contents and approach, highlighting its "Mendelssohnian discussion of 'natural religion'" as a "'religion of reason'," "its marked stress on the universality of the 'moral law'."[84] "its presentation of Judaism as 'a religious confession'," and its emphasis on good citizenship, which enabled the Jew to be comfortable affirming the particularity of his own spiritual allegiance to Judaism without threatening his civil loyalty to Austria. Rainey emphasizes too that this presentation of Judaism was clearly "religious" in that it sought to strengthen the student's "faith in God and to interpret for him the ethics and ritual practices of Judaism; it was not a dispassionate analysis in the spirit of *Religionswissenschaft.*"[85] Therefore, Rainey continues, although Freud certainly rejected most of these "religious" aspects of his Jewish education, and so can imagine that he had always been an unbeliever—that is, brought up "without religion"—nevertheless "he maintained throughout his life some of its 'ethical' contents in the form of a staunch commitment to such precepts as the brotherhood of mankind and the alleviation of human suffering."[86] These ideals were reaffirmed and strengthened for Freud in the early period of the formation of his Jewish identity, when he joined the Vienna B'nai B'rith after his father's death. The content of Freud's Jewish education in the *Gymnasium* under Samuel Hammerschlag's tutelage emphasized a strong sense of Jewish identity based in ethics and the classical (i.e., biblical) story of the Jewish people, while teaching the harmony and relevance that tradition had for the larger humanistic culture.

On the other hand, Freud's sense of participation in and claim to that larger humanistic German classical culture was strengthened and established even more by the larger part of his studies at the *Gymnasium*, namely, his classical studies. To Latin and its literature, a student generally devoted eight hours a week for eight years, whereas to Greek and its classics he gave six hours a week for six years. In addition, Freud read much more on his own.[87] Thus the time given to classics far outweighed that given to Jewish studies. When Freud was nearly sixty, he wrote that his knowledge of classical culture, into whose extinct civilization he had gotten his first glimpses at the *Leopoldstädter Obergymnasium*, had brought him "as much consolation as anything else in the struggles of life."[88] This training formed a kind of "admission ticket" to European society (instead of Heine's conversion to Christianity), for as Sterba says, "one could consider oneself as belonging to the cultural and intellectual elite only if one was well versed in the Latin and Greek authors."[89]

Freud was an excellent student, at the top of his class for seven of his eight years in the *Gymnasium*, hardly ever needing to pass examinations,[90] and winning prizes and honors.[91] Sterba has published the curriculum of Freud's classical studies at the *Gymnasium* for the years 1868–73, and even without the additional reading material that professors were likely to have suggested for students of Freud's caliber, the extent of Freud's classical reading is impressive. Trosman summarizes:

> After a two-year preparatory period in Latin, which Freud began at nine, he was assigned Livy's *History of Rome.* Freud read much of Ovid's *Metamorphoses,* with its poetic rendering of many of the Greek myths. Sallust, the Roman historian, Cicero's *Orations,* Virgil's *Eclogues* and *The Aeneid,* Horace's poems, and Tacitus's *History* rounded out a rather full exposure to Latin. In Greek, Xenophon's *Anabasis* and *Cyropaedia* familiarized Freud with the Greek struggle with the Per-

> sians and with the character and education of Cyrus. In Herodotus he read of the death of Darius, Xerxes' invasion of Greece, and the Battle of Thermopylae. Demosthenes' orations, Sophocles' *Ajax* and *Antigone*, Homer's *Iliad* and *Odyssey*, and Plato's *Apology* and *Crito* were read in the original over a period of almost six years.[92]

The reading list conveys a sense of the cultural patrimony to which Freud must have felt entitled. This curriculum would have given him the sense of being an heir to the values and ethos of this "extinct civilization," and its discipline served him well. As Trosman says, speaking of the intention of the classical *Gymnasium*, "the formal discipline acquired by the mind in the mastery of the rudiments of the literature and language of Greece and Rome would carry into other modes of thinking and provide a basis for an educated outlook."[93]

Sterba argues that the therapeutic goal of psychoanalysis, which combined the lifting of repression with the watchful eye of a mature and prudent reason, was an eminently humanistic one. This was so both in reflecting the hedonistic trend of humanism against the asceticism of the medieval Church and in embodying the "age-old conflict between desire and restraint" which was both accentuated by and contained in the humanistic *Weltanschauung* itself.[94] Precisely how this humanistic education is reflected in Freud's correspondence and later in *Moses and Monotheism* will be elucidated in later chapters. At this point it is sufficient to observe the formation of a cultural allegiance. By education, Freud is both a humanist Jew and a Jewish humanist.

The Correspondence

Having presented a sketch of the argument for the development of Freud's Jewish identity, and a look at Freud's Jewish and humanist educations, I will turn now to a detailed chronological study in biographical and cultural context of selections from Freud's published correspondence (which is only a small portion of that extant), to demonstrate and illustrate this development. In this process, a picture of Freud's Jewishness will emerge, and its dual allegiance will become clear. The surviving correspondence that has been published covers the major part of Freud's life, from 1872 until his death in 1939, some sixty-seven of his eighty-three years. The letters are addressed to about 170 correspondents,[95] an indication in itself of the social breadth of Freud's identity. From this vast amount of material, selected passages will illustrate with Freud's own statements the nature and qualities of his Jewish identity.

Freud's Letters to Emil Fluss

The earliest published letters extant are those Freud wrote to his boyhood Jewish friends, Emil Fluss and Eduard Silberstein in the summer of 1872, occasioned by his return to the town of his birth, Freiberg, Moravia (now Príbor, in the Czech Republic). Clark quotes from letters written to Silberstein on 17 August and 4 September that reveal how passionate an adolescent Freud was, and how attracted to Gisela Fluss and her mother the sixteen-year-old felt.[96] These "passions" (*Leidenschaften*), in which Freud had "translated esteem for the mother into friendship for the daughter,"[97] came to nothing. However, the strength of Freud's emotions in connection with these incidents is indicated by his "Screen Memories" paper (1899), in which he conceals his own memories behind those of a "patient": "It was my first calf-love and sufficiently intense, but I kept it completely secret."[98]

These details provide a context for understanding Freud's "confidential" letter to Emil Fluss of 18 September 1872, written shortly after Freud had returned to Vienna from Freiberg by train ("my memories of yesterday").[99] Much of the letter relates Freud's flirtation with a twelve-year-old beauty on the train (the main reason for his insistence on the letter's secrecy), but this story is preceded by descriptions of Freud's fellow travelers. First, he describes a woman whose face was so disfigured from boils that, despite his initial forbearance for the sake of her feelings, Freud left her compartment in disgust to seek another, where he meets a family of Jews.

These Jews hail, like him originally, from a small town in Moravia. Thus it is to be wondered whether Freud's disappointments in love in Freiberg, coupled with the negative experience he has just undergone towards the disfigured woman might have influenced his attitude toward these Jews from Meseritsch, the focus of our interest here. It is clear that Freud seeks to distinguish and distance himself from them, because he attacks them with irony and venom, in a style typical of newly emancipated western Jews trying to make clear to other Europeans (and to themselves, anxious to join modern culture) that they are not like their "country cousins." In this Freud is somewhat typical, but even so his emotions seem extreme. He finds their company also "unbearable," and he says, "A remark I made, red with rage, could not sweeten my boredom." Why is Freud so angry at these people? Preceding this statement he describes them:

> This being my unlucky day, I ended up in the company of a most venerable old Jew and his correspondingly old Jewish wife with their

> melancholy, languishing little daughter and impudent "promising" son.

Freud is in a bad mood. Is this mood related to his experiences in Freiberg?

It is clear by his further description that these Jews remind Freud of something in his own past:

> Now this Jew talked in the same way as I had heard thousands of others talk before, even in Freiberg. Even his face seemed familiar [*mir bekannt*]. The man was a type. So was the boy, with whom he talked religion.

As discussed above, Freud himself as a young boy was taught religion by *his* father. Has this fact influenced Freud's choice of language as he now turns on this boy?

> He was hewn from the wood from which fate makes swindlers when the time is ripe: cunning, lying, supported by his dear relatives in the belief[100] [that] he is a talent, but unprincipled and without a *Weltanschauung*.

Freud's antisemitic language could have been drawn from any anti-Jewish tract, so familiar to Jews. But in 1872 it is more likely that Freud learned such attitudes from fellow West European Jews anxious to differentiate themselves from East European Jews. Western Jews resented the *Ostjuden* because the latter represented a threat to their liberal assimilationist ideals, and they blamed immigrant Jews for the antisemitic environment and insecure position of Jews in Vienna at the time.[101] The high rate of immigration forced Jews to abandon their assimilationist goals and concentrate on distinguishing themselves from East European Jews. Since Freud himself is in fact being supported in a special way by *his* family and fellow Jews in the belief that he is a great talent,[102] in his case rightly so, Freud's aggressive words serve this purpose of distinguishing himself from his "country-cousins." One wonders if he feels any guilt at his own special treatment, as he felt ashamed at first later in life when receiving money from Hammerschlag.[103] In any event, Freud must pride himself on his difference from this provincial boy. Unlike him, Freud has principles and a *Weltanschauung*, a humanistic Enlightenment outlook, and he is a cosmopolitan young man about to enter the university, not a boy from the provinces.

These "relatives in the Faith" are too close for comfort, and when he spies a "cook from Bohemia with the most perfect pug-face" he had ever seen, that is, a lower-class peasant, Freud can no longer contain himself: "I have enough of this mob" *[Gesindel]*. Freud's aspirations for influential participation in cultured Austrian society are threatened by his own family's provincial origins, of which these unassimilated provincials remind him. He sees himself differently. As he will write his fiancée in 1883, "the mob *[das Gesindel]* gives vent to its appetites and we deprive ourselves . . . in order to maintain our integrity."[104] Freud sees himself as a part of an elite. As will be seen, he sees himself in this way precisely *as* a Jew, and that is why these "mob-Jews" are a threat to his identity and why he must put them down so vehemently. As he says, "Madame Jewess and family hailed from Meseritsch: the fitting dung-heap [*der rechte Misthaufen*] for this sort of growth." These Jews grew from shit; Freud seeks to eliminate this past from his own Jewish self-understanding, in order to become a humanist. Nevertheless, it is interesting that Freud also feels disgusted when he sees Vienna again. As a Jew perhaps he cannot simply assent to Vienna's culture, for its expectation of German humanist assimilation requires Freud's own self-abnegation. This is disgusting to the defiant Jew in Freud, even if he is also disgusted by his provincial roots.

Sandwiched between these two rejections in this letter to Fluss is the story of Freud's flirtation on the train, an indication that his "calf-love" for Gisela Fluss was nothing more serious, but also perhaps that his erotic interests are aroused. It also indicates that Freud is a typical adolescent, given to strong emotions and opinions, full of secrets and secret shared meanings (e.g., the cluster around "Ichthyosaura," meaning for them, "flirtation"), carrying on exciting but innocent and naïve affairs, all the while posing with pretensions to worldly wisdom. In these shared dramas an adolescent search for self-definition can be seen. Though Freud is only sixteen when he writes this letter, his dislike of East European Jews will continue in evidence throughout the early period, and will influence Freud's view of himself as a Jew by contrast. However, in the late period Freud will mellow on this point, asserting his Galician origins proudly.

A desire for self-definition may also contribute to Freud's pleasure in another letter to Fluss in "discerning the closely knit web of connecting threads which chance and fate have woven around us all."[105] The young man's choice of words to refer to the ultimate power governing our relations, namely, *"Zufall und Schicksal,"* points to Freud's agnosticism, a prominent feature of his adolescence. Freud describes himself as "an old philistine" (at age sixteen) in his next letter to Fluss, and he goes on to comment ironically at the coincidence of Emil's finding the girl he has been dreaming of "as if driven by fate":

> And there—oh wonderful concatenation of circumstances![106]—you find Ottilie. Truly, any more such dispensations could convince even me of the unfathomable workings of a divine Providence.[107]

Freud's humor mingles with his unbelief in these higher providential powers. It is "Nature" rather which gifts us with her "benevolent solicitude." Thus when we hear in a letter written three months later that Freud has decided to become a "nature-explorer" (or natural scientist) [*Naturforscher*] in order to "gain insight into the millennia-old records of Nature, perhaps even listen in on her eternal processes,"[108] we understand that "Nature" here includes Freud's broadest horizons.

Freud writes in his *Autobiography* that it was hearing "Goethe's beautiful essay on Nature read aloud at a popular lecture by Professor Carl Bruehl just before [he] left school" that persuaded him to become a medical student.[109] A few lines from this Romantic poem,[110] now thought to have been written by Swiss theologian Georg Christoph Tobler, will give a sense of the spirit which moved Freud, whose own words are reminiscent of this poem:

> Nature! We are surrounded and embraced by her,
> powerless to separate ourselves from her,
> and powerless to penetrate beyond her.
> Without asking, or warning,
> she snatches us up into her circling dance,
> and whirls us on until we are tired,
> and drop from her arms.
> She is ever shaping new forms:
> what is, has never yet been;
> what has been, comes not again.
> Everything is new, and yet nought but the old.
> We live in her midst and know her not.
> She is incessantly speaking to us,
> but betrays not her secret.
> We constantly act upon her and yet
> have no power over her . . .

As R. C. Clark comments, "this was heady stuff for a young man of seventeen."[111] Its mysterious, sexually tinged images must have expressed something of Freud's own feelings, a Romantic inversion of his unbelief in "God." As noted above, "Nature" replaces "God" in Freud's mind. Such passion for "Nature" may also express a transference of Freud's deep attachment to his mother.

Freud's skeptical agnosticism is formulated in writing to Fluss in a witty, humorous form: "The next time you feel a 'burning' desire for something, pray to God 'Grant me this or that,' and add 'but not too soon.'"[112] He remarks in the same letter that the coincidence of the entrance of the newly married daughter of the Kaiser Franz Josef into Munich with the burial of a well-known German chemical scientist was "an exceedingly witty [*sinnreiches*] arrangement contrived by fate." Freud's sense of humor, often accompanying his agnosticism, may be a "Jewish trait" in his mind, balancing his rejection of theology with ethnicity.

Freud brings this ironical wit to his description of the "theatrical" preparations for Purim (when humor would be most appropriate) in his home in March 1873:

> We had a little theater performance at our house for Purim (which moreover came out on the 13th of March, so sacred to us all; the day too when Caesar was murdered). A bored lady from the neighborhood drilled my sisters, brother, and a few other children into actors and forced us to earn the Purim-dinner (well-known to be not among the worst) laboriously by an artistic treat of the most "marvelous" kind. May you never find yourself in the position of being the brother of such ambitious actresses![113]

Judging by Freud's words, he was included himself in this *Purimshpiel* and we can hear in his ironic complaint the "world-weary" tone of a seventeen-year-old who thinks himself "too old" for such games. The parricidal reference to Caesar's murder may be less out of place than it seems at first, since Purim also commemorates the day when the Jews avenged themselves on their enemies by slaying thousands of them (Esther 9:5–6, 10, 16). Nonetheless, to juxtapose "the 13th of March, so sacred to us all," that is, Purim day given over to familial and public festivity and frivolity, with "the day when Caesar was murdered," is a grim (or "sick") and aggressive kind of humor, again somewhat typical of the bravado of adolescents. It does indicate Freud's youthful disaffection with the practice of Judaism, but on the other hand, Rainey draws attention to the fact that Freud makes no mention of any conflict with his parents over the festivals or his mocking attitude towards them.[114] Furthermore, Ismar Schorsch points out that at about the same time that Freud is poking fun at Jewish festival observances, he is earning the highest possible grades in religion in his classes with Samuel Hammerschlag at the *Gymnasium*.[115] Thus it is clear that even at an early age, Freud's relationships with his Jewish heritage on the one hand, and the practice of Jewish religion on the other, are independent and complex. Agnosticism and Jewish identity are not contradictory for Freud (as is also the case for many modern Jews), and his sense of humor supports both. Note too that Freud uses a classical reference (i.e., to Caesar's murder) to deflate or undercut a Jewish observance. He will use that technique again.

There is a revealing mock outburst on Freud's part in a letter to Fluss from 15 June 1873 that shows how much Freud has come to admire the German humanistic (and Christian Romantic) culture in which he has immersed himself. Waxing nostalgic and sentimental at the thought of Emil's imminent departure from home, at "how painful the parting must be for you when the time comes," Freud says,

> I can well imagine your frame of mind. To leave the beautiful native place, beloved kinsmen—the most beautiful surroundings—ruins close by—I must break off or I'll be as sad as you—and you yourself know best what you must leave behind!

Freud ends this paragraph with an outcry that conveys his sense of the superiority of Enlightenment Christian culture over the Jewish:

> Oh, why are you a prosaic Jew, Emil? Young tradesmen imbued with Christian Germanic fervor have composed beautiful ballads in similar circumstances.

We must not miss Freud's humor here again, but at the same time there is a recognition that the Jew has a "*prosaisch*" character, as opposed to the soul of the Christian-Teutonic folk (like Goethe). The Jew is down-to-earth, unable (or unwilling) to be carried away by Romantic raptures (perhaps Freud had not yet read Heine). This hardheaded sense of Freud's Jew will emerge in a more positive form later; here in his adolescence, when he is "neither this nor that," it seems to him something of a liability. It is of course also a bit antisemitic.

Despite the fact that he felt disgusted at his first return to Vienna a month-and-a-half earlier, Freud is now charmed by the Prater: "What genteel manners! How cosmopolitan and how refined!" And at the end of this letter he jokes about Freiberg being indifferent to the goings-on in town: "Oh, in what a perfidious town was I born!" The contrast between town and country is thus drawn as one of competing allegiances. Freud's contrast between the "prosaic Jew" and the poetic soul of the Christian Teuton expresses his admiration for the sophisticated life of Vienna as compared to the rural simplicity of the country town, in spite of his nostalgia. The young Freud sees little in his provincial Jewish origins to admire—typical, as noted, of liberal assimilated Western Jews.

Before we leave the Fluss correspondence, it is worth mentioning, in light of the previous discussion of Freud's Jewish and humanist educations, the frequent literary citations and allusions that Gedo and Wolf find in their survey of the seven letters: three allusions to Horace, four to Shakespeare, two quotes from Goethe, one from Heine, a line from the Mass for the Dead, and six allusions to or quotes from the Bible (the highest number).[116] Furthermore, "many other phrases call to mind a cultural heritage without pointing so directly to a literary source."[117] The presence of so much literary tradition in so small a corpus indicates the extent to which Freud was immersed in his Jewish and humanist cultural heritage, and the six biblical references suggest again that the Jewish part was not insignificant for Freud's sense of himself, even when writing in a self-consciously humanist vein. Theo Pfrimmer, scanning both Freud's psychoanalytic writings and his published correspondence, found 488 different Biblical references,[118] indicating that this influence remained strong throughout Freud's life.

Freud's Letters to Eduard Silberstein

Let us look now at Freud's correspondence with Eduard Silberstein. Again there is a mix of Jewish and humanist references, both kinds maturing and developing as Freud does. The correspondence with Silberstein is much greater in size, with seventy-eight letters and postcards, as opposed to seven letters and two postcards to Fluss. Freud's relationship with Silberstein is more intimate and more intellectual, as their two-member "learned association," the "Academia Española Castellana," indicates. The two learned Spanish together and developed their own mythology and private language. Freud described their "intimer Freundschaft" in a letter in 1928 to the B'nai B'rith Lodge in Braila, to which Silberstein had belonged, as a "brüderlicher Gemeinschaft,"[119] and he tells Martha that they "became friends at a time when one . . . needs a friend with whom to share things. . . . We used to be together literally every hour of the day that was not spent on the school bench."[120] Freud discusses with Silberstein his philosophy, politics, and scholarly pursuits in a manner that conveys the respect and esteem in which he held his friend.

In the summer before Freud matriculates at the University of Vienna, he writes a letter to Silberstein that reveals his growing attraction to humanism:

> About the first year at the university I can tell you that I shall spend it entirely in studying humanistic subjects, which have nothing at all to do with my future profession, but which will not be useless to me. . . . I am joining in the first year the faculty of philosophy.[121]

This curriculum helps illuminate Freud's remarks in the Silberstein correspondence about religion and Jewish practice, almost all of which have a skeptical and mocking tone, as though Freud had found another place to "stand." With the cynicism typical of late adolescence, he mocks the idealizations of his elders in an effort to free himself from his past.

On the other hand, evidence of Freud's attachment to Jewish life and tradition (or its attachment to him) is also present in these letters. As when writing to Fluss, Freud makes use of biblical references and quotations to illustrate his meaning and declare his patrimony, even in a casual way. For example, in a letter of 2 August 1873, teasing Silberstein about a philosophy teacher he admires, Freud asks, referring obliquely to 1 Sam. 10:11f.,

> How is it that Saul has fallen in with the prophets, and how have you become his disciple? Is philosophy his area of study, does he hope to earn his bread by it or does he live by manna that our Lord God lets rain down daily for him,[122] and is he purely a philosopher out of love of the subject?

Similarly, on 8 November 1874, complaining of his situation, Freud asks in mock-heroic vein:

> Is there anywhere a refreshing brook in this desert, or an angel who will point out to Ishmael, dying of thirst, a fresh spring, please tell me about it . . .

And again, referring to the demise of a journal he helped found, Freud speaks ironically of himself, recalling Job's words in Job 1:21: "I called it into life, I called it out of life, so my name be praised to all eternity, Amen." The ease with which Freud makes use of these allusions, adapting them wittily to suit his purpose, shows how comfortable he is with the Bible. His references are well-known and so do not imply a familiarity beyond what would ordinarily be expected growing up in his environment, but my point is precisely that: Freud is familiar as a Jew with his Bible, and he refers to it in a native way. His father's example serves him well.

That this environment has affected him deeply, in spite of his teasing, is clear from his conviction, disclosed in a biblical allegory he develops for Silberstein, that a Jew must choose a wife from among the daughters of Israel, and that this was one of the few commandments of Abraham which must not be broken.[123] As Walter Böhlich comments, "Freud was proud of his allegory. . . . Although he was a 'completely Godless Jew' already even in his youth, nevertheless he was very conscious of being a Jew," and once having been born Jewish, Freud believed that one should remain so. It was like "an indelible character."[124] Thus Freud's feeling of belonging to his people is evident at an early age, in spite of his agnosticism.

Information about the religious practice of Freud's boyhood home has been hard to come by, but there are hints in the correspondence. Did the family ever attend synagogue? In a letter to Silberstein of 17 July 1873, Freud says, "You know, don't you, why the Jews in Temple do not remove their hats before God. Because he is omnipresent equally." Since he knows of this practice, perhaps Freud attended occasionally with his family.[125]In a letter of 24 July 1880, Freud uses the Jewish idiom by which the time before a holiday is called that holiday's "evening" (*ereb*), referring to it as the manner in which "los antiguos Castellanos" (the old Spaniards—i.e., Sephardim)[126] spoke. Yerushalmi notes a letter to Carl Koller the day before (23 July), when Freud wrote of "the fateful eve of examination approaching (*eref* examination as they said in olden times)."[127] "What Freud must have heard in his childhood was *'Erev Shabbes,' 'Erev Pesach,' 'Erev Yomtev,'* and it was so natural to him that he could conjure it up with ease and wittily apply it to the eve of the *rigorosum*."[128] Again, evidence for a pattern of observance rather than assimilation seems to emerge.

Did Freud have a bar mitzvah? Yerushalmi argues that given "his father's orientation . . . the norms of the time and of his parents' Jewish milieu, [and] his studies with Samuel Hammerschlag," it is "almost inconceivable that he should not have prepared for and experienced" one.[129] He cites as additional evidence Simon's clue from Freud's third person remark about himself in "Note on the Prehistory of the Technique of Analysis" (1920) that

> in his fourteenth year he had been given [Ludwig] Börne's works as a present, that he still possessed the book now, fifty years later, the only one he had retained from his childhood.[130]

Simon claims that he was able to convince Anna Freud that this passage contains a screen memory of Freud's bar mitzvah, for "only on the Bar-Mitzvah would one receive a gift of classics"[131] such as Börne's collected works. If these clues do not mislead us, sometime around 1869 Freud conformed to Jewish convention in this regard.

In any event, clear evidence of the observance of the Jewish holidays in Jakob and Amalia Freud's household, and of Freud's attitude toward them at age eighteen, is found in a postscript Freud writes in a letter to Silberstein of 18 September 1874. Apparently because Freud did not mention the upcoming Jewish New Year in his recent letters, Silberstein accused his friend (probably teasing him) of a certain "tastelessness" or "tactlessness" (*Geschmacklosigkeit*). Freud replies with a parody of a *d'var Torah*, a Jewish homily, emphasizing the role that food plays in his appreciation and understanding of the Jewish holidays (thus he is not "tasteless" when it comes to Rosh HaShanah):

> One reproaches religion unjustly in saying that it is of a metaphysical nature and so lacks the certainty of sensual perception. On the contrary, religion addresses itself exclusively to the senses, and even the God-denier who has the good fortune to belong to a somewhat [*leidlich*] pious family [i.e., himself] cannot deny the holiday when he puts a New Year's morsel to his mouth.[132]

Gay points out that Freud is proffering here not so much a serious thought (although one ought not underestimate Freud), as he is making a culinary joke.[133] Freud's wit is reminiscent of Heinrich Heine, whose apostate Jew in *The Rabbi of Bacherach* insists, "My nose has not been unfaithful," and who says to his Jewish Sabbath hosts, "I love your cooking far better than your faith; it [the latter] lacks the proper sauce."[134] Freud will refer to Heine in 1928 as "my fellow in disbelief."[135]

In any event, Freud echoes the experience of nearly all Jews when he goes on to say that

> religion, moderately consumed, stimulates the digestion, but taken in excess, harms it. Goethe already knew: "Nothing is more difficult to bear than a sequence of holidays."[136]

Interestingly enough, as a note in Böhlich's edition of these letters reveals,[137] Freud had originally written *leichter*, "easier" to bear, instead of *schwerer*, so we may assume that in spite of his complaint, he also enjoyed the holidays. Note too Freud's use of a humanist text to confirm his Jewish experience. The two traditions meet here to shape Freud's identity. As Feuerbach says, we are what we eat.[138]

Freud continues with an overview of the holidays of the Jewish year, seen through the "lens" of foods associated with them. The speech is a parody of Jewish Torah homilies, as will become clear below in the "Nathan" letter.

> It is remarkable how certain holidays distinguish themselves by an entirely particular religious effect on the organs of the abdomen. For example, Easter [i.e., Passover] causes constipation through unleavened bread and hard-boiled eggs. Yom Kippur is such a gloomy day not so much because of God's wrath, as because of the stewed plum preserves, which produce diarrhea. However, such signs are not sufficient to distinguish all the holidays from one another, and an empiricist such as I will often, as again this year, mix up New Year and Purim, since nothing specific is eaten on either of them.[139] But today the death rattle of two fishes and a goose outside in the kitchen appraised me of the fact that the Day of Atonement is drawing near (I am exaggerating however, for the sake of vividness, for the beasts arrived dead in our house).

Freud's humor is characteristically associated in his mind with his Jewishness. He uses it in relation to religion often, for example when he draws three crosses after mentioning *der liebe Gott* in a letter discussing the reason God created the world in six days rather than in one second.[140] Humor enabled one to bear the difficulty of life, he tells Silberstein's B'nai B'rith brethren in 1928.[141]

Without humor life seems grim. In the body of the letter that contains the humorous postscript about the Jewish holidays, Freud advises his friend to enjoy his youth in the following chilling and rather humorless pronouncement reminiscent, as Rainey notes, of Gloucester's words in *King Lear* (act 4, scene 1) about the sport of the gods in killing us as boys do flies:

> Youth is only the closed season which fate grants to strengthen us so when it gets the whim to hunt us we amuse it with our resistance.[142]

The agnosticism of humanistic studies leads Freud to a skeptical view of the divinity in another letter: "For God's dark ways no one has yet found a lantern," he tells Silberstein. "Like Herodotus," Freud reports, he is beginning to believe in "the maliciousness of destiny."[143] This heaviness is absent from Freud's remarks about the Jewish holidays. In some way, the latter seem easier to bear than theology. In spite of his complaints, Freud does not mention any conflict with his parents over the festivals, and Rainey offers the impression that Freud "grudgingly submitted to them in an attitude of ironic detachment."[144] In any event,

Freud is clearly growing up in a household where the major Jewish festivals are being celebrated, with food being an important focus (as is traditional). Remember Freud's comment to Fluss about the Purim feast being well known as "not among the worst." In a letter to Silberstein of 21 February 1875, Freud will make playful use of the *Mah Nishtanah* from the Passover Haggadah, making clear his own familiarity with the tradition. Theodor Reik will remember Freud comparing the Maori taboos described in Frazer's *Golden Bough* to the *Chad Gadya*, the closing children's song of the Haggadah.[145]

Freud continues his parody in his 1874 postscript, suggesting that this alliance between religion and the stomach works to the advantage of religion. Yet he believes that "the stomach would start a revolution, if religion were abolished." Furthermore, perhaps "in this alliance between digestion and edification [*Verdauung und Erbauung*] may be found the reason why piety agrees so well with the clerics." Probably referring to the common girth of priests, Freud's pun expresses his playfulness. In addition, this transposition from "the high" to "the low," and the hidden connection between them, is an anticipation of Freud's psychoanalytic method for interpreting all culture,[146] as well as being reminiscent of Feuerbach, whom Freud reports two months later he is reading in the university.[147] Freud tells Silberstein in 1875 that "among all philosophers, I worship and admire this man [Feuerbach] the most."[148]

Freud breaks off in the postscript now:

> But we are lost here in cultural-historical questions that do not concern us. The truth is eating is the most entrenched practice. Our festivals have outlived our dogma like the funeral meal has outlived the dead. And the question—What will the last man do?—I can answer, what the first man did: he will eat.

This attention to eating in the Garden of Eden will come up again in the Nathan letter below. Freud concludes here by saying that although both the pious and we *Weltkinder* eat equally on "Sundays and holidays," yet there is one difference:

> though the pious think they have done a good deed [i.e., a *mitzvah*, a commandment], we children of the world are aware: we have eaten a good dish.

So although the Jewish religion is "dead" as far as Freud is concerned, and only the pleasure of eating persists, nevertheless he can in his own way enjoy its good dishes. Such eating is a Jewish pleasure that should not be underestimated in its power to form Jewish identity independently of belief, a phenomenon to which Heine's apostate testifies. Jewish cooking has contributed its potent share to Freud's sense of himself as a Jew: *Der Mensch ist, was er ißt.* As noted, later in life Freud will report that even though he is estranged from the religion of his fathers, he still perceives his own particularity as Jewish *(seine Eigenart als jüdisch empfindet)* and that this Jewishness is so in the most important respect *(die Hauptsache)* in spite of its ineffable quality.[149] Thus here in the early period, the roots are formed for Freud's distinction between Jewish faith and Jewish "essence." Though he is an unbeliever, a "child of the world," Jewish festivals are still "ours," as is the dogma over against which Freud defines himself.

A few years later, in September 1877, Freud will discuss the holidays again, and this time he admits that the previous year, when he was doing research for the first time at Carl Claus's experimental station for marine biology in Trieste, Italy, he had let "the whole spectacle" of Rosh HaShanah pass him by without participating. This contrast tells us that in the past the observance was a regular feature of Freud's life. He now remembers his freedom from the holiday with pleasure, complaining that the result of all the cooking and baking in his home now will be that he will sleep worse than he otherwise would. The benefit he sees to these festive occasions, on the other hand, is communal:

> Such an abundance of feasting [*Fressen*] can only be justified if a great company of people who do not otherwise gather at one table get together. The better food [*Essen*] is then a means to merrymaking, like the finer clothes, dancing, games and other entertainments.

Yet, Freud continues, if all one gets from this is a bellyful of acid, it's a pretty poor way to enjoy oneself. Again we see the focus on the stomach's relation to the holidays, but now with less humor. He concludes by saying,

> We young people, who have half left their own families and not yet entered into a new one, are above all the most unsuited persons to appreciate holidays.

Without a familial context, Jewish holidays are hard to enjoy, and so their effect on the stomach is harder to bear.

Freud finds the value of order and discipline rooted in the Jewish Bible, when he interprets the creation story for Silberstein. "Theologians have asked themselves for a long time, why the dear God † † † needed six days to do the work of creation, which He could have done entirely in one second. None of the explanations given until now hold up," Freud insists, "only I can give the correct interpretation." Again Freud's humor mediates his relation to Jewish religious tradition. God wanted, says Freud,

> to show the children of human beings that with every work one must maintain a rational order and succession of individual tasks. In one second, God would have created everything at the same time, and this teaching would have been lost to human beings in their striving to imitate God.

Thus, in spite of (or by means of) his humor, the discipline of Freud's life has its roots partly in Jewish tradition. That he takes this teaching to heart is evident from the words that follow in his letter, where he says that "this order should also show itself in our letters . . . the order of a work of art."[150] Significantly, Freud's interpretation is methodologically reminiscent of traditional Jewish exegesis.

Evidence of Freud's negative views of East European Jews, which we saw in his letters to Fluss, is also present in the Silberstein letters. Freud seems to have met Nahum Sokolow,[151] the Hebrew writer, journalist, and later Zionist leader, and was impressed with the scholar's knowledge of Hebrew, French, English, Italian, and Spanish, as well as his literary writings, including an upcoming geography of Palestine. "He is without a doubt brilliant," Freud admits, "but unfortunately a Polish Jew."[152] Why is this descent "unfortunate"? Freud's mother was also a Polish Jew, from Brody. In the mind-set of assimilated West European Jews, Polish Jews were crude and uncultured, apparently incorrigibly so. Admittedly, Freud may just be thinking of the antisemitism that will hinder this talented man because of his Jewish descent. In another letter, Freud refers to an old man as a *grober Jude*, an uncultured, crude Jew,[153] and while praising Friedreich Hebbel's skillful depiction of Jewish characters, he does so for his gift for describing *die Starrköpfe*, stubborn or hardheaded persons. In other words, Freud sees Jews as typically headstrong or stubborn. Admittedly, this might be a Jewish asset in Freud's view, since he later expresses admiration for Jewish "tenacity."

A chronicle of Freud's changing theological views is present in his correspondence with Silberstein. In Freud's letter of 30 January 1875, referred to above, he tells his friend that as a child he used to believe in the jealousy of the "so-called Gods" (Freud's quotes), who would oppose the fulfillment of expensive wishes and bring about their opposite. But "today," by contrast, "the world appears more cheerful, and I dare think something possible without holding back, which to my greatest joy promises to be fulfilled." So liberation from belief in the gods and their jealousies has freed Freud for a happier, more self-confident outlook on life.

Three months later in the same year (1875), Freud writes about his discussions with his professor, Franz Brentano, about materialism versus theism, saying that for the moment he has had to admit the possibility that theism is true, only because he has not been able to counter Brentano's arguments. "For the present, I am no longer a materialist, but not yet a theist."[154] Later, he will become a confirmed atheist, but his superstitions and lifelong interest in religion, as well as the very vehemence of his rejection of it, lead us to think that his atheism was qualified in his mind by other possibilities.

The influence of humanistic *belles lettres* on Freud's view of Jewish law and social convention is clear from a letter he writes to Silberstein on 22 August 1874. Speaking against those who, from a "moralistic" point of view, deny value to Alexander Dumas's *Dame aux camélias* (even though he agrees it is "trash"), Freud has this to say:

> Yet by no means do I think, as some aesthetes do, that everything considered immoral according to the bourgeois or Mosaic law must also be unpoetic. Gottfried's *Tristan and Isolde* is the most brilliant refutation of this dictum. On the contrary, poetry, supported by the authority of our own passion, could quite well poetically transform by far that which is immoral, or better, that which society considers impermissible.[155]

Poetry and the law here are independent. Poetry is able to idealize and lend an aspect of beauty to things "immoral" and thus show us something of value in spite of their conflict with the conventions of society or with *das mosaisch Gesetz*. In this way "poetry," or the aesthetic sensibility, is able to transcend Jewish law, to be about something valuable that the law can even obscure. As Freud says further on, "Where poetry has not established its position of exception [to the laws of morality] firmly enough, there morality enters into its own authority." But when poetry does establish this position, it takes its own legitimate stand based on its independent perception of value. Aesthetic values are not subordinate to religious or social values; in fact, they have the power to transform the impermissible. Note Freud's suspension of the authority of the Law. His loyalty to this Romantic humanism expresses his early intellectual independence of inherited convention and Jewish religious law.

The absence of any particular allegiance to Jewish law as an absolute standard parallels Freud's atheism. Writing several months later, Freud describes himself to Silberstein as "the godless, the empirically minded man of medicine" (who is nevertheless studying philosophy and reading Feuerbach), and though he admires his Professor Brentano, he mocks the scientist's belief in the existence of God, his support for "this airy existence of a divinity."[156]

Whatever the role of Freud's humanistic studies in his intellectual effort for freedom, the antisemitism of the university strengthened Freud's Jewish identity in its defiance of Gentile norms. As Freud put it in his *Selbstdarstellung* (1925), recalling the time in 1873 when he first joined the University of Vienna,

> I found that I was expected to feel myself inferior and an alien because I was a Jew. I refused absolutely to do the first of these things. I have never been able to see why I should feel ashamed of my descent or, as people were beginning to say, of my race. I put up, without much regret, with my non-acceptance into the community. . . . [Thus] at an early age I was made familiar with the fate of being in the Opposition and of being put under the ban of the "compact majority." The foundations were thus laid for a certain degree of independence of judgment.[157]

It will become clear how closely this defiance and independent spirit are linked to Freud's sense of himself as a Jew. But it is also significant that these traits are developed in tandem with Freud's allegiance to humanistic and agnostic thinking.

For alongside of Freud's solidarity with his Jewish descent, the humanistic correlate of Freud's atheism is the existential *human* solidarity and responsibility that follows morally from it. As he writes graciously to his friend William Knöpfmacher, who has lent him some money,

> I thank you for the friendly way in which you helped me out of my embarrassment. If there is a God he will take note of your deed and repay you a thousandfold, and if there is not, then there exists at least one man who will remember it and consider it one more reason for remaining fond of you.[158]

In the absence of God, we must depend on each other.

That Freud's humanism has taken over many of the traditional functions of religion becomes even clearer in this letter when Freud cautions Silberstein not to become frivolous and profligate when he goes away to law school in Leipzig:

> Stop—and I say this very seriously—at the limit appropriate for a member of the A[cademia] E[spañola]. Don't become, in Leipzig, too much of a *Tannhäuser*. Nobody today believes in the absolving power of the Pope. Do not think of the futility of all being, but rather of the significance of all earthly things and that an easygoing mind will not be able to cope with our serious task.[159]

Though Freud may be teasing his friend, note the sense of moral limit conveyed by membership in their "learned society."[160] Furthermore, since religion no longer has the power to absolve the responsibility for or the destructive effect of "sins," we must take responsibility ourselves for the consequences of our actions: we are on our own. Nevertheless, do not despair, Freud goes on, for human life on earth is full of meaning and still addresses its moral challenge to the young: "our serious task." The sense of mission is palpable. Although it is facile to call Freud's humanism here a "religion," it is clearly a source of value that commands Freud's loyalty. In this respect it functions in the place of religious allegiance.

A postcard in March 1880 illustrates the skeptical position Freud adopted toward religion as he grew older. At age twenty-three, Freud writes in Spanish to Silberstein, consoling him over what seems some lack of success in love by ironically citing "el sabio Rabbi Don Akiba," from Karl Gutzkow's play, *Uriel Acosta* (1846):

> "Everything has happened before," as the sage Rabbi Don Akiba used to say. He was a very wise man and he saw into the depth of the matter.[161]

In the context of Gutzkow's play, these words from "Rabbi Ben[162] Akiba" convey a slightly foolish impression, as the ninety-year-old rabbi assures his fellow rabbinical judges in the trial overseeing the recantation of the excommunicated "heretic," Uriel Acosta[163] that

> "All hath already been!"—believe me Rabbis,
> Epicureans, Doubters, Skeptics,—though
> Our youth may think: "See these are novel things!"
> "All hath already been!"—believe me Rabbis,
> Of everything our Talmud gives account—
> "All hath already been,—already been!"[164]

Yet when Uriel Acosta turns the rabbi's example of Elisha ben Abuya—*Acher*—on its head, to say that doubt—"the Other"—is the basis of true faith ("For pious faith from doubt alone proceeds"), Ben Akiba is bewildered, and cannot understand the young man's meaning. So it seems that indeed here is something new that the old tradition cannot understand or cope with, and must reject with blind force. The scene probably reflects Freud's view as a young man of his own "enlightened" understanding against the Judaism of his forebears.

In the play, the rabbi is a figure not to be taken seriously or respected by the young, who know new things. Freud seems to be telling Silberstein not to take his disappointment too seriously, while poking fun at Jewish tradition. In the early period, Freud mocks the rabbis of Jewish tradition, using Enlightenment and humanist perspectives. In the late period, on the other hand, he will instead *identify* with the only rabbinic figure mentioned in his correspondence or published psychoanalytic writings, namely, Rabbi Yochanan ben Zakkai. Significantly, these references appear in correspondence in 1938 and in *Moses and Monotheism*, providing evidence for recapitulation in the periodic development of Freud's Jewish identity.

Freud's Letters to Martha Bernays

Freud wrote more than nine hundred letters to his betrothed, Martha Bernays,[165] over the four-and-a-half years they waited before finding the means to marry in September 1886. These letters disclose Freud in his most personal voice, writing to define himself to his fiancée while courting her. One of the most significant of these letters features an encounter with an old merchant whom Freud calls "Nathan." Freud's conversation with him discloses much about his own attitudes toward Judaism and his understanding of himself as a Jew in the early period, at age twenty-six.

The "Nathan" Letter

On 23 July 1882, shortly after his secret engagement, Freud writes a letter to Martha, in Hamburg, describing his meeting with an old Jewish stationery merchant. Freud has come to buy engraved stationery for his betrothed to use in writing to him, and in the course of his conversation with the merchant (whom he calls Nathan, from Lessing's *Nathan the Wise*), Freud discovers that the old Jew is a disciple of Martha's famous grandfather, Chacham Isaac Bernays (1792–1849), the former Chief Rabbi of Hamburg. The encounter provides Freud with an opportunity to woo his beloved and clarify for her (and for himself) his Jewish identity and allegiances in relation to the traditions of Jewish scholarship and religious practice to which she is heir. Freud's letter thus gives us a vivid picture of his Jewish self-understanding as a young man. Though Freud's Jewish identity develops and changes over the course of his life, the Jewish-humanist dual allegiance established in the early period sets the stage for more mature later developments.

The letter closes with a promise from Freud to his fiancée:

> And as for us, I believe that though the form in which the old Jews found comfort no longer offers us any shelter, something of the kernel, of the essence of this meaningful and life-affirming Judaism will not be absent from our home.[166]

Our study of this letter is primarily an attempt to understand both what Freud means by this statement of Jewish belief and its significance for his Jewish self-understanding in the first period of his Jewish development. As will be seen, despite his humanist allegiances and atheist beliefs, Freud sees himself in his youth (at twenty-six) as he does in his old age (at eighty-two), as "a good Jew, who has never denied his *Judentum*."[167]

Biographical Context of the "Nathan" Letter. It will be helpful to establish the biographical context for this letter, in order to assess its import accurately. Much of the following is taken from Ernest Jones's biography.

Sigmund Freud, age twenty-five, living at home with his family while doing research and working as a "Demonstrator" (sort of a teaching assistant) in Ernst Brück's Physiological Institute, returns home from work one evening in April 1882. His usual habit was to head straight for his room to resume his studies, but on this occasion his attention was arrested by the presence of a lovely young girl peeling an apple while chatting gaily with family members at the table. Contrary to his usual habit, and to the surprise of the family, Freud joins them. Martha Bernays is twenty. She and Freud become engaged secretly on Saturday, 17 June 1882, that is, within three months of their meeting. The next day, however, Martha leaves with her family for Wandsbek, a suburb of Hamburg, for a ten-week summer holiday with her uncle, not to return to Vienna until September 11.[168] The Nathan letter is written in Hamburg on 23 July 1882, slightly over a month after Freud and Martha have gotten engaged (N.B., without their parents' consent), when Freud travels to Wandsbek for a rendezvous with his fiancée to iron out some misunderstandings that have arisen between them.

On 15 June 1882, Freud wrote his first letter to his fiancée-to-be, on his father's stationery, in effect proposing to her in gentle and delicate, even shy language:

> The last time that we see each other [i.e., before Martha leaves on holiday] I should like to address the loved one, the adored one, as 'Du', and be assured of a relationship which perhaps will have for long to be veiled in secrecy.[169]

He got his wish. The assurance came in the form of a ring, reference to which figures prominently in the Nathan letter, bearing meanings drawn from Gotthold Lessing's play, *Nathan the Wise.* Jones says, "Martha's response to the letter when he saw her in his home on the Saturday [i.e., on Shabbat] was to present him with a ring of her father's which her mother had given her—perhaps for such a purpose."[170] Freud wore it on his little finger and had a copy made for her, lest its absence give cause for suspicion.

Freud and Martha kept their engagement secret, in part because Martha's family was not entirely pleased with Freud as a prospective husband for their Martha, undoubtedly preferring someone more traditionally observant.[171] Martha's father had died in 1879, and the family's finances were virtually ruined. As Peter Swales suggests, had it not been for this fall of fortune, Freud may not even have been considered as a suitor.[172] The Bernays family was heir to and had continued in a profound tradition of Jewish scholarship, and they were well known as descendants of Chacham Bernays. Freud acknowledges this descent and connects the notepaper to it:

> My girl came from a family of scholars,[173] and wrote—for the time being only letters—with untiring hand. . . . So I decided to acquire some notepaper for the dear industrious child and chose some on which she could write to me only.

Freud's gift seems to insert itself into the family's tradition of scholarship, as if to lead Martha aside, into his own tradition. Martha's family probably regarded Freud as something of an *am ha'aretz* (i.e., Jewishly unlearned to the extent that one is unable or unwilling to be observant), and so he is waging a subtle polemic along with his courting.

To help the betrothed couple maintain the secrecy of their relationship, a former admirer of Martha and friend of Freud, Fritz Wahle, addressed a number of envelopes to Martha for Freud to use. Thus it makes sense that Freud should assume the name of "Dr. Wahle" when buying notepaper for Martha's exclusive correspondence with him. However, Fritz was an artist, not a doctor. The conflation may indicate Freud's sense of victory, the "scientist" over the "artist." Samuel Jaffe has suggested that one of the underlying themes of the letter is Freud's relationship to other men,[174] a vehicle for his relationship to Judaism as well, and so worth our attention in this context.

Not only was Wahle an artist, but Martha had also once been his pupil. Freud, as a scientist, saw Fritz as a rival for Martha's love. He thought that artists possess in their art "a master key to open with ease all female hearts," whereas scientists were "helpless at the strange design of the lock and have first to torment ourselves to discover a suitable key to it."[175] Martha had given Freud some grounds for his jealousy, for she had once allowed Fritz to kiss her, in fact on the same day that she and Freud had walked arm in arm, perhaps for the first time.[176] Although engaged himself to a cousin of Martha's, Fritz had burst into tears on hearing of Martha's engagement, "and since then, however affectionate her letters, he had gone about complaining that Martha was neglecting him and that her letters were cold."[177]

A mutual friend of Freud and Wahle, Schönberg, called the two together for a talk in a café in an effort to help reconcile them. It didn't help. Fritz threatened to shoot Freud and then himself if Freud did not make Martha happy. A scene of strong emotions followed, during which Wahle wrote a letter to Martha in front of Freud and Schönberg, instructing her to dismiss Freud, using such language as "Beloved Martha" and "undying love," which he was apparently accustomed to using before Martha's engagement to Freud. Freud insisted on reading the letter, and upon doing so, tore it to pieces. At this point Wahle left, mortified. When his two friends caught up with him to bring him to his senses, he burst into tears. Freud comes to realize that Fritz loves Martha, in spite of her protestations that theirs is but a simple friendship. He decides that he must travel to Wandsbek to reestablish his harmonious relationship with Martha, even though he must borrow money to do so. Fritz's threat to order Martha to give Freud up "because he tormented her," raised Freud's doubts about his own hold on her, and another letter from Martha, assuring Fritz that "their friendship was quite unchanged" despite her engagement, drove Freud into such a frantic state that "he wandered through the streets for hours in the night."[178]

With this anxiety accompanying him, Freud arrives in Wandsbek on 17 July, staying for ten days in a hotel in great secrecy. It is several days before Martha can arrange a rendezvous in the marketplace in Hamburg, and it is after this meeting, on 23 July, that Freud writes the Nathan letter, probably delivering it in person (as we deduce from the absence of address or signature). We may assume therefore that this letter held special, personal importance for the newly betrothed couple, or at least that Freud felt that it did. It almost seems like a gift.

I have entered into such detail to show the important role the Nathan letter could have played at this particular point in the newly engaged couple's relationship. The first month after an engagement may easily be a time of self-doubt, especially if the couple are not together, and these scenes of jealousy and anxiety imply that Freud felt such doubts. Now, with the crisis past, Freud writes the Nathan letter in a playful and happy mood, confident of Martha's love. With his rival out of the way, Freud seeks now to cement their future together all the more firmly by giving his Orthodox fiancée some reassurance concerning his own relation to Jewish tradition. It is in this context that the closing sentence of the letter, quoted above, is to be understood. It is a fantasy of their future home, but it reveals Freud's wishes and intentions with regard to the place of Judaism or Jewishness in their future life together, and in so doing it defines Freud's Jewish self-understanding at this point in his life, at least in part. Freud's letter is full of humor, wit, and playfulness, with apt references to humanist literature and the scholarly historical tradition with which he identifies. Freud shows Martha that he too is a scholar worthy of her family tradition, and that in marrying him she will be winning a prize of great joy (*Freude*).

Analysis of the Nathan Letter. Freud opens the letter with a few lines intended to introduce the "Tale of the Three Rings" told by the Jew, Nathan the Wise, in Lessing's play[179] of the same name: "The Jew is called Nathan. (A strange Jew—hm)." Freud knows he does not have the quotation exactly, but he gets the gist of what he wants to say: "Continue, worthy Nathan." Freud evokes the scene in Lessing's play before the Moslem ruler, Saladin, who has asked Nathan which faith or law (Islam, Christianity, or Judaism) he "deems the best" (act 3, scene 5). After some thought, Nathan tells the "Tale of the Rings" (act 3, scene 7).

There was once, Nathan says, "in eastern lands" a man who had a magic ring, whose wearer, "trusting in its strength, was loved of God and men" (3.7.22). Note that the power of the ring derives not from the ring itself but from the faith of its wearer. This man bequeathed the ring to his favorite son, on condition that it be passed on in turn to that son whom the father loved best, regardless of order of birth. In time the ring came into the hands of a man who had three sons, all of whom he loved equally and none of whom could he bear to humiliate in order to favor one. Therefore he had exact copies made and gave to each son separately a ring to make that son believe he was "the prince of all his house." One wonders at the father's foolishness here, but since the king is God, the act may be intentional. As Nathan says, "Possibly the father wished / To tolerate no longer in his house / The tyranny of just one ring!" (3.7.129–31). In any event, since the effect is only reflexive, not outward ("Each one loves himself the most"), the judge in Nathan's tale counsels the quarreling brothers each to "believe his ring to be / The true one," and so

> aspire
> To emulate his father's unbeguiled,
> Unprejudiced affection! Let each strive
> To match the rest in bringing to the fore
> The magic of the opal in his ring!
> Assist that power with all humility,
> With benefaction, hearty peacefulness,
> And with profound submission to God's will!
> (3.7.134–41)

The true religion (to translate the parable) will only be known in a "thousand thousand years," when its practitioners' deeds make them obviously more beloved of God and human beings than others.

The play's moral point of brotherhood in spite of difference must have impressed Freud, as it did so many others, as a truth that transcended the particularity of "confessional religions." Freud's use of the ring allusion in his letter relates to his struggle with his rival, Fritz Wahle, but its context and origin in Lessing's play are important as well to Freud's Jewish identity.

Freud thought highly of Lessing. He writes to Martha a year after this letter that "everyone ought to have someone great and powerful to be his lord and protector, to whom he could turn in dark, heavy hours."[180] Turning from Milton, Freud says of Lessing that he has "nearer, older rights over me, and can direct us on this earth instead of leading us beyond it." Furthermore, he says,

> I am resolved to set up a statue of him in our future home . . . and to keep his works in a prominent place. I remember that with the last remains of my religious faith I put you under his protection when I came upon him unexpectedly in Hamburg.[181]

There is a monument to Lessing in the marketplace in Hamburg, the precise location of Freud and Martha's rendezvous on his mission for reassurance, and Freud refers to it at the beginning of his letter to his fiancée, confident, as he says, of Lessing's "forgiveness" for his not having the exact quote. Perhaps it was at their rendezvous that Freud put Martha under Lessing's "protection." Freud may be implying that

Lessing is a worthy replacement for traditional religious allegiance, from which he is seeking to wean Martha. In his later letter, he is using language that would in Jewish tradition usually be applied especially to God.

According to Freud, Lessing is someone who can direct them "on this earth." This guiding task is in traditional Judaism the special role of the *halacha,* the Jewish religious practice which has interfered with Freud's courting of Martha (e.g., preventing her at first from writing to him on Shabbat). It continues to do so, as he notes in his letter, with regard to Tisha B'Av. Thus we might see Freud offering Martha Lessing's humanist position as a substitute for the Jewish observance of her family. This suggestion seems plausible given Freud's opening lines, as though they introduce Freud's own "Tale of the Rings," answering Saladin's question in *Nathan the Wise* with Freud's Jewish humanism. Yet Freud notes that "the true ring" remained with Martha, in spite of the copy he'd had made for her. Though *halachic* observance was in fact absent from the Freud home,[182] Freud promises in the end that the essence of Martha's Judaism, "the true ring," will not be absent.

German Jewry regarded *Nathan the Wise* as its "spiritual Magna Carta,"[183] because its vision held forth the possibility of a society in which they participated equally, irrespective of their Jewish difference. However, as Dilthey noted, "the value of Nathan's personality . . . is independent of the historical religion to which he formally belonged," so that "Nathan's virtues have nothing to do with his Jewishness."[184] Lessing's point in *Nathan der Weise* is that whatever the particular claims each of the three religions makes with regard to revelation, religious differences are "utterly irrelevant to an individual's humanity and capacity to achieve cultural and moral virtue."[185] Ethical results are what count, and so if each religion's adherents would persuade others that they hold the true religion, the "true ring," then let them act with love and justice in the world (as the humanists will also do, without "religion"), the sign of the true ring. In this approach, Lessing is following Immanuel Kant (1724–1804), who persuaded a whole generation that beyond all historical religions there was "a single, unchanging, pure religious faith" dwelling in the human conscience—in essence the religion of the future—which made indifference to all specific elements of Judaism (and other historical religions, like Christianity and Islam) respectable. For as Michael Meyer explains, "if God required nothing more than steadfast diligence in leading a morally good life, in fulfilling one's duties to fellow human beings, then all ceremonial and symbolic expressions were ultimately superfluous."[186] Furthermore, for Kant, ceremonies designed "to please God," that is, rituals were "morally indifferent and historically representative of paganism." A house of God instead was properly a "meeting place for the instruction and quickening of moral dispositions."[187] Needless to say, this philosophy profoundly underestimates the role that ritual and symbolic expression play in shaping "moral dispositions."

This Kantianism was combined with an attitude developed by G. W. F. Hegel (1770–1831) and absorbed also by Lessing (and everybody else) that Judaism was a fossil, that though it had been a stage in the spiritual development of mankind, it had reached the end of its capacity for internal religious development during the Second Temple period (at which point Christianity took over). According to Meyer, the Judaism that was taught by the leaders of the Reform movement (who influenced Freud's teachers) became a kind of "reaction-formation" (my word) to Kant's caricature of a "no-morality Judaism." Judaism was presented by contrast as being exclusively concerned with morality, and so most worthy of the future.[188] Freud's rejection of the ritual practice of Judaism coupled with his respect for its ethical foundations can be seen as a reflection of the reigning Kantian and Hegelian conventions of his time. And *Moses and Monotheism* may be in part a recapitulation of this complex of ideas from the Judaism Freud was taught as a youth, especially so if Freud locates the ultimate source of all spiritual progress and morality in Judaism and Jewish tradition.

In the Nathan letter, in any event, Freud seems to be saying that the Judaism in his and Martha's home will be "wise," that is, based on the Enlightenment view of Lessing and that of his model for Nathan, Moses Mendelssohn, who presented Kant's position to their generation and respective communities. In addition, Freud's emphasis on the kind of Judaism that will be present in their *home* may reflect the compromise that Enlightenment-minded Jews like Mendelssohn developed, expressed succinctly by Judah Leib Gordon (1831–92) in his poem, "Awake, My People": "Be a human being [*Mensch*] when you go forth, and a Jew in your home." Jewishness is described here as a private matter, *"für uns beide."* Later, outside his home and private life, Freud will choose Carl Jung to "de-Judaize" psychoanalysis for the world.

Freud's *use* of Lessing's tale in relation to rivals for Martha's love points to Freud's struggle to establish his humanistic Judaism in their home. Jaffe notes that Freud deftly maneuvers his metaphor to talk about his own jealousy.[189] Despite the fact that Martha wears "the true ring," because "everyone who saw and spoke to her loves her," Freud "didn't like this much," and he wondered how he could make her less attractive. Freud's humor at himself is evident, and he goes on to celebrate Martha's devotion to him alone: "What mattered was whether she loved several people." This was precisely what he had come to Wandsbek to find out: "Is it Fritz or me?" He is now convinced that Fritz Wahle is not a serious threat, and he is "very happy in Hamburg."

As mentioned above, Jaffe infers from this passage that an underlying theme in the letter is Freud's relationship to other men, who are most immediately rivals for Martha's loyalty and love. Her obedience to the *halacha*, the "law of the fathers," also represents such a rival. The issue of religious allegiance, implied by the Ring Tale, is framed in terms of Martha's loyalty to rival suitors (a well-known topos in the Bible as well). So in Freud's mind, his victory over other men is also to lead Martha to his kind of non-*halachic* Judaism. This interpretation is supported by Freud's oedipal glee (expressed, *nota bene*, immediately after praising Martha's father, Berman Bernays) at the thought of what the merchant Nathan would think if he knew that his customer, "allegedly a Dr. Wahle, from Prague, had this very morning kissed the granddaughter of his idol." Martha's grandfather, an Orthodox opponent of Reform Judaism, would not have been pleased at Freud's nonobservance. In winning Martha, Freud is also victorious over *that* old man. As Jaffe puts it, Freud, with "despotic notepaper" in hand, is engaged in this letter in taking possession of his woman, combined with a put-down of the old father figure, and he seals his oedipal aggression with the memory of his kiss.[190] So Freud does express his wish to be free of Jewish tradition in the early period in "patricidal" images. But the expression is ambiguous, for killing the father is also a subtle form of identification, as Ernst Simon notes.[191]

After this introduction that leaves Freud in sole possession of his "Marty," he turns to the "jovial old gentleman" from whom he has bought some notepaper engraved with a special *M* and *S* monogram. Freud must wait for this paper until Sunday because Shabbat intervenes. Freud thus introduces the merchant to Martha as someone who observes Shabbat, as she does. He teases her: "Oh, I know that ancient tradition!" Shabbat observance has been and will continue to be a bone of contention between them, but in any event note Freud's assertion of familiarity with the practice. His own home may not have been as devoid of such observance as has sometimes been assumed.

Isaiah Berlin relates that even in 1938 the pair still argued over Martha's desire to light Shabbat candles on Friday night.[192] Martha's cousin, Elliott Philipp, recalls Martha telling him how "not being allowed to light the Sabbath lights on the first Friday night after her marriage was one of the more upsetting experiences of her life."[193] Freud thought such ritual nothing more than superstition.[194] Significantly, three days before this refusal to allow his new bride to perform this traditional ritual acknowledgment of the entrance of the Sabbath, Freud had been compelled to submit to the Jewish marriage ritual and recite its Hebrew phrases with the help of one of Martha's relatives.[195] Given his attitude toward religious ritual, the experience must have been humiliating for him. Freud's dogmatic refusal to allow this seemingly harmless (and beautiful) bit of Jewish observance into his new home may have been a reaction to the embarrassment of that marriage ritual, an insistence that their home would be ruled by reason, not ritual, by him and not by her relatives. But here at the beginning of their engagement, by contrast, Freud obtains a gift for Martha that is *associated* with the observance of Shabbat. This giving implies a recognition of its importance to Martha, and perhaps even some respect at this stage, in spite of Freud's teasing. After the marriage ceremony, Freud will be less flexible; here he is courting.

Next, Freud guesses at the old man's age, and learns that he is seventy-four. Freud's own father is sixty-seven at this time, and like the merchant, might also be described as *ein jovialer alter Herr*. One of the things Freud often mentions about his father is his good humor. He writes Wilhelm Fliess that Jakob was "very happy within himself," and characterizes him as having a quality of "playfully imaginative lightheartedness" [*phantastisch leichtem Sinn*].[196] Martin Freud recalls that Jakob had "a little twinkle in his great brown eyes, as if he wanted to say, 'Isn't everything we are doing and saying here a great joke?'"[197] This joviality links Freud to his father. As Freud tells Fliess, he begins collecting "profound Jewish stories," which later find a place in his book on jokes, around the same time he is writing *Die Traumdeutung*.[198] And we know by Freud's own report that his *Interpretation of Dreams* is very much bound up with his father.[199] Martin describes Freud himself as having *ein fröhliches Herz*, which he translates as "a merry heart."[200] Humor, especially Jewish humor, united Jakob Freud and his son, and it is a dimension of Freud's Jewish identity formed in the early period and present throughout his life.

The merchant is clearly a father figure for Freud, linked to him specifically by a sense of humor and his joy at life. Freud likes him: "Der Mann gefiel mir." The merchant's gusto for pleasure and work reminds us of Freud himself, who worked eighteen-hour days, but always took a long summer vacation, and smoked with a pleasure he would not deny himself. Freud tells Fliess in fact that his father, who remained a heavy smoker until the age of eighty-one, was his model in this pleasure, so smoking itself links Freud to his father.[201] This connection may explain Freud's resistance to relinquishing smoking, even when it threatened his health, though Freud related his refusal to the contribution smoking made to his ability to work.[202] The old merchant Nathan takes a fatherly interest in Freud, explaining the world of Hamburg banking to him, and he sits him down on a chair to give him friendly advice and "words of Torah" from his master and teacher, Chacham Isaac Bernays.

I suggest that Freud is in turn "giving over" these *divrei Torah* to Martha, sharing Jewish tradition with her in a way that strengthens the bond between them by creating common Jewish "ground" or "firmament." Freud is doing something in his own way that has delighted and united Jews for many centuries. He is of course doing so with tongue-in-cheek humor and a healthy dose of criticism, but he clearly admires the Torah of Martha's grandfather, as well as the man himself and his disciple, and he seeks to equal that esteem in Martha's and his own eyes. He does so on his own terms—that is, historical and literary ones—but he uses as well the Jewish traditions transmitted to him by the disciple of Chacham Bernays. In this way he forges a link between himself, his fiancée, and their forefathers. Despite his atheism, at age twenty-six Freud can take a delight in Jewish tradition and identify himself with it, even if he does so selectively.

Before Freud discusses Isaac Bernays however, he turns to the fast of Tisha B'Av, for which the old merchant is preparing himself by letting his beard grow as a sign of mourning for the destruction of the ancient Temple in Jerusalem. To Freud the fast day is a nuisance, preventing him from seeing Martha on Tuesday, the last day of his stay. It is clear that Martha too will observe the fast. Freud's comment is illuminating:

> Just because years ago at this time—according to a false chronological calculation—Jerusalem had been destroyed I was to be prevented from speaking to my girl on the last day of my stay here.

Again, Jewish observance interferes with his personal relationship with and access to his fiancée. This denial would be quite enough to earn Freud's resentment, but there is more.

First, it should be noted that Freud's initial criticism has to do with his claim that the observance is inaccurately related to the actual historical event on which the fast is based. By "false calculation," Freud may refer to the fact that the destruction of neither the First Temple in c. 586/7 B.C.E. nor the Second Temple in 70 C.E. actually took place on the 9th of Av.[203] That is, in Freud's eyes the observance is not based on an objective historical fact, which he sets up as a judge over the tradition. This elevation of history to a status of ultimate criterion is typical of the *Wissenschaft des Judentums* movement within Judaism, whose influence on Freud is clear. "History"—a humanistic discipline—tells us what is true, and religion should be based on that. Tradition, especially as a vehicle of authority or a mode of revealed truth, has no place in this approach, which seeks to be a "science" based on Reason. Here the Enlightenment supplants Jewish tradition in Freud's mind.

Freud's reaction is defiant, and somewhat callous:

> "What's Hecuba to me?" Jerusalem is destroyed and Marty and I are alive and happy/lucky [*glücklich*].

This last sentence sounds very much like one from Abraham Geiger, a leading historian in the *Wissenschaft des Judentums* and Reform movements whom we know Freud read: "Jerusalem is a tomb; you must draw from the living present and labor in it."[204] This similarity will lead us further into the influence of the teaching of Reform Judaism on Freud, but first let us turn our attention to Freud's quote from Shakespeare's *Hamlet* (2.2.559) to illustrate Freud's attachment to and use of humanist texts.

In the context of the play, Hamlet asks the question Freud quotes in relation to an actor who has just wept for Hecuba's grief at the slaying of her husband, Priam, in the piece the actor has just played: "What's Hecuba to him or he to Hecuba that he should weep for her?" Hamlet is upset at his own inability to act in relation to his uncle's fratricide, and he is puzzled by the emotional response of one who is not even related to those for whom he can nonetheless weep. How apt is Freud's allusion: the fall of Troy/the fall of Jerusalem. Both contexts, Shakespeare's and Freud's, speak of the denial of relation that would make one weep for the fallen and their loss; both speak of the denial of familial roots and filial obligation. Freud uses a humanist text to uproot the personal relevance of a Jewish observance and tradition being pressed upon him by a father figure ("Nathan"), a technique that reflects his own allegiance. Freud here reveals his humanist allegiances in relation to Jewish tradition or belief. As we have seen, Freud is Jewish on his own terms, namely, humanist ones.

Note that the player's piece in *Hamlet* recounts the murder of a father figure, an "old grandsire," and Hamlet's chagrin is over his own inability to act in revenge of his father's murder by murdering his father's brother. In the merchant's shop, Freud does not argue with Nathan, but sits listening respectfully, like a good son, perhaps telling Martha what he might have liked to have said. Freud seems to be saying, What is Jerusalem that I should weep [i.e., observe the mourning customs] for her? But the player does weep, as does Nathan. Freud does not—perhaps cannot—and is as helpless here as Hamlet is in the play. Freud's callous dismissal of the tradition expresses his denial of his connection to the old man and to the tradition of observance he embodies. His selfish and immature reaction is precisely what the tradition is trying to counter, by teaching a dependence on the past, on structures, meanings, and values that transcend our own lives and personal happiness. Freud does not see such lessons in his irritation at being limited by them.

Freud then offers two more defenses of his attitude (perhaps sensing its callousness), drawing from the tradition of historical scholarship of the Reform Judaism of his time. The first defense Freud labels specifically a historical one:

> And the historians say that if Jerusalem had not been destroyed, we Jews [N.B.] would have perished like so many peoples before us and after us.

I have not been able to locate the exact source of Freud's statement, or the identity of "the historians" he is thinking of, but his idea is clearly influenced by Geiger's work, and may derive from the history textbooks from which Freud was taught in his last three years at the *Gymnasium*, namely, those by David Cassel and Leopold Breuer. Rainey says that these scholars belonged to the second generation of the *Wissenschaft des Judentums* movement and were sympathetic to Reform Judaism.[205] A copy of Abraham Geiger's *Judaism and Its History* was found in Freud's library.[206]

Geiger writes that "Israel's mission was not accomplished by the establishment of its nationality."[207] If it had been, Israel would have vanished with the loss of its commonwealth, like other "nations which the World's History commissions only to establish and preserve commonwealths for a time, in order that they may do their allotted share in the world's work."[208] But, he continues,

> A nationality which is only a means for a higher object, an external form for a great Idea intended to comprise all mankind must, for a time gather all its forces, until a serried host is prepared, among whom the Idea may obtain its full manifestation, so that it may, fully strengthened, spread all over the world.[209]

It is this universal relevance that ensures Judaism's (and the Jews') survival, for "only that religion which is reconciled with free thought has . . . the guarantee of its continuance."[210] It is the universalization of Judaism that makes possible and worthwhile its survival, and this is accomplished by the destruction of the Temple in Jerusalem.

This view is similar to that articulated by David Einhorn, a more radical member of the Reform movement in Germany, who said, specifically with regard to Tisha B'Av,

> Reform recognizes in the flaming Temple mount not a curtailment but rather a continuation of the divine work of salvation, which had begun on flaming Mount Sinai, marking the real beginning of the priestly mission, the conveyance of the divinity to all the children of this earth, for which Israel had been ordained at the Sinaitic choice.[211]

Thus, the destruction of the Temple becomes an act by God for the reform of the law he had revealed to Moses. As Einhorn put it, "Only after the destruction of Jerusalem was it possible for Israel to become a kingdom of priests and a holy nation."[212]

Einhorn's words sound like Freud's second defense: "Only after the collapse of the visible Temple, did the invisible edifice of Judaism become possible." What exactly Freud means by "the invisible edifice of Judaism" may be clarified by comparing his words with Geiger's, who writes that "the temple [in this case, the one in Egypt] was the visible housing, but far above that was the spirit, the doctrine,"[213] and "the spiritual, being in mind and heart, is not visible in space."[214] Therefore, it was only when Israel's spirit became separated from the political state that "Israel's soul truly blossomed forth and entered into all parts of the world."[215] That is, as Einhorn says, the result of the destruction of the Temple was a "rich inner development," "an adequate replacement for that external pageantry."[216]

Views such as these from the early period of Freud's Jewish development remained with him into his later life, as can be seen from his words on the occasion of the opening of Hebrew University in Jerusalem (of which Freud was a trustee) in 1925:

> Historians have told us that our small nation withstood the destruction of its independence as a State only because it began to transfer in its estimation of values the highest rank to its spiritual possessions, to its religion and its literature.[217]

From this link, spanning forty years, it is clear that Freud's Jewish viewpoint was deeply influenced by and is the expression of thinking within the *Wissenschaft des Judentums* movement, especially as it found application in Reform Judaism. Though Freud's practical loyalties lie within this Enlightenment tradition, he is internally linked also to the Jewish tradition that Nathan represents, and he seeks in his letter to Martha to define that connection in a positive though critical way. Freud seeks this expression to gain Martha's trust and her allegiance, but he will not be severed from the larger humanistic cultural life that connects him to the world beyond the Jews, beyond the *shtetl* his father left so many years ago, and to what he believes is the truth.

Nathan claims that his own Judaism, learned from Martha's grandfather, holds fast to the religion without cutting him off from life, so we can understand why Freud admires the man. This conflict between the larger cultural "life" and the particular tradition is of course the modern tension. Isaac Bernays himself responded to this tension with an affirmation of modernity from within the Jewish tradition: "acculturation and halakhically permissible modernization in religious externals" (e.g., he wore the garb of Christian clergy, like the preachers of the temple), combined with "the preservation of inherited customs and ceremonies" (e.g., he opposed changes in the prayer book).[218] The method produced such disciples as Nathan, and Freud admires this achievement, though he himself cannot fully share in it. He must find his own compromise instead. Still, in some sense, Bernays' work is a model. Freud's admiration of Bernays leads him to a discussion of the Chacham and his talented family, whom he also clearly admires. That the grandfather was important to Martha is indicated by the fact that the rabbi's portrait "occupied an honorable place in her living room."[219]

It may be significant that neither Freud nor the merchant mentions the fact that Michael Bernays converted to Christianity (in 1856). In more traditionally pious Jewish circles, that is, those which are more exclusive, perhaps more "Orthodox," about their culture, one "sits *shiv'ah*" (a seven-day period of mourning) for an apostate as if he had died, and one no longer speaks of him. Jacob Bernays in fact did "sit *shiv'ah*" for his brother Michael.[220] Here Nathan speaks of the second son with a pride no different from that for Jacob, the eldest son, saying that Michael is "still teaching the appreciation of the subtleties and the wisdom [*den feinen Geschmack und die Weisheit*] which our great poets and teachers have put into their writings." Michael Bernays (1834–97) was a professor of German literature at the University of Munich (1874–90) who "wrote pioneering textual studies of Goethe."[221] "*Our* great poets and teachers" here are *German* ones, rather than Jewish. They are representatives of "the ideal of humanism of our German classical period," as Freud put it in his obituary for Hammerschlag. Freud is showing Martha (though perhaps she knew already) that his connection with the world of humanistic letters is something he shares with her own family tradition, and that there need not be a contradiction between being part of a

Jewish family and at the same time being an active worker in the world at large. In this context, it is only sensible that no one mentions Michael's conversion, for that fact undermines the argument that one can be Jewish *and* German humanist. In any event, Freud goes on to imply that all that scholarship (and Jacob [1824–81] was even more impressive) is little match in value for the treasure (*Schatz*) of a human being like Martha. For Freud, she is one of the *bedeutend Kinder* left behind by Berman Bernays, indeed the most distinguished: "Glory to the memory of him who presented me with my Marty!"

Immediately after honoring Martha's father in this way, Freud takes an oedipal delight in imagining what *mein alter Jude* would think if he knew that Freud had just that morning kissed the granddaughter of his idol. This secret "victory" may compensate Freud for some discomfort at humbling himself before the memory of Martha's father's (he had died in 1879). Oedipal victory protects Freud from the religious claim of Orthodox tradition, whose background he shares with Martha.

Now the image of Nathan the Wise emerges again in Freud's letter, as he says traits of Lessing's figure begin to emerge in *seinem Gemüte*, "his temperament." Whose? The merchant's or that of Isaac Bernays? The ambiguity is perhaps intentional, for Freud wants to link them both to Lessing's vision of progress and "natural religion." One wonders exactly what features of Nathan Freud sees. The merchant reports that Bernays taught religion with such *Geist und Humanität*, and Freud said of Hammerschlag that Jewish "religious instruction served him as a way of educating toward humanism" (*Humanität*). The particular serves as the access to the universal. Thus Bernays, like Hammerschlag, is able to combine Judaism with humanistic culture, just as Freud wishes to. Bernays can move in both worlds without losing his own Jewishness, as did Lessing's Nathan the Wise, and as did Mendelssohn. Perhaps this constituted their "wisdom." That is, Bernays could "step outside the law" without thereby ceasing to be Jewish. In fact, by doing so he can better defend, interpret, and explain the law. Freud seeks to do the same, though he steps further away. An example of Bernays's participation in both cultures and of his teaching of Jewish religion with "great imagination and humanism" follows in Freud's letter, in the form of Nathan's *d'var Torah* about *kashrut*, the dietary law. It will be helpful to examine it closely, both for method and content, to get a sense of how it relates to Freud's Jewish identity.

Bernays's opening question (at least as Freud reports Nathan's retelling of it) is, "What could be less important, of less consequence, than what one eats?" The question presumes no *a priori* allegiance to

Judaism. Bernays stands with the unbeliever, even perhaps outside the context of Jewish culture, demonstrating a humanistic solidarity. Bernays's effort is an attempt to respond to what seems on the surface to be *"unsinnig,"* "without meaning." "Meaning" [*Sinn*] is one of the components of the Judaism Freud promises will be a part of his Jewish home with Martha. It is the modern demand, but of course it has a strong place in the tradition as well (e.g., in Maimonides). In this case Bernays will discover Jewish meaning through *aggada,* story, instead of *halacha,* law. Story is of course more immediately accessible, since it requires no prior commitment on the part of the listener.

From this stance "outside the law," Bernays moves to the Creation story in the Bible, that is, to an appeal to a common, universal heritage that is at the same time a Jewish one. He goes back to the beginnings of Western culture. His approach opens with a concession to the Enlightenment: *Es ist vielleicht aus einer Fabel.* No ordinary Orthodox Jew would say that. Only a story? The literary contextualization reminds us of Michael Bernays's *feiner Geschmack.* We remember also that Michael's father was a *Schriftausleger,* "an interpreter of the Scriptures." Is this part of Nathan's wisdom? Bernays starts with a humanist appeal, grounding his argument in the larger, common culture. He then moves to a populist or democratic argument that has analogues in the Jewish tradition in reference to the evidence for the veracity of the revelation on Mount Sinai:

> what the whole of mankind [transferred significantly from the Sinaitic 600,000] has believed for centuries surely cannot be without meaning; it must hold a meaning [*Sinn*].

Again the demand or drive for meaning. There is an Orthodox view that rejects this approach for the very reason Bernays uses it, namely, it seems to place man and his needs at the center of the question, basing obedience on human capacities for understanding.[222] Bernays's approach is the opposite of the traditional *na'aseh ve nishma'*—"Do [the commandment] and *then* you may understand/hear meaning." Though Orthodox himself, Bernays is willing to argue from a position that has affinities with humanism and seems close to Reform Judaism's emphasis on modern perspective.

However, the next step in his argument seems to challenge Reform Judaism's emphasis on ethics over ritual. "Why is the first command God gives the first human beings in the Garden of Eden not about morals? Why instead is it about eating?" Bernays seems to be suggesting that the

Orthodox emphasis on obedience first conceals some wisdom that involves God's intention. Perhaps Judaism grounds itself in something deeper than ethics, something beyond ethical reason, and not initially accessible.

Significantly, therefore, the argument ends in God: "And if the first commandment God made was one about food, can it be of no importance what one eats?"[223] That is, must we not take God's *first* commandment especially seriously? Bernays's method begins with man's need and leads to God's act. It also begins with a story and ends with a commandment. The bridge between the two is an intriguing *question* that engages the listener and humbles him: perhaps there is more here than meets the Enlightenment's eye. The purpose of the method is to make one *think*. Note that we are left with a question, not an answer. Judaism is a life lived in the presence of great questions. Our response to those questions keeps the religion alive with fresh meaning.

If we step back and describe the method used here by Chacham Bernays, as reported by his disciple through Freud, we see that the method is a literary-rhetorical one that seeks to analyze a text and get at its underlying issues. We are reminded of Freud's own psychoanalytic method. Bernays's method uses the general assumptions and conventions of the larger humanist culture to lead the listener into a Jewish frame of reference and value, seeking to have the life of the text speak for itself. As we saw, Rainey describes the method of Freud's teachers of Jewish religion in similar terms.[224] Note also the method leads us to take the commandments, the *mitzvot,* more seriously, because we realize that they are full of meaning, *Sinn*. In this way, *halacha*, literally "a way of walking," becomes a deeply *enabling* dynamic, rather than being a "law" imposed externally from "above."

Methodologically, Bernays works on the basis of a sense of the essence or issue at stake in the story, and he adapts the form of his presentation to create access for a listener out of touch with that inner core. In other words, he uses the form/essence distinction on which Freud bases his Jewish promise to Martha at the close of his letter. In Bernays's hands, the method comes ultimately to support *halachic* observance, but this message is unacceptable to Freud, however entertaining the argument.

Freud dismisses it: "I knew the method." But what he is rejecting equally is the message, "the Scriptures' claim to truth and obedience." As he says, there is "no room here for Reform, only for a revolution [*Umsturz*]." Enlightenment humanism is his revolution. But how did Freud know the method? The answer seems clear: he learned it from Hammerschlag. As Rainey says, Hammerschlag

> was fond of drawing links between Jewish tradition and modern European culture. . . . For him Judaism was not a religion of authoritarian doctrine but of free and open enquiry. . . . He endeavored to confront his students with the "concrete material" of the Bible and to guide them in "abstracting" for themselves its essential concepts.[225]

As mentioned above, this approach conforms to the general method of teaching used in Freud's schooling in religion, which emphasized study of the Bible in order to "confront the students with the 'power and vitality' of their tradition."[226] This is why Freud says he knows the method. Even if he enjoys the game, however, Freud does not take its content too seriously. Given the two hours a week allotted to the study of Judaism in the *Gymnasium*, we can hardly expect Freud to have learned otherwise, in spite of his respect and affection for his teacher.

For when it comes to truth (what you expect from your parents and teachers) and obedience (what they expect from you), this method is not adequate in Freud's mind. He does not say why, but he feels the need for a complete break. *Umsturz* is a strong word, meaning "overthrowing" or "overturning"—in this case, the tradition of the fathers. Perhaps Freud feels that the Scriptures are not historically "true" and so cannot command obedience. In any event, it is clear that Freud takes his stand elsewhere, holding another, historical truth that judges the scriptural one, and pledging an allegiance to a different authority, namely, the moral authority of humanistic letters.[227] It is in these terms that Freud now praises Bernays's method, for he says that there lay in such teaching "tremendous progress, a kind of education of the human race in Lessing's sense." It will be helpful to examine Lessing's essay to illuminate Freud's meaning in his praise.

Beginning with the proposition "What education is to the individual man, revelation is to the whole human race,"[228] Gotthold Ephraim Lessing (1729–81) argues in his essay, "The Education of the Human Race" (1780), that progress in history depends upon "the development of revealed truths into truths of reason," and that this development is "absolutely necessary, if the human race is to be assisted by them."[229] Furthermore, the goal of this process of education is the realization of a "third age" which supersedes the first two (i.e., Judaism, "the old covenant," and Christianity, the "new"), much as Christianity claimed to have superseded Judaism (and Islam to have superseded both of them). This third age will overtake both the "sensual Jew" and the "spiritual Christian" to emerge as a common Enlightenment-based humanistic culture.[230] Again we find the search for the cultural whole so important to the liberals.[231] Lessing describes this age as "the time of a new eternal Gospel," when man "will do right because it *is* right, not because arbitrary rewards are set upon it."[232] That is, human beings will no longer need "religion." It seems possible that in 1882 Freud, like so many moderns, felt that he had already begun to enjoy the fruits of this humanistic age, the result of "human reason on its way," in spite of the setbacks political liberalism had begun to experience in Austria in the 1880s. But most simply, Freud recognizes in Bernays's method "the development of revealed truths into truths of reason," and so he recognizes an ally. Indeed, he gives it high praise when he calls it *Kritik,* for this implies the objective use of reason that Freud values so much. In addition, we may note that Freud's textbook in school on Jewish doctrine, by Leopold Breuer, contains the sentence, "Revelation is instruction [*Belehrung*] from God himself."[233] Judaism and the Enlightenment were brought to flow together into one stream in Freud's education.

But Freud tells Martha himself what he means by *in Lessingschem Sinne:*

> Religion was no longer treated as a rigid dogma, it became an object for the satisfaction of cultivated artistic taste and of intensified logical efforts, and the teacher of Hamburg recommended it finally not because it happened to exist and had been declared holy, but because he was pleased by the deeper meaning which he found in it or which he projected into it.

Rainey suggests that Isaac Bernays "probably would have found such an aesthetic transvaluation of his faith rather obnoxious,"[234] but Freud's emphasis on pleasure as the basis for supporting religion corresponds to Nathan's or Bernays's view (see below) that "the Jew is made for joy and joy for the Jew." Still, Freud's description is *his* view of what Bernays is doing and why it is progress. Religion is valuable here because of the pleasure it brings, like a work of art or a challenging math problem. It serves human ends and needs, and is subordinated to "cultural taste," that is, to the standards of modern culture. Judaism has been contextualized (some might say swallowed) by humanism. The Bible begins with a universal framework (Gen. 1–11) for its particular story and this perhaps makes Judaism eminently suited for a humanistic outlook, but in any event, as noted, this universalistic approach reflected the thrust of Freud's Jewish and classical education in the *Gymnasium.* As suggested above, Bernays may remind Freud of his old schoolmaster, who was like a father to him: "He always regards me as his son."[235] This relationship could be an immediate emotional basis for his admiration of Bernays's work, and it might contribute to why Freud is so "moved" by their encounter.

And now, with this appropriation of religion for the pleasure and enjoyment of the interpreter—religion now serves man, rather than man serving God through religion—Freud develops an increasing emphasis on pleasure and joy in Judaism, culminating in Nathan's *d'var Torah* about the growing importance of joy in the High Holiday festivals. Freud uses this Jewish tradition to present Martha with and include her in a picture of the kind of Jewish feeling she can expect from marrying and setting up a home with him. Thus the letter is very much part of Freud's courtship of Martha, wooing her to his way of life and thinking, while reassuring her that she will not lose what Freud sees as the essence of Jewish life, namely, meaningful, life-affirming joy.

This rhetorical character of the letter might lead one to assume that its phrases cannot be taken so seriously as a measure of Freud's Jewish identity. However, the letter does present a statement of values. Written in the context of prospective marriage and family, its values are heartfelt and serious, and therefore relevant for a picture of Freud's Jewish identity in this early period. Values form the infrastructure of identity and so provide a lens for bringing it into focus. Admittedly, the Nathan letter involves Freud's idealizations; but idealizations shape the self, especially in a young man.

Freud now begins to explain these Jewish connections. He reports Nathan's wisdom:

> The Jew . . . is the finest flower of mankind, and is created for enjoyment [*Genuss*]. He scorns anyone who is unable to enjoy.

Note the pride in being Jewish that this statement conveys. It recalls the superiority of the Jew as portrayed in works like Yehuda HaLevi's *Kuzari*. Freud admits later in life to such partisan prejudice, for example, in a letter to Sabina Spielrein in August 1912.[236] The merchant's last phrase is reminiscent of the one by Rav in the Jerusalem Talmud, that in the world to come, a man will be required to give an accounting for every opportunity he had to enjoy a legitimate pleasure that he refused without sufficient cause.[237]

Freud is reminded at this point of a line by the Roman poet Terence (also a favorite of Montaigne's) that Martha's brother Eli once made when he was drunk in reference to his own worldview: *Homo sum.*[238] Freud universalizes Nathan's particular message by a reference to a verse from the Latin classics: *Homo sum: humani nil a me alienum puto* ("I am human; I consider nothing human alien to me"). Instead of the *Jew* being the bearer of this "finest flower," the capacity for enjoyment, it is now in Freud's association a universal *human* trait, foreign to none. Yet it is through Jewish identity that Freud gains access to this feeling. Again he uses a classical humanist reference to alter and thus affirm a Jewish identification. This combination, which will reappear throughout Freud's life, supports Jaffe's observation that although Freud's intellectual tools came from his classical *Gymnasium* education, the impulses and motivations that put those tools in motion came from Freud's Jewish tradition and its inheritance.[239]

Solidarity on the basis of common humanity can be seen as a goal of Freud's psychoanalytic science, which he will try to protect from being identified as a "Jewish national concern" in the middle period. At that time he will be unable to overcome the false dichotomy between the particular and the universal that was so characteristic of his cultural milieu. As noted, Freud also eliminated the emphasis on Jewish particularity in his description of Hammerschlag's teaching. Even though Freud feels proud of being Jewish, if his identification interferes with the realization of a larger solidarity based on a core humanity, he will deemphasize its particularity. Nonetheless, in this letter the Jew remains the paradigm for the human.

Freud's association of the pleasure of drinking with Nathan's *Genuss* is a natural Jewish one also, because wine is "the symbol of joy" in Jewish tradition, and the blessing or sanctification over wine is ubiquitous at Jewish festivals. It is characteristic of traditional Judaism to mingle physical pleasure with spiritual pleasure and meaning, and the *kiddush* (sanctification over wine) is a good example. Freud must have heard his father "make *kiddush*" many times at home using the family's kiddush cups, and as mentioned above, what are probably the Freud family's kiddush cups found a prominent and honored place among Freud's antiquities collection. In the photographs by Edmund Engelman of Freud's home and offices at Bergasse 19 in 1938, the two kiddush cups stand prominently on the table in front of Freud's analytic chair.[240] They are placed in front of the many statuettes and *objets d'art* that make up part of Freud's collection of antiquities, perhaps a reflection of his affection and respect for his father, and they appear as a symbolic statement of the balance Freud found between Judaism and humanism: they stand together. Yet the kiddush cups are placed among antiquities, objects given to the satisfaction of cultivated artistic taste, rather than being actively used for the weekly sanctification of Jewish festivals, like Shabbat. Religion, like the ancient world, has been superseded. Nevertheless, Freud remains attached to it in some important way. Humanism is Freud's most active faith, but he is proud of his roots, and the fact that they are roots related to the pleasures of eating and drinking is not insignificant for Freud's Jewish identification. We recall again Heine's apostate, Don Isaak, who asserts that his nose has "kept the faith."[241] And again Feuerbach's dictum seems to fit: *Der Mensch ist, was er ißt.* Even if Freud's reason for saving the kiddush cups was only sentimental, their placement with the antiquities deserves our attention because of the value Freud placed on his collection.

What role did this collection play in Freud's identity? Besides the obvious parallel to the archaeology of the psyche that so fascinated Freud, his antiquities collection may also be understood as an expression of his identification with German *Kultur.* As Paul Mendes-Flohr explains, "*Kultur* was a syncretistic summary—or *Aufhebung*, as Hegel would put it—of all previous cultures."[242] The inclusion of Freud's kiddush cups, as a symbol of Jewish culture, in his antiquities collection may be precisely this kind of "raising." As Mendes-Flohr points out, the educated German would have regarded himself as "a custodian of world-culture, a privileged curator of the cumulative wisdom of distant and not so distant cultures."

> Refracted through the learned perspective of German *Kultur*—that is, through the consciousness of a thinking, reflective humanity—these cultures would gain a refinement and depth they presumably lacked when isolated in the place and time of their emergence. A Sumerian Temple placed in the Pergamon Museum of Berlin was said to acquire not only a dignity but a cultural significance far surpassing its original impact or intent.[243]

Freud's parlor is of course not the Pergamon Museum, but nonetheless the combination of Jewish and classical objects in one aesthetic display may be a visual representation of Freud's dual allegiance as an expression of enlightenment *Kultur*, an expression of thinking, reflective humanity.

In any event, now Freud brings his presentation in the Nathan letter to a climax with an epigram: "Der Jude ist für die Freude, und Freude ist für den Juden."[244] The pun is obvious, and it is confirmed later by Freud's reference to his fiancée as becoming "eine andere Freude" to the merchant, providing him with pleasure. Freud's illustration of this maxim culminates in "the festival of the joy of God," namely, *Simchat Torah.* In a tremendous display of wit, Freud himself becomes the joy of the Torah, and a worthy substitute for the tradition: "See what you'll be getting if you marry me!" he seems to say. In spite of his nonobservance of Jewish ritual and his intellectual opposition to its theology, Freud can still imply wittily that "the Jews are for Freud, and Freud is for the Jews." Before one dismisses this suggestion as too fanciful, remember that humor is a primary connection for Freud to both his father and to Judaism. Freud is telling Martha in a delightful way that in spite of his split from the kind of Orthodoxy she is rooted in, nonetheless there are Jews who support his kind of Judaism, that she will not lack a Jewish community, and that furthermore, Freud too affirms an allegiance to his people, one that can be well expressed through wit. Wit was considered to be a particularly Jewish trait in nineteenth-century Germany.[245]

The climax of Freud's tour de force, his *Freude–an Torah,* as it were, which began with his assessment of the significance of Bernays's contribution to the education of the human race and continued under the rubric of *Er war kein Asket,* "he was no ascetic," is now reached in the illustration of this motto linking Jews and joy, namely, the growing importance of joy in the High Holiday festivals. We saw from Freud's correspondence with Fluss and Silberstein that his own household celebrated these festivals as he was growing up.[246]

The discussion begins with the situation in which the *Christian* finds himself at the beginning of his New Year. This image functions as a foil for the Jewish meaning: contraries placed together shine the more. There is thus a quiet polemic present beneath the illustration. We are reminded of Jones's impression that Freud's opening of his medical practice on Easter Sunday 1886 was "an act of defiance." Freud shapes his own Jewish identity throughout his life using defiance as a mode of Jewish expression, often against Christian and German antisemitism.

Freud's Nathan describes Bernays's interpretation of the sequence of the High Holidays, i.e., Rosh HaShanah, Yom Kippur, Sukkot and Simchat Torah, as expressing an ascendance of joy through the different emphases of the festivals. Rosh HaShanah is the Festival of the Fear of God, because one's fate for the whole year is decided. Yom Kippur is the Festival of the Love of God, because only love can motivate the self-sacrifice of the fast (or as Freud would say later, the renunciation of drive). Sukkot is the Festival of the Joy of God, as is evident by its climax in the festival called The Joy of the Law (*Simchat Torah*).[247] Freud does not interject any of his own comments among Nathan's explanations of this last festival, perhaps because he does not need to, with the pun on his name carrying his message playfully and delightfully: *das Fest der Gottesfreude.*

This passage tells how good it feels to be a Jew, especially when compared with the paltry spiritual life of the Christian. The best the Christian can hope for is a better year to come, and it is implied that he knows no analogue of the rich spiritual pleasure the Jew feels in the rhythm of his life as the journey of the year begins. There is a depth to the Jewish life described in this *d'var Torah* that Freud seems to assent to by the absence of any criticism or gainsaying. Indeed the very fact that Freud "tells over" this homily is a participation in its Jewish life. James Kugel points out that Jews will tell each other *midrashim*, Jewish Torah-stories, almost the way people pass jokes around for mutual pleasure.[248] But with midrash, part of the pleasure is in teaching an ongoing Jewish tradition. It is the pleasure of ongoing participation, and Freud gives and shares that pleasure with his Orthodox fiancée while at the same time wooing her away from its ritual practice with his humanism. His charm worked. Martha at the age of eighty-six described Freud when he was young in these words: "Oh, he was the most charming and fascinating man I ever met. Everybody who came to know him wanted to do something nice for him."[249]

The kind of interpretation Nathan gives Freud may not support a claim to truth or evoke Freud's obedience, but it does make the practice of Judaism more meaningful and enjoyable, and it seems to silence Freud's quibbling for once. As he says, "When I took my leave I was more deeply moved than the old Jew could have guessed." Why was he moved, and how? On the one hand, as mentioned above, it seems likely that Bernays's method reminded Freud of that of his friend and teacher, Hammerschlag, to whom he was deeply indebted in more ways than one. Freud says he felt uneasy when Nathan was talking about banking. Was this partly because he himself was deeply in debt to Hammerschlag and Breuer? On the other hand, it also seems likely, again as suggested above, that "the old Jew" reminds Freud of his father, and the oedipal games he plays support this idea. The emphasis on joy is a prominent part of the Chassidic tradition from which Freud's father came, and so Freud has probably been put in touch with his own paternally mediated Jewish roots, even if only unconsciously. His awareness that he is nevertheless severed from these origins by his humanist allegiances may be part of the reason for his emotion. To identify and yet not be able to take part fully is painful. Even though Freud himself will not observe these festivals, he identifies with and is moved by their meaning as explained by the disciple of his fiancée's grandfather, even if only nostalgically. Perhaps it is easier to admire this father figure, competing with him less, needing to overthrow him less. Freud can therefore feel a moving connection to the tradition and religion of the fathers with less ambivalence, whereas when they interfere with his personal life, he feels resentful.

When at this point Freud introduces Martha as *eine andere Freude* for Nathan, one almost senses that he is telling her something about Judaism, answering Saladin's question in *Nathan the Wise* with his new joy: Martha wears the true ring. Judaism, with its life of meaningful joy, seems far superior to the life of the Christian (as far as Freud knows), and Freud is pleased with this gift of *Freude* that he prepares for Nathan. He makes up for his demeaning deceit of the old man by making him a gift of his Marty, giving him back, in atonement for his oedipal aggression earlier, the woman he has wrested from the tradition of this father figure through his wit and charm.[250] Martha must visit the old merchant to pick up her gift and bring it to Vienna, so that "Nathan" will see that "the stock of his master has not deteriorated since he sat at his feet."

Spurred by this identification with the male side of the oedipal conflict, Freud now turns to his vision of his own male role in his future home with Martha: that of a Jewish husband of the essence without the external forms. To close the letter, he brings all this playfulness home to make his fiancée his serious promise about their future:

> Und für uns beide glaube ich: wenn die Forme in der die alten Juden sich wohl fühlten auch für uns kein Obdach mehr bietet, etwas vom Kern, das Wesen des sinnvollen und lebensfrohen Judentums, wird unser Haus nicht verlassen.

Rainey says that this metaphor of husk/kernel or form/essence expresses

> the leitmotif of Freud's understanding of his Jewishness. . . . He sought to preserve the "core" of his Jewishness while casting off its outer form, which for him was its theology and ritual observances.[251]

The metaphor was very popular in Reform circles (often used to jettison ritual observances), and was raised to the status of a method by Geiger when he argued for the need for biblical criticism and in support of the *Wissenschaft des Judentums* movement.[252] Speaking of the "Synagogue of the Spirit," Zecharias Fraenkel (1801–75) writes in 1842:

> In Judaism we distinguish between kernel and shell, matter and form, the lasting and the ephemeral, the eternal and the temporal manifestation.[253]

This way of thinking clearly influences how Freud thinks about religion. His distinction in *Moses and Monotheism* (1939) between a material and a historical truth[254] may ultimately derive from it. In fact, Freud's psychoanalytic method of interpretation itself resembles this metaphor, whereby a seemingly meaningless form is revealed to be meaningful by virtue of its inner, essential significance. With this method Freud interpreted such things as dreams, jokes, symptoms, slips of the tongue or pen, even neuroses, which were considered meaningless or absurd by most of his contemporaries. Thus Freud's personal and professional spheres intertwine.

Freud's statement of belief connects him not only to his own Jewish education, but also to his father, Jakob, and to his parents' home as the model for this "meaningful and life-enjoying Judaism" that he promises his fiancée for their future home. As mentioned above, Freud writes to Fliess of his dying father, "He was an interesting human being, very happy within himself." Martin Freud tells us,

> Every member of my family loved Jakob and treated him with great respect. He was tall and broad-shouldered . . . terribly nice with us children. He brought us small presents and he used to tell us stories, mostly with a little twinkle in his great brown eyes, as if he wanted to say, "Isn't everything we are doing and saying here a great joke?"[255]

Jakob was a "life-enjoying" Jew, one from whom Freud could have learned his own joyful feeling for life. As Dorothy Burlingham said of Freud,

> I felt the greatness of his spirit and the warmth of his feelings, and above all, how he met life. Another quality which I learned to value was his ability to enjoy, whenever there was something to enjoy.[256]

So Freud too was a life-enjoying Jew. Recall Martin's description of his father as having had *ein fröhliches Herz*. Jakob therefore is Freud's model, at least in part, for a *lebensfrohe Judentum*.

After his father has died, Freud writes to Fliess about how deeply "the old man's death" has affected him:

> I valued him highly and understood him very well indeed, and with his peculiar mixture of deep wisdom and imaginative light-heartedness he meant a great deal in my life . . .[257]

The similarity in this description of his father's character to Freud's fantasy of his future home with Martha is striking, for both mention the combination of joyful ("phantastisch leichtem") and meaningful ("tiefer Weisheit und . . . Sinn") elements. Contrary to what many interpreters have said about Freud's negative attitude towards Judaism on the basis of a negative relationship with his father, it can be seen here that he *consciously* has a deeply positive relationship with his father and a positive side to his relationship with Judaism as well. These positive relationships must be taken into account in any assessment of Freud's relation to Judaism and the Jewish tradition of his fathers, for they contribute a positive dimension to Freud's Jewish identity, overlooked by many interpreters in the past.

According to his son Martin, Freud's own home had a strong sense of "Jewishness," despite the absence of Jewish ritual observance or Jewish religion. Yet, the family festivals were Christmas and Easter (presumably without their Christian meanings adduced), and they never attended synagogue.[258] Instead, their Jewish identification was established socially: "We moved in Jewish circles, our friends were Jews, our doctor, our lawyer were Jews."[259] All Freud's fellow tarock card players were Jews too. These social contexts are a familial reflection of Freud's sense of his own Jewishness in solidarity with other Jews, independently of his estrangement from Jewish religion. Many of his friends of course were equally estranged from religion. Despite the fact that Martin describes his mother as "very hospitable" (a traditional Jewish value), he can hardly remember a non-Jewish person among the many guests in their home until his father became internationally recognized.[260] "Jewishness" for Freud was conveyed and confirmed by personal relationships with other Jews, even independently of Jewish observance or texts. Thus Freud's social and commercial encounter with the merchant he calls "Nathan" functions for him as a way of defining his own Jewish identity, playfully, yet with depth. At the same time, judging from Pfister's description of the "happy-free spirit" of the Freud household,[261] Freud fulfilled his promise to Martha that their home would not lack something of the essence of a joyful, life-affirming Judaism, even in the absence of religious observance or belief.

Through his identification with *mein alter Jude,* Freud is able to define his conditional relationship with Jewish tradition and the Jewish people. In some essential way related to his solidarity with Jews and their meaningful enjoyment of life, Freud is a "good" Jew and he is proud of it. Furthermore, this essence is located in his home, the traditional root of Jewish life. But the outer form of his life is humanist, a new form of shelter for a Jew. Like Mendelssohn, and as J. L. Gordon advised, Freud is a Jew at home and a humanist abroad.

Thus, in his own way, Sigmund Freud the Jew identifies with and seeks to add to the "tradition of the fathers,"[262] even though he must root his contribution in an Enlightenment humanism that is at odds with Jewish tradition, especially in its agnosticism. We see Freud's identification with the Jewish people throughout the Nathan letter, even when he rejects the tradition—as for example when he refers to himself and Martha as "we Jews" immediately after disassociating himself from the mourning for the destruction of the Temple on Tisha B'Av. We are Jews even in disbelief and rebellion. Freud participates in the Jewish tradition by reinterpreting it through the lenses of Enlightenment humanism (which he may see as a fruit of Jewish prophetic tradition in any event), and he will apply a psychoanalytic version of this same method to Judaism at the end of his life in *Moses and Monotheism.* Here, while using Nathan's *d'var Torah* primarily as a means of wooing his fiancée, he also sees in Isaac Bernays's teaching an ally for "progress," and he learns from him, as he did from his teacher, Samuel Hammerschlag, that one can identify an inner "essence" and seek to remain faithful to it, while adapting its outer form to speak to changed circumstances—in this case, an Enlightenment humanist culture.

The Nathan letter provides abundant evidence for Freud's strong and proud Jewish identification at this stage in his life, in addition to or perhaps even in spite of, his humanist identification. Freud's sense of himself is to be found in the balance he strikes in the midst of these tensions.

Further Letters to Martha Bernays

This analysis of the Nathan letter serves as an extended introduction to Freud's correspondence with his fiancée. These intimate letters contain many Jewish references relevant to our discussion. In fact, all of the letters in the years before Freud's friendship with Wilhelm Fliess (which began in November 1887) relevant to our study are to Martha (1881–86), and all but one or two of the rest in the early period are addressed to Fliess (up to 1902, after which there are none until 1907 and the beginning of the middle period). This fact itself (which may be a function of selective publication) suggests a confirmation of two significant aspects of Freud's Jewish identity in the early period: it is intensely personal and familial, and it is defined by and expressed within Jewish social relationships.

Freud's youthful immersion in the "Bible story" and his Jewish tendency to identify with biblical characters are reflected again in a letter he writes to Martha on 14 August 1882, in which Freud compares the two of them to Adam and Eve in the Garden of Eden. Freud's father Jakob has invited his family to visit the Prater with him, a beautiful park on the outskirts of Vienna, to "compensate" them for "some less good days" when "our old Herr" had been grouchy. Freud comments that when his father is not in a grumpy mood, "he is the greatest optimist of all us young people." The son's affection and admiration for his father, in spite of the old man's irritability or glumness, is clear. The visit to the park has reminded Freud of a visit with Martha to the Wandsbek grove: "Oh yes, the Prater is a paradise; but the Wandsbek wood is more beautiful, because there we were alone like Adam and Eve. . . ." For Freud thinking of his father, the association to the first "Bible story" is a natural one.

With the couple in the grove there were

> only a number of animals who did nothing to us, mild venerable clergymen, curious and tactful old women, and also helpful animals, cows which gave milk and hostesses who brought butter and cakes and so forth. The little Eve wore a brown dress in keeping with the changed times . . . the Eternal had placed benches under the beautiful tall trees, all of which belonged to us, and nowhere was there to be seen an angel with a flaming sword, only one little tender angel with emerald eyes and two sweet lips. . . .

Perhaps every newly engaged couple feels like the original pair in a garden of their own making, attended to by God and all His host. In fact the Jewish wedding ceremony that Freud was to resist so much casts bride and groom in the same roles, so Freud's metaphor has both a natural human and a Jewish resonance. The humor and playfulness that Freud brings to the text indicates both his comfort with it and his sense of ownership: it all belongs to them.

It is revealing that when Freud draws on the Bible story again later to insist on Martha's allegiance to him over that to her family, he reverses the biblical text:

> For how has it been prescribed from time immemorial? The woman shall leave father and mother and follow the man she has chosen.

Freud sounds like he is quoting Gen. 2:24, but of course that verse is cast in reference to the man and *his* leaving parents and cleaving to the woman. Clearly Freud feels free not only to cite Scripture to support his own authority, but also to alter its reference to suit his purposes. In this Freud acts no differently than Sholom Aleichem's Tevye, so we should not think of his act as either pernicious or un-Jewish. Rather it indicates that Freud is at home with the Bible; it is in fact his deepest patrimony.

Ernst Simon notices also a significantly altered paraphrase of Prov. 31:30 when Freud responds to a self-deprecating remark Martha has made about her own beauty. Freud seems to have in mind "Charm is deceitful and beauty is vain" when he writes,

> Don't forget that "beauty" only stays a few years, and that we have to spend a long life together. Once the smoothness and freshness of youth is gone then only the beauty lies where goodness and understanding transfigure the features, and that is where you excel.[263]

But Freud does not include the ideal of Proverbs's praise, namely, "A woman that fears the Lord, she shall be praised." Instead Freud talks of "a kind heart and common sense." Morals and intelligence have taken the place of religious faith.[264] Again Freud feels free to make subtle but significant alterations in the biblical text in order to express his own convictions. Recall his humanistic recontextualization of the biblical lesson with his mother (also from the Garden Story) about human earthly origins: "Thou owest Nature a death." Beginning at an early age, a feeling of easy familiarity with the Bible has enabled Freud to feel free to use it to express his own views.

In discussing the books Freud shared and talked about with Martha, Jones mentions that George Eliot's *Daniel Deronda* (1876) "amazed him by its knowledge of Jewish intimate ways that 'we speak of only among ourselves.'"[265] Eliot's last novel was notable for its Zionist theme and its open sympathy for Jewish life and future, a positive portrayal "unique in English fiction of the period."[266] One wonders which details Freud is referring to. Eliot has carefully researched her topic and has been given access to intimate details of Jewish observance and family life, for example the Friday evening Sabbath blessing:

> Cohen . . . stood still while the two children went up to him and clasped his knees: then he laid his hands on each in turn and uttered his Hebrew benediction; whereupon the wife who had lately taken baby from the cradle brought it up to her husband and held it under his outstretched hands, to be blessed in its sleep.[267]

Given the ubiquity of "*bensching* [blessing] the children" in Jewish homes on Shabbat eve, it is quite possible that Freud had experienced such intimacy himself in his childhood.

Commentators and biographers have pointed out Eliot's references to rabbinical literature, Jewish historical writing, and her acquaintance with and study of Hebrew with Emanuel Deutsch, a well-known nineteenth-century Jewish scholar. The overall effect has been to create a novel in which a Jewish reader feels at home, among friends:

> Cohen now washed his hands, pronouncing Hebrew words the while: afterwards he took off the napkin covering the dish and disclosed the two long flat loaves besprinkled with seed—the memorial of the manna that fed the wandering forefathers—and breaking off small pieces gave one to each of the family . . .[268]

These are intimate Jewish ways that an insider could appreciate, even one from a household whose Jewish observance was occasional.

But Freud's amazement may also be a result of the novel's bold Zionist vision, so many years before Zionism became popular:

> The divine principle of our race is action, choice, resolved memory. Let us contradict the blasphemy and help to will our own better future and the better future of the world [note the combination]—not renounce our higher gift and say "Let us be as if we were not among the populations"; but choose our full heritage, claim the brotherhood of our nation, and carry into it a new brotherhood with the nations of the Gentiles. The vision is there; it will be fulfilled.[269]

In 1882, when Freud read this, these may have been words that Jews spoke only among themselves. Given Freud's later sympathy for Zionism, his amazement at *Daniel Deronda* may be conditioned by a shock of self-recognition mediated by the novel of a Gentile outsider.

In this first year of his engagement, Freud also wrote Martha about his admiration for and friendship with his mentor Josef Breuer, the only Jew among his medical seniors. When Freud's friend Ernst von Fleischl-Marxow had a particularly bad time with his cocaine addiction (to which he was brought unintentionally by Freud's attempts to lessen his dependence on morphine), Freud wrote to Martha,

> Breuer has again behaved magnificently in the Fleischl affair. One does not adequately characterize him by only saying good things about him; one has to emphasize the absence of so much badness.[270]

Freud visited Breuer in his home often, and Jones reports "how happy and comfortable he felt in the peace there; they are such 'dear good understanding people.'" 'To talk with Breuer was 'like sitting in the sun'; 'he radiates light and warmth.' 'He is such a sunny person, and I don't know what he sees in me to be so kind.' 'He is a man who always understands one.'"[271]

Breuer's kindness was matched by his generosity. He often lent Freud money, and his attempts later to have the debt represent Freud's compensation for treating one of Breuer's relatives show that he really intended the money as a gift.[272] The total debt eventually reached 2,300 gulden, a considerable sum.[273] Breuer once entered Freud's name in a guest house book as his brother, "so that Freud would not have to tip the waiter,"[274] and on another occasion, when Freud asked for an extra fifty gulden for a month's holiday in Wandsbek with Martha, Breuer delayed lending/giving him the money out of a paternal concern for Freud's welfare.[275] There was thus a familial feeling of responsibility between the two, even one of father and son. That they were both Jews contributed to this feeling. Freud learns early that being Jewish is a familial kinship, an intermingling of selfhood.

As mentioned, Freud felt equally positive about the Hammerschlags. As he says,

> I don't know any people kinder, more humane, further removed from any ignoble motives than they. . . . I have always felt more at home with this family than with the wealthy Schwabs, quite apart from the deep-seated sympathy which has existed between myself and the good old Jewish teacher ever since my years in the *Gymnasium*.[276]

As with the Breuers, Freud often visited the Hammerschlags in their home,[277] and the letter quoted above from January 1884 discusses his teacher's and Breuer's generous charity:

> The old professor . . . informed me that a rich man had given him a sum of money for a worthy person in need, that he had mentioned my name and he was herewith handing it to me. . . . It is not the first time the old man has helped me in this way; during my university years he often, and unasked, helped me out of a difficult situation. At first I felt very ashamed, but later when I saw that Breuer and he agreed in this respect, I accepted the idea of being indebted to good men and those of our faith without [the feeling of] personal obligation.

Elliott Oring finds fault with Freud for *not* feeling a sense of "personal obligation" about his debts.[278] But in fact Freud's position is traditional, one to which his Jewish teachers have guided him. In the Jewish understanding, the poor person has a *right* to the money he receives. Giving is a form of justice (*tzedakah*), a redistribution of God's wealth, not "charity" (from *caritas*, "love"). The poor actually enable the giver to fulfill a divine commandment. Thus Freud expresses a link to Jewish ways of thinking on this issue, even if unknowingly, and he is shaped in its generous image. Freud in turn becomes a generous Jewish giver himself, as he promises he will later in this letter. Note that Freud widens the Jewish principle to include the fact that his benefactors are "good men" and not only "those of our faith." Freud remains loyal to his humanism and its universalism even when he is most traditionally Jewish.

These generous Jews were role models for Freud, and he tells Martha that he intends to emulate their example by being charitable himself when he can afford it. Freud's son Martin confirms that Freud carried through his intention:

> Once my father had begun to earn money, that is, more than he absolutely needed for the support of his family, he behaved in an unbelievably generous manner. He enjoyed giving. There must have been literally scores of students for whom he made it possible to finish their studies.[279]

Freud also extended this generosity to his psychoanalytic practice. Max Graf reports that it was Freud's

> fundamental rule always to treat at least one patient without compensation. It was his way of doing welfare work . . . Freud knew how to live with people; he was a person with social feelings.[280]

Freud's social feeling has a Jewish root, based in his Jewish social relations with father figures like Breuer and Hammerschlag. It is an extension of the familial solidarity of the Jewish people.

Freud's generosity may also express a positive link to his father, who despite his perennial problems with money was, Micawber-like, even *luftmensch*-like, "always hopefully expecting something to turn up."[281] Freud writes to Martha on 10 January 1884 that he had "met Father in the street, still full of projects, still hoping." He adds that he took it upon himself to write to Jakob's sons by his first marriage, Emanuel and Philipp, "urging them to help Father out of his present [financial] predicament."[282] Yet in spite of financial difficulties, Jakob was generous to his son Sigismund, enrolling him in a Jewish private school and sending him to England as a graduation present. Freud's attitude toward money was that it was not important in itself, but had value only as a means to an end,[283] and this attitude may reflect his father's too, who was "happy in life" despite his lack of funds. To Martha "Freud remarked that he was the duplicate of his father physically and to some extent mentally."[284] Freud's charitable and generous treatment of those in need reflects a link with his father and his father figures, and behaving in this humanitarian way is an expression of Freud's Jewishness learned in relations with other Jews. As mentioned, Anna Bernays reports that Jakob's motto was "Think ethically and act morally."[285] On this basis, joining the humanitarian B'nai B'rith would have been a natural culmination of the early period, one which partly reconciled Freud to his father, burying the guilt and anger he felt at the old man's death, by expressing a Jewish humanitarian impulse.

Jones observes that Breuer and Hammerschlag have the distinction of being the only ones for whom Freud has no word whatsoever of adverse criticism in his letters (at least in the early period), despite the fact that "Freud was not sparing in this."[286] On the one hand, this fact must reflect Freud's affection and admiration for these two men, implying the strength of their influence on him. But on the other hand, Jakob Freud is reported to have once rebuked a young man arguing with his father in the street: "What, are you contradicting your father? My Sigmund's little toe is cleverer than my head, but he would never dare to contradict me!"[287] Father figures, especially Jewish ones, would have had a tremendous amount of respectful authority invested in them for Freud, especially if they were generous and deserved that respect. Therefore when Freud thought of converting to Protestantism to avoid the Jewish marriage ritual, Breuer was able to dissuade him by saying simply, "Too complicated."[288] Freud still resented having to go through it, and this conflict between allegiance to and resentment of fathers and their traditions clings to Freud throughout his life.

Next we turn to a letter to Martha dated 29 August 1883, in which Freud reveals how the two of them differ from "the masses" *(Das Gesindel)* or the poor folk *(Die Armen/Volk). Das Gesindel* recalls Freud's letter to Emil Fluss of 18 September 1872, and so suggests that Freud is making a Jewish distinction in his self-understanding here, one that expresses the difference between "enlightened," partially assimilated Jews like Freud and Martha (whom Freud depicts as a kind of elite) and the unassimilated provincial Eastern European Jews who reminded Freud of a "mob."

The difference between Freud and Martha and "the rabble" is radical:

> The rabble *[Gesindel]* gives vent to its appetites *[ausleben]*, and we deprive ourselves. We do without in order to maintain our integrity, we economize with our health, our capacity for enjoyment, our emotions; we save ourselves *[aufheben]* for something, not knowing what. And this habit of constant suppression of natural drives gives us the quality of refinement.

At first glance one might not think that Freud is talking about Jews or Jewish characteristics at all, referring instead to a distinction between "the nobility" and "the masses," a dichotomy between the boorish and the cultivated. But Freud's distinction has much in common with his attitude toward East European Jews. In this letter, Freud is defining the kind of refined Jewish identity in which he takes pride. It is a kind of nobility that he relates to his Jewishness. He contrasts it with another kind, the unassimilated *Ostjuden*, who behave like *das Gesindel* of the Fluss letter of 18 September 1872.

Freud also expressed his disdain for *Ostjuden* at age forty-one in a letter to Fliess dated 27 April 1898. Writing about his sister Marie's husband Moriz, who hailed from Eastern Europe (Bucharest), Freud refers to the fellow Jew as "half-Asian." Freud's term recalls a popular book published in 1876 by Karl-Emil Franzos (1848–1904) entitled *Aus Halb-Asien* ("Out of Half-Asia"), which consisted of tales of East European Jews. As Wistrich explains, "Asia" was pictured as

> a jungle of darkness, barbarism and violent hatreds. The *Ostjuden* were "half-Asian" precisely because they lived within these social and cultural boundaries. They were an unfortunate *product* of this unredeemed world of religious fanaticism, national oppression, superstition and backwardness.[289]

Freud's condescension reflects this mind-set. The context of Freud's remark is a discussion of the role of seduction by the father as the cause of hysteria, and Freud doubts that *this* father, Moriz, is innocent in this case: the mob gives vent to its appetites.

Freud may also share the prejudices common to assimilated Western Jews about the "bad manners of the [unassimilated] Jews."[290] Freud refers to a figure he met on a train who "gave evidence of his primitive state of culture and level of education."[291] Bad manners are a sign of low culture, and Jews are a proverbial example. *Ostjuden* are typically the kind of Jew Freud is thinking of. For example, Freud's joke about the Galician Jew traveling on a train associates a lack of civility with Jews among each other (N.B., especially ones who practice Judaism):

> The entrance into his compartment of a man in modern dress has brought the Jew to sit up straight and take his feet from the bench. But when the stranger asks, "*Wann haben wir Jomkipur?*" ["When will we observe Yom Kippur?"], the Jew responds, "Aesoi!" and puts his feet back onto the bench before replying.[292]

On the one hand, the joke implies a certain disrespect of Jews for other Jews; but it also conveys an intimacy and comfortable familiarity, like that of members of the same family. The joke's pleasure lies in the recognition of kinship as well as in the truth of its criticism. Freud probably appreciates both.

Freud sees himself and Martha as Jews who are different from the masses, however. They develop a refinement of character as a consequence of constantly suppressing their "natural drives" (the couple had been engaged now for over a year and two months). Freud lists pleasures in which the *Volk* indulge, but which he and Martha do without: drinking, promiscuity ("falling in love with a different person every month"), making friends with everyone," that is, indiscriminately, and indulgence in pleasures of the moment without moderation or consideration of their consequences. "Thus," Freud says, "we strive more to protect ourselves from pain than to provide ourselves with enjoyment [*Genuss*]." This self-restraint is in tension with the life-enjoying Judaism of the Nathan letter, so it is an important addition to our image of Freud's sense of himself as a Jew. Self-restraint is the hallmark of traditional Jewish life, as the regimen of halakhic life makes natural. The ethic is well-expressed by Ben Zoma in *Pirkei Avot* (Ethics of the fathers) 4:1: "Who is the mighty hero [*gibbor*]? The one who conquers his impulse, as it says [in Prov. 16:32], 'Better the one who is slow to anger than the mighty warrior [*gibbor*], and the one who rules his spirit than the one who captures a city.'"

In this letter, Freud develops his sense of himself independently of the enjoyment he associated with Martha's grandfather, and he makes no explicit reference to Jewish tradition.[293] Freud takes pride in a character based on the renunciation of drive for the sake of something higher, even not knowing what that something is. As he tells Martha, "We raise ourselves [*aufheben*] for something, not knowing what."[294] This character trait will recur, both in the middle and in the late periods, in connection with Freud's interpretations of Moses. "There is a psychology of the common man which differs considerably from ours," Freud says, for "*das Volk* judge, believe, hope, and work in a manner wholly other than we do." This distinction in the early period forms the basis of Freud's view of the character of the Jew in the late period's *Moses and Monotheism*.

A similar distinction recurs in a letter to Martha five days later:

> I think I will in the future, for the remainder of my apprenticeship in the hospital, live according to the manner of the *goyim*, modestly, studying and pursuing the ordinary things, not struggling for discoveries and delving so very deeply.[295]

Yerushalmi notes Freud's "sense of otherness vis-à-vis non-Jews which cannot be explained merely as a reaction to antisemitism. . . this feeling seems to have been primal, inherited from his family and early milieu, and it remained with him throughout his life."[296] Freud thinks that non-Jews work in a manner and aspire to things wholly different from the manner and goals of Jews. Specifically, they have little ambition or imagination; they don't strive for "higher" things. Furthermore, the word that comes naturally to Freud to describe these Gentiles is *Goyim*. As Yershalmi comments, "The hand is the hand of Sigmund; the voice is the voice of Jakob."[297]

By contrast, as Freud has told Martha, "We raise ourselves for something, not knowing what." The two of them will achieve what they need for their independence and beautiful life together "by honest, steady work without any gigantic efforts." In this determined resolve to work hard and consistently toward a better life, Freud presents a stark contrast to the attitude of "the rabble" of whom he speaks in his letter of 29 August. Freud will retain this view of the masses, and it will reassert itself explicitly in the late period. As Freud writes in *The Future of an Illusion* (1927), "The masses are lazy and unreasonable; they do not love the renunciation of drive."[298]

In a letter of 23 October 1883, Freud again makes clear that a refined Jewish character is different from that of the masses. Freud writes to Martha about Benedikt Stilling (1810–79), a pioneering German-Jewish anatomist and surgeon, and after describing the man's success as the result of patient and steady hard work undertaken in addition to his regular duties as a doctor, Freud continues:

> All this shows the diligent industry, the tenacious passion of the Jew, not even coupled with so much talent as is normally not scarce with Jews. This we can also do.[299]

"We Jews"—tenacious, passionate,[300] hard-working—have a psychology that differs completely from the character of *das Gesindel* or *die Masse*. The attitude was widespread and conventional in Jewish circles, especially given Jewish experience of persecution by Gentile mobs and Eastern European peasants.

The next letter reveals again Freud's disdain for Jewish religion. On 8 September 1883, a little more than a month before Yom Kippur (on 11 October), Freud queries Martha, "What can it be that you want and do not dare to mention?" First Freud speculates in a fantastic vein, teasing her:

> A tooth out of the Caliph's jaw, a jewel from Queen Victoria's crown, a giant's autograph, or something equally fantastic which would mean putting on my armor at once and setting out for the Orient?

Freud sounds like Don Quixote speaking to his Dulcinea, and indeed Gedo and Wolf have shown that "Cervantes . . . served as one of the principal conduits through which the humanist tradition was acquired by Freud."[301] This context may influence Freud's attitude when he goes on to ask,

> Or is my sweetheart's wish nearer [home]; could it possibly be a deed of self-conquest? Am I to fast on Yom Kippur, reconcile myself with someone I don't like? O pfui, my Marty would not take unfair advantage of her power in order to move me to actions that lack meaning [*Sinn*] as well as sincerity.

As when he scorned Tisha B'Av, Freud's attitude has blinded him to the point of the *ritual* denial of drives and the opportunity for personal growth that the ritual of commanded reconciliation on Yom Kippur makes possible. In the tradition, with repentance, fasting on the Day of Atonement can only atone for sins between man and God. Since sins committed against one's fellow also involve a sin against God, one must first ask for the wronged party's forgiveness before asking forgiveness from God for having wronged one of His creatures. Yom Kippur therefore becomes an opportunity to face up to oneself and one's own guilts and deal with them sincerely, honestly, and meaningfully, by apologizing to the person one has hurt. This requires some courage, and it promotes the growth of character if taken seriously, *especially* if one does not like the person one has wronged. The ritual teaches that higher values exist than those based only on one's own feelings and self. In the name of those higher values, God commands deeds of self-conquest for Yom Kippur, for the good of His creatures and their social life together. Since Freud struck his friends as a person with "social feeling," one who "knew how to live with people," why does he resist this meaningful and life-affirming side of Judaism in Yom Kippur?

The answer may be related to the relationship between humanism and Judaism in Freud's mind. Both humanism and Judaism intend the shaping of the human personality around self-transcendent, civilizing values, the values of *Humanität* (German) or *Menschlichkeit* (Yiddish). But Freud, schooled in the *humanitas Romana*, does not see the practice of Jewish religion as this kind of personal instrument. Perhaps this is because he associates Judaism with the *shtetl* that his Galitzianer parents left behind and whose emancipated movement toward the fruits of the Enlightenment Freud is continuing.[302] In other words, although Freud can appreciate and even admire the *ideas* within Judaism, especially when they are presented in a modern way that resonates with Enlightenment humanism, he cannot appreciate Jewish religious *ritual.* This incapacity may be related to the nature of ritual itself, for it de-centers the ego, requiring a surrender to its form in order for its meaning to be experienced. It stands upon an irrational base. The rational humanist Freud rebels against this particular de-centering because he does not believe in the God who speaks to Jews through such commandments. Humanism places man at the center instead, making him the measure of all things, and charging him with self-cultivation in the name of humanity and civilization, i.e., *Bildung* ("education") for the sake of *Kultur*. At this point, Freud does not see how the practice and tradition of Judaism contribute to this process. In *Moses and Monotheism,* he will imply that in fact at least Jewish tradition does.

Here instead Freud rejects Jewish religion, and especially Jewish ritual. Even this rejection forms Freud's Jewish identity in a Jewish mold, however, for we define ourselves as much by what we hate as by what we love. When Freud's friend Joseph Paneth married Hammerschlag's niece, Sophie Schwab, Freud attended the Jewish wedding ceremony. Jones reports from an unpublished letter to Martha dated 16 May 1884 that "he gazed at the scene with a fascinated horror and then wrote a letter of sixteen pages describing all the odious detail in a spirit of malign mockery."[303] The young man doth protest too much. The month before, in April, Paneth had set aside 1,500 gulden ($600) for Freud and Martha as a contribution intended to shorten the delay of their marriage.[304] Was Freud uncomfortable with the debt he owed Paneth for this charitable deed? He commented at the time, "Isn't it splendid that a rich man should seek to ameliorate the injustice of our birth and the illegitimacy of his own favored position?"[305] Again, Freud expresses the traditional basis of Jewish *tzedakah* ("justice") exactly. It was only three months earlier that he had accepted "the idea of being indebted to good men and those of our faith without the feeling of personal obligation."[306] But does not Freud's reaction to the wedding ceremony seem extreme and ungrateful in this context? Perhaps Freud feels threatened by the ritual whose irrational and (for him) meaningless power he hates, and this feeling overwhelms his gratitude towards and affection for his friends when he mocks their Jewish marriage ritual.[307] Freud's first psychoanalytic study of religion, "Obsessive Acts and Religious Practices," is a negative assessment of ritual or "ceremonial" as an expression of obsessional neurosis. Coming in 1907, it is perhaps an appropriate professional close to Freud's Jewish view of the early period.

Freud's atheism sometimes even leads him to admire Jews who bring up their children "outside of the faith" (*Konfessionlos*). This word occurs in a letter to Martha from 20 December 1883, in relation to Freud's visit with the family of one of Frau Hammerschlag's sisters. Freud describes the father as "an ardent freethinker," and the man's practice with his children follows like an achievement. Appropriately so, for Freud sees it based on a stand for the truth of an idea, namely, that religion is an illusion (or a superstition) from which we must free ourselves, in spite of the difficulty. Freud identifies with the Jewish *Freidenker.* Significantly, this Jew has not converted to Christianity; he is still a Jew, whose two boys have "the most delicate Jewish faces." This combination of atheism, earnest commitment to the truth of an idea, and undiluted Jewish ethnic identification lives in Freud's mind as a positive response. It is a combination he is proud of. Note in particular the opposition to the Jewish "confession" does not obstruct a full identification with the Jewish people.

At the same time Freud also knows of a darker side to Jewish identity. Freud's friend Nathan Weiss hung himself in a public bath, in anguish over his unhappy nuptials. The father, Isaac Weiss, was a great talmudic scholar who lectured at the Vienna Beth HaMidrash, an Orthodox college of Jewish studies.[308] At the funeral, his colleague Meir Friedmann, ironically, known by his book of the same title as the "Ish Shalom" ["Man of Peace"],

> began in clear words to accuse the other family of having dealt the fatal blow. And all this he spoke with the powerful voice of the fanatic, with the fire of the savage, pitiless Jew. We were all paralyzed with indignation and shame in the presence of the Christians who were among us. It seemed as though we had given them a right to believe that we worship the God of vengeance, not the God of love. Pfungen's thin voice was lost in the echo of the savage accusation of the Jew.[309]

Freud's horror and anger are palpable. Yet there is something very Jewish in Freud's reaction. There is no embarrassment so deep as that dealt by a member of one's own family, and Freud's reaction is of just that kind, a feeling based on Jewish belonging, in spite of differences in *Weltanschauung.* The traditional phrasing of this relationship, "All Jews are responsible for one another," points to the root of such a feeling, for the word translated as "responsible" derives from a root meaning "mingled together" [*'rb*]. Jews feel a sense of "familial" responsibility for and consequent vulnerability to one another because they are somehow bound up together into one family, one Jewish people or nation. They *participate* in each other, as a family does, whether they choose to or not. Freud's anger and shame bear witness to his Jewish depth. Note too his plural pronouns: "*We* have given them reason to believe that *we* worship. . . ." In spite of his humiliation, Freud's feeling of belonging is inalienable.

Freud's reaction is also typical of assimilated Jews who adopt the standards of Gentile culture (especially their good manners and courtesy) as their own. Why should it be the presence of "the Christians who were among us" that evokes Freud's anger and shame? Is such public humiliation of a fellow Jew acceptable from a Jewish standpoint? On the contrary, the rabbis compare embarrassing someone with shedding his blood.[310] But Freud feels ashamed because this "merciless Jew" is "uncivilized" [*wild*]; he is exhibiting bad manners in the presence of Christians. "What will the *goyim* say?" has always been the watchword of Jews who seek to be accepted and even admired by those same Gentiles. Though this reaction is related to fear of antisemitism, it is rooted too in Jewish tradition, since the Jewish people are to be a "light unto the nations." An awareness of Christian polemic thus underlies Freud's feelings, for he knows the popular Christian characterization of the "God of the Old Testament" as a "God of Wrath" in contrast to the New Testament's "God of Love." Freud feels responsible for his fellow Jews, and he identifies with their inherited "chosen" status among the nations. He also has a sense that these Jews are equally responsible to him, and his angry words are rooted in a sense of betrayal by their uncivilized behavior. Freud cannot help but identify with Jews even when their behavior offends him.

This letter points to the negative side of Freud's image of the Jew, who is not only "savage," but also "pitiless." Freud seems to speak paradigmatically—almost "mythically"—when he refers to "the Jew" in this passage, as though he were speaking of a type. This passage therefore raises the possibility of Jewish self-hate in Freud, an idea that must be considered, since so many interpreters have seen Freud as a self-hating Jew.[311]

Freud harshly criticized the provincial Jews he met on the train back from Freiberg in September 1872, but I argued that Freud's words reflected not so much self-hate as the rejection of his own unassimilated Jewish past, the "boorish" *Ostjude.* Freud knows that he himself has a cultivated *Weltanschauung.* Though he seeks to distance himself from his identification with his "country-cousins," he does not hate his own Jewishness because of them. Instead, Freud locates his sense of Jewish identity in the expression of liberal ideals. Sander Gilman notes that though Freud read avidly Otto Weininger's expression of his self-hate, *Sex and Character* (1903), he "seems not to have responded to Weininger's self-hatred as the reflection of his identity crisis."[312] Freud resolved his own Jewish ambivalence through self-creation rather than by self-destruction.

Gilman has drawn attention to the stereotypical images of Jews in this period. Jews were pictured as typically uncivilized, even criminal, immoral, liars, rootless yet "cosmopolitan," sexually deviant, typically comic or witty, devoted to money, without aesthetic sense, and neurotically ill. "Neurasthenia" (nervous exhaustion from overwork or prolonged mental strain), a special concern of Freud's work, was seen as an especially Jewish malady.[313] In light of Jaffe's thesis that Freud sought to vindicate the Jews through the recovery and interpretation of "typically" Jewish texts such as the joke and neurotic illness, it is significant that Freud writes to Martha on 10 February 1886 of his own family's "neuropathological taint" [*Belastung:* "handicap" or "encumbrance"] to be found in the family of a younger brother of his father. He is happy to say that there is not much to report in his immediate family, except that he and Rosa "have a generous propensity for neurasthenia." It almost sounds like a boast. In any event, Freud concludes, "These stories are very common in Jewish families." "As a neurologist," Freud says, he is about as worried by it "as a sailor is by the sea." Indeed, he seems comfortable with this image of "neuropathological handicap." It is a part of his self-image that he acknowledges. In fact, such a propensity may point to greater sensitivity and so be a secret source of pride in a Jew. Although it is a negative stereotype drawn from antisemitic Gentile culture, it does not produce self-hatred in Freud; rather it becomes a resource for creative advance. The Jew turns the tables on his opponents, as in Purim.

Far from indulging in self-hatred, what Freud admires in Jews is their lack of shame at being Jewish. He states this explicitly when writing to Martha on 5 August 1885, telling her the story of one Moritz Kohn, a man whose father was "as poor as only a Jew can be." In spite of the poverty of his origins, the young Moritz worked hard, and upon acceptance to the Pressberg *Gymnasium* was found to have brought with him into the world "a so-called Jewish brain" [*jüdischen Kopf*]. His "Jewish head" and "diligent industry" kept him always at the top of his class. Sounds like Freud himself. Kohn was "a typical little Jew, with crafty features, a boundless vivacity, an unrestrained speech, rather a wholly honest fellow." "Naturally," the "clever Jewish boy" came to Vienna and took up medicine, eventually marrying his Viennese professor's daughter. "In short, Kohn, son of the *Schammes*,[314] became Kohn, the *Dozent*, associate Professor and finally, since 1881, J.'s [his father-in-law's] successor." Freud's conversation with this successful Jew was unrestrained, "for the vain, easily transparent man has his respectable sides, among them no shame at being a Jew."

Freud's psychological insight is subtle, for he implies that Jewish formality and pompousness in such a social setting (among a mixture of Jews and Gentiles, where Gentile social norms would prevail) imply a defensive reaction-formation (as he would put it later) to an unconscious sense of shame at being a Jew. Being from "uncultivated," that is, Jewish origins, the Jew feels self-conscious if seeking to join Gentile society as an equal and compensates for it by suppressing his Jewish characteristics.

The similarity of the story to Freud's own[315] is patent, and so Freud's description discloses elements of his Jewish identifications. Jews are again typically intelligent and hardworking, crafty, diligent, ambitious, talkative and full of life. In spite of all these good qualities—or perhaps because of them—Jews might have reason to hide the fact of their Jewishness when successful in Gentile society (an achievement to be expected of Jews in Freud's mind), and so Freud admires the man who has kept such social pressure at bay and can be Jewish openly and honestly. Freud will be proud of just this posture himself later in life.

Three months later, Freud's sense of the typical intelligent cleverness (and affable nature) of Jews is confirmed again, when he learns sometime after meeting "Mr. Barney Sachs" that he is a Jew. He is "an especially affable and clever sir."[316] Though the young Freud is aware of the social norms of the dominant Gentile society, and he identifies with and feels bound by them to a certain extent, he respects the man who will live and work openly as a Jew. This response is evidence for an inherited sense of Jewish self-worth and for Freud's dual allegiance to free Jewish expression in an enlightened Gentile polity.

The strength of this pride can be gauged by the intensity of Freud's defiance of antisemitism throughout his life, a pattern established in the early period. Wistrich says that antisemitism functioned as "a catalyst in Freud's growing inner affirmation of Jewish identity during the mid-1880s."[317] On 16 December 1883, Freud writes to Martha of an "adventure" on his train ride to Leipzig to meet his brother Emanuel, "unpleasant in the experiencing, pleasant in the contemplating." We will do well to let Freud tell the story at length, not only because he is such a good storyteller (a skill that will serve him well later), but also because it conveys a sense of Freud's Jewish personality in response to antisemitic attack. Freud sets the scene:

> You know that I am always thirsting after fresh air and am always at pains to open windows wide, especially in railway carriages. So I opened also here a window and stuck my head out in order to feel at ease. Whereupon there were shouts to close it (it was the windy side), especially coming from one particular man. I declared myself willing to close it, provided that another someplace opposite were opened—it

> was the only open window in the long carriage. While we thus parleyed and he declared himself willing to open the ventilation slit in place of the window, there rang out from a man in the background the shout: "He's a rotten Jew!" [*ein elender Jude*]. With that the whole affair took a different turn. My first opponent also became an antisemite, declaring, "We Christians have a sense of the public weal. You had better subordinate your precious Ego," and similar such things. And my second opponent proclaimed under insults corresponding to his education that he would climb over the seats to show me, etc. A year ago I would have been unable to utter a word from the excitement, but now I am different. I felt no fear of the mob [*Gesindel*], invited the one to keep his common phrases to himself, since they commanded no respect in me, and the other to trouble himself to come up to me and fetch the answer he deserved. I was quite prepared to kill him, but he did not step up. That I did not join in with insults pleased me; that one must leave to "Gentlemen." With the compromise, ventilation slit versus window, the first Act closed.

Before turning to "act two," let us examine this incident. Until the issue became one of antisemite versus Jew, Freud was willing to "parley" [*parlamentieren*] and to compromise. As long as two human beings with equal rights can discuss together their conflicting wishes, Freud is willing to be "civilized," to work within the "rules." But when his status is degraded to that of a "wretched Jew," implying that for a Jew to assume a public claim to equal rights is an affront to social norms, an arrogance, Freud then becomes defiant of all social norms, ready to kill. And let not the reference to poverty and dirt in *elender Jude* be lost on Freud, the ambitious doctor, trying to maintain a hygienic and fresh environment in the railway carriage, contrary to the typical condition of Jews portrayed in Jewish jokes.[318] "For Freud, these are fighting words, whereas they were not for Freud's father."[319]

Freud's Jewish identity is grounded in the Enlightenment and the Emancipation that guarantee him equal rights *as* an individual Jew. When the antisemite shows that he does not accept these premises, Freud no longer feels bound by "civilized" behavior. But in fact he is loyal to what he considers a higher set of norms, those namely not of the masses, *das Gesindel,* but of the educated, those with *Bildung.* These norms are humanist values, according to which all are equal on principle. Freud is outraged at being told to subordinate himself to Christian chauvinism, especially in the name of the *Gemeinwohl,* for he is himself committed to a public weal based in humanism. In the late period, describing his reaction to the antisemitic expectation he encountered at the University of Vienna that he should consider himself inferior because he was a Jew, Freud says "I absolutely refused to do [this]."[320] Freud's language in this letter to Martha, which makes clear that he conceives of the confrontation as one between the uneducated Christian mob and the cultivated Jew able to exercise self-control, supports the contention that Freud's letter to Martha four months earlier (29 August 1883), discussing the difference between "us" and *das Gesindel,* is related to Freud's sense of what a Jew is (or should be). The "rabble," whether Gentile or *Ostjuden,* is "the other" in Freud's mind.

In the present letter, Freud reveals a sense of the development of his Jewish identity and his pride in defending it on humanist grounds, for he admits that a year ago he would have been speechless, unable to use language to fight for himself. Gilman points out the importance of the skillful and correct use of the language of the host culture for the immigrant Jew's sense of self-respect. Freud's capacity for speech in such a situation confirms his place in educated German society precisely as the kind of Jew he believes he is, namely, one who triumphs over the "appetites" of the mob.

Before we leave this story (which Freud dismisses as "stupid" [*dumm*] at its conclusion), let us look at "act two." The conductor whom Freud has summoned refuses to take sides, but he offers to escort Freud to another compartment. Freud declines; he will not budge. In fact, when several people leaving the train later through a window leave it open, Freud sits down boldly [*keck*]—one might say provocatively—beside it. As he says, "I felt very ready for a fight [*sehr rauflustig*]." At this,

> the antisemite, this time with ironic civility [*Höflichkeit*], renewed his demand. "No," I responded, [and] he received no answer, rather [I] told him he should turn to the conductor, and I stood my ground until the next station. There the conductor again refused to say anything, but another official who after all had heard only about the issue and not of the row ruled that in winter all windows had to be closed. Whereupon I closed it. After this victory, I seemed lost; there rained slanders, insults and insinuations, until I turned round and shouted at the ringleader and told him furthermore that he should come on over and make my acquaintance. I was really uncertain of the outcome.

The outcome seems to be that Freud was ignored, and "from then on everything was quiet." Freud is proud of his behavior:

> I do think however that I held my own worthily and made use of the means at my disposal courageously; in any case I did not become vulgar [*gemein*].

The means at his disposal, Freud notes, were not physical size, wild and threatening appearance, or roaring voice, not even a distinguished presence with which to intimidate the crowd. Rather he had only his lack of fear and undaunted temper to oppose the mob. That is, he had character. He did not lower himself to the mob's level. Freud's Jewishness is expressed by a poised civility. But note too Freud's stubbornness, his aggressiveness, his defiance of the antisemites, and his rude and provocative challenge in sitting down "boldly" next to the open window, almost daring anyone to say something to him. These are "bad manners" for anyone, but for Freud as a Jew they represent "courageous" and "worthy" behavior, because he is making a point in battle for his rights as a *human being* who happens also to be Jewish. His Jewishness is the means by which he makes his point, but it is the humanist—and modern—claim to universal equality as the basis of a cultural whole that fuels Freud's stubborn allegiance to his seat by the open window. Again, the Jewish particular is necessarily and unavoidably Freud's access to the universal. As mentioned above, Martin Freud characterizes his father as "a fighting Jew," and this phrase does capture an important element of Freud's Jewish self-conception.

This aspect of Freud's personality emerges again in his response to an antisemitic attack on his medical colleague Carl Koller, who through Freud's somewhat unwitting help became famous for discovering the use of cocaine as an anesthetic in eye surgery. Freud writes breathlessly of the incident to Martha on 6 January 1885, breaking off three times while writing the letter because he is too restless and impatient to continue. A Gentile surgeon had lost his temper and called Koller a "Jewish swine" [*Saujud*]. Freud says that "we would all have retorted in the same way as Koller—in short, with a slap in the face." Because both men were reserve officers, they were honor-bound to fight a duel, and Freud is writing to his fiancée even as the duel with swords is taking place. He promises he will not post the letter until he can report the outcome of the fight. "So much could be said about all this," he adds. Freud's excitement must be seen against the background of the declaration of the German student fraternities that Jews were by nature incapable of insult and unable to defend their honor by dueling because they were without honor. Freud has sent Koller a bottle of fine wine "to strengthen him for the fight." He breaks off now to see if the duelers are back and is delighted to report that Koller is unharmed, while his opponent has two deep gashes. It is "a proud day for us," and he and his colleagues are going to send Koller a present as a lasting reminder of his victory.

On the same day Freud is moved to write to Koller himself,[321] asking that his colleague accept his proposal that in their conversation henceforth they use the familiar pronoun *Du* "as an external sign of honest friendship, sympathy and readiness to help." This gesture is not insignificant as an indication of Freud's feeling. For all his "fatherly fondness" for Jung (as Gay puts it), Freud never offered this "emblem of Germanic familiarity" to his Gentile psychoanalytic "crown prince."[322] Furthermore Freud praises Koller as "a helper to men and a source of pride to friends." Freud clearly identifies with his Jewish colleague and his defiant defense. As he says, Koller did what he himself would have done. Freud is proud that a Jew has stood up for himself, fighting like a soldier. We recall Freud's childhood admiration for Hannibal and Napoleon's marshal, Massena. As Freud advised his children, "Do not tolerate insults. Defend yourself!"[323] Note however that Freud praises Koller as a helper to "human beings" [*Menschen*], rather than as a "defender of our people." On the other hand, his "friends" are Jewish, and this fact is related to their pride. Koller is clearly defending his people too, so Freud's language implies again that his identification with his Jewish particularity is his access to the universal human kinship. Although Freud feels Jewish pride here, his allegiance includes at the same time a humanist horizon realized through his Jewish identification. Thus he does not seem bothered by the obvious assimilation of the decidedly "un-Jewish" practice of dueling that so offended Jewish critics (like Jellinek) of the student Zionist societies. His identity straddles both worlds.[324]

That Freud's sense of himself as a fighter is rooted in his sense of his own *Jewishness* is not to be doubted. Freud links this trait himself to Jewish tradition and history when he writes to Martha from Paris a little over a year later, on 2 February 1886, referring to a conversation he had had at some earlier time with his mentor, Josef Breuer:

> You know what Breuer told me one evening? I was so moved by what he said that I disclosed to him the secret of our engagement. He told me he had discovered that hidden under the covering of shyness there lay in me an extremely daring and fearless human being [*Mensch*]. I had always thought so, but never dared tell anyone. I have often felt as though I had inherited all the obstinate defiance [*Trotz*] and all the passions with which our forefathers defended their Temple, and I could gladly [*mit Freude*] throw down my life for one great moment [in history].

Freud demonstrated his fearless courage and obstinate defiance on that train, so he isn't just boasting. Freud's word *Trotz* perhaps recalls the biblical "stiff-necked," and he seemed quite stubborn then, when threatened as a Jew, bold enough to defy all comers and all conventions. In moments like these he may indeed have felt as though he were defending values that were in a way sacred like the Temple. Freud will use this metaphor in the late period to describe his defense of psychoanalysis. And he will respond to antisemitic threats with such defiant courage again.

In this same letter from Paris to Martha, written later that night, Freud reports a political conversation he had with Giles de la Tourette, a famous neurologist, at a party at Charcot's residence (with whom Freud was studying). Gen. George Boulanger had just been appointed the French minister of war and was heading the *revanche* movement against German occupation of Alsace-Lorraine. In such a context, Freud's German accent may have been a temptation in cocktail-party conversation to try and get a rise. In the course of the conversation, Tourette

> naturally prophesied the most ferocious war with Germany. I disclosed my identity as a Jew [*als juif*], [one] who is neither German nor Austrian.

Given the first part of Freud's letter, it is clear that his pride and strength in being Jewish are connected to his sense of Jewish history, and that his identification with the ancient patriotism of his people supports his reply to his French challenger. The Jews who defended their Temple were doing so in defense of their national sovereignty. So even as early as 1886, Freud's Jewish identity has a political and a *national* horizon. It is analogous to German or Austrian citizenship. Even in the early period, Freud's Jewish identity contains an indigenous element of national pride that enables him to assume a place for himself as an independent among other nations. Though a humanist abroad, Freud is a *Jewish* humanist. Or is he a humanist Jew? The ambiguity will stand as a part of Freud's poise.

Lest we think that things are just that simple with Freud, the letter continues:

> Such conversations are always very awkward [*peinlich*] for me, for I feel what is German stir itself within me, something I long ago decided to suppress.

Freud's identity is not simply Jewish and humanist; he is also part German and has been passionately so. As he confesses from Paris to Martha's sister Minna, "As you realize, my heart is German-provincial" [*deutsch-kleinstädtisch*]. Until 1878 Freud was a member of the *Leseverein der deutschen Studenten*, a German nationalist debating society.[325] But as German-nationalist students begin increasingly to regard German Jews as their enemies, Freud suppresses his allegiance to the Fatherland, rejecting its rejection of the Enlightenment and its logical consequence, the Emancipation, and this separation sets him free to define himself politically as an independent. This independence is Jewish, for that is a patrimony too natural to him to deny; it need only be defended.

Freud's Letters to Wilhelm Fliess

At this point let us turn to Freud's letters to his friend and early collaborator, Wilhelm Fliess. Frank Sulloway has shown how profound was Fliess's scientific influence upon Freud, despite the "bad press" Fliess has received in the self-serving "mythical" histories of psychoanalysis written by Freud's followers.[326] Here we are concerned with the extent to which the friendship between the two men can illuminate Freud's Jewishness in the early period.

Freud first writes to Fliess in November 1887, a month after his first child is born. In the next eight years (1887-95), Martha will bear him five more children. In all, therefore, Freud fathers six children, three girls and three boys, naming the girls after Jewish friends and the boys after Gentile mentors.[327] Before turning to the Fliess correspondence itself we might do well to pause and consider this choice of naming. The division between Jews and Gentiles may reflect Freud's sense of the primary location of his Jewishness, at home with those connected to family and birth. Out in the world, the boys' names reflect Freud's participation in Gentile culture. Peter Gay goes so far as to specify "the anti-metaphysical, determinist tradition of nineteenth century positivism" as the tradition that the names Martin and Ernst honor.[328] Gay connects all six of Freud's choices for his children's names—and it seems clear that they were Freud's choices—with his effort to free himself internally from his father Jakob, in order that he might become a father himself. The combination of Gentile and Jewish names was Freud's way of putting "his Jewishness into the largest possible context,"[329] namely, Gentile society and scientific humanism.

Although it is true that in these years and those that follow in the early period Freud is seeking to resolve his ambivalence towards his father (a maturational step every man must take), Gay does not place enough emphasis on the positive connection to Freud's own Jewishness that the girls' names represent. They are all named for close Jewish family friends, perhaps a reflection of matrilineal descent in the biological transmission of Jewishness. It is a measure of the regard in which Freud held

Wilhelm Fliess at the time that had the sixth child, born 3 December 1895, been a boy, Freud would have named it after Fliess.[330] This fact supports Gay's contention that Freud is trying to resolve his ambivalence towards his father in intending to name his child after the man to whom he had attached such a strong "father-transference." Interestingly enough, Fliess's birthday (24 October) fell on the day after Freud's father died (23 October 1896). But in addition, Freud's intention points to the importance that Jewishness and Jewish friendships had for him at this time, less than a year before his father's death and two years before Freud's subsequent involvement in the Vienna B'nai B'rith, which he joined on 29 September 1897. The choice of Fliess represents the coming together of Freud's Jewish and Gentile (viz., scientific humanism) attachments in one Jewish friend and professional colleague, an apt symbol of the harmony of his dual allegiance.

Freud is indeed ambivalent about his father; but in the end this ambivalence does not alter his attachment to his own Jewishness, especially in the increasingly antisemitic environment of Vienna in the 1890s. Instead, the discovery of a way to express a Jewish commitment without compromising his humanism enables Freud to resolve that ambivalence into a coherent sense of identity. Is seems apt therefore, that Anna Freud, who acted as Freud's stand-in at the end of his life, in her inaugural lecture for the Sigmund Freud Chair at Hebrew University in Jerusalem in 1978, should accept the appellation "Jewish science" for psychoanalysis as a "title of honour."[331]

There are commentators who dispute Freud's view of the presence and influence of antisemitism in Vienna and how it impeded his own progress (e.g., Drucker, Sulloway). Whatever the objective truth may be—and there are certainly voices that support Freud's view—it is clear that Freud saw antisemitism opposing him in Vienna. How this factor contributed to the formation of Freud's Jewish identity may be seen in his letters to Fliess. On 4 February 1888, Freud writes about "a major scandal" in the Vienna medical society to which he belonged. "Honorable Christendom is very indecent," Freud begins, protesting that

> they wanted to force us to subscribe to a new weekly journal, which is intended to represent the purified, exact, and Christian views of a few *Hofräte* [high civil servants] who have long ago forgotten what work is like. Of course, they are succeeding; I feel very much like resigning.

Jeffrey Masson, who edited and published the complete edition of the Freud-Fliess correspondence, notes that the first issue of this journal contained nothing obviously Christian about it, but that its initial editorial spoke "rather ominously of the 'fatherland' and the 'honor of the Vienna school'."[332] Perhaps Freud associates such views with Christianity. Clearly he resents the society's action, and his desire to resign reflects a self-understanding. Nonetheless, Masson notes, "it seems he never did resign."[333]

As Vienna reached middecade in the 1890s, political antisemitism grew more popular. Karl Lueger, cofounder and leader of the Christian Social Party, was elected mayor of Vienna three times in 1895–96, supported by an antisemitic and nationalist political platform, but confirmation was withheld by Emperor Franz Joseph for two years. Freud writes to Fliess on 23 September 1895 of the results of the first election. The liberals lost 46 to 0 in the third district (where 6 per cent of Vienna's Jews lived) and were outvoted 32 to 14 in the second (i.e., Leopoldstadt, the district where 41 percent of Vienna's Jews lived at this time).[334] Freud says, "I voted after all. Our district[335] has remained liberal." A month and a half later, Freud mentions that he is following Fliess's prescription that he refrain from cigar smoking, but he "overindulged out of joy only on the day of Lueger's nonconfirmation,"[336] when the emperor overturned Lueger's second election in 1895. As noted, smoking is a point of identification with his father, so Freud's act joins his father's image to this Jewish triumph.

Ernst Simon says that in the exchange of letters between Freud and Fliess, "this election constitutes the only political topic."[337] Yet on 11 September 1899, Freud comments on the retrial of Alfred Dreyfus, who was found guilty again in spite of the discovery of forgery in the case against him:

> The outcome [of the Dreyfus affair] in France also saddened and embittered me. Respects are due to the action of the German government![338] There is no question on whose side the future lies.

Freud's interest in European political life, at least judging from his comments to Fliess, is confined to matters affecting the Jews. His interest in Zionism will follow this pattern.

Around this same time, when Karl Lueger was "popular," Max Graf was considering having his newborn son baptized, in an attempt to shelter him from such antisemitism. He reports Freud's advice:

> If you do not let your son grow up as a Jew, you will deprive him of those sources of energy which cannot be replaced by anything else. He will have to struggle as a Jew, and you ought to develop in him all the energy he will need for that struggle. Do not deprive him of that advantage.[339]

Freud's Jewish pride here is remarkable. In the context of antisemitic opposition, the certainty of being Jewish is an *advantage* that a father owes to his son, a source of strength, according to Freud. The unavoidable particularism of Jewish identity is an energetic resource in the struggle for life, especially since the boy will be seen as Jewish by the antisemites anyway. To some extent, Freud's defiance may simply be realistic; but one senses that Freud would not choose to be anything other than Jewish.

The Death of Jakob Freud. The death of Freud's father was a major turning point in his life, one that determined his career in many ways. He admitted that *Die Traumdeutung* was in part a reaction to his father's death, and he characterizes the latter as "the most important event, the most poignant loss, of a man's life."[340] With all the negative things that have been written about Jakob Freud and Freud's relation to him, it is worth noting that Freud himself almost always speaks of his father in glowing terms, his admiration and respect obvious. He is "a tremendous fellow" [*Riesenkerl:* a "giant of a man"],[341] "an interesting human being," "very happy within himself,"[342] "an extraordinary human being."[343] The death of the old man on 23 October 1896 at age eighty-one moved Freud deeply: "I treasured him very much . . . he had a significant effect[344] on my life . . . I feel now quite uprooted."[345] In speaking a few years later about Jakob's manner of dying, Freud admires his father and seeks to emulate his example: "My father was fully aware of it [his coming death], did not speak about it, and retained his beautiful poise until the end."[346] As may be inferred from Freud's stoic composure at his own death,[347] Jakob's example remained a positive model to the end of Freud's days. Freud's words and later behavior reveal that whatever ambivalence he discovered buried in his unconscious, he loved the Jewish father whose duplicate he claimed to be. To be unwilling to contradict his father reveals a tremendous love and respect, and not just fear.

Jakob's death impelled Freud to rediscover his "roots." His search combined his effort both for professional recognition and success and for Jewish self-understanding and expression. This combination reflects Freud's dual allegiance to Jewishness and humanism; it also reflects a dual allegiance to his father. Marianne Krüll and Marthe Robert argue that Freud's drive for success in the Gentile world is rooted in an allegiance to a kind of psychological "mandate" from his father, following Jakob's own move from the *stetlach* of Galicia to the big city of Vienna. Freud's involvement with the B'nai B'rith, especially since he joined the lodge at "the first possible moment after he recognized the pervasiveness of antisemitism in Viennese politics and academic life,"[348] also reflects an allegiance to

Jewishness and to the Jewish people in relation to his father. Freud's activity in B'nai B'rith honors his father's memory and is an expression of the liberal values learned in his home.

This two-pronged development can be seen clearly in a letter to Fliess dated 22 June 1897.[349] Having been proposed for an associate professorship (*Extraordinarius*) by a medical faculty committee on 12 June,[350] Freud is thinking of the possibility of a new title. "At our next congress you shall call me 'Herr Professor'," he jokes with Fliess, and then more seriously, "I mean to be a gentlemen like other gentlemen." Freud is determined to be a member of the cultural elite, successful in Gentile society. Yet in the same letter he affirms the importance of his being Jewish both by his use of Yiddish—a language that Jews used only among themselves—and by his reference to his collection of Jewish jokes:

> We parcel things out like two *Schnorrer* [beggars], one of whom gets the province of Posen [in Poland]; you, the biological; I, the psychological. I must admit [as if to explain his reference to *Schnorrer*] that I have recently started a collection of profound Jewish stories.

Given that this collection eventually gave rise (in 1905) to Freud's book, *Wit and its Relation to the Unconscious,* this conjunction of professional aspirations, Jewish solidarity through humor, and Yiddish is not insignificant. As discussed in chapter 1, in the early months of 1897 Freud had a series of dreams that expressed "a longing to visit Rome."[351] Freud saw these dreams as ultimately rooted in the struggle for Jewish emancipation from the antisemitism of the Catholic church, and he alludes to this struggle through Jewish jokes. As Klein says,

> Frustrated by the dreary daytime reality of academic and political anti-Semitism, Freud internalized this "perseverance and single-mindedness" of Hannibal's Roman siege. In the dream that, at last, took him to Rome, he recognized the influence of a Jewish anecdote that communicated this prototype of Jewish tenacity. It concerned a Jew who, despite poverty and external restraint [he keeps getting thrown off the train], was determined to reach his destination. "To Karlsbad," he told an inquiring acquaintance, "if my constitution can stand it."[352]

Defiance of those in power and getting the better of them is a common feature of Jewish jokes in relation to antisemitism.[353]

Another Jewish joke occurs to Freud at the end of his dream, one that stressed the importance of Jewish solidarity in defiance of antisemitism. In the joke, a Jew who cannot speak French asks a Jew in

Paris his way, speaking French so badly that his fellow Jew responds in Yiddish, *Men ken Shabbes makhn mit dos* ("You can make the Sabbath with that")[354] (and it's useless for anything else). Klein observes that the response in Yiddish affirms the common tie between the two Jews in the joke (as it does between Freud and Fliess), conveying a sense of support and familial reassurance—*Heimlichkeit* perhaps—that only a fellow Jew could provide.[355] The humorous Yiddish reference in Freud's letter to Fliess functions in the same way.

A word about Freud's use of Yiddish is not out of place here. Freud responds to a query from A. A. Roback in 1930, saying, "I have never learned or spoken Yiddish,"[356] but Yiddish words are sprinkled throughout Freud's correspondence with Fliess. Yerushalmi counts at least thirteen in the portions of Freud's correspondence published to date, most of them in the Fliess correspondence, "where Freud is at his most uninhibited."[357] In 1930 Freud may just mean that he never mastered the language, for Theodor Reik reports that Freud's mother "did not speak in high German but Galician Yiddish,"[358] and as Yerushalmi says, "If this be so, even though Amalie Freud had grown up in Vienna, what shall we say of Jakob Freud, who grew up in Galicia?"[359] Noting words that were not common coinage, like *Knetcher* (wrinkles), *Stuss* (nonsense), *Dalles* (poverty), or *tomer dokh* (perhaps, after all), Yerushalmi suggests that it is reasonable to assume that Freud heard Yiddish commonly in his home, and that "he could speak or at least understand it."[360] Of course, as Gay writes, "*not* to speak Yiddish was one thing a German Jew, as a good German, did,"[361] since Yiddish was associated with the "primitive state of culture" of Eastern Europe, and this prejudice may account for the defensive sound of Freud's remark to Roback. Actually though, Freud's use of Yiddish seems like a way of "touching base," a tacit recognition of a shared (counter-) culture, so the social disdain for Yiddish did not interfere with Freud's use of it to create a (private) feeling of shared Jewishness. Freud also used Yiddish occasionally when writing to Martha and other Jewish friends—for example, to Ferenczi. In additions to the ones mentioned above, I noticed such words as *meschugge, meschuggene* ("crazy"), *chutzpah, Chazan, schadchan* ("marriage broker"), *schigan*, and *parnosse* ("livelihood"). So perhaps he picked them up at home from his father and mother. If so, Yiddish would be linked to his Jewish home, literally *mame-loschen* ("mother-tongue"), the affectionate term among Jews for Yiddish. Freud would also have heard such Yiddish growing up in the Jewish district, Leopoldstadt (II), where he lived until he moved out in 1883 at the age of twenty-seven. In any event, he uses Yiddish expressions in his correspondence with Fliess often enough to suggest that experiencing and expressing his Jewishness is important to him at this time. That he is in a process of self-formation Freud expresses vividly himself in the 22 June letter to Fliess: "I believe I am in a cocoon, and God knows what sort of beast will crawl out."

Christopher Hutton suggests that for assimilated Jews like Freud, telling Jewish jokes with Yiddish punch lines was "the vehicle for a controlled regression to an image of the Eastern European self," involving "an interplay between the identity of the 'little Jew' and that of the intellectual or 'outsider' Jew. In telling the joke, Freud . . . identifies with both sides, seeing each inside the other."[362] Freud allows himself "a controlled lapse of identity," whereby the hidden self underneath emerges to ease the transition from Eastern European Jew to "Viennese bourgeois intellectual Jew." Similarly, psychoanalysis uncovers the infantile self in order to manage the transition from neurosis to health, from childhood to adulthood. "For Freud . . . the Jewish joke is a kind of therapy. It parallels to a degree the aims and methods of psychoanalysis."[363]

Thus Freud's Jewish-Yiddish jokes in the Fliess correspondence both express his anxiety as he moves further away from his Eastern European roots and also function to bring about that transition by confirming their authentic connection: each is inside the other. When these jokes become a book in 1905, Freud has basically completed a kind of self-translation, whereby the language, culture, and psychology of the Eastern European Jew are brought to a wider audience and presented as universally relevant. The characters and contexts of the jokes remain Jewish, but as Freud says, utilizing the form-essence distinction we saw in the Nathan letter, "the core belongs to humanity in general."[364] As Hutton says, "this is clearly a statement of the 'universal' nature of Jewish psychology, that fundamentally the same processes are at work in the Jew as in everyone else."[365] Again the Jew is the paradigm for the human and the particular is the access to that universal. No wonder "a fondness for relating Jewish jokes and anecdotes" is the one overt Jewish characteristic that Jones says a Gentile would notice in Freud.[366] In telling such jokes, Freud expresses a sense of Jewish triumph in the discovery of humanist allegiance.

Jewish jokes also provide Freud with consolation and courage to face the opposition. On 21 September 1897, Freud confides to Fliess the collapse of his seduction theory. After quoting the verse from 2 Samuel discussed above, Freud says, "A little story from my collection occurs to me: 'Rebecca take off your gown; you are no longer a bride.'" Masson agrees with Anna Freud that her father meant by this joke that with his seduction theory for the neuroses he had felt as happy as a bride. "Those days were now over and he had to return to his earlier status; he had made no discovery."[367] In such a situation, he says, "To be cheerful is everything!" and putting into practice this twist on the humanist reference to Hamlet's "Readiness is all," Freud tells a Jewish joke. In this way he consoles himself with the Bible, Shakespeare, and Jewish humor, and so finds the courage to move on, his identity as a humanist Jew confirmed.

Freud finds such courage again in another Jewish joke he shares with Fliess in a letter of 28 May 1899. Freud is hard at work on his "Dream Book" (*The Interpretation of Dreams*), and he is aware that its contents will shock some in his audience. Yet he has decided that he cannot disguise his material, nor can he afford to relinquish his discoveries and not publish them because, he says, "I am not rich enough to keep my finest and probably my only lasting discovery to myself. In this dilemma I behaved like the Rabbi in the story of the cock and the hen." Freud proceeds to tell Fliess the joke, sharing a Jewish pleasure:

> A married couple who owned one cock and one hen decided to celebrate the holidays by roasting a fowl, but they could not make up their minds which was to be sacrificed and therefore turned to the rabbi. "Rebbe, what should we do? We have only one cock and one hen. If we slaughter the cock, the hen will grieve; and if we slaughter the hen, the cock will grieve. But we want to eat a fowl on the holiday; Rebbe, what should we do?" The Rabbi: "So slaughter the cock." —"But then the hen will grieve." —"Yes, that's true; so slaughter the hen." —"But Rabbi, then the cock will grieve." —The Rabbi: "So let him grieve!"

As Freud comments, "So the dream [book] will be." Through sharing the warmth, wisdom, and humor of a Jewish joke with a friend, Freud consolidates his courage to face the opposition. This immediacy contrasts sharply with the "scientific" and distant tone of the jokes in the psychoanalytic *Witz* book (1905). The Rebbe in this joke reflects Freud's own Jewishness in his attitude towards facing painful necessity: one bears with it. So Freud's stoicism also has a Jewish root. In this way, Freud's identification with Jewish jokes serves as an important source of Jewish moral support.

The years immediately following Freud's father's death in October 1896 were crucial for Freud's development, both personally and professionally. They were also characterized by his sense of antisemitic ostracism. As mentioned, Freud felt that antisemitism was blocking his appointment to a professorship in the University of Vienna. Just as he responded to the "Christian views" of the Society of Physicians in the Fliess letter of 4 February 1888, Freud also considered resigning from the university in a letter of 24 January 1897 ("Perhaps it will hasten my final break with the university"), when the proposal for his professorship was rejected due—as far as he was concerned—to antisemitism. As Nothnagel, who authored the proposal, told him, "Being an intelligent man, you are aware of the further difficulties."[368] "Denominational considerations,"[369] as Freud put it in *The Interpretation of Dreams*, were delaying his promotion. In fact, Freud discontinued teaching in the university from July 1898 until October 1903, ten consecutive terms.[370]

Freud had his series of "Rome dreams" during these early months of 1897. He admits that his longing for Rome is "deeply neurotic," connected, he tells Fliess, "with my *Gymnasium* idolization of the Semitic hero Hannibal."[371] As mentioned in chapter 1, Robert Gordis suggests that Freud's ambivalence over reaching Rome is related to a conflict between the classical Rome he loved, whose culture and language had given Freud such humanistic "consolation," and the antisemitic Rome he hated (and whose successor in Freud's mind was the Catholic church) as the ancient enemy and destroyer of his people.[372] Freud's maturation depends upon a resolution of this conflict.

This division in Freud's feeling for Rome comes out clearly in a letter he writes to Fliess on 19 September 1901, when he finally reaches Rome. Freud says then,

> While I was completely untroubled by antiquity (I could have worshiped the little piece of the Temple of Minerva near the forum of Nerva in its degradation and mutilation), I found I could not freely enjoy the second [i.e., the medieval, Christian] Rome; the inclination [to enjoy] troubled me. Unable to be rid of the thought of my own pain and all the other misery I know about, I could not bear well with the lie about the salvation of mankind, which raises its head to high heaven.

One wonders why Freud felt a desire to worship the remnant of classical culture in the form of the Temple of Minerva, even in (or perhaps because of) its mutilated and degraded state. Perhaps the Jewish Freud realizes that he is present in Christian Rome because of the triumph of the classical humanism of the Enlightenment, which took its inspiration and primary texts from classical culture. The goddess of wisdom would in this case be an appropriate patroness. Freud may feel impelled to give thanks to his benefactor. Yet the undisturbed presence of the Christian Rome bothers him, for its antisemitism is still at this point blocking his appointment to a professorship. Therefore his pain.

As mentioned, Freud sees his professional success as a battle for Jewish victory over the ancient and present-day enemies of the Jewish people. In *Die Traumdeutung* Freud's association for the joke about Herr

Zucker's difficult train journey with Christian antisemitism is clear. On 3 January 1897, Freud writes to Fliess, "We shall not be shipwrecked . . . if we do not prematurely capsize, if our constitutions can stand it, we shall arrive." It is possible that Freud refers here to his frustration in not finding the key to the neuroses, but considering Freud's associations to the Rome dreams, Klein suggests that Freud is also thinking of being repeatedly "derailed" by antisemitism in the professional societies and the university. Freud demonstrates his humanist cultural credentials (as if to defy any antisemitic accusation of language incompetence)[373] by promising in French, *Nous y arriverons.*

At this point in his life Freud joins the Vienna lodge of the International Order of the B'nai B'rith; he entered it on 29 September 1897, "the first possible moment after he recognized the pervasiveness of antisemitism in Viennese politics and academic life."[374] Freud discovers his deepest Jewish sense of himself in response to antisemitism, in defiance of its attack on his worth. Indeed, antisemitism brings out Freud's strongest Jewish self-assertions. At the end of his life, in 1926 and 1935, he writes to his Jewish lodge brethren explaining his reasons for seeking them out. "Surrounded by extreme hostility," "outlawed, shunned by all," he sought Jewish brotherhood—in fact his only formal connection with the local Jewish community.[375] His hostile professional reception and general sense of isolation aroused "the longing for a circle of excellent men with high ideals who would accept me in friendship despite my temerity." Finding what he sought in B'nai B'rith, Freud says,

> I soon became one of you, enjoyed your sympathy, and almost never neglected to go to the place, surrounded by extreme hostility, where I was certain to find friends.[376]

As he writes to Fliess on 23 March 1900, "Every second Tuesday I spend among my Jewish brethren, to whom I recently gave another lecture."

This last sentence makes it clear that Freud's association with B'nai B'rith was not solely for the sake of Jewish companionship; it was also a Jewish forum for the development of his scientific ideas. Freud's friendship and correspondence with Fliess should also be understood in this context, namely, as both Jewish companionship and intellectual forum. That these fora (Fliess and B'nai B'rith) are related is implied by Freud's frequent mentioning of his lectures to Fliess: "Last Tuesday I gave a lecture on the dream to my Jewish society (an audience of laymen). It was received enthusiastically. Next Tuesday the continuation."[377] On

29 December 1897, Freud again reports, "My second and last lecture on the dream is over and was acclaimed enthusiastically by the Jews." Despite their status as laymen and their stupid questions (as his letter continues to relate), these Jews are important to Freud. As he tells them in 1926, "You were my first audience." The same words of course apply to Fliess.

Freud lectured to his B'nai B'rith brethren many times on his psychoanalytic ideas and research, and at least five times he presented these ideas before he published them as an article in a professional journal or as part of a book.[378] His first two lectures mentioned above, given on 7 and 14 December 1897, were on the interpretation of dreams, indicating Freud's trust of and regard for his Jewish audience and the role they played in the initial stages of his work.

In fact Freud lectured to B'nai B'rith twenty-one times over a period of twenty years, on such topics as "The Psychology of Forgetting," "The Psychic Life of the Child," "On Dreams," "On Jokes," and "We and Death," with his most active participation coming in the early period (fifteen times through 1908, ten times through 1902). Furthermore, Freud took an active role in defining the ideals and goals of the order. He introduced a series of discussions on this topic in the fall of 1901 with a talk entitled "Goals and Purposes of the B'nai B'rith Order," and he spoke the following year on "The Role of Woman in our Union," also an introduction to a series of discussions.[379] In addition, in 1902 Freud helped found a second B'nai B'rith lodge in Vienna, named *Eintracht* ("Harmony"), participating in the planning stages and serving on the search committee to help establish it.[380] He got many of his friends to join the lodge, including his brother Alexander. Thus Freud's investment in B'nai B'rith was considerable, and his contributions indicate "how highly he prized the Jewish society as a viable center for intellectual discussion."[381]

And just as he will respond later to Fliess, when Freud's Jewish audience rejected his work, he scorned them in turn. Freud writes to Fliess on 25 April 1900 about his lecture to B'nai B'rith on Zola's *Fecondite*. He uses language that implies he did not take his lodge members very seriously:

> I am always ill prepared; actually I start only an hour before—much as one writes a German composition in school.

Yet he continues, "During the night from Monday to Tuesday, I dreamed inordinately [*ausgebig*] of this lecture." If Freud takes the lecture so lightly, why does he dream so much about it? Freud himself answers:

"The brethren, moreover, were unkind and scornful of me—conduct that is apt, quite surely, to reduce my interest in the success of the lecture." His first audience is finding his views too much to take and is skeptical. Admittedly Freud's indifferent attitude seems to precede his audience's reaction, but it is likely that he anticipated it. Fliess will also respond with skepticism and finally scorn ("the reader of thoughts merely reads his own thoughts into other people"),[382] and this will be a major reason for their parting.[383] Yet Freud's displeasure here with his Jewish brethren, who after all are laymen, does not end his involvement in the lodge; in fact it increases after this point. Therefore, in spite of the importance of Freud's lectures to B'nai B'rith for the birth of psychoanalysis, as Klein documents, the role of Freud's membership in the formation of his Jewish identity is really more social and personal than it is intellectual or professional.

The members of B'nai B'rith saw themselves as men chosen from "the best circles of Vienna Jewry," a phalanx of high-principled, intelligent, and educated Jews, an ethical society."[384] The Viennese lodges were devoted to the idea that one could be both a Jew and a "modern man." As such, Marsha Rozenblit says, "B'nai B'rith provided . . . an opportunity for secular Jews to experience their Jewishness profoundly."[385] Therefore the society became an appropriate crucible for the formation of Freud's liberal humanist identity in a Jewish form, enabling him to identify his Jewishness with the expression of liberal ideals. This may be one reason why Freud was later unashamed to acknowledge a Jewish link to psychoanalysis,[386] namely, because his science was in part an expression of his own Jewish ideals, his contribution to the (messianic) search for the cultural whole. As Klein says, "Psychoanalysis provided Freud with a basis for . . . determining the common basis of all human life."[387] On this basis, it could be argued that in the early period, Freud developed psychoanalysis as an expression for the values that constituted his identity as a humanist Jew.

Yet Freud is also a Jewish humanist. On 26 August 1898, he writes to Fliess of "a small point that [he] had surmised to be so for some time," namely, that memory lapses, especially in the process of name recollection, are due to the interference of threatening unconscious or repressed thoughts. This insight spurred Freud to write a paper entitled "The Psychical Mechanism of Forgetfulness"[388] a month later, and to deliver a lecture to B'nai B'rith on the same subject on 3 February 1899, a few months after its being published. It eventually formed the basis of the first chapter of *The Psychopathology of Everyday Life* (1901). The beginning of this sequence is found in this letter to Fliess in August, based on Freud's forgetting the name of Julius Mosen:

> You know how one can forget a name and substitute part of another one for it; you could swear it was correct, although invariably it turns out to be wrong. That happened to me recently with the name of the poet who wrote *Andreas Hoffer* ("Zu Mantua in Banden"). . . . Of course, the man's name is Julius *Mosen;* the "Julius" had not slipped my memory. Now, I was able to prove (1) that I had repressed the name Mosen because of certain connections; (2) that infantile material played a part in this repression; [and] (3) that the substitute names that were pushed into the foreground were formed, like symptoms, from both groups of material. . . . Unfortunately, I cannot expose it to the public anymore than my big dream [which Fliess had warned him not to include].

Julius Mosen (1803–67) was a well-known German poet and dramatist. He also happened to be Jewish, and his poem on the Wandering or Eternal Jew, "Ahasver" (1838), may have been known to Freud.[389] But Mosen was more widely known for works that link him to German culture than to Jewish culture. None of his writings besides "Ahasver" are related to Jewish themes, and "Andreas Hofer," on the contrary, is a nationalistic Romantic poem about a Tyrolean patriot on his way to his own execution, hardly a Jewish theme (though perhaps appealing to German Jews anxious to identify emotionally with *Deutschland* and Austria). Julius Mosen may represent for Freud an example of a successfully assimilated German Jew, part of a growing humanist culture in which Jews can play an influential part.

But why does Freud forget (i.e., repress) the poet's name? Freud felt guilty at the infant death of his brother Julius in 1858, as he admits to Fliess in a letter dated 3 October 1897. Yet the "Julius" had not slipped his memory. Perhaps the similarity of the name "Mosen" to "Moses" was an additional connection that brought about the repression. But why can't Freud "expose it to the public"? Why does Freud hesitate to disclose an identification with Moses, whereas he is willing to reveal sexual and aggressive impulses that many would have balked at? Perhaps Freud refrains from making this association public here in the early period because this element of his Jewish identity does not fit into the humanist coherence he has found; it is "too Jewish."

In other words, this letter reveals a conflict that Freud the humanist feels in relation to that Jewish inheritance that separates him from Gentiles and Gentile culture, namely, his identification with Moses, the lawgiver of the Jewish people. Freud rejected Jewish religious laws; but these laws create the Jews as a separate people, and Freud feels a solidarity with them. In addition, Moses is a great moral hero in the Bible, and Freud is given to hero worship. Freud's Moses-identification, present *in nuce* here in the early period, confronts him with the perceived exclusivity of the Jewish people, so it is in conflict with his allegiance to universal humanist culture. Therefore this identification must be repressed at this stage of Freud's development. Indeed, its particularity will remain a problem for Freud. In the middle period, Freud will publish his analysis of the *Moses* of Michelangelo anonymously in part for the same reason, namely, because he does not want to associate the deepest symbol of his unassimilated Jewish identity with his universal humanist science, especially having just lost the "Gentile facade," Carl Jung. It is not until the end of his life, in *Moses and Monotheism,* that Freud finds a way to bring this identification into line with his humanist, psychoanalytic vision, and then it involves a sacrifice of Moses' ethnic Jewishness.

Another example of Freud's discomfort at being associated too closely with Judaism can be found in a letter to Fliess dated 16 April 1900. In the year 1900, Passover fell on 14 April and Easter the day after, on 15 April. On 16 April Freud wrote to Fliess about a hoped-for meeting the following year in Rome:

> If I closed with "Next Easter in Rome," I would feel like a pious, believing [*frommgläubiger*] Jew. So I say rather until we meet in the summer or fall in Berlin or where you will.

One need not be a "frum," that is, a pious Jew, to recognize immediately, as Fliess surely does, Freud's reference to the closing line of the Passover Haggadah, "Next year in Jerusalem!" Had Freud attended a Passover seder two days before? Did Martha give up seders also? Judith Bernays Heller recalls attending a Freud family seder in which Jakob Freud recited the Haggadah by heart.[390] She does not say whether Freud was present then or not, but he surely was during his youth, and so it is unlikely that the date would have passed now unnoticed. Easter was associated in Freud's mind with the defiant opening of his medical practice on Easter Sunday 1886 (which Freud observed on subsequent Easters regardless of the date),[391] and Freud's twist on the closing hope from the Haggadah for national restoration combines these associations. It must have delighted him with its heretical humor and freedom, and perhaps in its very declaration of intellectual independence it expresses Freud's identification with "Jewish" character.

Like the name-forgetting symptom, the alteration here is a perfect "compromise-formation," enabling Freud to express his dissent from Jewish belief and ritual,[392] while holding out hope for an eventual Jewish triumph of his own over the enemies of his people. The association of Jewish religion is still too close for comfort, however, so Freud rephrases his wish in language that removes any Jewish (or Christian) reference. Freud is most comfortable on his own (atheist) terms.

On the other hand, a month later (7 May 1900) Freud is thoroughly at ease the day after his birthday identifying with the biblical namesake of the Jewish people (and his own father, of course), Jacob, in the scene where the patriarch receives the name of Israel by wrestling with the "angel" (Gen. 32:24–32). Discussing his dissatisfaction with his work and the problems he sees in its conclusions, Freud says that it will be a fitting punishment for him that "none of the unexplored regions of psychic life in which I have been the first mortal to set foot will ever bear my name or obey my laws." Furthermore,

> When it appeared that my breath would fail me in the wrestling match, I asked the angel to desist, and that is what he has done since then. But I did not turn out to be the stronger, although since then I have been limping noticeably. Yes, I really am forty-four now, an old, somewhat shabby Israelite [*etwas schäbiger Israelit*] . . .

In spite of Freud's atheism, he is still a Jew who identifies with the founding fathers. In the Bible, Jacob is left alone at the Ford of Wrestling (Gen. 32:24ff.) where he wrestles with "a man" until daybreak, and Freud begins this letter with a reference to his own "splendid isolation" (English in the original). But Freud fails in the wrestling match in which Jacob prevailed. The patriarch did not yield until he had received the angel's blessing and the destiny of a new name, receiving his wound in his victory.[393] Freud, by contrast, seems to admit defeat and speaks of a modest assessment of his work. Still, his "limping" leads him to explicit "Israelite" self-identification, which, strangely enough for Freud, was a designation for Jews as adherents of a particular faith rather than a nationality.[394] He seems to be speaking ironically, in any event.

In addition to Freud's identification with Jacob/Israel, there may also be a subconscious identification with Moses in the reference to "my laws" that is picked up again at the end of Freud's paragraph. He speaks of his own "best consolation" in not depriving his family of "all future achievements." He has, he says, "left them a foothold for a start, but [is] not leading them to the peak from which they could climb no farther." Is Moses' peak experience on Mt. Nebo (Deut. 32:48ff.) in the back of Freud's mind?

Freud and Herzl

We have already discussed the role antisemitism played in pushing Freud to assert himself as a Jew. Freud's identification with Theodor Herzl gives us further insight into this role and suggests that Freud's sympathy for Zionism is related to his defiance of antisemitism. At the same time, "by his own admission, national pride was at least sufficiently strong in Freud to require suppression,"[395] even in the absence of antisemitism.

On 4 January 1889, Freud writes to Fliess of a rare night out at the theater:

> On Wednesday we shall go with your entire family (Bondy and Rie) to a Jewish play by Herzl, in the Carl Theater—a premiere, which has already played a role in my dreams.

For it to have entered his dreams, Freud must have read it before the Viennese premiere, as Yerushalmi notes. Freud discusses the play's influence on his dream, "My son, the Myops," in *The Interpretation of Dreams:*

> This dream was constructed on a tangle of thoughts provoked by a play I had seen, called *Das Neue Ghetto* ["The New Ghetto"]. The Jewish problem, concern about the future of one's children, to whom one cannot give a country of their own, concern about educating them in such a way that they can move freely across frontiers . . . [396]

Note that Freud neglects to mention the author of the play, an omission unusual for him.[397] The omission may be of no import, but some (e.g., Simon, Falk) think that it points to a complex of identification and conflict where Herzl is concerned. As Wistrich says, "Herzl, who opted to repeat the Mosaic epic through political action, must have struck a sensitive nerve in Freud which he preferred to repress."[398] In his report of the dream to Fliess, Freud laments not being able to give his children a Jewish country of their own (just what Herzl is working for)—an expression of Jewish particularism—but at the same time he is concerned that they receive the kind of education that will enable them to transcend the boundaries of such nationalism—an expression of Freud's humanism. Yet, as Peter Lowenberg has pointed out, Herzl's play was not about persecution, but rather about reconciliation between Jews and non-Jews.[399] For Freud to have produced the dream he must also have already read or at least been fully aware of Herzl's *Der Judenstaat* ("The State of the Jews"), published in 1896. The death of the hero at the end of Herzl's play proves the failure of assimilation as a strategy for solving "the Jewish problem,"[400] so Freud's anxieties are understandable.

Freud's identification with Herzl is evident also in a letter he writes to the well-known literary editor of Vienna's *Neue Freie Presse,* when at the suggestion of an editorial colleague, Max Nordau, Freud had his publisher send Herzl a copy of *Die Traumdeutung,* "as well as a smaller treatise on the same subject," for review. Freud concludes his letter to Herzl by adding,

> I cannot know whether you will find the book suitable for the purpose Mr. Nordau had in mind; but in any case I ask you to keep the book as a sign of the high esteem with which I—like so many others—have for many years regarded the poet and fighter for the human rights [*die Menschenrechte*] of our people.[401]

Simon notes that Freud praises the poet before the statesman and avoids explicit identification with Zionism as a national movement, characterizing Herzl's struggle as one for *human* rights rather than national rights. Nonetheless, we note the combination of Jewish solidarity, *unseres Volkes,* with the commitment to human rights as the basis for modern community.

In addition, on the basis of his dreams, it is clear that Freud did identify with Herzl's efforts to "save the Jews," even if not entirely in accord with Herzl's solution. Leo Goldhammer reports that he heard Freud lecture at the University of Vienna either in 1905 or 1907 on the subject of "Dreams and their Interpretation," and that on this occasion Freud related a dream he had had about Herzl:

> Theodor Herzl appeared, a majestic figure, with a pale, dark-toned face framed by a beautiful, raven-black beard, with infinitely sad eyes. The apparition strove to explain to him [to Freud] the necessity of immediate action if the Jewish people was to be saved; the words were surprising in their strict logic and the feeling ringing through them.[402]

In spite of Freud's humanism and support for Enlightenment-based emancipation, he knows that the Jewish people must be saved, and he identifies with this aim in the early period, revealing it publicly at the ("antisemitic") University of Vienna through a dream that implies an identification with Herzl, the father of political Zionism. Perhaps here is evidence for Jacob Meitlis's claim that Freud was "sympathetic towards Zionism from the very first days of this movement when Herzl was still alive."[403]

Freud, the Fighting Jew

And lest we overlook the importance of Freud's praise for Herzl as a "fighter," a description of an incident at the end of the summer in 1901 leaves us with a vivid image of Freud himself as a fighting Jew.

Freud and his family were on summer holiday at Reichenhall, a large health spa in the Bavarian highlands near Lake Thumsee. One morning Freud's sons Oliver and Martin were fishing on the side of the lake opposite their lodging and were heckled by antisemites. They returned home early, and when they told their father about it, "he became very serious for a few moments, remarking that [that] kind of thing could happen to us again, and that we should be prepared for it." Freud himself was. That same afternoon his sons rowed him across the lake to save him the walk to the spa. The men who had abused Oliver and Martin in the morning were waiting on the other side, "now reinforced by a number of other people, including women, and [they] stood on the road near the primitive landing-place, apparently prepared to block the way to Reichenhall. As we moored the boat, they began shouting antisemitic abuse." Recall Freud's confrontation eighteen years earlier on the train to Leipzig in Martin's description of Freud's response to the antisemites at the landing place:

> Father, without the slightest hesitation, jumped out of the boat and, keeping to the middle of the road, marched towards the hostile crowd. When he saw me following him, he commanded me in so angry a voice to stay where I was that I dared not disobey. My mild-mannered father had never spoken to me in anything but kindly tones . . . the enemy . . . numbered about ten men, and all were armed with sticks and umbrellas. The women remained in the background, but cheered on their men-folk with shouts and gestures.
>
> In the meantime, father, swinging his stick, charged the hostile crowd, which gave way before him and promptly dispersed, allowing him a free passage.[404]

The Jews who defended their Temple would have recognized a brother in Freud.

Years later Martin recalled that Freud turned to his sons after this incident, saying, "We are Jews. You will often have such experiences. Prepare yourself for it in time."[405] The oppositional stance seems almost typological in Freud's understanding of what "Jews" are, but it has been confirmed repeatedly in his experience. Freud does not mention this incident to Fliess when he writes him on 7 August. The encounter could have taken place after this date, but Martin writes, "There is no evidence that father was affected in the least. He never recalled the incident at home, and I am not aware that he ever mentioned it in any of his letters to our family or friends." The incident confirms Freud's attitude as a Jew toward antisemitism, namely, defiant and courageous in defense of "free passage." The Jew has a right as a Jew and as a human being to full participation, and Freud will fight for that right. In this sense Freud is a *modern* Jew.

The Obituary for Hammerschlag

On 11 November 1904, an obituary Freud wrote for his old teacher of religion, Samuel Hammerschlag, appeared in the morning edition of the *Neue Freie Presse.*[406] Though discussed briefly above, another look at its language will be worthwhile, because Freud's description of his teacher combines a Jewish root with a humanistic horizon. "In his soul glowed a strong spark of the spirit of the great Jewish seers and prophets," Freud writes, but "fortunately," "the passionateness of his character was tempered by the ideal of humanism [*Humanitätsideal*] of our German classical period, which governed him." Hammerschlag's Jewish passion was made milder and governed by the *Humanität* he had learned through the philological and classical studies of his youth. The description sounds like Freud himself. "Religious instruction served him as a way of educating towards *Humanität,*" Freud assures his liberal readers, "and from the material of Jewish history he was able to find means of tapping the sources of enthusiasm hidden in the hearts of young people, making it gush forth beyond national or dogmatic narrowness." Judaism serves humanism in this description, acting as an element of *Bildung.* Furthermore, serving the larger whole is the purpose of the particular tradition. Such an ethic reflects the values of the B'nai B'rith lodge in which Freud had been so active in these years. But as Rainey points out, Freud does not mention his teacher's emphasis on the need for preserving Jewish particularity, and that omission reveals Freud's own agenda and bias. At the end of the early period, Freud's commitment to serving the humanistic cultural whole is strong, and it will fuel his Jewish self-restriction in promoting psychoanalysis as a universal science in the middle period. Freud links this service towards *Humanität* with his Jewish teacher, whom he describes in closing as a "fatherly caring friend," perhaps linking this humanistic thrust with the memory of his own father.

Jewish Jokes and Jewish Identity

The significance of Jewish humor for Freud's Jewish sensibility and identity has been noted above. To close our study of the early period, a brief look at Freud's understanding of Jews that is revealed in his analysis of their wit and jokes in his book, *Wit and its Relation to the Unconscious* will be helpful. The work was published in 1905, but as noted, its roots go back to 1897, when Freud began collecting Jewish jokes after his father's death, perhaps in unconscious tribute. Basing himself on a section of Freud's book,[407] Ernst Simon notes six characteristics of Jewish jokes and suggests that they constitute Freud's view of what a typical Jew is like, "'a theory of the Jewish soul' in miniature."[408]

According to Freud, Jewish jokes reveal that Jews are typically self-critical. This may be uniquely so of Jews in Freud's mind, for he says, "I do not know whether there are many other instances of a people making fun to such a degree of its own character."[409] Jews admit that they are "comic figures," says Freud, but they know the connection between their faults and their good qualities.[410] They tell such jokes as much to remind themselves of their virtues as to wallow in their failures, and so the note of pride in Freud's observation. Secondly, Freud speaks of "the democratic mode of thinking of Jews, which recognizes no distinction between lords and serfs."[411] Simon notes Freud's passage from "self-criticism to self-defense" in describing Jewish indifference to class distinctions, "a typical combination for a Diaspora Jew."[412] As we have seen, Jewish self-defense is particularly typical of Freud. Though this democratic thinking "upsets discipline and cooperation," the rejection of class differences between Jews affirms the familial equality that Freud knows he shares with Jews, feeling the way they are "mingled together."

There is a Jewish legend that all Jewish souls were present together at the giving of the Law on Mt. Sinai. This essential equality of all Jews is one root of the laws of *tzedakah* ("justice") that require the redistribution of wealth within the community, and it is to jokes about this situation that Freud now turns. These laws gave rise to innumerable jokes about Jewish beggars who treat the money of the rich as though it were their own. Freud correctly notes that "according to the sacred ordinances of the Jews," the *Schnorrer* almost has "a right to make this confusion."[413] Simon suggests that Freud must have heard such jokes and discussions of their ethical underpinnings told around the dinner table, growing up in a Jewish household,[414] perhaps told by a father who himself struggled with poverty. The social legislation on which these jokes are based reflects a deep Jewish commitment to the ethical care of the poor by the rich. Simon's analysis implies that Jakob's motto, "Think ethically and act morally," is typically Jewish in Freud's mind.

According to the theology of *tzedakah*, as Freud notes, the rich man should be grateful to the poor "for giving him an opportunity for beneficence" (and obedience to the Law). But the Jews also typically rebel against their religion in their jokes:

> The rich Baron, deeply moved by a *Schnorrer*'s tale of woe, rang for his servants: "Throw him out! He's breaking my heart!"[415]

So although the Jews are proud of the justice of their laws, they feel an inclination to "throw them out" because of the trouble they bring: "There is really no advantage in being a rich man if one is a Jew. Other people's misery makes it impossible to enjoy one's own happiness."[416] Also implied in these jokes is an image of Jews as typically poor,[417] which reflected Freud's own familial experience as well as that of his people's.

The rebellion characteristic of Jews leads Freud to jokes that express "a profoundly pessimistic cynicism," which he sees rooted in "the manifold and hopeless miseries of the Jews."[418] Such cynicism leads him to jokes that "attack religious dogmas and even the belief in God," and he cites Heine's flippant deathbed joke about God: *"Bien sûr qu'il me pardonnera: c'est son métier."*[419] Thus Freud can see his own skepticism as part of a venerable Jewish tradition, and this is a sixth characteristic that Simon isolates from Freud's text, namely, the "all-pervading skepticism" of Jews, expressed in their jokes. Freud's analysis of Heine's last joke reveals his own reading of Feuerbach:

> So in the dying man, as he lay there powerless, a consciousness stirred that he had created God and equipped him with power so as to make use of him when the occasion rose. What was supposed to be the created being revealed itself just before its annihilation as the creator.[420]

Freud's Jewish skepticism extends even further though, because he closes this section with a Jewish joke whose more serious substance is "the problem of what determines truth." It is typical of Jewish jokes that they not only make us laugh; they also make us think. In fact, they make us think *because* they make us laugh. The combination is certainly characteristic of Freud himself, who was known for both his merry heart and his deep thinking. In using a Jewish joke to discuss a philosophical problem, Freud is in fact expressing his sense of what a Jew is. "Is it the truth," Freud asks, "if we describe things as they are without troubling to consider how our hearer will understand what we say? Or is this only Jesuitical truth, and does not genuine truth consist in taking the hearer into account and giving him a faithful picture of our own knowledge?"[421] What more Jewish way of achieving that humanistic purpose could there be, Simon suggests Freud thinks, than through the pleasure of a Jewish joke?

At the end of the early period, Freud expresses a Jewish joke's understanding of truth that is profoundly communal and responsible, a reality that rises out of relationship, dependent for its existence as much on the hearer as on the speaker. In other words, genuine truth weaves the fabric of community and is discovered as a part of that fabric. No one knows this so well as the Jew, Freud seems to imply, whose community has survived on the strength of the truth of its ideas. We are reminded of Freud's remarks about the "invisible edifice" of Judaism in the Nathan letter.

Jewish jokes express the soul of Freud's Jew so well precisely because they combine an unabashed Jewish particularity with a deep wisdom that links the Jew to all humanity.[422] Freud's jokes remind us that self-criticism is really a form of high expectation based on a knowledge of self-worth. A democratic attitude is rooted ultimately in the opening chapters of the Jewish Bible, whose moral principles underscore the responsible brotherhood of mankind. But it is only human to rebel against such "unnatural" responsibilities, laughing at our childish impulses while the adult in us acknowledges the need for their guidance by higher principles. And of course the misuse of religion for selfish purposes is universal. Jews were not the only poor; but their example of humor in response to difficulty can give relief and hope to those beset by similar circumstances. Finally, having been bred on the truth and having hoped for so long for its messianic fulfillment, the Jew will not be easily fooled. Such skepticism could be a warning to the idolatries of any age. All of these characteristics of "the Jewish soul" link Freud proudly to his people, but they also link him to the larger human community to which he seeks to contribute.

Summary

We have reached the first turning point, the end of the "early" period, in which Freud consolidates a sense of himself as a Jew and so is ready and able to move psychoanalysis out into the larger world and have it take its place among other branches of science, a *Wissenschaft* on its own terms. Before moving on to discuss Freud's letters during the middle period (roughly 1907 to 1922), let us summarize the results thus far, in order to fix an image of Freud's Jewish-humanist identity. It is the base upon which the rest will be built.

The picture of Freud's Jewish identity that emerges from the early period is defined first of all from the Jewish Bible, a product of biblical history. This patrimony is the deepest intellectual base for his solidarity with fellow Jews, and it leads him to locate his Jewishness in the home, where he first studied the Bible, and in Jewish social relations, which have the Bible as their assumed deep context. The attachment Freud expresses in the late period to Jewish languages such as Hebrew and Yiddish, in spite of his ignorance of their vocabulary and syntax, also has its root here in the early period in relation to family and Jewish friends. This context in turn gives Jewish jokes and humor an important role in Freud's self-expression and Jewish pride, and Freud's joy at life and his ability to enjoy are part of this Jewishness. He would have known the toast over the kiddush cups: "To life!" All these traits link Freud's Jewishness to his father Jakob in a positive way.

Freud's defiance of antisemitism (associated in his mind with the Catholic church) is another basic characteristic of his Jewish identity, helping to shape him into a "fighting Jew" as an expression of his love for his father. Freud's ambitiousness too may be associated with seeking his father's esteem. Freud learned Jewish self-assertion at home, wrestling with fellow Jews. His mother's love fuels his ambition with high self-esteem, the confidence of a "conquistador."[423] Thus, Jewish tenacity is connected in his mind with a love of life experienced in the home, and with a determination to be faithful to familial oaths. This self-transcendent drive to succeed is grounded in Freud's commitment to disciplined self-restraint in the service of an unknown goal, the renunciation required by this attitude forming Freud's sense of himself as part of an elite in obedience to his own Jewishness.

Freud's Jewish identity in the early period also has a national and a political dimension. This Jewish self-assertion is related to a defiance of antisemitism, but it is also rooted in Jewish history. Freud is proud of the independence of this Jewish spirit, in spite of the ambivalence generated by his "small-town German heart."

Yet all these characteristics of Jewish emotional allegiance are contextualized by an Enlightenment-based humanism, an identity formed by *Bildung* and *Kultur*, learned at school and at home, and legitimated in both places by admired Jews and Gentiles. On the one hand, this humanist context provides the means to a just Jewish revenge against Christian antisemitism; on the other hand, its agnosticism fuels Freud's atheistic rejection of religion, including Jewish ritual and its foundation, the Law. The Enlightenment is thus a double-edged sword. This rejection does not diminish Freud's identification with biblical characters—an atheist Jew is a Jew nonetheless—but it probably does create some ambivalence toward these founding fathers. Along with such ambivalence, Freud's identification with Moses is present beneath the surface in the early period.

Freud is proud to be Jewish, but he sees the need to sift the kernels of meaning from the antiquated husks of the tradition. Thus in matters of religion, as a Jewish *humanist,* Freud gives precedence to humanism and its agnosticism over Jewish tradition and its ritual and belief. This conflict of allegiances is resolved in a preliminary way by Freud's discovery in the Vienna B'nai B'rith of a Jewish social forum for the expression of the liberal ideals that he learned to be proud of at home and at school. Through the B'nai B'rith Freud affirms that he is also a humanist *Jew.*

On the other hand, in spite of his humanism, Freud exhibits a prejudice against *Ostjuden,* East European Jews, who symbolized "the distinction between progress and reaction, Enlightenment and superstition, even beauty and ugliness."[424] The Jew sometimes seems "prosaic" in Freud's mind when compared to the Christian, and his "wildness" can lead to cruelty, especially when he is hurt deeply. Freud himself is quite capable of such "bad" Jewish behavior in defense of Jewish worth, however, so his disdain may conceal an identification. Another negative trait associated in Freud's mind with his own Eastern European origins is the image of the Jew as neurotic, suffering typically from neurasthenia. But Freud's psychological health with regard to his Jewishness enabled him to use this trait in the service of psychoanalysis. By curing himself, he created a universal method of cure, turning the tables on his enemies.

In Freud's mind, Jews are typically tenacious, talented, hardworking, self-critical, passionate, democratic, intelligent, even crafty, skeptical, given to rebellion against their religion, ambitious, talkative, diligent, energetic, humorous, and full of life. Thus even in the early period, Freud's Jew consists of a particular psychological and ethical character, independent of the content of Jewish religion or practice. It is no wonder that Freud admires and emulates the Jew who has no shame at being Jewish, for the antisemitism that would make the Jew hide this identity is an outrage to such obvious worth. Yet Freud is a Jewish fighter not only for the Jews, but also for the Gentiles. He sees himself, as psychoanalysis moves out into the larger world, fighting for *Humanität* and for the cultural whole based on such Jewish-humanist value. In the late period, many of the characteristics of Freud's Jewish identity developed in the early period will reassert themselves and be given a new form in *Moses and Monotheism.*

3

The Middle Period

Introduction

In his three-volume biography of Freud, Ernest Jones titles the period from 1901–6, "Emergence from Isolation." The designation is apt, for in this period Freud begins to move psychoanalysis out of an exclusively Jewish environment into the larger, Gentile world. But as psychoanalysis "goes public," Freud's Jewishness retreats behind a "Gentile facade" in a strategic effort to further the interests of psychoanalysis as a "universal" science, for Freud believes that his Jewishness contributes to the opposition psychoanalysis encounters.[1] This chapter will describe and analyze both these movements—the one outward, into the larger culture, the other inward, turned back towards Jewish tradition and Jewish ethnicity—as it follows the development of Freud's dual allegiance in the period 1907–23.

In early September 1901, Freud visits Rome for the first time, visiting for the first time too Michelangelo's *Moses*.[2] The combination is appropriate for the shape of Freud's Jewish identity, as will be seen. This success enables him on his return to take steps to secure for himself his long-delayed professorship,[3] completing his vengeance on Catholic Vienna as the representative of the antisemitism that had humiliated both him and his father Jakob. September 1902 brings Freud his second trip to Rome and an extended tour of Italy. Immediately upon his return, in October 1902, Freud founds the "Psychological Wednesday Society" as a forum for discussion of his developing psychoanalytic ideas. Although all five members including Freud were Jewish, Klein suggests that Freud's decision to form his psychoanalytic circle at this point reflects his desire to move psychoanalysis beyond the strictly Jewish setting in which he had been developing it "in isolation" (i.e., in lectures to the Vienna B'nai B'rith), in order to articulate his new science more broadly. Klein notes that Freud's activity in the lodge declines dramatically after this date.[4] In other words, once Freud has consolidated his own Jewish identity enough to breach the "walls of Rome," and he then has his professional identity confirmed by Rome's symbolic successor, that is, Catholic Vienna, Freud feels secure enough to "leave home," as it were, and make a new start, on new professional terms.

The Freud-Jung correspondence begins in April 1906, and Jung visits Freud personally in March of 1907.[5] When he and Ludwig Binswanger attend a meeting of the Psychological Wednesday Society on 6 March 1907, they are the first Gentiles to do so.[6] In September of this same year Freud, in Rome for the third time, writes a circular letter to his society. Its contents reveal to us the nature of the new terms on which Freud seeks to pursue the development of his new science, for he proposes that the society be dissolved and immediately reconstituted on a new voluntary basis.[7] This act symbolizes a new beginning for Freud and the vicissitudes of his Jewish identity. The Society is no longer exclusively Jewish (though it is still predominantly so), and its bonds are to be rational and chosen, not primarily inherited or "tribal." This is now science, not a Jewish support group, for in Freud's mind the Jewishness of psychoanalysis must in the interests of psychoanalysis itself be placed in the background. Therefore the middle period can be thought of as a "recessive" phase in the development of Freud's Jewish identity. Nonetheless some important things happen in this period that push Freud to a more mature and explicit articulation of his Jewishness in the late period.

Freud will articulate his belief in the need for Jewish deference explicitly later to his Jewish followers, most dramatically at the Psychoanalytic Congress in Nuremberg in the spring of 1910. As Wittels reported, Freud said then,

> Most of you are Jews, and therefore you are incompetent to win friends for the new teaching. Jews must be content with the modest role of preparing the ground. It is absolutely essential that I should form ties in the world of general science. I am getting on in years, and am weary of being perpetually attacked. We are all in danger. . . . The Swiss will save us—will save me, and all of you as well.[8]

Klein notes that this position affirms the belief in the pioneering function of the Jews widely held by Freud's B'nai B'rith brothers,[9] and so Freud's self-subordination here may be for him in context an essentially

Jewish act, learned from fellow Jews in B'nai B'rith. This suggestion will seem even more plausible when linked below with Freud's interpretation of the "*Moses* of Michelangelo" and later with *Moses and Monotheism.* In any event, Freud's Psychological Wednesday Society and his circular letter are the first steps on the path to "de-Judaizing" psychoanalysis. Seven months after Freud reconstitutes his Psychological Society on the new basis, its name will be changed too, becoming "The Vienna Psycho-Analytical Society," indicating a new, more professional basis for its activity and for Freud's self-conception as its leader.

The Correspondence

That Freud on this trip to Rome in 1907 is trying to put his Jewishness "behind" him (not to eliminate but subordinate it) is also indicated by a letter he writes to Martha on 21 September, describing his visit to the Roman catacombs: "In the Jewish ones the inscriptions are Greek, the candelabrum—I think it's called Menorah—can be seen on many tablets." That Freud almost forgets the Jewish name of this symbol of the Maccabean victory over the Jews' Greek enemies, celebrated yearly in the festival of Hanukkah, indicates the psychological distance Freud feels from his Jewish heritage at this time in the heart of Rome. He surely would have been familiar with the candle lighting of Hanukkah. Furthermore, Yerushalmi has discovered that Freud owned "a bronze or brass Hanukkah Menorah of the type that hangs on the wall and is lighted by oil and wicks," which he kept in his study during his lifetime.[10] So if that Menorah belonged to his family, Freud himself may have lit a Menorah for Hanukkah at some time during his youth, or at least have been present at a lighting. And we have seen that he identified with "our ancestors" who defended their Temple with passion and defiance.[11] In Rome at this point, Freud almost sounds like he is pretending to be Gentile, his identification with *Kultur* is so strong.

As discussed in chapter 1, the fact that Freud destroys his papers for the second time in this year, 1907, also indicates a desire to separate himself from his past, in order that he may, as he put it in 1885 in reference to his old papers, "think them" all over again, and in so doing "think himself" all over again too. It is also in 1907 that Freud published his first work on religion, an essay comparing religious ritual to compulsive obsessions.[12] Although Freud may have had Catholicism in mind in speaking about religious practices in his essay, when we recall his refusal to allow Martha to perform the ritual of lighting Sabbath candles, it seems plausible to say that this essay expresses Freud's position in general and so symbolically seals off psychoanalysis from Jewish religious "influence." Jones's chapter title for the period 1906–9 again seems appropriate: "The Beginning of International Recognition." A new phase has officially begun.

Freud and Jung's circumlocutions in letters written in August 1907 when discussing Karl Abraham's "descent" also indicate the recession of Freud's Jewishness in this period. Freud has not met Abraham yet and asks, as though it were incidental, "By the way, is he a descendent of his eponym?" Jung is equally circumspect, confirming Freud's query in parentheses—"Abraham (who is what his name implies)"—as though to speak the word "Jew" would spoil their communication, forcing them to acknowledge their difference. The world of humanist science is still the Gentile world, to which Jews have only recently been admitted as equal partners. But it seems that they have not been fully accepted *qua* Jews, only as humanists or pseudo-Gentiles.

Freud will again avoid the word "Jew" with Jung a year later when writing about Ernest Jones. His language is revealing:

> The racial mixture in our group is to me very interesting; he is a Celt and consequently not quite accessible to us, the Teuton [*dem Germanen*] and the Mediterranean man.[13]

Note Freud's perception of racial difference at the outset, as though he were recognizing a physical foundation. Freud's self-description ("Mediterranean man") is probably a private circumlocution for "Jew," one that contextualizes his Jewishness broadly enough to include the classical civilizations of Greece and Italy. On 30 March 1922, at the close of our middle period, Freud will write to Sandor Ferenczi and confess "strange secret yearnings" rising "from my ancestral heritage—for the East and the Mediterranean." In 1932 he writes to Arnold Zweig in Palestine and refers to that land as "our mother-earth," a description which Marthe Robert glosses as the "eastern Mediterranean matrix of Western civilization."[14] Thus there is probably a subterranean Jewish reference in Freud's *Mittelmeermann*. In this placement, Freud's deep Jewish allegiance is undisturbed by rational attachments to Gentile humanistic *Kultur*, so the two allegiances are free to pursue independent paths.

Karl Abraham and Jewishness

This "Freudian" recession of the Jewish character of psychoanalysis is possible for Freud because he is secure in his Jewish identity and its natural ethnic allegiances unfettered by religious beliefs. That Freud values his Jewishness in this context is clear from what he tells Abraham in a letter dated 8 October 1907 (only the fourth one Freud had written to him). Abraham writes to tell Freud that since his being Jewish has prevented his promotion "beyond a junior position," he is leaving Zurich for Berlin and will take up psychoanalysis as a profession, hoping for Freud's support and advice. Freud replies:

> No harm can come to a young man like you from being forced into a free existence *au grand air*, and the fact that things will be more difficult for you as a Jew will have the effect, as it has with all of us, of bringing to light the best of which you are capable [*all Ihre Leistungfähigkeit*].

As he had said to Max Graf in 1897 when the latter thought to have his son baptized in an attempt to protect him from antisemitic discrimination, Freud conveys to Abraham the conviction that being Jewish in a Gentile world is in a way an advantage, because it is an irreplaceable source of "energy" that helps stimulate one's productivity, bringing out the best in one's capacity for achievement. There is therefore an intrinsic compensation for which a Jew can be proud. It is worth noting too the switch to French: *au grand air*. The Jew will move into the open air of an international humanist community while retaining his allegiance to his Jewishness as a resource rather than a liability.

For at the same time that Freud sought to place psychoanalysis on a "neutral" scientific (or perhaps Gentile) footing, he recognized that nonetheless he shared a kind of "racial kinship" with the Jews in his psychoanalytic movement that facilitated "a mode of intersubjective communication between Jewish analysts,"[15] making it easier for Jews to understand each other. As Freud told Jung, their difference now out in the open,

> In connection with Abraham I believe that the burdens of Jewishness—which are to me so easily understood—and worries for the future hinder him from unfolding.[16]

Thinking that this understanding born of a shared predicament enabled Jews, like Abraham, to follow his ideas more easily than Gentiles, like Jung, Freud used this difference to political advantage in his attempts to have Jews and Gentiles work together in the psychoanalytic movement.

Indeed, as in his dramatic plea at the 1910 Psychoanalytic Congress, Freud felt free to draw on a shared sense of Jewish kinship to manipulate his followers into sharing his Jewish self-subordination. When Jung took offense at Abraham's failing to mention his and Bleuler's work on dementia praecox when Abraham read a paper that contradicted one of Jung's at the Salzburg Psychoanalytic Congress in April 1908,[17] Freud wrote to Abraham to ask him to "play his part" to placate Jung, "both for my sake and that of the cause."[18] Freud asks his fellow Jew to do him "a great personal favour" and inform Jung in advance of what he intended to write in the future, in order that Abraham could take Jung's objections into account. Freud characterizes this "self-conquest" as an "act of courtesy," but judging from the way in which he closes the letter, it is clear that he is asking Abraham to subordinate himself to Jung, in the interests of the advance of psychoanalysis. He speaks "interfamilially" when he writes,

> Please be tolerant and do not forget that it is really easier for you than it is for Jung to follow my ideas, for in the first place you are completely independent, and then you stand nearer to my intellectual constitution because of racial kinship [*Rassenverwandtschaft*], whereas he as a Christian and a pastor's son finds his way to me only against great inner resistances.[19]

Here we see a central element of Freud's Jewish self-understanding, significantly articulated in contrast to the Gentile and Christian Jung. Jews share an "intellectual constitution" because they are ethnically or "racially" kin, part of a kind of family. We recall Freud's joke about the poor Jew who hopes to reach his destination if his "constitution" can stand it. Jews are physically and intellectually bound up together, related as if by blood, in possession of a similar psychological character.

Freud's conviction of a shared intellectual or psychic structure based on *racial* kinship, his psychological Lamarckism, becomes the foundation of his argument in *Moses and Monotheism* about the transmission of the Jewish character, the infrastructure of the "Psychological Jew," as Yerushalmi terms it. The fact that Freud expresses this connection when differentiating himself from Jung strengthens the likelihood that, as Yerushalmi suggests, Freud's belief in Lamarckism is related to his subjective experience of his Jewishness,

> the feeling, harbored and expressed by committed and alienated modern Jews alike, of the enormous weight, the gravitational pull, of the Jewish past, whether it be felt as an anchor or a burden.[20]

Yerushalmi points out that Freud developed his psycho-Lamarckism as the dominant theme of his "Overview of the Transference Neuroses," the long-lost twelfth metapsychological paper of 1915, so it was "neither casual nor circumstantial."[21] Did he refrain from publishing it in the middle period because he sensed unconsciously its connection to his Jewishness and so suppressed its public expression? We will return to Freud's understanding of "constitution," but it is important here to note the strength of the recognition Freud feels. This feeling supports his Jewish identity in private, behind his acts of "self-conquest."

In any event though, in Freud's view, this "racial kinship" must be kept separate from the science of psychoanalysis. He continues his letter to Abraham, insisting that Jung's association with their group is all the more valuable because of his Christian background:

> I nearly said that it was only by his appearance on the scene that psychoanalysis escaped the danger of becoming a Jewish national concern [*jüdisch nationale Angelegenheit*].

Freud is afraid that psychoanalysis will be facilely reduced to and dismissed as a "Jewish science," therefore relevant only to Jews, pointedly not universal and by definition perhaps not even science.[22] Freud treated his strategy for overcoming this danger as a purely practical one, given the "natural"—or at least inbred—antisemitism of the Gentiles, but one wonders if he isn't being somewhat defensive, for there is an open recognition in Freud's words to Abraham that psychoanalytic ideas have a particularly natural place in Jewish souls, which share the same structure as that of the science's founder. That is, Freud himself seems aware of a special affinity between Jews and psychoanalysis, and he is concerned that this connection impugns its universality. Freud seeks officially to separate psychoanalysis from his own Jewishness, because as a science, it transcends the particular nature of its origins. As he will say in 1913, if the differences between "the Jewish and the Aryan spirit" "mirror themselves in the apprehension of objective relationships in science there must be something wrong."[23]

Freud's adjective *nationale* in his letter to Abraham may be significant. Freud is aware of the view held by some of his followers, most notably Otto Rank, that psychoanalysis is in fact an expression of a "Jewish missionary consciousness" and that Jews working in psychoanalysis constitute the "essence of redemption."[24] In Rank's view, psychoanalysis is to be the fulfillment of the Jewish people's "national" aspirations to redeem the world. Freud sees psychoanalysis differently, hoping in this period especially to distance his science from his people's religion and have it be the basis for *human* solidarity rather than just Jewish solidarity. Thus Freud's Jewish nationalism, as he expressed for example in 1886 to Giles de la Tourette, and to George S. Viereck in

1926,[25] is separate from his science. Freud is a Jew at home, but a humanist abroad. This dichotomy is particularly true in the middle period, but Freud will tell Jones even in 1926 that his Jewishness is, like his interest in telepathy, his "private affair."[26]

On the other hand, Yerushalmi wonders whether by the end of his life, with *Moses and Monotheism*, Freud has not come to believe "that psychoanalysis is itself a further, if not final metamorphosed extension of Judaism, divested of its illusory religious forms but retaining its essential monotheistic characteristics, at least as [he] understood and described them," and that just as Freud is "a godless Jew, psychoanalysis is a godless Judaism."[27] Yet Yerushalmi thinks that Freud, even at the end of his life, did not intend his public to know this. It was still part of his "private affair." This would be still truer in the middle period, if my thesis of developmental periodicity is correct.

Abraham's first response to Freud's letter, as he tells him when he finally replies on 11 May, was anger, perhaps sensing the injustice, however wise politically, of Freud's request. So he waited until he had cooled down and had sent Jung a conciliatory letter (a second draft), before writing back to Freud. He tells him now that he hopes his effort will "serve the cause." In any event, Abraham continues, he recognizes the Jewish kinship of which Freud speaks:

> That it is easier for me to go along with you than with Jung I freely admit. I too have always felt this intellectual kinship. After all, our Talmudic way of thinking cannot all of a sudden disappear from us.

Abraham immediately links Freud's sense of shared intellectual constitution with "our Talmudic way of thinking." Unlike Freud, Abraham seems to have learned some Talmud, for his father was a teacher of religion,[28] and he goes on to explain his gloss on this *intellektuelle Verwandtschaft* as follows:

> Some days ago a small paragraph in *Witz* strangely attracted me. When I looked at it more closely, I found that in the technique of apposition and its whole structure it was thoroughly Talmudic.[29]

It is clear from this passage that Abraham does not mean "Talmudic" in a negative sense, as Freud uses it in *Moses and Monotheism*.[30] Rather, he refers to a skill in deriving and expressing meaning through association and juxtaposition, both of which figure prominently in rabbinic exegesis and psychoanalytic hermeneutics. Susan Handelman has explored this relationship in her book, *The Slayers of Moses*,[31] where she writes in reference to Freud's confession in 1926 to his B'nai B'rith brethren of a "clear consciousness of . . . the same psychic structure," that "the Talmudic mode of thought became the ingrained model of the Jewish psyche."[32] She also cites as an example the "technique of apposition" that Abraham notices (*semuchin* and *hekkesh*).[33] Even if Abraham doesn't share Freud's psycho-Lamarckism, he believes that as a people nurtured on such literature (as Jakob Freud certainly was), Jews share certain traits of thinking that generate a sense of intellectual kinship.

Though Abraham does not indicate what paragraph in *Witz* attracted his attention, the following passage could be taken as typical. In a section on the technique of conceptual jokes—"representation by something *similar* or akin" [emphasis Freud's]—an "American anecdote" appears:

> Two not particularly scrupulous business men had succeeded, by dint of a series of highly risky enterprises, in amassing a large fortune, and they were now making efforts to push their way into good society. One method, which struck them as a likely one, was to have their portraits painted by the most celebrated and highly-paid artist in the city, whose pictures had an immense reputation. The precious canvases were shown for the first time at a large evening party, and the two hosts themselves led the most influential connoisseur and art critic up to the wall upon which the portraits were hanging side by side, to extract his admiring judgement on them. He studied the works for a long time, and then, shaking his head, as though there was something he had missed, pointed to the gap between the pictures and asked quietly: "But where's the Saviour?" (I.e., "I don't see the picture of the Saviour.")[34]

To understand the "indirect representation" of the joke-work, Freud explains, "Starting from the representation in the joke, we trace the path backwards through *a series of easily established associations and inferences*" (emphasis mine). This paragraph follows:

> We can guess from the question 'Where's the Saviour? Where's the picture of the Saviour?' that the sight of the two pictures had reminded the speaker of a similar sight, familiar to him, as to us, which however, included an element that was missing here—the picture of the Saviour between two other pictures. There is only one such situation: Christ hanging between the two thieves. The missing element is brought into prominence by the joke. The similarity lies in the pictures, hanging to the right and left of the Saviour, which the joke passes over; it can only consist in the fact that the pictures hanging on the walls are pictures of thieves. What the critic wanted to say but could not say was: "You are a couple of rascals" or, in greater detail:

> "What do I care about your pictures? You are a couple of rascals—I know that!" And he did in fact end by saying it by means of a few associations and inferences, using the method which we speak of as an "allusion."[35]

Note that the content of the joke itself is structured by juxtaposition, and so Freud's whole explanation unpacks this technique of apposition, spelling out the inference the joke makes by association.

Handelman cites as an *halachic* example of *semuchin* R. Chanina bar Chama's derivation of the thirty-nine categories of work prohibited on Shabbat based on the juxtaposition of the commands concerning Shabbat observance (Exod. 35:1–3) and the description of the erection of the Desert Sanctuary (Exod. 35:4ff.).[36] However, the exegetical technique is also commonly used to derive ethical teachings, for example, when explaining the placement of sections in the Bible, a type of explanation Freud may have been more likely to have heard himself.

For example, in Exod. 17:1–7, the Israelites quarrel with Moses at Massah and Meribah, complaining that they have no water and questioning his motives. Furthermore, in verse 7 they are reported to have tested God, saying "Is the Lord among us or not?" The next verse reports, "Then came Amalek and fought with Israel in Rephidim" (verse 8). Rashi (Rabbi Shlomo Yitzhaki of Troyes), the eleventh-century French *tradent*, comments,

> [Scripture] juxtaposed [*samach*] this section [about Amalek] to this verse [reporting Israel's taunt] to imply, "I am always among you and attendant to all your needs and [yet] you say, 'Is the Lord among us or not?' By your lives, [I swear] that the dog [Amalek] will come and bite you and you will cry out for me and then you will know where I am!"

That is, Rashi interprets the apposition to mean that the Torah intended to teach that misfortune comes to the Jewish people when they lose faith in or lose touch with the Presence of God. On the basis of a gap in textual continuity (i.e., Why is this section next to that? It doesn't follow logically), the rabbinic mind expects a teaching (a "word of Torah"), and the "omission," as it were, is made good on the basis of the principle of *semuchin*.[37]

The striking similarity between this "way of thinking" and the passage from *Witz* quoted above may represent the "thoroughly Talmudic" structure that attracted Abraham's attention and led him to feel a familiar "intellectual kinship" with Freud. Having had little or no experience with the Talmud himself, Freud may not know consciously what Abraham is referring to by his *durchaus talmudisch.* Still, Freud feels the Jewish link both ethnically and intellectually.

Freud distinguishes again between Jews and Gentiles, between himself and Abraham on the one hand and Jung and the Swiss on the other, in a letter of 23 July 1908. Freud has just read the published version of Abraham's paper on dementia praecox, and he responds enthusiastically:

> Thank you very much . . . I value so highly the decisiveness and the clarity in your publications, that I must ask you not to think that I overlook their beauty. May I say that it is consanguineous Jewish traits [*verwandte, jüdische Züge*] that draw me to you? We understand each other.

Again we see the recognition of a cultural kinship that seems almost biologically rooted (*verwandte*). The emotional bond occasioned by this kinship is clear too. Freud responds to Abraham's last letter and confirms that they do share a special intellectual sympathy based on their shared Jewishness. But what are these "Jewish traits"? Freud cites a resolute tone (*Entschiedenheit*), clarity, and elegance (*Schönheit*) in Abraham's writings. The same traits of course are characteristic of Freud's writings, which brought him the Goethe Prize for literature in 1930. These qualities require a certain intellectual discipline and skill with language, a value taught throughout Jewish tradition. But such skill is also testimony to their *Bildung* and membership in German *Kultur*, which became for many Jews almost a substitute religion.[38] On the basis of a kinship of Jewish impulses, something deeply embedded in the character of both men, Freud knows that they understand one another. It is as though the two Jews know they come from the same family, and so have an intersubjective familiarity with one another's thinking.

But having said this much, Freud goes on to worry about the conflict between Abraham and Jung now made manifest by this paper. By Abraham's approach in it, Freud says, he is forcing Jung into "the opposition." Freud himself, when he goes to Zurich in September, will "try to make good what can be made good," in spite of his agreement with Abraham's position. This tactic again reflects Freud's strategy for the success of the psychoanalytic movement. Freud argues that it would have shown "greater refinement of feeling" on Abraham's part if he had not made use of his right to write in just that way. That is, he would have shown better manners, been more tactful—been a better *goy,* Freud is almost saying. Yet he is not reproaching Abraham, for he suspects that "the suppressed antisemitism of the Swiss that spares me is deflected in reinforced form upon you." Freud seems to think that this is unavoidable, for he continues, explaining his displeasure,

> But I mean that as Jews we must, if we want to join in anywhere, develop a bit of masochism, be prepared ourselves to suffer some wrong. Otherwise it doesn't go together.

Again Jews must restrain themselves, suppress their natural right, develop a refined surface, a more sensitive way of dealing with Gentiles, and thus make room for the feelings and talents of the Gentiles, who will otherwise be forced into the opposition. It is this conviction that accounts for the recession of Freud's Jewish identity in the middle period, its separation from psychoanalysis, and its privatization.

Needless to say, Freud's attitude conceals an assumed Jewish superiority, a condescension that surely does not go undetected for long (if at all) among "the Swiss." Freud's posture is his practical solution to the problem of antisemitism within the psychoanalytic movement itself, for he knows he needs the Gentiles: "Rest assured that, if my name were Oberhuber, in spite of everything my innovations would have met with far less resistance." In Freud's mind, antisemitism is a natural reflex of his Jewishness, perhaps precisely because of his feeling of Jewish superiority.[39] Thus Freud believes he must tolerate antisemitism to some extent because of the structure of his Jewish identity. Again we see the need for Jewish concealment if psychoanalysis is to flourish in the wider world. This professional suppression has the effect of turning Freud's personal psychological attention away from exploring his Jewishness and developing it further, as he will do in the late period.

My rather literal translation of Freud's *Es geht sonst nicht zusammen* is conditioned, I think, by his meaning. Freud is trying to join Jews and Gentiles together in the service of psychoanalysis, and not just for practical reasons, but for ideological, humanist ones as well. In spite of the difference between Jews and Gentiles, they must learn to become part of a larger whole. The failure to fulfill this ideal is one reason why Freud is so bitter when the collaboration with Jung and the Swiss breaks down in 1911 and the years following. Freud will state this goal explicitly in these years to a number of his colleagues, both Jewish and Gentile, as Jung's defection (and so Freud's failure) becomes evident. He will close this letter too by asking Abraham,

> Why cannot I harness Jung and you together, your keenness [*Schärfe*] and his soaring [*Schwung*]?

A good question. The combination of these differences would clearly outdo their separate efforts. It is to be noted that these two qualities correspond to the two sides of Freud's own personality that he says he struggled all his life to keep in dynamic balance. He described this character to Ferenczi in 1915 when defining his own "mechanism of production" as "the succession of boldly playing imagination and ruthlessly realistic criticism."[40] Note the dialectical interplay. These intellectual activities parallel Freud's urge for speculation and his need for discipline.

This correspondence between Abraham versus Jung, on the one hand, and the two sides of Freud's own personality, on the other, helps us understand both Freud's attraction to Jung and his antipathy for the latter's "mysticism," for Freud saw Jung's soaring speculation as unchecked by ("Jewish") rationality. Abraham and Jung represent the two sides of Freud's own personality, and in both his own personality and in the psychoanalytic movement that expressed it, Freud sought to yoke them. Otherwise there was no hitting it off. In fact, the larger psychoanalytic cultural enterprise, the effort to create a cultural whole, depends upon this yoking, just as Freud's own work depends upon it. Thus, Freud's desire for uniting Jews and Gentiles in the service of psychoanalysis may have its origin in his own drive for wholeness.

Carl Jung and Mysticism

Three days before he wrote the letter discussed above, Freud had written to Abraham, worried about the vacillation of his Zurich followers. He thinks more favorably about Jung, but not about Bleuler. "On the whole," he reflects, "it is easier for us Jews, since we lack the mystical element."[41] Gay says that in Freud's view, "To be happily free of the mystical element meant . . . to be open to science, to have the only attitude suitable for an understanding of his ideas." But Freud's remark recalls the one he made to Abraham two-and-a-half months earlier about it being easier for Jews than Christians to follow his psychoanalytic ideas, so it may be that Freud associated mysticism with Christians and Christianity. In this prejudice, Freud was again probably influenced by his education. The *Wissenschaft des Judentums* movement associated mysticism with primitive and backward religion and so sought to disassociate it from Judaism. It was not until Gershom Scholem's work, *Major Trends in Jewish Mysticism* (1941), that the substantial role Jewish mysticism played in the history of rabbinic Judaism was recognized by the Jewish academic establishment.

To understand further what Freud means by "mysticism," let us examine an exchange of letters between Freud and Jung in April 1909, discussing their differing interpretations of what Jung called his "spookery" (*Spiritisterei*) and Freud called "the poltergeist knocking" (*Klopfgeisterspuk*).[42] On the evening of 30 March 1909, the last night of Jung's five-day visit with Freud in Vienna, the two men were discussing precognition and parapsychology in Freud's study, and after the latter had dismissed the subject as "nonsensical," there was a loud knock in the bookcase, which Jung insisted was an example of a "so-called catalytic exteriorization phenomenon." In other words, he thought that his own inner psychic state had caused the sound. Freud scoffed: "That is sheer bosh." Jung predicted that another report would follow in a moment, and indeed one did, demonstrating, Jung believed, the objective effect of inner psychic powers and their ideational correlates, the "spiritualism" he refers to in his letter of 2 April 1909.[43] Freud's response to this event after Jung had left is characteristic of his understanding of himself as a scientist: he examined the bookcase and the floorboards, carrying out what he considered to be an empirical investigation, finally concluding that it was "quite unlikely that such phenomena should exist."

Given Freud's later interest in telepathy and his own superstitions (omens, numerology, revenants, etc.), one cannot help but wonder if Freud is not being defensive.[44] He admits in print that he is quite capable of believing, at least temporarily, in such "occult" phenomena,[45] and in fact it is clear from his words following in his letter to Jung that at first Freud believed in what Jung was insisting on. But his belief vanished, he says, with the magic of Jung's personal presence, and he now confronted "the despiritualized furniture as the poet [i.e., Schiller] confronted undeified Nature after the Gods of Greece had passed away."[46] Freud speaks here as though he has surmounted the "spiritual" mode of thought, but as he admits is often the case with one who achieves this success, he may not feel quite sure of the finality of his achievement.[47] Freud regards Jung's belief condescendingly as a youthful illusion, wishful thinking, and cautions him against "such great sacrifices to understanding."

But then, demonstrating that he was not closed to the "scientific" investigation of such phenomena, Freud goes on to relate his own superstition about numbers, one that revolved around a conviction about the date of his own death. Freud analyzes this idea as though it were a symptomatic parapraxis, tracing its unconscious associations. In addition, he says, "the hidden influence of W. Fliess was at work; the superstition erupted in the year of his attack on me."[48] From this Freud concludes, "You will find confirmed again [?] the specifically Jewish nature of my mysticism," namely, its origins in the fellow Jew Fliess's speculations about numbers. Setting aside for the moment any possibly genuine link to the long tradition of Jewish mysticism to which Freud, as the son of a father from a Chassidic background, would have been heir, at least unconsciously, we note Freud's linking of "mysticism" with "superstition."[49] As Rainey shows, the "occult" and religion were closely related in Freud's mind,[50] and so it would be characteristic of Freud to reject a mysticism associated with the Christian Jung, while presenting his own "Jewish mysticism" in rational, psychoanalytic terms, suggesting further that he picked it up socially, from a fellow Jew, as a traumatic reaction to personal attack. Jung's youthful flights of fancy into "psychosynthesis" are contrasted in Freud's mind with his own sober "demystification" of nature and his careful empirical investigation of the material reality before him: youthful mysticism versus sober rationalism. Seeking to exclude entirely the possibility of any objective spiritual reality or mental processes external to or independent of the human mental apparatus and its organic bodily functions, Freud prefers to interpret such "adventure" as psychological obsession and the "compliance of chance." In other words, only the human is real; the superstitious belief in external "powers" is a flight from empirical reality, or "mysticism."

Perhaps this is why Freud seemed to equate Jung's defection from the "sexual theory" of psychoanalysis as evidence of Jung's mysticism, that is, a flight from empiricism. Jung reports that Freud told him that they must make an unshakable bulwark of the sexual theory "against the black tide of mud . . . of occultism."[51] (Remember Freud's linking of mysticism and superstition.) On the other hand, Jung thought that Freud's self-possession by the idea of sex was "a flight from himself, or from that other side of him which might perhaps be called mystical."[52] So although they did so in different ways, both Freud and Jung seemed to place mysticism and sexuality in opposition. An attraction to one indicated a flight from the other. Does this link provide an insight into Freud's distinction between Christians and Jews? Perhaps he felt Jews could accept the human reality of sexuality more easily because their religion was "life-enjoying," well-acquainted with the joy of pleasure, whereas the Christian sought to leave this world in search of another, less "empirical" one.

Jung's future investigations into the "spook complex" are to Freud "a charming delusion in which one does not oneself participate." This rather condescending statement sounds like the beginning of a separation from what Freud, writing to Abraham, will later call the "Aryan religiousness" of the Swiss.[53] Note the connection between a racial identification and a particular kind of "religiousness."

But in 1908 Freud still hoped that a working alliance would prosper.

He tells Jung explicitly of the advantage to psychoanalysis that he sees in him:

> The selfish purpose [in his coming to visit Jung in Zurich], which I frankly confess, is to persuade you to continue and complete my work by applying to the psychoses what I have begun with the neuroses. With your strong, independent personality, with your Germanic blood [*als Germane*], which enables you to command the sympathies of the public more easily than I, you seem better fitted for this than anyone else I know.[54]

Jung's assets here are personal and "racial," rather than intellectual. Freud hopes to use Jung to give him greater access to the larger culture, whose sympathies he hopes to gain and to which, as a humanist, he feels an allegiance. Freud is beginning the investiture of his "crown prince," in hopes that it will lead to a reign of psychoanalytic thinking.

Freud frames this choice five months later, in January 1909, with a Jewish metaphor of conquest drawn from the Hebrew Bible:

> We are certainly getting ahead; if I am Moses, then you are Joshua and will take possession of the promised land of psychiatry, which I shall only be able to glimpse from afar.[55]

We see both Freud's identification with Moses emerge clearly, and also his attempt to make the Gentile Jung an extension of it. Perhaps at some level he feels uncomfortable about removing psychoanalysis too far from its Jewish roots. Psychoanalysis is to be the "new law," not only for Jews (who follow easily, having been intellectually formed by the Law), but also for Gentiles, who need a leader from their own kind to identify with and persuade them. Freud therefore even "adopts" Jung as his "eldest son" and "anoints" him "*in partibus infidelium*" ["in the lands of the unbelievers," i.e., those who reject psychoanalysis] as his "successor and crown prince."[56] These metaphors express again the placement of Freud's Jewish identity in the background. "Moses" (a Jewish figure) will yield to his "crown prince" (arguably a Gentile image), just as the Jews must yield to Gentiles in the interests of psychoanalysis. At least it cannot be said that the leader asks his followers to do something he would not do himself.

In fact, this self-subordination may seem characteristically *Jewish* (or "Mosaic") to Freud, for to sacrifice something of himself for the sake of something higher is associated in Freud's mind with an imagined "Moses." As he will put it in 1913 in relation to the *Moses* of Michelangelo, such an act is "the highest mental achievement that is possible in a man, that of struggling successfully against an inward passion for the sake of a cause to which he has devoted himself."[57] Yet in his efforts to woo Jung, Freud will even use an analogy from Christianity so Jung can feel he is on familiar ground. In 1911 he writes to Jung of a convert to psychoanalysis, describing him as having been "transformed from a Saul into a Paul."[58] In his pleasure at winning adherents, Freud seems to have overlooked Paul's dim view of sexuality.

This reference to St. Paul, as though psychoanalysis were a kind of "New Testament," recalls also the role of the "Old Testament" in the Christian Bible, which is superseded by the "new covenant." To be content, as Freud urges his followers, with the "modest role of preparing the ground," may be in harmony with Christian *Kultur,* but it cannot help but generate Jewish resentment. And that anger would redouble, when the alliance falls apart, if the similarity to Christian supersessionism were sensed by Freud and his fellow assimilated Jews.

In the middle period, Freud thus alternates between images that attach psychoanalysis to Jewish roots and images that create distance from those roots. This ambivalence reflects a confusion in Freud's dual allegiance. In the late period, the combination will be clarified and reaffirmed on the basis of a renewed link to his own Jewish particularity.

Jewish Tenacity

Freud is able to yield place to Gentiles in this period because he is confident of his own Jewish worth. As he tells Abraham in reference to a case whose success is of special concern to Abraham,

> The opportunity of demonstrating our skill will come, even if it should fail in this case. Do not lose heart. Our ancient Jewish tenacity [*Unsere altjüdische Zähigkeit*] will prove itself superior also this time.[59]

Patient tenacity, characteristic of Jews and Jewish history *(altjüdische),* will enable them to succeed and show eventually that they are right. Freud refers to this same Jewish characteristic in not responding to a Gentile opponent's attack on psychoanalysis in 1916: "No matter! An old Jew is tougher than a Royal Prussian Teuton."[60] Thus one must not interpret Freud's yielding place to the Gentile Jung as half-heartedness; rather it is an expression of Freud's Jewish self-confidence in his cause. Recall the Hannibalian "tenacity of Jewry" in its struggle against "the organization of the Catholic Church" that Freud mentions in the *Inter-*

pretation of Dreams.[61] Freud's yielding to Jung may in fact be a part of his tenacious struggle to overcome the antisemitism of the Gentile world that opposes him and his new science. For the "fighting Jew," there are many ways to fight a battle.

Freud knows that the battle for psychoanalysis requires such tenacity and self-sacrifice. As he tells Abraham in 1913,

> I already see that the whole situation depends on our squeezing every ounce out of ourselves. There is the cause, and we shall sacrifice ourselves for it without complaint. C.C.!

"C.C." stands for *"Coraggio, Casimiro!"* ("Courage, Casimiro!"), and it refers to an experience Abraham had while mountain climbing. Two guides accompanying him had cooked some meat that had become spoiled on the trip, and one of them had encouraged the other to eat it anyway, with that exhortation to have courage for the deed. In spite of the distasteful nature of their self-subordinating task, Freud implies in this letter, Jews must have the courage for it because, as Freud tells Abraham in closing his letter in 1908, "Our Aryan comrades are really indispensable to us, otherwise psychoanalysis would succumb to antisemitism."

Letters to Oskar Pfister and Freud's Jewishness

Freud's correspondence with Jung's friend, the Swiss Protestant pastor, Oskar Pfister, began in 1909. The two became real friends, in spite of their religious difference. In fact, this "religious context" for their psychoanalytic friendship helps bring out for us more clearly Freud's Jewish self-understanding and his understanding of the humanistic activity of psychoanalysis. As an example of the latter, speaking about love, Freud tells Pfister that "our patients have to find in human beings what we are unable to promise them from above and what we must deny them from our own persons."[62] Freud was gratified at this unexpected new acquisition, but at the same time, it was "upsetting" to see psychoanalysis "stretched into the service of the battle against 'sin'."[63] Pfister's Christian use of psychoanalysis will drive Freud to define himself differently, bringing out his Jewishness and his humanistic atheism in opposition.

Freud makes clear to Pfarrer Pfister in his second letter to him that he is "profoundly" irreligious, and that he is, "as a wicked heretic" *(bösem Ketzer),* remote from religious ideas.[64] Note that Freud does not call himself either "wicked" or a "heretic" when writing to Jews about his atheism. Freud knows he does not have to be religious to be Jewish. Psychoanalysis is to be a secular science, "neither religious nor its opposite, but an impartial instrument which both the clergyman and the layman can use in the service of the sufferer." Therefore, as a "godless Jew,"[65] Freud can use psychoanalysis as an expression of his Jewish-humanist identity, for psychoanalysis is "not a religion." Freud tells Jung this explicitly in a letter of 13 February 1910, and again in 1913, when Jung claimed that psychoanalysis was in fact a religion. Freud wrote to Ferenczi at the time, saying "the Jewish spirit regrets that it cannot play along. A little mockery could do no harm."[66] Thus for Freud, the "Jewish spirit" can even oppose "religion." Beller points out that in the desire for truth, justice, knowledge and genuine intimacy with God, etc., "the break with organized religion could . . . be a natural consequence of Judaism itself."[67]

The non-religiousness of his Jewishness is so clear in Freud's mind that he was able, "years ago," according to Max Eitingon writing in 1913, to close a Psychoanalytic Congress with the "old Jewish New Year's greeting, *l'shanah tovah.*"[68] Even though psychoanalysis is not to become a "Jewish national concern," Freud can use the Jewish tradition to wish his followers well, without seeing this good wish as a religious act. It is instead an expression of friendly solidarity, an affirmation of a social bond between fellow Jews. Wishing Freud a Happy Rosh HaShanah himself, Eitingon recalled Freud's gesture in a letter to him on the day before the Jewish New Year. It is not clear when Freud's benefaction took place, but it may have been at an early stage, before the recession of the Jewish character of psychoanalysis became more politically important to Freud. More characteristic of this period was Freud's Rosh HaShanah wire to his family when he was in America for his lectures at Clark University in 1909. Although Freud's family was so irreligious (or so Jewish) that Pfister seemed like a "visitor from another planet,"[69] Freud sent them New Year's greetings from America.[70] On a journey in a foreign country, articulating his humanistic psychoanalysis before a largely Gentile audience, Freud reaffirms his Jewishness by invoking the Jewish calendar, the temporal context of Jewish life, with his family. In trying to cast psychoanalysis publicly as a part of humanistic *Kultur*, Freud feels the need to reaffirm and reconnect with his Jewishness in private. This difference is the structure of Freud's dual allegiance in the middle period. In the late period, both commitments will find public expression.

Though Freud is gratified at the adherence of a Christian pastor to his work, he is still a little nervous about it. Noticing an abundance of fire metaphors at the close of his second letter to Pfister, he tells Jung, with a certain irony,

> I couldn't help myself, respect for theology had nailed me to this quotation (!): "One way or the other, the Jew will be burned." I was still so unaccustomed to being on good terms with Protestant theologians.[71]

Freud's quote is from Lessing's *Nathan the Wise* (4.2.79ff.), the play that will come up yet again in connection with Freud's Jewish identity. In Lessing's play, Freud's line is spoken three times by the Christian Patriarch of Jerusalem in response to the Templar's question about what would happen to a Jew who raised a Christian child as a Jew. Even if the Jew did so lovingly, even if the child would have otherwise been reduced to misery and died, even if the Jew had "reared the girl not in / His faith, but rather in no faith at all, / And taught this child not more or less of God / Than reason would require," "All one!" the Patriarch answers; "The Jew must burn."[72] The Templar finds this hard. Does Freud feel that he has seduced these Christians to apostasy from their faith, and so in spite of his good intentions and the conformity of psychoanalysis to "Reason," he nonetheless will get "burned"?

A few years will prove him prescient on this point, and it will confirm again his Jewishness in opposition to Christianity. In 1913, when Jung is in the process of leaving the movement, in part because he rejects Freud's "sexual theory," Freud will tell Eitingon that he can see "some advantage in having psychoanalysis confined to 'our people'." It might provide, he says, the kind of strength one gains as one returns to one's "indestructible national feeling." However, Gay reports, "such reassuring 'racial' exclusiveness clashed with Freud's 'ideal desires—*Idealwünschen,*' desires for general relevance and general acceptance." "To make psychoanalysis cosmopolitan was high on Freud's agenda."[73] Yet he will learn that this cosmopolitanism must not and cannot replace his attachment to his own Jewishness. Freud is both Jewish and cosmopolitan. But since Freud seems to believe in the inevitability of Jewish "burning," we can understand why he also believes that Jews must develop "a bit of masochism" (without relinquishing their Jewishness), in order to work together with Gentiles and so achieve this cosmopolitanism. Otherwise his ideas won't catch on. In any event, he will learn that like Antaeus touching his feet to the earth again in order to regain his strength, so he needs his Jewish roots to gain access to psychoanalytic universality.

Freud and Talmudic Dream Interpretation

Further evidence of Freud's wish to distance psychoanalysis from Jewish tradition in this period can be found in Freud's reaction in 1910 to a Jewish correspondent from Palestine, who sought to assimilate Freud's theory of dreams to talmudic discussions. Freud tells the man that although "my attention has repeatedly been called to the observations in the Talmud about the problem of dreams," "the approximation to the understanding of dreams among the ancient Greeks is far more striking."[74] It is likely that Freud's attention was called to such talmudic parallels as these "repeatedly" when he lectured to the Vienna B'nai B'rith, twice in December 1897, on *Traumdeutung,* and again in April 1902, on "Dreams." Freud's disavowal in 1910 of a talmudic connection to his Jewish public in Palestine might lend support to my argument for the recessive Jewish character of Freud's middle period, though it seems he rejected the association in the early and late periods too.

Given Abraham's observation about the similarity in the structure and technique of Freud's thought to talmudic patterns, Freud's lack of interest in the talmudic material seems strange. Ken Frieden has discussed Freud's deep ambivalence towards this rabbinic material in his book, *Freud's Dream of Interpretation* (1990). He points out that the rabbinic view of the crucial role of the dream interpreter, and the belief that "no meaning inheres in a dream; all meaning depends on interpretation . . . a grafting of text upon text," would challenge Freud's belief in the objective meaning of dreams, striking at his theory.[75] Thus Freud's lack of interest in rabbinic dream theory may not be disinterested, if he was aware of and understood the material as Frieden does.

Though we do not know exactly what "observations in the Talmud" were pointed out to Freud, those in the last chapter of tractate Berachot in the Babylonian Talmud are indeed "striking" when compared with Freud's thought, because they both challenge and relate to it. A few examples: "R. Hisda said: A dream which is not interpreted is like a letter which is not read" (55a). In other words, dreams have a message, sent like a letter *to* someone, though they must be interpreted in order to be understood. Furthermore, "All dreams follow the mouth," that is, their interpretation (55b; 56a). The interpretation of a dream discovers and fixes its meaning. Though Frieden correctly perceives the challenge to Freud's overall theory here, still the role of the interpreter in psychoanalysis is crucial for disclosing the dream's meaning, even if that meaning is thought of as objective. In any event, sometimes dreams in the Talmud do seem to have an objective meaning that the interpreter discloses. For example, as in the following: "A certain Sadducee said to

R. Ishmael: I saw myself [in a dream] pouring olive oil on olives. He replied: [This man] has had sexual relations with his mother" (56b). The sexual symbolism of a man returning the thick liquid to its original source is clear to Rabbi Ishmael. Or again, an interpretation is given that one can expect to obtain "understanding" if one dreams of having intercourse with one's mother (57a) (based on a playful[76] alteration of the vowel pointing of one letter, *'im* to *'em*). Such interpretations do not seem so dissimilar from parallel psychoanalytic ones, and so we are led to wonder again about Freud's disinterest.

Such parallels can be multiplied easily, and are indeed striking. Though Frieden argues that Freud was threatened by rabbinic dream interpretation because its hermeneutics challenged his and its similar sexual interpretations might have led him to take those hermeneutics seriously, Freud may not have paid attention to the rabbinic system because he sought in this period in particular to free psychoanalysis from its Jewish roots and ally it with classical humanist culture. In the late period, by contrast, Freud will compare himself to Rabbi Yochanan ben Zakkai and present psychoanalysis, by analogy, as a "godless" rabbinic Judaism.

Building the Temple of Psychoanalysis

Yet as controversies within the psychoanalytic movement begin to multiply, threatening the movement's unity, Freud will reach for Jewish images to characterize his own situation. As he writes to Pfister in 1910,

> Building the Temple with one hand and with the other wielding weapons against those who would disturb its building—I believe it is a reminiscence from Jewish history.[77]

Indeed the memory probably comes from stories Freud must have heard during his Jewish schooling about the rebuilding of the Second Temple, for his language reflects Neh. 4:11 precisely:

> Those who were building the wall and those who were carrying burdens were laden so that with one hand he did the work and with the other grasped his weapon.

So although it can be misleading to see psychoanalysis as a kind of religion, nonetheless, here Freud did see his new science as parallel to the Jewish struggle for religious freedom and expression, the building of a kind of "Temple." As Paul Rosen says, psychoanalysis, "in many respects a growing shrine, sociologically reflected the age-old Jewish sensitivity and vulnerability to assault."[78] At some level, psychoanalysis was conceived in Freud's mind as an extension of, or in continuity with, his Jewish heritage and its history. Through "Gentile opposition," Freud comes to understand that though cosmopolitan, psychoanalysis is also in continuity with the *Jewish* struggle for the truth.

The Jewish metaphor becomes biological and parental in a letter Freud writes in 1913 to Sandor Ferenczi about the future of psychoanalysis now that "the Committee" (all of whom except Jones were Jews) has been formed to protect its development:

> That assurance that the children will be provided for, which for a Jewish father is a matter of life and death, I expected to get from Jung; I am glad now that you and our friends will give me this.[79]

A note by the editors (Ernst Freud, et al.) clarifies that "the children" here refers to the future of the psychoanalytic movement, Freud's "brainchild."[80] Thus as Freud's attempt "to amalgamate Jews and *goyim* in the service of Psa."[81] begins to fail, he looks to the predominantly Jewish "Committee" to ensure him psychoanalytic progeny. One can hear how bitter Freud feels at this failure when he writes to Sabina Spielrein in 1913: "We are and remain Jews; the others [e.g., Jung and the Swiss] will always simply exploit us and never understand or appreciate us."[82]

Yerushalmi characterizes this statement , which, as we can see, has been a long time coming, as "a kind of watershed in [Freud's] perception of the non-Jewish world,"[83] and it is an important moment in the development of his Jewish identity, crystalizing the impossibility of assimilation, even within psychoanalysis. The "voice of [his father] Jakob," which Yerushalmi detected in Freud's *Goyim* to Martha in 1883, is heard again alongside Freud's anger and disappointment. As Freud reports to the Gentile Binswanger, "Semites and Aryans or anti-Semites whom I wanted to bring to merge in the service of Psycho-Analysis separate from each other again like oil from water."[84] So in spite of Freud's hope to achieve "the integration of Jews and anti-Semites [N.B., the exchange for *goyim* above] on the soil of psychoanalysis"[85] in order for psychoanalysis to be ideally cosmopolitan, he admits to Eitingon that he can see some advantage in having psychoanalysis confined to "our people," for it might provide the kind of strength one gains as one returns to one's "indestructible national feeling." When Freud feels weakened by non-Jewish "assault" (in this case, by ideological—Freud would say unscientific—rejection), he returns to an identification with the Jewish "nation" for strengthening. In private, Freud the Jew is being forced to return to his people for sustenance and self-affirmation. As time goes on, this return will establish one firm, "fanatic" root for Freud's identity.

Yet Freud knows that the difference between Jews and Gentiles does not impinge on "science." As he comments to Ferenczi on the scientific differences between the Viennese and the Swiss, which Alphonse Maeder claims are due to "racial" differences,

> Certainly there are great differences between the Jewish and the Aryan spirit. We can observe that every day. Hence there would assuredly be here and there differences in outlook on life and art. But there should not be such a thing as Aryan or Jewish science. Results in science must be identical, though the presentation of them may vary. If these differences mirror themselves in the apprehension of objective relationships in science there must be something wrong.[86]

Thus in Freud's mind, psychoanalysis *qua* science is not an expression of his Jewishness, but rather a transcendence of its ethnicity. Yerushalmi asks, "With all the talk of German science and French science, neither of which implied that its contents are not universally accessible or applicable, why not Jewish science, especially in the case of psychoanalysis?"[87] The answer of course is that Freud, at this time at least, has not overcome the false dichotomy characteristic of his antisemitic age between the particular and the universal. True, the results of "Aryan" and "Jewish" science should not differ, and if they do there is something wrong (as time will tell). But Freud does not seem to see that it may be the very Jewishness of psychoanalysis that gives it its access to the objective reality his science claims to mediate. As Yerushalmi says, altering the line from Terence (or Montaigne), "Why not say, with psychoanalysis in mind, *Judaeus sum, nihil humani a me alienam puto.*"[88] Why not, indeed?

Freud's Jewish sensibility comes out all the more strongly when his effort to unite Jews and Gentiles fails, due (at least in Freud's mind, judging from his comments to Jews and Gentiles alike) to antisemitism. Thus Freud's postcard to Abraham in September 1913, on his now annual pilgrimage to Rome for a renewed sense of personal triumph, takes on a certain poignancy and illuminates the image of Freud as a defiant Jew. On a picture postcard of the Arch of Titus in Rome, showing the Roman legions carrying off the spoils of the Temple in Jerusalem (including most prominently its large Menorah), Freud writes to his fellow Jew,

> The Jew survives it!
> Cordial greetings and coraggio, Casimiro!

Freud's Jewish pride is profound here, and the implied identification of opposition to psychoanalysis with the Roman sack of the Jerusalem Temple makes it seem once again that Freud's psychoanalytic "cause" is a Jewish one, even if he doesn't want to call it a "Jewish science." Freud's identification with the Jewish people, Jewish history, and the tenacious and somewhat miraculous persistence of Jewish survival in spite of more powerful enemies is clear and palpable. Temples can be destroyed and a whole commonwealth can disappear, but the Jew survives it. Did the collapse of psychoanalytic collaboration with Jung seem to Freud like the destruction of the "Temple" he fought so hard to build, as implied by his analogy to Pfister in 1910? Never fear, Freud tells Abraham, the Jew will survive, as he has throughout history, because that is the nature of the Jew. Freud sounds here like a Jewish patriot who has gained strength from renewed contact with his "indestructible national feeling" (N.B., in Rome—contraries placed together shine the more).

Totem and Taboo

Though this study focuses primarily on Freud's correspondence, it is also worth examining at this point Freud's comments about two essays he wrote in this period that are important to his Jewish identity, namely, *Totem and Taboo* (1912–13) and "The *Moses* of Michelangelo" (1914), the latter published anonymously until (*nota bene*) 1924, just as our "late period" begins.

Freud began work on his "psychology of religion" in the summer of 1911. He first mentions it to Jones and then to Ferenczi in early August: "I am entirely Totem and Taboo."[89] But writing to Jung on 20 August, he alludes secretively to his new research:

> Since my mental powers revived, I have been working in a field where you will be surprised to meet me. I have unearthed strange and uncanny things and will almost feel obliged *not* to discuss them with you. But you are too shrewd not to guess what I am up to when I add that I am dying to read your "Transformations and Symb[olism] of the Lib[ido]."

Indeed it is not until March 1912 that Freud tells Jung anything specific: "My paper on Taboo is coming along slowly. The conclusion has long been known to me. The source of taboo and hence also of conscience is ambivalence."[90] Why is Freud so secretive about his "psychology of religion"?

Jones argues that Freud took up this research in an effort to distinguish his own work from that of Jung. If true, it would be further evidence that Freud feels driven to define his own relation to religion in opposition to Christianity. That the impulse to write a "Freudian" psychology of religion beyond the 1907 essay originated with Jung seems clear from Freud's own words to Jung. Complaining that the work is hard going, Freud bursts out, "Why in God's name did I allow myself to follow you into this field?"[91] Ten days earlier Freud used one of Jung's favorite metaphors for doing research, namely, that of giving birth,[92] to describe his own labors. Freud reports "constant *douleurs d'enfantement*" (labor pains).[93] Indeed the two men are so close that Freud worries that his own ideas may in fact belong to Jung and that he is "appropriating something that might just as well have been acquired by [Jung]."[94] Jung admits Freud is "a dangerous rival."[95]

In any event, Freud's work has a personal motive too, and not just a professional one. As he tells James Putnam in November 1911,

> I am trying to comprehend the psychogenesis of religion from an analytic point of view, and to use psychoanalysis to explain my own lack of a religious need.[96]

Thus Freud's "psychology of religious faith and ties"[97] seems also intended to be a way of distinguishing his own "religiosity"—or the lack of it—from Jung's, to separate Freud the Jew from Jung the Christian. It may not be coincidental that Freud mentions this "religious" motive to the Christian Putnam. Perhaps this purpose too is why Freud "hides" the work at first from Jung.

Freud will state this purpose explicitly in 1913, when things between him and Jung are much worse. The "Totem," he tells Ferenczi on 8 May of that year, "comes at the right moment to deepen the gap" (between him and Jung),[98] and he writes to Abraham on 1 July: "The gap between ourselves and the Swiss is likely to be substantially widened."[99] That Freud comes to see this gap as one over *religion* is clear from what he writes to Abraham on 13 May 1913. The essay, Freud tells his fellow Jew, "will serve to cut us off cleanly from all Aryan religiousness." On 4 November 1913 Freud gave a lecture to the B'nai B'rith entitled "What is Psychoanalysis?" Klein says that Freud's lecture was "most likely his first effort at defining psychoanalysis in light of Jung's stirring challenge."[100] I would argue that *Totem and Taboo* is really the first attempt, but it is significant in any event that the Jewish society played a role at this time, as Freud sought to differentiate himself and psychoanalysis from "Aryan religiosity." Psychoanalysis is nonreligious (i.e., humanistic) in Freud's mind, and so different from "Aryan religiousness," but Freud's Jewishness is also bound up in this difference.

Freud's refusal in *Totem and Taboo* to follow his conclusions into a more specific treatment of Judaism may also be seen as evidence of the Jewish "recessiveness" of this period. As Ernst Simon notes, Freud purposely neglects "all the later developments,"[101] adding that "a great number of powerful motives" restrain him from pursuing "the further development of religions from their origins in totemism to their condition today."[102] Simon argues that it is the presence of Freud's unconscious attachment to his Jewish heritage that accounts for the "lengthy intellectual process" that Freud has to undergo in order to formulate his theory about the "historical" Moses.[103] *Totem and Taboo* is the beginning of this long process, whose origins lie in Freud's need to differentiate himself from the Christian "psychoanalytic" goals of Jung. The long-deferred application to Judaism will of course occur when Freud is ready to explore his own Jewishness more deeply in *Moses and Monotheism.*

Jung's "Aryan Religiosity"

What this "Aryan religiosity" might be is made clearer by an exchange of letters a few years earlier, in February 1910. Freud has suggested that supporters of psychoanalysis "affiliate with a larger group working for a practical ideal," namely, "to fight for common progressive ideals of world improvement and practical reform while opposing the injustice practiced by reactionary States and by the Catholic Church,"[104] and he mentions Alfred Knapp's, "International Fraternity for Ethics and Culture."[105] Jung's response is noteworthy: "I imagine a far finer and more comprehensive task for psychoanalysis than alliance with an ethical fraternity." What he has in mind may have alarmed the Jewish Freud. At least it divides Freud and him. Jung wants

> to revivify among intellectuals a feeling for symbol and myth, ever so gently to transform Christ back into the soothsaying god of the vine which he was, and in this way absorb those ecstatic instinctual forces of Christianity for the *one* purpose of making the cult and the sacred myth what they once were—a drunken feast of joy where man regained the ethos and holiness of an animal.

Jung is musing on "the ethical problem of sexual freedom," and he continues enthusiastically,

> Yet what infinite rapture and wantonness lie dormant in our [*sic*] religion, waiting to be led back to their true destination! A genuine and proper ethical development cannot abandon Christianity but must grow up within it, must bring to fruition its hymn of love, the agony and

> ecstasy over the dying and resurgent god, the mystic power of the wine, the awesome anthropophagy of the Last Supper—only *this* ethical development can serve the vital forces of religion.[106]

Freud answers this soaring outburst two days later, hastening to drop the whole idea, and saying,

> I am not thinking of a substitute for religion; this need must be sublimated. I did not expect the Fraternity to become a religious organization any more than I would expect a volunteer fire department to do so![107]

The spark has indeed caught fire, and the Jew, in finding psychoanalysis subordinated to Christianity, has been "burned" (i.e., eliminated—"our religion") again. In making this suggestion, Freud, for his part, had hoped "to draw the moralists to psychoanalysis rather than let the psychoanalysts be turned into moralists." Thus it is clear to Freud at least by this time (months before the 1910 Congress) that his and Jung's conceptions of psychoanalysis are moving in radically different directions, and that their difference is related to Freud's sober Jewishness over against Jung's ecstatic Christianity. As Freud will tell Jung upon reading his *Wandlungen,* "Sometimes I have the feeling that his [i.e., the author, Jung's] horizon has been too narrowed by Christianity."[108] That he ignores this difference and presses Jung's leadership on the psychoanalytic movement indicates how strongly Freud felt he needed the gentile Jung for strategic purposes. But as their differences begin to become irreconcilable in public, *Totem and Taboo* becomes Freud's attempt to show how the line between him and Jung must be drawn. That *Moses and Monotheism* is as it were the "Jewish child" of *Totem and Taboo* indicates that something Jewish has begun to grow here under the surface that will only be fully articulated later.

That this line is connected in Freud's mind with a difference between Judaism (or Jewishness) and Christianity is made clear also by a Jewish joke Freud told Theodor Reik during the Psychoanalytic Congress at Munich in 1913:

> A rabbi and a parson agree to found a new common religion and set about listing the changes the other will have to make. The parson wishes to change the Sabbath service to Sunday, wants its language to be Latin instead of Hebrew, and he goes on to enumerate other concessions concerning Jewish ritual and religious observances. The rabbi agrees to them all, as though they were inessential, and has only one demand in return: Get rid of Jesus Christ.

As Reik comments, "If Jesus Christus is 'radically' out, what remains then but Judaism?"[109] Freud told Reik this joke earlier in relation to his conviction that "Jung's theological history" (i.e., his Christianity) was a decisive factor in his denial of the forces of sex.[110] Thus "Jesus Christus" in the joke represents Freud's psychoanalytic theory of sex, which is central to his system. Though in the joke Jung is the rabbi (wishful thinking?), it is not hard to see that things are really reversed, and that Jung's rejection of "the forces of sex" is connected in Freud's mind with Jung's allegiance to Christianity, an allegiance from which psychoanalysis must separate itself. And without "Jesus Christus" (i.e., the rejection of psychoanalytically conceived sexuality), what remains then but "Judaism" (i.e., psychoanalysis)? The irony here is that Jung is really all *for* sexuality, as his Dionysian paean to the instinctual powers lying dormant in Christianity shows. Furthermore, Jung's promiscuous and adulterous behavior (e.g., with his patients Sabina Spielrein[111] and Toni Wolff, among others) indicates that he indulged himself in this area, whereas Freud was more self-disciplined.[112] Perhaps what was unacceptable to Jung in Freud's theory is the discipline and self-control required by a rational, rather than a mystical, relationship to these drives. If so, we would again be faced with Freud's dichotomy of a rational "Judaism" and a mystical "Christianity."

That Freud's research into the psychology of religion represents for him a new beginning is indicated by Freud's comments to Putnam and Ferenczi that in taking up the subject he has contracted "a second marriage late in life."[113] That is, his humanistic attempt to amalgamate "Jews and *goyim*" in the service of psychoanalysis having failed, Freud must return to reconsider his own foundations, to establish a conscious psychoanalytic relationship to religion. This almost implies that his attempt at union with Gentiles involved a kind of "conversion," in which his atheistic Jewishness was subordinated to Jung's Dionysian Christianity. Freud will learn from this failure that his attachment to his Jewishness is more important than he had realized and is not negotiable. This realization, along with the historical and political stimuli, will contribute to the origins of *Moses and Monotheism*.

We can understand further what Freud meant by Jung's "Aryan religiousness," and why he was so repelled by it, through a deeper look at the role that Jung's affair with Sabina Spielrein played in their relationship. Yerushalmi provides an excellent summary of the affair, based on Aldo Carotenuto's book, *A Secret Symmetry: Sabina Spielrein between Jung and Freud.*[114] The Jewish girl was nineteen and Jung thirty when she was admitted to the Burghölzli in 1904 and given into Jung's care, who diagnosed her condition as psychotic hysteria. "I was still a baby,"

Sabina wrote, "and ran around in very simple dresses with a long, dangling braid, since I wanted to elevate my soul above my body."[115] Jung fell in love with her, and the two had a passionate affair. "It is my misfortune," Jung confessed, "that my life means nothing to me without the joy of love, of tempestuous, eternally changing love." "Return to me," he begged her later, "in this moment of my need, some of the love and guilt and altruism I was able to give you at the time of your illness. Now it is I who am ill."[116] "He told me that he loved Jewish women, that he wanted to love a dark, Jewish girl," Spielrein wrote in her diary.[117] No wonder that she began to imagine later that she could mediate between Jung and Freud by having Jung's child.

Yerushalmi describes Jung's behavior:

> The second time Jung ever wrote to Freud (October 23, 1906), he described Spielrein's case briefly without mentioning her name and, more important, without disclosing that he was involved in a love affair with her that must have begun while she was in the hospital and then continued after her release. The affair was at its height in 1908–09 and came to the attention of Spielrein's parents, almost certainly through Jung's wife, Emma. The mother wrote to Jung demanding that he end the affair. Whereupon Jung sent her the astonishing reply that in a normal doctor-patient relationship certain bounds apply, but since he is paid no fee, the relationship is not in the same category.[118]

Jung went on to suggest that "if you wish me to adhere strictly to my role as doctor, you should pay me a fee as suitable recompense for my trouble."[119] Jung lies to Freud about the affair (who is too willing at this point to take his side), until finally in June 1909, after Spielrein has written of the affair in detail to Freud, Jung admits that his behavior "was a piece of knavery which I very reluctantly confess to you as my father."[120]

When Spielrein finally abandons her fantasy of having a child by Jung and marries a Jew in 1912, Freud confesses to her that "your fantasy about the birth of the Savior to a mixed union did not appeal to me at all. The Lord, in that anti-Jewish period, had him born from the superior Jewish race. But I know these are my prejudices."[121] Freud's Jewish chauvinism will lead Freud to produce a justification and an explanation in the late period, when the fate of psychoanalysis and that of the "Jewish race" coincide in Nazi persecution. A year later in 1913, with Sabina pregnant, Freud writes that he is cured of his "predilection for the Aryan cause" and hopes that "if the child turns out to be a boy he will develop into a stalwart Zionist." Furthermore, he tells her, "I shall not present my compliments to Jung in Munich [at the Psychoanalytic Congress], as you know perfectly well." We can now appreciate the impact of Freud's words when he continues, "We are and remain Jews. The others will only exploit us and will never understand and appreciate us."[122]

Yerushalmi writes that this juncture "could have marked the public emergence of the full Jew within [Freud]," that is, that Freud could have realized that it was his Jewishness that gave him access to the universal humanity that psychoanalysis predicates. But significantly, Freud's full Jewishness does *not* emerge publically—that is, maturely in full consciousness—at this time. Instead that realization only comes—if it comes at all—when Freud writes his "deliberately Jewish" book and so develops a vision of the human bases of Western civilization, locating the universal root of all spiritual progress in Jewish tradition. It may be that only we can complete what Freud adumbrates.

But we can also glimpse in Freud's words his view of Jung's "religiousness," implied by his words about the birth of the "Savior" through Jung, recalling as well Jung's words in 1910 about "those ecstatic instinctual forces of Christianity" and regaining the "holiness of an animal." Jung's "religiosity" permits him to take unethical advantage of the young Sabina Spielrein, exploiting her shamelessly and betraying his wife, Emma. Freud now identifies with Spielrein and sees himself betrayed by Jung in a similar way. Thus the image of self-restraint that Freud sees in the *Moses* of Michelangelo (see below) also serves to draw the line between his tradition's "religiousness" and Jung's "Aryan" kind.

"*The* Moses *of Michelangelo*"

The next step in this process comes in 1914, when Freud writes his essay, "The *Moses* of Michelangelo," and publishes it, appropriately enough in the middle period, anonymously. That Freud's study of the *Moses* statue should be anonymous in the middle period, and owned publicly at the beginning of the late period (i.e., in 1924), is evidence both for the recessive character of Freud's Jewishness in the middle period and for Freud's reencounter with it in the late period. Many have commented on how personal the "*Moses*" essay is.[123] It is one in which Freud seemed to let himself go to play in his imagination with the statue and the images it evoked.[124] The result was a "Moses" that Freud could admire deeply, a suitable ideal to emulate in his own situation, when he needs to overcome his anger at Jung, the "Aryan antisemites," and Viennese "defectors" like Stekel, for the sake of the psychoanalytic cause. That Freud related his interpretation of the statue to his own situation is clear from what he writes to Ferenczi in October 1912, a month after having written his *"Moses"* essay:

> At the moment the situation in Vienna makes me feel more like the historical Moses [i.e., the biblical one, who smashed the Tablets of the Law in anger] than the Michelangelo one [i.e., the one Freud saw in Michelangelo's statue].[125]

Interestingly enough, "the Michelangelo one," that is, Freud's interpretation of the statue, may have been influenced by the guidebook he owned (published in the year he visited the statue, 1912), *Rom und die Campagna,* by Dr. Th. Gsell Fels.[126] As Molnar notes, Freud marked with blue crayon the section describing the statue (the only marking in the entire book), where the author stresses his view that "Michelangelo has depicted not an outburst of wrath but a moment of self-restraint."[127] Gsell Fels also reports that "Roman Jews regarded this particular statue as a religious image of their leader," so Freud might have been led to regard it not only as historically accurate, but also relevant in particular to Jewish group identity.

On this basis, being of the "Mosaic persuasion" meant for Freud, especially in the middle period, subordinating himself and his ego-impulses to the dictates of the *Über-Ich* and its ideals: saving himself for something self-transcendent, this time knowing what. As mentioned, in this essay Freud describes this act of self-restraint and self-transcendence as "the highest mental achievement that is possible in a man." Freud's perception of this work of art forges a new identification with his father's self-restraint in the hat-in-the-gutter episode, and it will lead him in *Moses and Monotheism* to see this drive renunciation as *the* Jewish contribution to spiritual progress in the history of Western civilization. In this perspective, Freud's last book becomes a testimonial tribute to the Jewish character of his father, Jakob Freud.

On the other hand, Yerushalmi notes that in his essay, Freud also identifies with the idolatrous mob upon whom "the hero's" "angry scorn" has fallen. "Sometimes I have crept cautiously out of the half-gloom of the interior," Freud writes, "as though I myself belonged to the mob upon whom his eye is turned—the mob which can hold fast no conviction, which has neither faith nor patience, and which rejoices when it has regained its illusory idols."[128] In this almost "hallucinatory statement," Yerushalmi asks, who else can Michelangelo's *Moses* be but Jakob Freud? Sigmund cringes under the impact of "Jewish guilt,"[129] singled out by "Moses'" rebuking stare because he has not fulfilled his father's mandate, implied in the birthday inscription of the Philippsohn Bible, to return to the Jewish Bible and its teachings.[130]

So Freud identifies with both Moses and the mob. At some level, Freud is both this "Moses," restraining his impulse to "kill" Jung, for the sake of a purpose that transcends his own gratification (unlike Jung), and part of this "mob," which cowers at their leader's (i.e., psychologically, their "father's") anger at their failure to live up to his expectation. Whatever Jung's faults, Freud feels that he hasn't done enough himself. Both identifications strengthen Freud's attachment and allegiance to, as well as his respect for, his father. If the identification with Moses effects "an intrasystemic change within Freud's own superego," as Bergman argues,[131] by which Freud sees his father as a kind of spiritual hero whom he can admire, the identification with the mob underscores his submission to the authority of that ideal, which he takes as his own. Out of this crucible emerges a renewed Jewish identification with his own past, both personal and cultural or national. A new path is opened for a reassessment of the value of his Jewishness. Furthermore, the content of this Jewishness is defined in psychological terms, as the capacity for self-transcendence in the renunciation of drive. The "Psychological Jew" finds a voice.

In the past, Freud used humanist texts to uproot Jewish observance and Jewish religion; here he has used a humanist "text" (i.e., Michelangelo's *Moses*) to find what he will identify in the late period as the essentially Jewish root of that civilization's progress. In the middle period, the Jewish origins of this achievement of self-transcendence (that is, his father Jakob's example) may not be clear to him, but it has had its intrasystemic effect on Freud's Jewish identity, so that he is opened to a new sense of Jewish wholeness that he will develop and articulate in the late period, in *Moses and Monotheism.* Note too that Freud the Jewish humanist discovered this achievement of drive-renunciation in an image of Moses (at this time still Jewish) sculpted by a great Italian humanist in the heart of Christian culture. Freud's most personal Jewish identification has led him to the root of humanist civilization. Again, the particular has provided an access to the universal. This configuration is the basis of Freud's dual allegiance, whether he realizes it or not. Again, his Jewishness is a resource, an entry point, rather than a liability.

Freud seems to have had a sense of humor about his "*Moses*" essay—appropriately so if it is related to his Jewish identity. Commenting on the work's anonymity, Freud writes to Jones, "Why disgrace Moses by putting my name to it? It is only a joke, but perhaps not a bad one."[132] To Abraham he wrote, "The '*Moses*' is anonymous partly as a joke [*Scherz*]"[133] (presumably those familiar with Freud's style would recognize its author immediately). And in May 1914, having sent Putnam a copy of the essay, Freud jokes, "Its author does not publicly acknowledge having written it because in this exceptional instance, it does not deal with sexuality."[134] Freud seems to see this foray into applied psychoanalysis as a form of play, and this attitude may be particularly well-suited for psychoanalytic expressions connected to his Jewishness. But this is so in general too. In November Freud comments playfully on a lithograph portrait of himself done by Hermann Struck that "Whatever is Jewish about the head has my full agreement, but something else has struck me as alien . . . a hybrid phenomenon . . . of Jew and orchid!"[135]

As we saw in our study of Freud's correspondence in the early period, Jewish jokes express an important element of Freud's Jewish identity, a taste inherited or learned from his father. Reik points out that such jokes served Freud as a way of expressing and enjoying a subterranean tie between himself and other Jews, a tie that carries with it by the nature of its Jewish origin an emotional intimacy.[136] In continuity with the early period, this role of Jewish humor can be seen in a letter Freud writes to Reik on 24 July 1914 in reference to the latter's critical review of Pfister's article on psychoanalysis in the *Theologische Literaturzeitung.* Pfister had said that psychoanalysis deals not only with aggressive and sexual drives, but also with "unconscious moral trends." Reik used a joke whose punch line underscored their differences. Freud writes,

> The *'à qui dites-vous ça'* ["You're telling me?"] is a Jewish joke, too good for those *goyim,* and makes a bad impression. I am, of course, in agreement with the content of your criticism.[137]

Freud likes the Jewish joke, but nonetheless it makes a "bad impression," presumably because it seems proud or chauvinistic, reminding Gentiles that Jews know better than they. Freud mentioned to Reik his belief that Jewish humor, often self-deprecating, concealed "an unconscious or preconscious awareness of the high value and worth" of the Jewish people, "a concealed national pride."[138] What emerges clearly from Freud's handling of Jewish wit, Reik says, is his "deep sympathy for the unbroken spirit and dignity of the Jewish people."[139] Here in the middle period, Freud was still concerned to keep that pride concealed. In the late period, it will be less disguised.

Freud, the German Jew

Freud is a Jew, but he is a German-Jew, in spite of his protestations. World War I at first brought out Freud's latent German-Austrian patriotism:

> For the first time in thirty years I feel myself to be an Austrian and I feel like giving this not very hopeful Empire another chance.[140]

We recall Freud's letter to Martha Bernays of 2 February 1886, when he reported declaring himself neither German nor Austrian but *juif*, and as a consequence felt something "German" stirring within him. In August 1914 he declares that "All my libido is given to Austro-Hungary."[141] This initial response Jones characterizes as "a re-awakening of the military ardors of his boyhood." Remember that those ardors were associated with "Semitic" figures. But Freud's mood lasted little more than a fortnight, and then he "came to himself." "Very characteristically," Jones says, Freud described this change of mood by means of a Jewish joke, in which a Jew who had lived in Germany for years and had adopted German manners returns home to his family, where the old grandfather, "by examining his underclothes, decides that the German part was only veneer."[142] Jewish humor again reminds Freud who he is under the surface; it enables him to return to "himself." Though Freud is Austrian, his Jewish identity is a deeper identification, which Jewish humor discloses. It is noteworthy too that what brought about the reversal in Freud's feelings was "a loathing for the incompetence his newly adopted fatherland was displaying in its campaign against the Serbians."[143] That is, they were bad soldiers. This martial incompetence disgusted the fighting Jew, and he returns to his Jewish roots with a self-deprecating Jewish joke about assimilated German Jews (like himself).

Freud's feeling of disgust is similar in 1917. As he tells Abraham,

> I am at daggers drawn . . . [with regard to] your dear German fatherland. . . . in the struggle between the Entente and the Quadruple Alliance I have definitely adopted the viewpoint of Heine's Donna Blanca in the disputation at Toledo: "But I rather suspect . . ."

The quotation from the closing lines of Heinrich Heine's "The Disputation" (1851),[144] to which Freud alludes, continues ". . . that both the Rabbi and the monk stink alike." Politics, like religions, are equally bad, no matter which side one is on. Rosen says that Freud was "in the end an apolitical person."[145] Yet in this letter to Abraham, Freud continues,

> The only thing that gives me any pleasure is the capture of Jerusalem and the British experiment with the chosen people.[146]

Though perhaps apolitical in general, Jewish politics arouses Freud's interest. Remember his lighting up a cigar at Lueger's nonconfirmation in 1895, and his mention of the Dreyfus trial. Freud is referring here of course to the Balfour Declaration of 2 November 1917, which stated in part that "His Majesty's Government view with favor the establishment in Palestine of a national home for the Jewish people." In spite of, or perhaps because of, Freud's disgust with politics and his German "Fatherland," the prospect that the Jewish people (Freud himself adds the "chosen") might find a home in the land of Palestine gives him pleasure. Part of this pleasure comes from the military victory, the capture of Jerusalem. Freud remains the fighting Jew, even at sixty-one.

At the end of the middle period, in 1922, Freud writes to Ferenczi,

> Strange secret yearnings rise in me—perhaps from my ancestral heritage—for the East and the Mediterranean and for a life of quite a different kind: wishes from late childhood never to be fulfilled . . .[147]

In view of Freud's phylogenetic theory of Jewish identity developed in *Moses and Monotheism* that man carries "with him at birth fragments of phylogenetic origin, an archaic heritage,"[148] and that Jewish character is an expression of a particular historical development acquired and passed on "genetically" over the centuries, Freud's recognition in this letter to Ferenczi of a deep attachment to the land and Eastern origins of that heritage points toward his growing interest at the end of the middle period in the issue of his own Jewish identity, bound up as it is with the history of the "Chosen People."

Freud's Jewishness and Christianity

But in addition to this ethnic focus, Freud's psychoanalytic Jewish identity also finds definition in contrast to Christian religion, as we saw in relation to Jung. In an exchange with Pfister in October 1918, Freud discusses his criticism of Pfister's *Psychoanalysis in the Service of Education*,[149] mentioning specifically the latter's objection to Freud's "sexual theory." He suspects that Pfister wants a "synthesis without a previous analysis." Given Jung's "Christianizing" efforts at a "psychosynthesis," when Freud goes on to say to Pfister that "the relics of your resistance to sexuality must have crept into this," we are probably not mistaken to suggest that Freud associates Pfister's resistance with his Christianity. Remember that Freud thought Jung's views had been "too narrowed by Christianity."

This suggestion gains credence when we see the challenge with which Freud closes his letter to Pfister:

> Incidentally, why was it that none of all the pious ever discovered psychoanalysis? Why did it have to wait for a completely godless Jew?[150]

Given Freud's view of the relationship between Christianity and sexuality, it may be that Freud felt that Christians (here, "the pious") were less able to be in touch with their own sexuality in a rational, conscious way that could lead them to create a "science." But a "godless Jew," by contrast, by virtue of his life-enjoying heritage on the one hand and his atheism on the other, indeed could be so in touch.

Pfister responds in a different way. First he denies that Freud is a Jew, because he does not correspond to Pfister's Protestant definition of a Jew drawn from the "Old Testament" prophets (he mentions Amos, Isaiah, and Jeremiah) and wisdom literature (Job and Ecclesiastes); secondly, he denies that Freud is "godless," bringing language and ideas from the New Testament as proof: "for he who lives the truth lives in God, and he who strives for the freeing of love 'dwelleth in God' (First Epistle of John, iv, 16)." These Christian premises lead Pfister to say of Freud what the Friar in *Nathan the Wise* says of Nathan. If Freud only understood his own place in the larger scheme of things, Pfister says, he would see that "a better Christian there never was."[151] In Lessing's play, the Friar identifies the Jewish Nathan as a "Christian soul" because Nathan rises above hating the Christians who have slaughtered his wife and seven sons, in order to raise an abandoned Christian child as his own daughter. Does Pfister see Freud performing an analogous rescue for Christian civilization? Gay says simply that Pfister's quote is his way of saying that he had discovered some substantial affinities between his version of Protestantism and Freud's thought, namely, the role of love.[152] Freud tells Jung in a letter of 6 December 1906 that psychoanalysis is "essentially a cure through love." But Freud's words in 1909 have proven prophetic: "The Jew [working with Christians] must be burned."

In any event, Freud does not respond himself to Pfister's characterization of him as a "Jewless Christian" until 1929, in the late period. Then, in a letter to Pfister discussing once again the psychoanalytic role—or lack of it—in the teaching of an ethics, Freud insists that the scientific *Weltanschauung* of psychoanalysis is incompatible with the religious one, and that the latter's ideals are a pious illusion in conflict with reason. On the other hand, no difficulties for the scientific outlook of psychoanalysis are created by patients' demands for ethical values, for "ethics are not based on an external world order but on the inescapable exigencies of human cohabitation." That is, they are only practical. Rejecting as "excessively friendly" Pfister's view of him in this 1929 letter as one who acts "as if" there were "one universal meaning to life," Freud goes on to say that it always reminds him of "the friar who insisted on regarding Nathan as a Christian through and through." "I am a long way from being Nathan," Freud continues in a gentle, affectionate rebuff, "but of course I cannot help remaining 'good' towards you."[153]

Pfister's *einen Lebens- und Weltsinn,* the drive to find one meaning that can apply to all things may seem a particularly Christian approach to the matter, expressed paradigmatically of course in the life and crucifixion of Jesus Christ, and it may be this thrust that has reminded Freud of Pfister's well-meaning "defense" of him ten years earlier as a preeminent Christian. Freud rejects this characterization, perhaps because he cannot accept such a "spiritual" definition of his Jewishness, as Nathan does in Lessing's play.[154] Freud's Jewishness is not based on "religion," but rather on something deeper, more embodied, namely, an ethnically transmitted archaic heritage. Such an identity is not so easily identified with those of a different heritage. Also, Freud's biblical self-definition comes as much, if not more, from the stories and figures in the Pentateuch (e.g., Moses and Joseph), as it does from the prophets of the Hebrew Bible.

Yet Freud did express in this period a "special sympathy" for one of the founders of Christianity, namely, Paul. Writing to Pfister in May 1920, Freud praises Pfister's psychological "sketch" of the Apostle Paul,[155] saying he likes it very much. Furthermore, he goes on to say,

> I have always had a special sympathy for St. Paul as a genuinely Jewish character. Is he not the only one who stands completely in the light of history?[156]

Paul's "authentically Jewish character" seems to be the reason for Freud's "special sympathy." Pfister's essay includes sections on Paul's Jewish background. Because Paul is Jewish, Freud feels a kinship with him, even across a Christian boundary and even mediated by a Protestant pastor. But in addition, the "historical" nature of the figure of Paul attracts Freud. This historical base helps Freud feel attached to Paul, for as we saw in the Nathan letter, "history" determines for Freud what is true about a religious tradition, perhaps because it is a *rational* attachment. Therefore, in spite of the vicissitudes of Paul's influence, the man himself is "genuinely Jewish," and so Freud feels a sympathy for him, in spite of Christianity. A Jew always remains a member of the family. Recall Freud and the merchant in the Nathan letter treating Michael Bernays as if he were still a Jewish member of the family, even though he had converted.

Considering this comment about the historicity of Paul, we remember too Freud's comment to Ferenczi, thinking of himself and "the situation in Vienna," about the "historical Moses." Freud knows that Michelangelo's creation is not the biblical one (which he labels "historical") that is a part of his "ancient heritage." This allegiance to historicity, so characteristic of modernity, is as basic to Freud's self-understanding as it is to his view of the world, his *Weltanschauung.* When Freud first begins to write *Moses and Monotheism,* he refers to it as a "historical novel,"[157] meaning that "given the extreme paucity of reliable historical facts concerning Moses, [Freud's] reconstruction must be based to such an unusual extent on psychoanalytic probability."[158] Later he drops this subtitle, perhaps because he wants his book to refer to historical events and not just psychoanalytic probability. In *Moses and Monotheism,* Freud describes (his) Jewishness as a genetically transmitted fact of history and a psychological infrastructure, not a religious faith. He will discover however that as a result it also has powerful irrational roots. Freud's last book will attempt to trace the historical vicissitudes of this historical psychological infrastructure, so that he can die with a sense of Jewish wholeness (*shalom*), his "racial kinship" united with his "intellectual constitution" in a historical framework.

Sophie's Death

Freud describes himself in this period to the Gentile James Putnam as "a God-forsaken 'incredulous Jew'."[159] If Freud is indeed "godless," how might we characterize his attitude towards man's ultimate horizons? To answer this question, whose answer should shape our view of Freud's identity as a whole, let us consider his response to his daughter Sophie's sudden death. On 25 January 1920, Freud's fourth child, his "dear, blooming Sophie," died of influenza complicated by pneumonia, pregnant with her third child. Freud writes to Sophie's bereaved husband, Max Halberstadt, himself an observant Jew,

> it was a senseless, brutal stroke of fate that took our Sophie from us, in the face of which it is useless to recriminate or brood; we can only bow our heads under the blow like the poor helpless creatures we are, mere playthings for the higher powers.[160]

Freud's stoicism here reminds us of his words to his friend Silberstein in 1877 about the amusement of fate in hunting us at its whim, and "the maliciousness of Destiny," which he drew from Herodotus.[161] As an "unbeliever," Freud faces only "Blunt necessity, mute submission."[162] As he tells Ferenczi,

> Since I am the deepest of unbelievers, I have no one to accuse and realize there is no place where one can lodge an accusation."[163]

"Indeed," Freud says sadly to another friend, "to outlive a child is not agreeable. Fate does not keep even to this order of precedence."[164] Freud's personal religious outlook, what he is committed to at the ultimate horizons of his world, is a kind of atheistic stoicism, expressing a lifelong link to the classical *Gymnasium* of his youth. Yet, as he tells Pfister in 1922, "it is only in old age that one is converted to the grim heavenly pair *logos kai ananke*" [Reason and Necessity].[165] Thus at the end of the middle period, we see that Freud's identity is rooted in this stoic and existential atheism, a position that seemed to him only reasonable. He could not be farther away from the providential view of things taken by Judaism. Therefore, when in the following year death stalks Freud himself, it may be only human that he seeks to touch base with his Jewish roots, to draw strength from his "indestructible national feeling," perhaps one reason for Freud's only "deliberately Jewish" book.

Summary

Before we move on to the third and final period in the development of Freud's Jewish identity, let us summarize the results of our study of the middle, "recessive" phase. In spite of the fact that Freud placed his Jewishness in the background, "behind" Gentiles in the psychoanalytic movement, in order that Gentiles like Jung might lead the way in bringing psychoanalysis to the larger world, nevertheless Freud's Jewishness was clear as an identification in his own mind, and it developed under the surface and in his private life in response to events in his psychoanalytic life. Certain characteristics, familiar to us from our study of the early period, reappear here behind the "Gentile facade."

For example, in the middle period, Freud's sense of the Jew rooted in Jewish history, as one who survives and eventually triumphs on the basis of patient tenacity, is put into practice. Freud's subordination of the Jewishness of psychoanalysis to Gentile leadership in an attempt to further psychoanalysis as a humanistic science expresses this tenacity, as well as a sense of Jewish worth and ultimate probity (therefore the Jew can afford to wait). The self-restraint and renunciation of ego-impulses in the name of something higher is the fulfillment of a Jewish value Freud had defined with Martha as an element of the "higher" calling they bore over against the nature of "the mob." This value becomes more explicitly associated with his Jewishness in the middle period, because it recalls Jakob Freud's self-control in response to antisemitic attack and is identified with a "Moses" of Freud's imagination, even as Freud imagines that he himself is also part of "the faithless (Jewish) mob." These two sides represent respectively Freud's Jewish superego and his equally Jewish id. The final task of course is the achievement of a whole Jewish ego.

Freud is still the fighting Jew, and he is pretty cagey too, waging a strategic battle against antisemitism. His "national" or latently "political" Jewishness is also present, as he watches "the British experiment with the chosen people" from afar. Freud is still attached to Jewish dreams, and he continues to draw strength from that "indestructible national feeling." Jewishness is a source of pride for him and a source of energy, a certain advantage in the real world, stimulating one's productivity. Though he is still an atheist, Freud is again nonetheless Jewish, and he still feels comfortable and natural using biblical figures to express and define himself. Jewishness is still related to humor and Jewish jokes (especially in situations of personal difficulty and self-definition), and biblical identifications (e.g., with Moses) still express this play. Thus there is considerable continuity in Freud's Jewish identity between the early and middle periods; the difference is one of presentation and structuring. In the early period, Freud often (but not always) explores and experiments with his Jewish identity in public fora, like the B'nai B'rith, the university, or fighting with antisemites. In the middle period, Freud's Jewishness fights and incubates behind the scenes, privately, anonymously. The major difference between these two earlier periods and the late period, on the other hand, is maturity.

In the struggle to make psychoanalysis successful in the Gentile world, Freud articulates what he shares in common with fellow Jews. He recognizes a Jewish "intellectual constitution" and a "racial kinship." "Consanguineous Jewish traits" link him to other Jews, among them decisiveness, rational clarity, and a skill with language. Religiously, Jews lack a "mystical element," in Freud's view, and so they can be rational more easily and defined historically. Freud expresses this rationality in his own religious outlook through a form of stoicism. Because Jews lack the "mystical element," they have an easier time accepting psychoanalytic ideas, especially ones related to sex. A connection in Freud's mind between "mysticism" and a flight from sexuality characteristic of Christianity colors the division between Jews and Gentiles in the psychoanalytic movement in this regard. Also in relation to Gentiles, Freud develops part of his sense of his own Jewishness over against inevitable and ever-present antisemitism. Whether Freud's condescending sense of Jewish superiority is a consequence or a contributing cause (or both) of this antisemitism cannot be decided here, but that chauvinism too is a part of Freud's Jewishness, even as a prejudice.

Though Freud sees his Jewishness expressed especially by a sober rationalism, he admits that he is superstitious, especially about his own death, and he suggests that his numerology—or to use the traditional Jewish term, *gematria*—is a form of Jewish "mysticism." He means by this term that it is irrational and superstitious. Freud's expression of his fear of death and his superstitions through play with numbers both expresses a connection to his Eastern European Jewish folk background (though he does not acknowledge it publicly in this period) and bears witness to the continuing influence of his most powerful Jewish friendship with Wilhelm Fliess (whom he holds responsible for this "Jewish" mysticism). Typically, he avoids a rational link with the talmudic tradition, preferring to find "striking" parallels to dream interpretation in the tradition of the Greek classics.

Though not a "Jewish science," psychoanalysis is for Freud clearly in continuity with Jewish history, and the metaphor of building a new "Temple" makes psychoanalysis seem indeed like something of a specifically *Jewish* "cause." If Dennis Klein is correct about Freud's link with the "messianic" Jewish liberalism of the B'nai B'rith, then Freud's sacrificing himself for "the cause" also expresses a deep identification with Jewish tradition.

Freud's identification with Moses becomes explicit in this very context of self-sacrifice and subordination, a form of knowing renunciation that now is linked to the most prominent leader of the Jewish people, their original lawgiver. Moses becomes for Freud the figure who yields place to another who will outlive him, and who renounces his impulse to destroy in order to preserve something—a cause to which he has devoted himself. Significantly, he keeps this identification from the public until after he knows he is dying. When in 1924 Freud acknowledges the *Moses* essay as his own, the unconscious identification with his father that underlies it can affect Freud's Jewish identity more completely, opening the way for a greater integration, connecting this emotional image rationally to Jewish history. The path to *Moses and Monotheism* is thereby opened. In the middle period too, Freud begins through *Totem and Taboo* to develop his conception of his Jewishness as a kind of ancient, phylogenetic Jewish heritage, and this concept may be his way ultimately of overcoming death, through an identification with the "eternal" germ-plasm. Again the culmination of this idea finds its place in Freud's last book.

4

The Late Period

The Encounter with Death

The years 1920–23 were painful ones for Freud, full of the deaths of loved ones and friends, culminating with the threat to his own life. Following the devastations of World War I, it is little wonder that Freud is pessimistic and bitter. On 20 January 1920 Freud's friend and great benefactor to psychoanalysis, Anton von Freund, died of cancer at the age of forty. Freud visited him daily in his illness, watching him die. "He bore his hopelessness with heroic clarity, did not disgrace analysis," Freud wrote Eitingon the day after Freund's death.[1] Though Freud felt the loss "keenly," his admiration is also clear, for Freund had died "as Freud's father had died and as he himself hoped to die," that is, stoically.[2] Five days later Freud's daughter Sophie died, pregnant with Freud's third grandchild. Hilda Doolittle remembers Freud saying in 1933 that he had lost his favorite daughter in an epidemic in the last year of the Great War. "'She is here,' he said, and he showed me a tiny locket that he wore, fastened to his watch-chain."[3]

Less than two years later, Freud's niece, Caecilie Graf, pregnant and unmarried, committed suicide. She was Freud's "best niece," "a dear girl of 23."[4] Six months later, in February 1923, Freud writes Jones that he had detected "a leucoplastic growth on my jaw and palate, right side," that he suspected was cancer ("My own diagnosis had been epithelioma, but this was not accepted").[5] When Freud finally showed this growth to two medical friends in April, both advised excision of the lesion but did not tell Freud he had cancer. A minor operation was performed badly on 20 April 1923 to remove the growth, and X-ray and radium treatments followed, belying the supposed harmlessness of the condition.[6] Freud was not told of the malignant diagnosis of the excised growth, but he probably understood enough. It is just after this operation that he announced plans by circular letter for a two-week trip to Rome in September with his daughter Anna.[7] The gesture may have indicated Freud's awareness that his time was running out and expressed a desire to set foot on the soil of Rome once more to renew his strength.

Then on 19 June 1923 Freud's grandson, Sophie's second son Heinz Rudolph, died of tubercular meningitis, and Freud wept—according to Robert Hollitscher, for the only time in his life.[8] This loss obviously affected Freud deeply, and he described himself in mid-August to Eitingon as now a stranger to life and a candidate for death.[9] The boy, he told lifelong friend Oscar Rie, "meant the future to me and thus has taken the future away with him."[10]

At this point, in September the true diagnosis of his cancer now being withheld from him by "The Committee" as well, Freud takes his planned trip to show Rome to his daughter Anna, thinking it might be his last opportunity. To Anna too it had been "plain enough" from a conversation she had had with his doctor, Felix Deutsch, that her father had cancer,[11] and even if Freud had not acknowledged his condition, his mood after Heinerle's death was enough to make the significance of the trip clear. And when at breakfast on the train from Verona to Rome "suddenly a stream of blood spurted from Freud's mouth," "there was no doubt of its significance in either of their minds."[12] Yet they continued on and did not return to Vienna until a few days before the scheduled oral surgery with Hans Pichler.

Facing death, Freud returns to the scene of his first triumph, both to say good-bye and to begin again with renewed strength, like Antaeus touching the earth. He certainly would have shown Michelangelo's *Moses* (and perhaps too the Arch of Titus) to Anna, who more than any other now must have appeared to be his real successor. As Freud says, "Anna was splendid. She understood and enjoyed everything, and I was very proud of her."[13] Freud is passing the mantle of psychoanalysis to Anna, who would serve until his death as his nurse and public representative. The final period of the development of Freud's Jewish-humanist identity begins here in Rome, appropriately enough. For it is in Rome that Freud can find confirmed together both his "indestructible national feeling" and his identification with the classical civilization that grounds his humanism.

When Freud returned to Vienna, he was examined by his oral surgeons on 26 September and told definitely that his ulcer was malignant. He wrote on the same day to Abraham, Eitingon, and Jones, facing the future with composure and adding, "You know what it all means."[14]

Major operations were performed 4 and 12 October, a large section of the right side of Freud's upper jaw was removed, and he was fitted with a prosthesis.[15] On 30 October 1923, following his return home from this radical surgery, Freud drafted a will in the form of a letter to Martin, so clearly Freud realized that he might die soon. A few days later, on 5 November, he began a systematic list of the translations of his works. He also kept lists of letters received and answered, visitors, patients, and a "Shortest Chronicle"—a kind of "list of lists." Michael Molnar suggests that Freud's keeping these lists was a way of his holding onto his life as he felt it begin to slip away.[16]

The Correspondence

With this biographical context as an introduction, let us turn to Freud's correspondence. While he was vacationing in July of 1923 at the summer resort at Badgastein, he received a letter from a young German Jew named Erich Leyens, who said he was alarmed at the growth of antisemitism in Germany. The young man had been a member of the German Youth Movement and had fought on the German side in World War I. One of the leaders of the now antisemitic Movement, psychiatrist Hans Blüher, had quoted Freud in support of his opinions, having called in the preceding year (in his *Secessio Judaica*) for the separation of all Jews from the German people.[17] Freud replies to Leyens on 4 July:

> I believe I understand you and your situation. That I have full sympathy for you requires no corroboration. But I would dissuade you from consuming yourself in the hopeless struggle against the present "spiritual" currents in Germany. Folk psychoses are immune to arguments. Precisely the Germans had the occasion to learn it in the recent World War. But they appear not to be capable of it. Let us leave them to themselves . . .

Repudiating Blüher, Freud continues,

> Turn yourself toward the things that can lift the Jews over all these insanities and—don't take amiss the advice that is the upshot of a long life!—don't impose yourself upon the Germans.[18]

One gets the sense from the last phrase that Freud regards Jews in German lands almost like "guests in someone else's house," so a kind of Jewish succession seems to have already taken place in his mind (unless of course he had always felt that way). Freud feels a *volle Sympathie* for this young Jew, whose shifting German-Jewish allegiances and encounters with antisemitism mirrored Freud's own as a youth.[19] Understanding Leyens, Freud identifies with him. Freud's words remind us of those he wrote to Abraham at the beginning of their correspondence. He advises Leyens to turn away from the Germans—they are crazy—lest he be "consumed" (*verzehren*). Instead, Freud says, turn to the Jews and lift them up, elevate them above this madness. Leave the Germans alone; help the Jews. Freud's advice, the experience of a long life, is a kind of "projective identification," whereby he uses the young Jew to do for him what he wants to do for himself. For as the final period unfolds, Freud does the same thing in his own life that he advises Leyens to do in his, namely, he turns from the Germans and toward the Jews and his own Jewishness in an effort to help his people, and in so doing discovers the nature of his own Jewishness. *Moses and Monotheism* may itself be an attempt to 'lift the Jews out of the insanities' that were engulfing Germany, in spite of its "ambivalent" form. This letter to Leyens stands at the beginning of our late period as suggestive evidence of a shift in Freud's attitude as he faced his own death in the summer before his last trip to Rome.

The following year, the City Council of Vienna bestowed upon Freud the *Bürgerrecht* of Vienna for his sixty-eighth birthday. It was the first civic honor with which the city saw fit to acknowledge him. Freud explained his view of the city's motives by telling Abraham that "the idea that my coming sixty-eighth birthday may be the last must have occurred to other people too."[20] To Ferenczi he dismissed the honor this way:

> There is little to be said about the Vienna *Bürgerrecht* you mention. *(Man kann Schabbes davon machen* ["One can make *Shabbes* with it"]).[21]

As mentioned in chapter 2, Freud made oblique reference to this Yiddish proverb as part of a joke in *The Interpretation of Dreams*.[22] The import of the proverb is to say "big deal," for the honor is useless for doing any "work" during the week. That is, as far as Freud is concerned, it means nothing for psychoanalysis. It does not indicate an acceptance of psychoanalysis, but is rather a kind of ritual blessing, of no use in earning a livelihood or in promoting psychoanalysis.

The conjunction of these two responses to Viennese recognition is significant in relation to Freud's Jewishness. Freud thinks on one hand of his own imminent death, and on the other of a Jewish joke with a Yiddish punch line (which, significantly, he renders in German). In the face of the threat of personal extinction, Freud affirms his ethnic roots and a kind of solidarity with a popular Jewish tradition. As Kurt Schlesinger says,

> Jewish humor as an oral tradition handed down over generations of joke telling is a form of secular communal ritual which both binds and characterizes the community, and acts adaptively for its survival.[23]

In letters to Abraham from 1924 dated 22 August and 8 December, Freud's interest in another Jewish tradition appears, namely, the symbolism of the number seven, so prominent in the Jewish Bible. Freud wants to take a "historical view" of the matter, and he proposes "a period when men counted in sixes," though he admits that "here ignorance sets in." In other words, Freud is letting his imagination play. As a result of being the first of a second series of six, the number seven is "like first things, subject to taboo." That the initial number of the third series, thirteen, is "the unluckiest of all numbers would fit in with this," Freud adds. Freud's idea has its origin in a book he is reading on the history of Assyria, in which "19 was also one of the suspect numbers"—as Freud remarks, it is "the beginning of a fourth series of sixes." He notes also that many prime numbers occur in this series, concluding with "49 which is again 7 x 7." He adds in December, "The problem of 7 still interests me greatly." Why? Freud is using this play with numbers in an attempt to get at ancient historical facts, to probe "Assyria" or perhaps "the Babylonians" (where Abraham looks),[24] in an effort to get a glimpse into an age that is "pre-astronomical."[25] This numerical interest is to be understood as part of Freud's long look backwards in time into the origins of human civilization, and this is tied up with his growing interest in the roots of the Jewish people. But as mentioned, the rabbis too used the play with numbers in a serious attempt to uncover the secrets of reality (in their case, the divine reality of Creation; Freud wants history). Freud may be closer to Jewish tradition than he knows.

The Return of the Suppressed: Letters from 1925

In the following year, 1925, Freud makes a number of significant and forthright statements about himself as a Jew, and all but one of these—importantly for my thesis of periodicity—are made to the public. Freud "comes out" as a Jew from behind the "Gentile facade." In this year Freud publishes his *Selbstdarstellung* ("An Autobiographical Study") in Grotes's *Die Medizin der Gegenwart in Selbstdarstellungen*, though Jones tells us it was written in August and September, 1924.[26] Freud notes in the "Postscript" he wrote for the work in 1935, "Shortly before I wrote this study it seemed as though my life would soon be brought to an end by the recurrence of a malignant disease,"[27] so he is clearly aware at this time that his own death is on the horizon.

At the beginning of the essay, Freud mentions that he has already published "the essence of all that I can say on the present occasion" ten years before, in *On the History of the Psycho-Analytical Movement* (1914).[28] But a difference in phrasing that is important for us is evident. In 1925 Freud writes, "My parents were Jews, and I have remained a Jew myself."[29] In his essay written in 1914, the word "Jew" does not appear, in spite of a clear allusion to Freud's Jewish origin in the context of his suspicion that antisemitism has played a role in an opponent's criticism of psychoanalysis as "typically Viennese." This charge, Freud suspects, is "a euphemistic substitute for another reproach which no one would care to put forward openly,"[30] namely, that psychoanalysis is the work of a Jew. In 1925, in the late period, Freud states openly the Jewish origins he only alludes to in 1914, in the middle period.

This contrast appears stronger when Freud describes here his experience of antisemitism in the years following his entrance into the University of Vienna in 1873:

> I found that I was expected to feel myself inferior and an alien because I was a Jew.

No circumlocutions here. Freud's reaction is characteristically defiant:

> I refused absolutely to do the first of these things. I have never been able to see why I should feel ashamed of my descent or, as people were beginning to say, of my "race."

Gay notes that around Christmas 1923 Freud had read an advance copy of Fritz Wittels's biography of him and had marked with strong disapproval a statement by Wittels that Freud's "fate as a Jew in the German cultural area made him sicken early with the feeling of inferiority, which no German Jew can escape."[31] Gay suggests that Freud's emphatic claim that he did *not* fall prey to this sickness was "an indirect response to Wittels's characterization."[32] Freud rejects the subordination because he expects to have a place to work within the "framework of humanity." He "relinquished, without much regret," the acceptance of the community, apparently accepting that he did not belong to the German *Volk,* as was evident in his letter to Erich Leyens in 1923. Belonging to the Jewish people functioned as compensatory support in this loss.

Rather than crushing Freud's Jewish identity, this antisemitic rejection helped form his character:

> . . . for at an early age I was made familiar with the fate of being in the Opposition and of being put under the ban of the "compact majority." The foundations were thus laid for a certain degree of independence of judgement.[33]

A character trait formed in the early period is given explicit public articulation in the late period. We will see that Freud identifies his "*Unabhängigkeit des Urteils*" as a specifically Jewish element of his character for which he is grateful.

Freud's reference to Henrik Ibsen's play, *An Enemy of the People*, recurs in the following year, when Freud addresses the Vienna B'nai B'rith. At that point we will discuss its context in detail. Here it is sufficient to note that being excluded from the community of the "solid majority," of finding himself socially marginalized, worked to his advantage in his eyes, strengthening his "intellectual constitution." He was willing to forego the "pleasure" of the community of the antisemitic majority.

There is one other sentence in this text that will reward our attention. Discussing his youth, Freud says,

> My early familiarity with the Bible story (almost as soon as I had learned the art of reading) had, as I recognized much later, an enduring effect upon the direction of my interest.[34]

Freud added this sentence too to his text in 1935.[35] Just as he is himself engrossed in his revision of the "biblical" or "historical" Moses that will appear in *Moses and Monotheism*, Freud acknowledges the early influence of his Bible reading on the direction of his later interests, and he includes this sentence in these paragraphs that relate to the givenness and formation of his Jewish identity. Freud realizes anew in the late period that he is a Jew whose identity is rooted in the Bible.[36]

But as Freud, facing death, re-encounters his own Jewishness, he repeatedly also reaffirms his atheism, lest there be any mistake about his allegiances, both of them deep. He writes at this time to the editor of the *Jewish Press Centre*, a Jewish-Swiss weekly in Zurich (from what cause we don't know, perhaps a query from that editor):

> I can say that I stand as far apart from the Jewish religion as from all other religions; that is to say, they are of great significance to me as a

> subject of scientific interest, but emotionally I take no part in them. On the other hand, I have always had a strong feeling of belonging together with [*Zusammengehörigkeit*] my people and have also nourished it in my children. We have all remained in the Jewish denomination.[37]

Echoing his words in his *Selbstdarstellung*, Freud says with a certain pride that he and his family have remained Jews. He knows how common conversion to Christianity was at the time, especially among liberals and freethinkers. As noted above, Freud considered this a great loss to one's potential; as we shall see below, he also considered it "unworthy" and "senseless." He is explicit in affirming the nature of his Jewish allegiance to "peoplehood" and not religion, a dichotomy we have seen Freud use before. Religions are a subject of *wissenschaftlichen Interessen* (not "national interests," as he will say in *Moses and Monotheism*). That is, they engage Freud *intellectually;* emotionally he claims to keep his distance. Yet since Freud defines himself to such a great extent in terms of the information that comes from intellectual "crafts of knowing," such interest is not insignificant for Freud's Jewish identity, even if he denies an emotional participation (which we have reason to question, in any event). In fact, Freud will use precisely this "scientific" method when he comes to define for himself (and his public) what a Jew *is* in *Moses and Monotheism*. And a little over a year later, Freud will admit that "Jewishness is still very important to me emotionally."[38] Presumably he refers here again to his feeling of "belonging together" with Jewish people.

Freud's letter continues with perhaps the first of many statements attesting both to his lack of Hebrew language ability and to his regret at this lack of knowledge:

> In the time of my youth our free-thinking [or "liberal"—*freisinnigen*] instructors of religion placed no value on the acquisition of a knowledge of the Hebrew language and literature by their pupils. My education in this field is therefore quite left behind, which I have since often regretted.[39]

As mentioned, Rainey points out that it is an exaggeration on Freud's part to say that his liberal Jewish teachers placed no value on a knowledge of Hebrew. "In principle," he says, "they valued Hebrew instruction highly, but they were forced to curtail it drastically because of the small amount of class time [two hours per week] allotted to them in the public schools."[40] This curricular decision itself, however, reflects a value—or rather, not valuing Hebrew and its religious traditions as compared to "secular" or even humanistic studies. The fact that there was no study of the Talmud and its commentaries also points to this choice. Although Freud's words are an exaggeration in their evaluation of his teachers' ideals, nonetheless he is right about the *Gymnasium*'s overall values. His education in this area was indeed minimal and inadequate, and his sorrow is understandable, especially later in life. Feeling a solidarity with his people and yet having no part in their language highlights the loss. As Freud's teacher Hammerschlag wrote,

> Precisely because he [the Jew] knows that he is one in language, customs, and way of life with the people among whom he lives, and directs his efforts toward the realization of the same political, national, and cultural goals, precisely for this reason he must preserve and protect with that much greater fervor and devotion the only means through which he remains conscious of his connection with his brothers in the faith [*Glaubensbrüder*] and his own religious particularity [*Besonderheit*],[41]

namely, the study of the Hebrew language, which binds Jews of all nations together. So Freud's regret can be traced to his teacher's unrealized ideals. A practical expression of this emotional connection is found in the fact that Freud refused to accept any royalties whatsoever whenever any of his works were translated into Hebrew or Yiddish and published or printed.[42]

Freud's respect for intellectual life and its *Wissenschaften* may also be related to his Jewishness. On 1 April 1925, inauguration ceremonies were led by Lord Balfour for the Hebrew University in Jerusalem. Freud himself was elected to the board of trustees for the university in 1925 and 1926, but because of ill health he was unable to attend these opening ceremonies. Instead he wrote a letter, dated 27 March 1925, to the Chief Rabbi of Vienna, Dr. Zvi Hirsch Chajes, for the occasion:

> Historians have told us that our small nation withstood the destruction of its independence as a State only because it began to transfer in its estimation of values the highest rank to its spiritual possessions [*geistigen Guter*], to its religion and its literature.
>
> We are now living in a time when this people has a prospect of again winning the land of its fathers with the help of a power that dominates the world [i.e., Britain], and it celebrates the occasion by the foundation of a University in its ancient capital city.
>
> A University is a place in which knowledge [*Wissenschaft*] is taught above all differences of religions and nations, where investigation is carried on, which is to show mankind how far they understand the world around them and how far they can control it.

> Such an undertaking is a noble witness to the development to which our people has forced its way in two thousand years of grievous fortune [*schwerer Schicksale*].
>
> I find it painful that my ill-health prevents me from experiencing in person the opening festivities of the Jewish University in Jerusalem.[43]

This extraordinary document deserves several comments. First, it is clear how moved Freud is by this event, and one can imagine that the pain of which he speaks at not being able to be present himself was indeed heartfelt. "Religions" may not claim Freud's emotional allegiance, but the "spiritual" (*geistig*) strivings of his people do. The man to whom this letter was addressed, Chief Rabbi Zvi Hirsch Chajes, was a liberal biblical scholar born in Brody, Galicia (Freud's mother's birthplace), and educated in part at the University of Vienna. He was an ardent Zionist and outspoken supporter of Herzl from his youth, and during nine years of office of Vienna (1918–27), he was "the undisputed spiritual leader of Austrian Jewry,"[44] recognized for his "love of truth" and his "pride at being a Jew."[45] Like Freud an honorary member of the Hebrew University's board of trustees, Chajes was a natural choice to receive Freud's letter.

Freud's opening words here in 1925 recall of course the Nathan letter of 1882 written to his fiancee. What was private in the early period becomes public in the late period. In 1882, Freud scoffed at the ritual fast of *Tisha B'Av*, not only because the date of its observance was based on a "historical miscalculation," but also because

> the historians say that if Jerusalem had not been destroyed, we Jews would have perished like so many peoples before and after us. Only after the collapse of the visible Temple, did the invisible edifice of Judaism become possible.

The "invisible edifice" from the Nathan letter in 1882 appears in 1925 as the Jewish people's "spiritual possessions, its religion and its literature." At the end of his life Freud will clarify these "spiritual goods" even further, identifying them specifically as "ideas."[46] Jewish survival is made possible only by its devotion to ideas, and the university, as a place dedicated to the teaching of *Wissenschaft* independently of religious or national differences (in sharp contrast to Freud's experience at the University of Vienna), is an institution that therefore supports Jewish survival and expresses its lifeblood. Two years later, in 1927, Freud will characterize religious ideas as an illusion, opposed to science; here religion is part of what made Jewish survival and development possible throughout two thousand years of "grievous destiny," and Freud is proud of that. The fact that this founding is taking place in his people's "ancient capital city," Jerusalem, is no small part of Freud's pride, stirred on by the fighting prospect of again winning its *"väterlichen Boden"* with Britain's help.

Lord Balfour, speaking on this occasion, referred to Freud as one of three Jews who, along with Einstein and Bergson, had had the greatest beneficial influence on modern thought. Eight months later, in December, Freud wrote to his nephew in England, Samuel, with bemused pride: "I am considered a celebrity. . . . The Jews all over the world boast of my name, pairing me with Einstein."[47] Freud acknowledged his thanks for the "honorable reference" by having Jones send Lord Balfour an offprint of his *Selbstdarstellung,* not insignificantly, considering the proud affirmation of his Jewishness that it contains. He also donated a signed copy to the Hebrew University Library.[48]

Karl Abraham, Freud's Jewish friend and psychoanalytic collaborator, died on 25 December 1925, apparently of an undiagnosed lung cancer.[49] The next issue of the 1926 *Internationale Zeitschrift für Psychoanalyse* was to have been a special issue commemorating Freud's seventieth birthday. But Freud, Jones tells us, instructed its editor to postpone the issue and to devote it "to the memorial notices of Abraham which Rado had wished to publish at the end of the year." As Freud said at the time, "One cannot celebrate any festival until one has performed the duty of mourning."[50] Freud's sentiment here is conditioned by Jewish law and custom, which rules that when one enters a state of mourning for a deceased blood relative (e.g., a brother), one cannot participate in any joyous festivity, particularly for the first seven days. Freud's response indicates how close he felt to Abraham: he was like a member of his family.

Statements and Letters from 1926

In 1926 Freud made a number of revealing statements about the nature of his Jewish identity and its allegiances, an act perhaps particularly appropriate for this Jew in his seventieth (7 x 10) year. Freud had achieved a kind of Jewish wholeness and could look back and observe some definitions. One aspect of that definition was his "sympathy" for Zionism, even if, he told Friedrich Thieberger, he could make "no judgement on it, on its chances of success and of the possible dangers facing it."[51] Yet he wrote in February 1926 to Enrico Morselli that he was able to read

Morselli's pamphlet on "the Zionist question" "wholly without mixed feelings, with unqualified approval." Freud is pleased at Morselli's sympathetic, humane [*Menschenfreundlichkeit*], and understanding discussion of an issue so often "distorted by human passions." In fact, he feels obligated to send him his "personal thanks for it." Though Freud does not become actively involved in the Zionist movement, nevertheless his positive emotional response must be noted, for it is a deep part of his Jewishness. Freud's public statements on the Zionist question will be less enthusiastic, as we shall see, but that may be accounted for by his political strategy for the advancement of psychoanalysis.

Freud's letter to Morselli, an Italian psychiatrist and anthropologist who wrote the first Italian textbook on psychoanalysis (which he had just sent to Freud), continues with Freud's customary complex of ethnic pledges of allegiance and religious denials:

> I do not know whether your judgement, which recognizes in psychoanalysis a direct product of the Jewish spirit [*Geist*] is correct, but if it were so I would not feel ashamed. Although I have been estranged from the religion of my forebears for a long time, I have never given up the feeling of solidarity with my people and realize with satisfaction that you call yourself a pupil of one of my clansmen—the great Lombroso.[52]

In contrast to those who would derive psychoanalysis from the Jewish "mind" in order to disparage and dismiss it, Freud is proud of the root—if it be there in fact. Yet since any statement of Jewish allegiance unavoidably raises the question of Jewish religion, Freud repeats his atheism, while returning immediately to his never-renounced feeling of belonging together with his people, whose "tribal" nature he acknowledges. Cesare Lombroso (1835–1909) was an Italian physician and criminologist who had an interest in Zionism and was a friend of Max Nordau. Freud feels a sense of "satisfaction" at finding psychoanalysis being promoted in Italy by a pupil of a "tribesman," and he would have liked to visit Morselli—had he been able to travel.

Freud feels this sense of satisfaction because of his Jewish and humanistic experience in the Vienna B'nai B'rith. Insofar as Freud regards psychoanalysis as a humanistic science, he regards its dissemination as a victory for *Humanität.* Klein notes that the Vienna B'nai B'rith interpreted their Jewish mission in terms of *Humanität:*

> We in Austria have not called ourselves *Humanitätsvereine* for nothing: we are the champions of the ideal of humanity.[53]

Thus when Freud finds that psychoanalysis is succeeding on the strength of the Jewish "tribal" connection, he can feel a sense of satisfaction at the fulfillment of Jewish ideals.

Freud's effort to insulate the scientific status of psychoanalysis from the irrationality of tribal affiliation, while at the same time taking pride in its Jewish origins, also comes to the fore in connection with his interest in telepathy and the occult. On 7 March 1926, Freud writes to Jones about the latter's distress over Freud's paper, "Dreams and Telepathy," saying,

> If someone should reproach you with my Fall into Sin, you are free to reply that my adherence to telepathy is my private affair, like my Jewishness, my passion for smoking and other things, and the theme of telepathy—inessential [*wesensfremd*] for psychoanalysis.[54]

The elements of this group—Jewishness, smoking, and telepathy—are not unrelated in Freud's mind, since all three relate to the irrational side of Freud's personality. All three also seem connected with his father. Freud reveals in a letter to Fliess written in 1929[55] that his model for cigar smoking was his father, who remained a heavy smoker until the age of eighty-one.[56] On 7 May 1930 Freud complains to Ferenczi that the "autotomy" ("self-amputation") of tobacco and cigar abstinence leaves him "feeling noticeably depersonalized,"[57] indicating how deeply smoking carries the identification with his father. It generates Freud's sense of personhood. So we can understand too why smoking and working are inextricably linked in his life.[58]

With regard to telepathy, we recall that in a letter to Jung in 1909,[59] Freud described his numerology superstitions as "Jewish mysticism." And as we have seen, Freud equated "mysticism" with "occultism."[60] Freud's obsession with numbers was connected with Jewish folk superstitions that link him to his father and his Eastern European background,[61] and so suggests a paternal link between Freud's Jewishness and his interest in parapsychological phenomena. Jewishness itself will become "para"-psychological for Freud in becoming phylogenetic in *Moses and Monotheism*.

This link between his Jewishness and irrationality might explain Freud's tendency to emphasize his atheism (i.e., his commitment to rationality) whenever he expressed his irrational feeling of solidarity with the Jewish people. Once in a late-night conversation with Jones before the first World War, Freud allowed for the possibility that the existence of mental processes independent of any organic bodily functions—whose reality he was not prepared to deny on this occasion at least—could lead to a belief even in *der liebe Gott.* [62] Though Freud may have gone this far to shock or tease Jones, still it seems to be evidence of an underlying tendency towards a belief in manifestations of the irrational "beyond" the merely psychological.[63] This leads Rainey to wonder whether Freud's agnosticism is not in fact in part a reaction-formation against an undesired propensity for belief.[64] If so, then Freud's interest in religion leads him quite naturally to a consideration of his own "non-religious" Jewishness as a manifestation of a "para-rational" solidarity. We recall his remark to Putnam that his motivation in writing *Totem and Taboo* was to explore his own lack of religious belief. Twenty years later this beginning will lead him to explore the irrational nature of his own Jewishness.

As Freud's seventieth birthday approached, his B'nai B'rith lodge published a commemorative issue of their periodical,[65] whose articles friendly to psychoanalysis Freud pronounced harmless.[66] We would expect this strengthening of the Jewish bond to produce a negative statement about religion from Freud, and indeed he continues his letter to Marie Bonaparte by saying, "I regard myself as one of the most dangerous enemies of religion, but they don't seem to have any suspicion of that."[67] But Freud does not see the B'nai B'rith as a "religious" society, for he tells Friedrich Thieberger in January of this year, "Our lodge is based on national foundations and pursues mainly ethical aims."[68]

Note that a Jewish foundation is a national one in Freud's mind. In his address to B'nai B'rith in May 1926, Freud makes this national dimension as clear publicly in the late period as he did privately in the early period, forty years earlier, in his letter to Martha in 1886. As he tells George Viereck in an interview in June 1926,

> My language is German. My culture, my attachments are German. I considered myself German intellectually, until I noticed the growth of anti-Semitic prejudice in Germany and German Austria. Since that time, I consider myself no longer German. I prefer to call myself a Jew.[69]

As mentioned, the pride Freud expresses in being Jewish may be related to the humanitarian ideals of the B'nai B'rith, which sought to be "a single nation of brothers" committed to "the active support of the ideals of humanity which our prophets laid down but which have been ignored by European mankind."[70] Note again that Freud's self-conscious Jewish identity emerges in response to antisemitism.

Antisemitism was in fact a crucial factor in the formation of the B'nai B'rith in Vienna. "Without antisemitism," William Knoepfmacher claimed, "we would never have formed this union in the first place."[71] Freud himself will reportedly tell Joseph Wortis that he believes that as long as there is an antisemitic movement, Jews must "band together" to fight it.[72] When in 1935 Freud writes of his joining the lodge, he says,

> I soon became one of you, enjoyed your sympathy, and almost never neglected to go to the place, surrounded by extreme hostility, where I was certain to find friends.[73]

So one reason for Freud's seeking out Jewish friends was that "he sought refuge from anti-Semitic ostracism."[74] In fact, as noted, Freud's joining the lodge on 29 September 1897 was at "the first possible moment after he recognized the pervasiveness of anti-Semitism in Viennese politics and academic life."[75]

The 1926 Address to B'nai B'rith. But Freud's association with the B'nai B'rith went beyond consolation; it also helped him define his own Jewishness. And when in May 1926, in addition to the commemorative issue of their periodical, the B'nai B'rith lodge organized a celebration in honor of Freud's seventieth birthday, Freud wrote an address, which his brother Alexander (also a member of the lodge) delivered for him, entitled "On Being of the Sons of the Covenant" (i.e., B'nai B'rith).[76]

As Klein shows, Freud's address must be read in the context of the one that preceded it, namely, that given by his friend and former physician, Ludwig Braun, for Freud had read Braun's address two days before the celebration,[77] and it clearly influenced his own remarks.

Braun attempted to define Freud's Jewish identity. He asked, "Can anyone even imagine Freud as not Jewish?" Braun went on to define Freud's Jewishness as typical and paradigmatic in three respects. First, Freud's spirit of moral and religious independence kept him apart from the world, as was characteristic of the Jew. The idea of the moral role of the Jew as the conscience of society, awake at the periphery, is also expressed. It is clearly a proud position, and seems rooted in the Biblical idea of being a "light unto the nations." Secondly, Freud had a courageous determination to oppose the rest of society, "his enemy." This determination involved a steadfast persistence (remember Freud's "tenacity"), dignity, and composure, as well as a spiritual optimism rooted in the Jewish will to survive. The third Jewish characteristic was "wholeness" (*das Ganze*), which constituted in Braun's mind the essence of the Jew "precisely." "The *Ganzejude* was able to discern, behind the fragmented and discordant surface, the unity and indivisibility of nature." This enabled the Jew in Freud to see all men equally, to recognize that "the mind and soul of every person has the same organization." Again the particular gave Freud a universal insight. Furthermore, Freud's refusal to "devote himself to Zionism, to religious piety, or to any other partial expression of Judaism," and instead to commit himself to the whole of humanity, was an expression of this essential Jewish characteristic, and it explained why "Freud feels at home here," namely, because of the humanitarian ideals of B'nai B'rith.

Though he will express certain reservations to friends later, in his address Freud does not dismiss or even qualify Braun's words. In fact, he admits to Marie Bonaparte that the speech "cast a spell over" (*bezaubern*) even his own family, implying a tacit Jewish self-recognition that accounts for his family's response. Freud in his address seeks only "to add something to what has been said by one who is both my friend and the physician who cares for me." Freud describes his loneliness and isolation after his initial psychoanalytic discoveries and publications: "I felt as though I were despised and shunned." He sought "a circle of chosen men of high character" who would befriend him. "That you were Jews," Freud tells them, "could only be desirable to me; for I was myself a Jew, and it always seemed to me not only unworthy but positively senseless [*unsinnig*] to deny it." The denial of his Jewishness is unreasonable or absurd, the severance of meaning.

Yet once admitting his bond to Jewry, Freud must define it more precisely over against other passions:

> What bound me to Jewry was—I am duty-bound [*schuldig*] to admit it—not the faith, nor the national pride, for I have always been an unbeliever, and was brought up without religion, though not without respect for what are called the "ethical" demands of human civilization. Whenever I felt an inclination towards national exaltation, I tried hard to suppress it as being harmful and unjust, frightened by the warning example of the peoples among whom we Jews live.

Freud says he feels "obligated"[78] to be honest about his true attachments, lest his brothers credit him with a piety or a kind of loyalty he cannot in good conscience profess. Yet based on the facts of Freud's life, his words are exaggerated in places. For example, he was not brought up "without religion." As we have seen, Freud's instruction in Judaism was "clearly 'religious' in the sense that it sought to strengthen his faith in God and to interpret the ethics and the ritual practices of Judaism; it was not a dispassionate analysis in the spirit of *Religionswissenschaft*."[79] So Rainey suggests that Freud is describing here his response to parts of this kind of instruction. For even though he rejected its "religious" aspects, nevertheless, his curriculum's heavy emphasis on the ethical teachings of the prophets and on "the moral laws" of the Bible made a lasting impression on him.[80] We recall Freud's eulogy for Hammerschlag, in which he wrote that "religious instruction seemed to him a way of educating towards *Humanität*." In Freud's childhood home, "religion" was present in the observance of Jewish festivals, but it is clear that such observance did not include a belief in God, at least for the young Freud, who was openly critical in his letters to friends. And his astonished belief in his mother's "proof" that we are made of clay gave way to a stoic belief in Nature's *Ananke*, and to atheism.[81] So he seems to describe this upbringing through the lenses of his own unbelief, perhaps a kind of wish-fulfillment.

Freud's denial that national pride bound him to Jewry must also be qualified—as he perhaps does in his own way—by the evidence from his letters that show a great deal of national pride, and even (as we shall see again) a sense of Jewish superiority. Freud's rational mind tells him that this feeling is harmful and unfair, but he admits that he feels it: *Ein nationales Hochgefühl habe ich*. His "sympathy" for Zionism also suggests that national feeling is part of what binds him to Jewry, but here in a public forum Freud the Jewish humanist tries to strike a balance. We recall the feeling of personal gratitude Freud expressed in response to Morselli's presentation of Zionism with such *Menschenfreundlichkeit*. Freud will say in his next paragraph that he took his share in B'nai B'rith's "humanitarian and national interests." Freud's national interests, like those of the lodge whose ideals he shares, are mingled with his humanitarian interests. Actually, as Klein shows, the former are an expression of the latter. This interdependence is also expressed in the last phrase quoted. Though proud to be a Jew, Freud wants to learn from "the peoples among whom we Jews live," and so be a better Jew. As the tradition in *Midrash Rabbah* says, "If you hear that there is wisdom among the Gentiles, believe it."[82]

But Freud goes on in his address to define *psychologically* what binds him to his people, what makes "the attraction of Jewry and of Jews irresistible." He speaks of "many dark emotional forces, all the more powerful the less they could be expressed in words." Freud feels powerfully drawn to his fellow Jews by deep emotions (*Gemachtfühlen*). But in addition, he has

> a clear consciousness of an inner identity, the intimate familiarity [*Heimlichkeit*] of the same psychological structure [*der gleichen seelischen Konstruction*].

In Freud's mind, Jews have the same inner psychic structure, or "soul-construction." They are psychologically "built" in the same way. As a result, they share a feeling of a common "home." Exactly what this structure of the Jewish psyche or soul consists of, Freud does not say, but the concept clearly underlies his project in *Moses and Monotheism* to say "how the Jew has come to acquire the character he has," the definition of the Psychological Jew.

As mentioned in chapter 2, Simon has suggested that Freud's theory of Jewish wit in his *Wit and Its Relation to the Unconscious* (1905) presents a "theory of the Jewish soul" in miniature. The rather conventional portrait there included sharp self-criticism, a democratic mode of thought, an emphasis on social justice rooted in Jewish religious tradition, revolt against the oppressiveness of religion itself, a consciousness of the experience of poverty, and an all-pervading skepticism.[83] As discussed above in connection with the early period, these conventional Jewish characteristics certainly reflect Freud's own personality, and this is why he uses Jewish wit so often in situations related to his Jewish identity. Jewish jokes are a means by which Freud feels and thus confirms his Jewishness. In the early period this implicit understanding was enough to convey a sense of coherence, or at least attachment. But in the late period, in 1934–38, Freud's need for a deeper understanding of his Jewish psychic constitution (and for a deeper attachment to the tradition of his father) will drive him to write *Moses and Monotheism,* a work that will help him understand why he feels so "mingled" or bound up together with other Jews. In 1926, he can only say that something is there.

Freud continues his address, saying that it was to his "Jewish nature alone" that he owed two character traits that had helped him in his struggles with life:

> Because I was a Jew I found myself free of many prejudices which restricted others [i.e., Gentiles] in the use of their intellect; and as a Jew I was prepared to join the Opposition and renounce [or "relinquish"—*verzichten*] agreement with the "compact majority."[84]

Freud attributes to his Jewish "nature" his independence of thought and his courageous capacity to oppose social convention and relinquish solidarity with the majority. In the context of an address to the B'nai B'rith, Freud seems to be talking about prejudices and agreement within Gentile society, though the same qualities will enable him to analyze Jewish history and reach conclusions that will require him to relinquish agreement with the majority of his fellow Jews. Thus *Moses and Monothe-*

ism, in its very independence of and challenge to accepted conventions, may be a quintessential expression of Freud's Jewish identity.

Freud's closing reference to Ibsen's *An Enemy of the People*, mentioned above in connection with Freud's use of it in his *Selbstdarstellung*, is also significant. The play's central character, Dr. Stockman, struggles throughout the story to enlighten the people of his town about a danger that threatens their livelihood, but whose solution threatens those in power with loss and so arouses their oppressive opposition. By telling them the truth Stockman struggles to free the townspeople from their self-serving masters, who want to keep them in ignorance of the facts. The parallel with Freud's view of himself teaching the disagreeable "facts" of psychoanalysis is patent. The play closes with Dr. Stockman's discovery that the strongest man in the world is he who stands alone. ("Father!" his daughter responds in breathless admiration at this discovery, her "eyes full of faith," as the play ends.) As Freud will say, no one is more familiar with that solitary position than the Jew, and it has made him strong indeed. Freud is proud to be a Jew, and his reference reveals it. He will stand alone again at the end of his life in asserting the Egyptian origins of a Moses who was himself the disciple of "the first individual in history,"[85] Akhnaton, who stood alone in *his* struggle to proclaim the truth. So Freud attaches himself to a long tradition of ideological opposition in the name of the truth. That Freud finds non-Jews at both the beginning and the end of this chain (Akhnaton and Ibsen), with Jews as the links in between, is not surprising given his hopes for humanistic culture and the instrumental role of Jews in "preparing the ground." *Moses and Monotheism* is Freud's last attempt to contribute to that cultural whole, and he will do so in what may be for *him* a characteristically Jewish way, namely, as a solitary individual.

A word might be said too about Freud's word *Heimlichkeit* as it applies to his Jewishness. Literally, it means "home-ness," and through the private nature of the home, it has come to mean secret or hidden, a reality shared only by those who live in the same home together. The word points to the family-like intimacy that Jews experience among themselves, a closeness that "the same psychic constitution" would produce. *Heimlichkeit*, as something both familiar and congenial (like the home) and yet concealed and secret (as Freud describes it himself in his essay, "Das Unheimlich," "The Uncanny"),[86] is a fitting word for Freud to use to characterize his Jewishness, for not only is he aware of its private nature, but he also has felt a need to keep it private. As we have shown, in the middle period Freud sought to keep the Jewishness of the psychoanalytic movement hidden behind Jung's "Gentile facade," and he bid his Jewish followers to suppress themselves to the advantage of Gentiles. We remember too Freud's comment about George Eliot's *Daniel Deronda* that it contained things that "we speak of only among ourselves."[87] Freud's sense of Jewishness is familial in nature, *heimlich*.

David Bakan has an epilogue to his speculative book on Freud and the Jewish mystical tradition,[88] in which he notes that Freud associates *Heimlichkeit* with the experience of the uncanny, *Unheimlichkeit*, to such an extent that Freud says *unheimlich* is in some way or other a subspecies of *heimlich*.[89] Bakan then goes on to show that Freud associated *Unheimlichkeit* with the sense of impending death. Now if *Heimlichkeit* is associated with being Jewish, and *Unheimlichkeit* with death, and the two ideas are related, then, Bakan reasons, "Freud's Jewish feeling is related to his sense of impending death."[90]

Bakan's conclusion supports my thesis that Freud's concern with and public statements about his Jewishness in the late period are related to his awareness of his approaching death. In characterizing his Jewishness by the "home-feeling" of *Heimlichkeit*, Bakan argues, Freud is reflecting a natural and common association in the Jewish experience. Furthermore, "with his sense of impending death Freud is then *returning home*," and since Freud gives this address to B'nai B'rith, Bakan concludes that Freud is in fact "returning to membership in the body of Israel."[91] This movement of return corresponds to my thesis about the periodicity of Freud's Jewish identity, namely, that having spent the middle period with his Jewishness in the background (and that didn't work out well), in the late period Freud brings it to the foreground, an interest that culminates in *Moses and Monotheism*. That book, as Emanuel Rice also argues, is Freud's return. Its seemingly ambivalent form is in part a reflection of Freud's dual allegiance as a modern Jew, and it is for this reason all the more interesting to us.

Four days after the B'nai B'rith celebration, Freud writes to Marie Bonaparte,

> The Jewish societies in Vienna and the University in Jerusalem (of which I am a trustee), in short the Jews altogether have celebrated me like national hero, although my service to the Jewish cause is confined to the single point that I have never denied my Jewishness.[92]

In other words, by openly affirming his Jewish origin, Freud allowed psychoanalysis to be an advocate for the inclusion of Jews in the humanistic culture liberal Jews like him sought. This was Freud's idea of *die jüdische Sache*, namely, that the Emancipation should reach its full horizon, a "glorious time" of freedom and unity, as envisioned by many in

Freud's B'nai B'rith lodge.[93] If Freud is Jewish, then people (especially Jews) can point to the valuable contributions to civilization that Jews are capable of, and Freud has served "the Jewish cause." The proud way in which many Jews today point to men like Freud, Einstein and Marx for their role in the construction of modernity seems a confirmation of Freud's view.

Freud can write similarly later in the same month to Arthur Schnitzler,

> Jews of all types and from many different places have adopted me with enthusiasm, as though I were a famous God-fearing Rabbi. I am not opposed to this, since I have left no doubt about my attitude towards religious faith; Jewishness is still very important to me emotionally.[94]

As long as the Jews accept Freud on his own non-religious terms, he does not mind being their "Rabbi"; he even seems pleased. As he says, "Das Judentum bedeutet mir noch sehr viel affectiv." Why? Though the word *Judentum* can mean "Judaism," as well as the collective, "Jewry," Freud makes his meaning clear. He feels emotionally connected to his people, not to his people's religion or its doctrine. "Affectively," they are still an extension of his family. *Judentum* is still important to Freud because it is a primary link to his roots, his parents and family, and in the years leading up to his death, he seems to connect himself to his past—as Bakan says, "returning home"—rather than sever himself from it (*contra* Marthe Robert). Furthermore, the Jews' attachment to him will prompt interest in psychoanalysis among the Jewish people, and so the psychoanalytic "cause" and the "Jewish cause" can unite in celebrating Freud's seventieth birthday.

Letters in 1927

Given Freud's strong affirmation of his Jewishness in 1926, perhaps it is no wonder that in 1927 he publishes his most sustained attack on religious belief, *The Future of an Illusion*. He is glad he has no religion, Freud tells Pfister in April 1926, lest he be divided in his allegiance.[95] It may be that Freud is in fact tempted unconsciously toward a belief in the supernatural, but publically he insists on his atheism (proudly, because he believes it is the truth). As he will tell Pfister in 1929, the essence of the religious *Weltanschauung* is "the pious illusion of providence and a moral world order, which reason contradicts."[96] Having been adopted like *ein gottesfürchtiger grosser Rabbi,* Freud may feel the need to clarify again his attitude to religious faith. On 16 October 1927 he writes to Pfister of the imminent publication of a "pamphlet" "which has a great deal to do with you" and whose subject matter is "my completely negative attitude to religion, in any form, and however attenuated." He hopes that his friend will nevertheless be able to have some tolerance and understanding for "the unholy heretic." Freud has told Romain Rolland in 1923 that he is a "destroyer of illusions" and that he has "spent a great part" of his life destroying his "own illusions and those of mankind."[97] Yet he writes Pfister six days after his letter cited above, "We know that by different routes we aspire to the same objectives for poor humanity."[98] Freud seeks to serve humanity, but he does so on his own terms, as an "infidel Jew."[99] Yet he can recognize his own goals in the Christian Pfarrer, for his humanism transcends this difference.

Georg Brandes

A respect for the Jewish Bible continues to be a part of Freud's identity, in spite of his atheism. On 4 March 1927, Freud writes to his niece, Margit Freud, a journalist in Copenhagen, about the death of the Jewish-Danish literary critic and writer, Georg Brandes. Saying that he too had been hurt by Brandes's death, Freud recalled one of their conversations "as he lay in the hotel room in Vienna":

> When he modestly tried to take second place behind the "scientist" [*Forscher,* i.e., Freud himself], I pointed out to him his position among the descendants of our prophets.

The "prophets" still take precedence over the "scientists" in Freud's mind.

But the fact that Freud will rank Brandes with the biblical prophets is indicative in itself of the cosmopolitan character of Freud's "prophetic line." Georg Brandes (1842–1927) was one of Denmark's greatest writers, and he had an enormous influence on European literature, opposing Romanticism and demanding that literature should stimulate discussion of modern problems. He wrote studies of major cultural personalities, such as Shakespeare, Goethe, Ibsen, Heine, Börne, and Michelangelo, and his essay on Nietzsche marked the starting point of the philosopher's world fame. Like many assimilated European Jews, he was ambivalent about his own Jewish identity, though he did not convert. He denounced the pogroms in Eastern Europe, but he repudiated his own Jewishness (he was born "Morris Cohen"), and he disliked "Jewish" characteristics in others. He defended Dreyfus, but did not take Herzl or Zionism seriously until after the Balfour Declaration, expressing this change in an article, "Das neue Judentum" (1918).[100] Thus Brandes was a European humanist who had only a tangential relationship to the Jewish tradition. It is significant that the Jewish figures whom he tried to understand were Heine and Börne (both of whom converted to Lutheranism), Disraeli (baptized at age thirteen), and Lassalle (who openly repudiated his Jewishness). Yet Freud gives Brandes a position "among the descendants of our prophets," clearly indicating a belief in the confluence of the Jewish prophetic tradition and that of European humanism. In this Freud is following the ideals of his instructors in Jewish religion in the *Gymnasium*.

The overlap with Freud's own literary and cultural interests is also clear, and Freud indicates the "unclouded respect" he had for Brandes by associating him with "great Jewish personalities" like Einstein and Popper-Lynkeus. The point with respect to Freud's Jewish identity is twofold. Despite his tremendous respect for science, at some level Freud's respect for the Jewish prophets outweighs that which he has for scientists. Secondly, despite a humanist's distance from Judaism, as far as Freud is concerned the Jew is still the proud descendent of biblical prophets. To Freud, he and Brandes share the same culture and the same roots. They are still "family."

YIVO

In 1925 the "Institute for Jewish Research" (*Yidisher Visenschaftlikher Institut,* YIVO) was founded in Vilna, dedicated to collecting and preserving Jewish and Yiddish culture, and to promoting scholarly research connected with it. Known also as the "Yiddish Scientific Institute," it sought to have Jews participate in scholarly research in their own language (i.e., in Yiddish) and to have the results of world scholarship made available to those Jews unfamiliar with languages other than Yiddish. The institute was guided by three principles:

> 1) the peoplehood of Jews all over the world; 2) the enrichment of the life of that people by means of Jewish scholarship; and 3) the application of the most modern methods of social science in the quest for a better understanding of Jewish identity and Jewish group phenomena.[101]

This agenda and these guiding principles make Freud's interest in and support of YIVO quite understandable, and significant for his Jewish self-understanding. On 29 December 1929, he wrote to the institute and offered his help:

> If you can still use my name in your World Presidium, avail yourselves of it. I wish you best success in your endeavor.
>
> Your devoted Freud[102]

Jacob Meitlis reports that Freud became "a member of the honorary praesidium [of YIVO] and showed great appreciation for its research work."[103] Freud may have hoped to have the results of psychoanalytic research made available to Yiddish-speaking Jews; or, he may simply have identified with the interests and goals of the institute. In any event, Freud's warm support and identification are clear, and they will reappear later.

Romain Rolland

The year 1930 begins Freud's last decade of life, and it is full of evidence of his Jewish identity, expressed both publically and privately. This flurry is not unexpected, for death confronts us with the question of our ultimate commitments, what we think it has meant to have lived. Jewish humanist, humanist Jew, Freud seeks in the last years of his life to state the truth about himself. The compromise-formation expresses his dual allegiance.

Freud's multifaceted sense of identity appears in a letter he wrote in 1930 to Romain Rolland, the French novelist, dramatist, essayist, and one of the great mystics of contemporary French literature. An exchange of ideas about religion and religious sensation began between them when Freud sent Rolland a copy of *Future of an Illusion* in November 1927 (the same month it was published). Rolland replied, saying that although Freud's analysis was "fair," he would have liked to have seen Freud deal with the real source of religion, namely, religious feeling or religious sensation, "the simple and direct fact of the *sensation of the 'eternal'* (. . . simply without perceptible limits, and in that way oceanic)."[104] Rolland documented and explored this mystical "sensation of the eternal" in a three-volume study of Hindu mysticism and its modern Indian personalities,[105] and he sent Freud a copy in January 1930, in response to Freud's analysis of Rolland's mystical feeling in *Civilization and Its Discontents*.

Freud replies on 19 January, thanking Rolland for the gift, and though aware that they are utterly different, he tells his friend that he will now try

> with your guidance to penetrate into the Indian jungle from which until now a certain blending of Hellenic love of measure (*sophrosune*), Jewish sobriety [*jüdische Nüchternheit*], and philistine uneasiness has kept me away.

This three-part self-description of the "limits" of Freud's "nature" reveals both his classical humanist training (and the expectation of cultivation that attends upon it) and his natural Jewish inheritance, a sober outlook on life. *Sophrosune*, Freud's Greek gloss on his *Massliebe*, refers to a "soundness of mind, prudence, discretion, moderation in sensual desires, self-control, temperance,"[106] which accords well with "sobriety." "*Nüchternheit*" literally means "emptiness," that is, empty of intoxicating drink, temperate, and so it implies a kind of clear-headedness, sobriety. Perhaps because Jews use wine almost exclusively in religious rituals, or perhaps because they could not afford the indulgence of getting drunk, Jews as a group have traditionally had a low incidence of alcohol abuse. They have been "typically" sober or temperate (or at least they have seen themselves that way). As Freud will reportedly tell Joseph Wortis in 1935, "The Jew does not drink."[107] Thus there is a certain convergence here between these "Hellenic" and "Jewish" traits in Freud that have, along with an uneasiness that Freud identifies as a function of cultural narrowness (*philiströse*), kept him from exploring Indian mysticism. This convergence again seems to reflect the Jewish-humanist mix of Freud's *Gymnasium* education. Freud's rationality and distrust of intuition have also made mysticism unattractive.

Yet we can also see in the very fact of his correspondence with Rolland (in spite of the standoff on the issue of religion),[108] the humanist, cosmopolitan dimension of Freud's identity. As Freud wrote, "Across all boundaries and bridges, I would like to press your hand."[109] David Fisher has pointed out that "for many men of Freud's generation, Rolland was the ideal 'European', the man who was committed uncompromisingly to internationalism, Franco-German reconciliation, and genuine cooperation among human beings."[110] For this reason Freud respects him and is willing to define himself in relation to Rolland's work on mysticism, even though it represents a form of spirituality so utterly different from his own self-conception. Freud sent Rolland a copy of the second edition (1931) of *Civilization and Its Discontents* with the dedication: "To His Great Oceanic Friend, The Land Animal."[111]

The month following his correspondence with Rolland, Freud received A. A. Roback's book, *Jewish Influence in Modern Thought* (1929), in which Roback honors Freud by including him, as Freud puts it, "among the greatest names of our people," such as Bergson and Einstein. Freud questions the justice of the comparison, especially since he feels Roback does not understand psychoanalysis. But what is interesting is Freud's last paragraph. Responding to Roback's characterization of him as "the *Chassid* in the history of modern psychology,"[112] Freud says,

> It will interest you to hear that my father actually did come from a Chassidic milieu.

But then, as if to cast doubt on Roback's interpretation of him, Freud continues,

> He was 41 years old when I was born and had been estranged from his home-town connections for almost 20 years.

Roback associates Freud's psychoanalytic hermeneutics with rabbinic techniques of biblical interpretation, such as *gematria, notarikon, At-Bash,* and *Ik-B'khar* (though he thinks the rabbis' interpretive acrobatics seem like "common sense" when compared with "the palpable absurdity of [psychoanalysts'] speculations"),[113] and he connects Freud's "humanitarian interest," "the catholicity of his views," "as well as the mystical halo" with "*Chassidism* in its philosophical and historical aspects."[114] Freud says, somewhat irritated, that he does not recognize himself in such characterizations ("no one has as yet reproached me with 'mystical leanings'"), and so we can well understand Freud's attempts to distance himself from his Jewish background. He continues,

> I had such an un-Jewish upbringing that today I am not even able to read your dedication which is evidently Hebrew characters [*jüdischer Schrift*]. In later years I have often regretted this gap in my education [*Unbildung*].

Roback himself notes Freud's surprising statement about his Jewish education ("he did have a Hebrew tutor in his childhood"). "Evidently" (*offenbar*) also seems a little forced. Admittedly, Freud will refer often in these years to his inability to read "our sacred old and now renewed tongue,"[115] but here he seems to be trying to imply that Roback's thesis of an influence of the Jewish mystical tradition and rabbinic hermeneutics is unlikely, given his father's estrangement and his own un-Jewish upbringing. Roback's claim is too close to home, as Freud will admit in a later letter trying to explain why he found himself arguing with Roback over his interpretations.[116] Yet Freud closes with a sympathetic note of admiration for his fellow Jew:

> With the expression of that sympathy which your valiant championing of our people calls forth.
>
> Yours in deep respect, Freud[117]

It is clear that Roback (who was active in YIVO) touched a chord in Freud, as he says explicitly on 24 March 1930, puzzled at himself for having been drawn into argument over psychoanalysis with Roback: "You have struck the Jewish chord, which reverberates so sensitively in me [*bei mir so empfindlich nachklingt*]. My sympathies were aroused."[118] Roback argues that psychoanalysis is "a Jewish production," and that Freud "was merely giving expression to the *hankering after purpose* [emphasis his], which has characterized the Jewish race from the days of the Prophets."[119] We remember Freud telling Enrico Morselli (in February 1926) that he would not be ashamed if psychoanalysis were indeed a product of the Jewish *Geist*, so we can understand why Freud's *Sympathie* was aroused by Roback's words, even if he quibbled at the "reproach" of "mystical leanings."

Freud is sorry, however, to find "a discrepancy between the high position you wish to grant me and your knowledge of my person and your understanding of my work."[120] Though Roback says he would be pleased to know that Freud spoke, read, or at least understood Yiddish—he says, "I think the nation cannot exist without its separate language"[121]—Freud closes his letter saying, "I have never learned or spoken Yiddish." This is a bit curt given Roback's reason for asking (he also says "the treasures of our fine literature are worth preserving"), and so Freud's words may indicate some pain at being cut off from his people through his Yiddish illiteracy. He will admit his regret explicitly in 1936 (see below).

We should note too in this letter another Jewish character trait that Freud identifies: "Jewish '*Chuzba*'." Roback suggests that this Jewish expression, whose meaning ranges from audacity and self-confidence to impudence, is best translated by "nerve."[122] The trait can be related to a willingness to act independently of social conventions in pursuit of one's goal. Freud himself would have certainly needed his share of *chutzpah* to have launched psychoanalysis.

Freud and Zionism

In February 1930, Freud writes nearly identical letters to both Albert Einstein and Dr. Chaim Koffler about his mixed attitude toward Zionism. In 1929 there were Arab riots in Palestine, in which 133 Jews were killed and 339 wounded by Arab gangs, 110 Arabs killed and 232 wounded in the repression of the attacks by the police and 6 Arabs killed by Jews in a counterattack.[123] The events were related to British irritation at the inherent contradictions in the Balfour Declaration (support for a Jewish homeland; support for non-Jewish, chiefly Arab rights and sensibilities)[124] and the cooling of support for Zionism with the return of the Laborites under Ramsey MacDonald to office in Britain.[125] The commission appointed to investigate the Arab massacre of the Jews was inclined to halt or limit immigration in order to mollify the Arabs. In an effort to elicit criticism of British policy and create favorable public opinion in Western Europe and America, the Jewish Agency sent appeals to prominent European figures, seeking to safeguard both Jewish religious rights of access to the Western Wall and immigration quotas to meet the needs of Eastern and Central European Jewry. The public nature this response was to take may have conditioned Freud's reaction. He wrote to Koffler on 26 February 1930:

> I cannot do what you wish. I am unable to overcome my aversion to burdening the public with my name and even the present critical time does not seem to me to warrant it. Whoever wants to influence the masses must give them something rousing and inflammatory and my sober judgement of Zionism does not permit this. I certainly sympathize with its goals, am proud of our University in Jerusalem and am delighted with our settlements' prosperity. But on the other hand, I do not think that Palestine could ever become a Jewish state, nor that the Christian and Islamic worlds would ever be prepared to have their holy places under Jewish care. It would have seemed more sensible to me to establish a Jewish homeland on a less historically burdened land. But I know that such a rational viewpoint would never have gained the enthusiasm of the masses and the financial support of the wealthy. I concede with sorrow that the baseless fanaticism of our people is in part to be blamed for the awakening of Arab distrust. I can raise no sympathy at all for the misdirected piety which transforms a piece of an Herodian wall into a national relic, thus offending the feelings of the natives. Now judge for yourself whether I, with such a critical point of view, am the right person to come forward as the solace of a people deluded by unjustified hope.
>
> Your obedient servant, Freud[126]

Given the situation in Palestine, Freud's response seems rather restrained. Nonetheless, this combination of sentiments is typical of the Jewish Freud we have come to know, especially when speaking for publication. His sober and somewhat overly rational, pessimistic assessment of the situation will not allow him too much enthusiasm, in spite of all his "sympathy" and pride. He prefers a "rational" solution, even though he is aware that it is unrealistic. He is explicitly proud of "our" university, where rational solutions are found for problems. And though "our" settlements give him pleasure, he rejects Jewish religious "fanaticism," mocking its " misdirected piety" with his historical positivism, much as he mocked *Tisha B'Av* in the Nathan letter of the early period.

The "Herodian wall" is of course a symbol of Jewish sovereign independence and freedom of worship, evidence of *Jewish* native presence, and it is for the possibility of recovering those that the Jews would challenge the Arab "natives," so perhaps their "fanaticism" was not baseless. Furthermore, Orthodox Jews about to pray on the eve of Yom Kippur in September 1928 with a *mechitza* (ritual prayer divide; the innocent origin of the riots), as they had done many times in the past, was hardly intended to offend the Arabs. And their piety was no more misdirected than the Muslim hallowing of the same area as "al-Buraq," where the Prophet Muhammed is thought to have "tethered his miraculous horse, Buraq, after his flight from Mecca to Jerusalem, and before his ascent to Heaven."[127] Rather, the wall represents a joining of the national and the religious horizons of Jewish identity.

Ernst Simon, in commenting on Freud's letter, notes "a certain blindness to the power of symbols characteristic of many intellectuals," but on the other hand he suggests that perhaps Freud implicitly recognized this power and is apprehensive of its being exploited for political purposes.[128] Yerushalmi points out that Freud's positions were shared by many Jews, even Zionists, who doubted the feasibility of a Jewish state in Palestine.[129] It is fair to say that Freud is characteristically a little shortsighted when it comes to Jewish religion. Still, even when he is judging the Jews and their aspirations, he does so on what are for him Jewish terms, that is, soberly, without illusions.

And Freud remains attached to Zionism. He will write to his Hebrew translator in Jerusalem, Yehuda Devosis, at the end of the same year, in December 1930, that "Zionism has awakened my strongest sympathies, which remain faithfully attached to it today."[130] Freud's reason for supporting Zionism is directly related to his concern about antisemitism; it is, he says, "something the present-day situation seems to justify." But he goes on to say, "I should like to be mistaken about this." Freud would prefer that there be no need for Zionism, in other words, that Jews be a part of a humanistic cultural whole as Jews, contributing their part, without the need to press their separate claims. As he will reportedly tell Wortis in January 1935, "Jew and Christian ought to meet on the common ground of irreligion and humanity," but "as long as Jews are not admitted into Gentile circles they have no choice but to band together."[131] So antisemitism is one reason for Freud's support of Zionism as an expression of his Jewishness.

Yet in June of this same year (1935), Freud writes to Leib Jaffe, president of the Keren HaYesod, the financial division of the World Zionist Organization in Jerusalem, to help celebrate the fifteenth anniversary of the founding of the agency dedicated to supporting Jewish immigration and colonization in Palestine in order to lay the foundations for a Jewish National Home. "I want to assure you," he writes,

> that I know how great and blessed an instrument this foundation has become in its endeavor to establish a new home in the ancient land of our fathers. It is a sign of our invincible will to survive which has, until now, successfully defied two thousand years of severe oppression! Our youth will continue the struggle.
>
> Your devoted Sigm. Freud[132]

So clearly Zionism also symbolized for Freud the positive Jewish will to survive and flourish (arguably a *non*rational drive for life). It is not only a rational defense against antisemitism. Freud's joining the Zionist youth group Kadimah in 1936 expressed his identification with this struggle by "our" Jewish youth (see below).

Freud and Hebrew

In the same letter to Devosis in which Freud discussed his attitude toward Zionism, he spoke of his father's Hebrew and his own lack of Jewish education, as well as the role of antisemitism in creating his Jewish self-awareness. Again Gay reports Freud's words:

> "My father spoke the sacred language as well as German or better. He let me grow up in complete ignorance of everything that concerned Judaism." It was only as a mature man, he added, that he had taken this neglect in bad part. "But I had already felt as a Jew earlier—under the impact of German antisemitism, whose more recent outbreak occurred during my university days."[133]

Perhaps Freud's age (seventy-four) and his anger at his father ("in bad part") interferes with his memory of his years of schooling with Hammerschlag, not to mention his father's reading the Bible with him.

Note that Freud calls Hebrew "the sacred language" (his German reflects the Hebrew terminology, *lashon ha-kodesh*). Perhaps without being fully aware, Freud is evoking and affirming an ancient Jewish tradition about the Hebrew language (particularly prominent in Kabbalah, but basic to rabbinic Judaism too), namely, that Hebrew is holy above all other human languages; it is the language spoken by the angels (Hag.

16a), even by God himself, the language with which the world was created. Freud spoke in the same terms in 1928 when writing to Devosis about his Hebrew translation of *Group Psychology and the Analysis of the Ego*. An unnamed relative "who is master of our sacred old and now renewed tongue" assured him that "the translation was really excellent."[134] In spite of Freud's ignorance, he is pleased at an "excellent" Hebrew translation of his work, whereas he was relatively indifferent about the English translations, even when his colleagues complained. The "sacred" language has a deep resonance for him, even though he insists again in 1929, "I adhere to the Jewish religion as little as to any other."[135] He is probably thinking of the conscious, rational adherence to religious doctrine and its ritual expression, but adherence is often irrational and unconscious in his case. Freud's ignorance of Hebrew contributes to his sense of "non-adherence," and the father's role as the child's teacher is traditionally important in this regard. The rabbis say that if a father does not speak to his child (i.e., teach him) in the Holy Tongue, "it is as though he had buried him."[136] So Freud's annoyance with his father's Jewish failure is understandable.

*Prefaces to Hebrew Translations.*In December of 1930, Freud wrote prefaces for Hebrew translations of *Totem and Taboo* and *Introductory Lectures to Psychoanalysis*. The former is moving and personal; the latter more distant and professional, perhaps because its subject matter is more general, whereas the *Totem* book "deals with the origin of religion and morality." Freud writes to Dvosis on 15 December 1930, "It is a source of extraordinary joy and satisfaction to me that some of my books are going to be published in Hebrew,"[137] so it is safe to assume that both prefaces will reward our attention.

Freud begins his preface to *Totem and Taboo* with a description of himself and his feelings:

> No reader of this book will be able so easily to place himself in the emotional position of the author, who does not understand the holy language, who is completely estranged from the religion of the fathers—as from every other religion—who cannot take part in nationalist ideals, and yet who has never denied belonging [*die Zugehörigkeit*] to his people, who feels his own nature to be Jewish and who does not wish it otherwise.

Though we grant Freud's ignorance of Hebrew and his atheism, what are we to think of his statement that he "an nationalistischen Idealen nicht teilnehmen kann," given Freud's repeated confessions of sympathy for Zionism, his participation in B'nai B'rith (which he says is "based on national foundations"),[138] as well as his wish at times to return to the Jews' "indestructible national feeling"? Perhaps Freud strikes this pose to differentiate himself from the "unrealistic fanaticism" of his fellow Jews living in Palestine who are making "a national religion" of Herod's wall and challenging the Arabs, as he wrote to Einstein and Chaim Koffler ten months earlier.[139] Perhaps Freud is speaking rhetorically to focus on why he is so moved in the absence of conventional allegiances, and to affirm his Jewishness on his own terms, using his published psychoanalytic work to establish a connection with his fellow Jews as they settle the ancient land.

For he continues by replying to an imagined skeptic's question (perhaps Freud's alter ego) about what is left to him that is Jewish if he has abandoned Jewish language, religion, and national ideals:

> He would reply, "Still very much, probably the most important thing" [*die Hauptsache*].

One wonders if this "most important thing" that Freud is thinking of is related to the "intimacy of a common psychic structure" that Freud spoke of in 1926. He admits that he cannot define the essence he is speaking of here more precisely, "but someday surely it will become accessible to scientific insight." *Moses and Monotheism* may be Freud's attempt to provide that access.

If *Totem and Taboo* is the beginning of this access, we can understand why Freud says that this translation put into the hands of readers of that "living tongue" is "an experience of quite a special kind." In spite of his Jewish illiteracy, irreligion, and "scientific" neutrality,[140] he has with this translation formed a bridge with his people across formidable boundaries, perhaps the most important thing to him. In so doing Freud hopes to make a contribution, through "unprejudiced science," "to the spirit of the new Jewry."[141] Given Freud's letter to his niece Margit in March 1927, in which he placed Georg Brandes among "our prophets," one wonders if Freud has in mind Brandes's essay expressing his reassessment of Zionism, "Das neue Judentum" (1918).

In contrast to *Totem and Taboo,* Freud's preface to the Hebrew translation of his *Vorlesungen* begins with a presentation of the historical background to the lectures and a sketch of the progress the "young science" has made since their initial delivery. Freud describes not himself, but his work. And when he mentions Hebrew, he describes it as "that ancient language [*jener uralten Sprach*] which has been awakened to a new life by the will of the Jewish people." Freud's language is more "intellectual," as it were, and distant, the voice of the humanist scientist, almost as if Freud were not himself a Jew. But lest there be any doubt, he refers to the likelihood that these Hebrew lectures would be unintelligible to "Moses and the prophets," and he explicitly numbers himself among their descendants [*Ihren Nachkommen*]. The indirect mode of Jewish self-reference recalls the middle period (when the lectures were originally delivered [1917–18]), and it is interesting that it occurs in association with Moses. In any event, Freud's humanism is more prominent in this preface than his Jewishness, as is evident from its close. Freud does not speak of "the new Jewry," but of the value these lectures in Hebrew have "for one who wants to understand the soul [*Seele*] and human life." Through his science of psychoanalysis, Freud seeks to link the Jewish people—the descendants of Moses and the prophets—with the larger life of all human beings. These two prefaces, written in the same month in 1930, vividly express Freud's dual allegiance and the role that Hebrew plays in disclosing it.

Freud, the Fanatical Jew

For the occasion of Freud's seventy-fifth birthday in 1931, the Chief Rabbi of Vienna, Rabbi David Feuchtwang, wrote to Freud, saying, "The author of *Future of an Illusion* is closer to me than he believes."[142] One wonders what the Rabbi could mean, given that book's sustained attack on religion. Freud in any event seems to have understood Feuchtwang (who like Freud was originally from Moravia), for he replied,

> Your words aroused a special echo in me, which I do not need to explain to you.

It seems that Freud could have said here, as he did to Abraham in 1908, "We understand each other." He continues,

> In some place in my soul [*Seele*], in a very hidden corner, I am a fanatical Jew [*ein fanatischer Jude*]. I am very much astonished to discover myself as such in spite of all efforts to be unprejudiced and impartial. What can I do against it at my age?[143]

Freud may realize that he has more in common with the Jews in Palestine than he had thought.

What has Freud discovered, much to his own surprise (*sehr erstaunt*), that makes him realize that he is a "fanatical Jew"? Jozef Hes, who published the letter, suggests that Freud means his "relatedness" with other

Jews, his feeling of "being-at-home" (*Heimlichkeit*), "being of the same mental make-up as other Jews."[144] But Freud has been aware of this characteristic for a long time, at least since 1926, when he stated it to B'nai B'rith. Now he is "astonished" at the discovery "in a very hidden corner" of his "soul." It stands over against the lack of prejudice and the impartiality that Freud has struggled to maintain as a humanist and a scientist. It represents apparently an element of inner Jewishness that cannot (or will not) be assimilated to Enlightenment (i.e., Reasoned) humanism, but will take the Jews' part in an unabashedly biased and emotional way. Such a discovery at his age is indeed something amazing to the man who claimed to have no share in "nationalist ideals" only six months earlier. It seems that what Freud has discovered is not the *presence* of his Jewish belonging, but its hidden *depth,* a depth that transcends Reason. This astonishes the arch-rationalist Freud, and may be part of the emotion that drives him to write *Moses and Monotheism* in an effort to explain that depth rationally.

For this reason we might wish to date the beginning of *Moses and Monotheism* to this time, when Freud discovers a hidden "fanatical" depth to his Jewishness that goes beyond his scientific will to reason. If *Totem and Taboo* was undertaken in part to explain Freud's own "lack of a religious need," then *Moses and Monotheism* will be undertaken to explain the depth of Freud's Jewish *Zugehörigkeit* independently of that lack of belief and its rationality. It is no wonder, therefore, that Freud locates his Jewishness in phylogenesis, for what could be deeper in scientific humanist consciousness?

Correspondence with Arnold Zweig

With this in mind, let us turn to a letter Freud writes to Arnold Zweig (1887–1968), a well-known German author and former analysand, in May 1932, after Zweig has just returned from a month's visit to Palestine (to which he will emigrate when the Nazis come to power in 1933). The correspondence between Freud and Zweig (which began in 1927) will concern us repeatedly as we focus on the genesis of Freud's last book, for as Freud confesses, "I write to you with pleasure and with special ease and I notice that I write many things to you which I withhold from others."[145] The link is probably not coincidental, given Zweig's Zionism, literary stature, and German-European humanism. In Freud's letter to Zweig dated 8 May 1932, having just referred to his "soon-to-be boundaried life span" and then to his birthday just past, Freud speaks almost in a rapture of Palestine:

> How remarkable this tragic raving mad land which you have visited must have been for you. Just think, no other progress is connected with this strip of our mother-earth, no discovery or invention—the Phoenecians are said to have invented glass and the alphabet (both doubtful!), the island of Crete created Minoan art, Pergamon reminds us of parchment, Magnesia of the magnet and so on endlessly, but Palestine has cultivated nothing but religions, holy mad absurdities [*heiligen Wahnwitz*], presumptuous attempts to overcome the outer world of appearances by means of the inner world of wishing, and we spring from there (though one of us considers himself a German as well; the other [i.e., Freud himself, N.B.] does not); our ancestors lived there for perhaps half, perhaps a whole millennium (but this [residence] too is only a perhaps), and it is impossible to say what we have taken over from the life in this land as an inheritance into our blood and nerves (as is mistakenly said). Oh, life could be very interesting if only we knew and understood more about it.

The first thing that Jaffe notes about this lyric tribute to "Palaestina" is how often Freud qualifies his expressions, as though the two sides of his personality—the one soaring, the other rationally disciplining—were wrestling with each other, first the one and then the other winning to expression.[146] Note too how Freud names what Palestine has cultivated: "progress" *(Fortschritt)*. Needless to say, that word is not used to describe religion in *The Future of an Illusion*. Here by contrast these "sacred delusions" are "daring" or "presumptuous" (*vermessene*) attempts. That is, they are characterized by a kind of "nerve" or "impudence," perhaps Jewish *chutzpah*. The difference in Freud's attitude here from that in *Future of an Illusion* may be because in that work Freud is thinking primarily about Christianity; here he may have Judaism in mind. True, this religion's holy ravings are still the products of wishing *(Wahnwitz)*, but precisely because of his own root in this history, Freud is struck by the contrast between his self-understanding based in Reason ("Logos is our god")[147] and his origins in this *tragisch-tolle Land*, this *Muttererde*. He almost seems to be reassessing himself, as though he has seen something new, perhaps something related to the (Jewish) "heritage in our blood and nerves." His nervous qualifications after each admission of connection only serve to confirm our suspicion that Freud has touched a nerve in his own Jewish identity, one that will become very interesting to him as he tries to understand it more deeply.

We should note too that though Freud has never repudiated belonging to the Jewish people, he has repeatedly denied that he is German, and he does so again. In his interview with Viereck in 1926, Freud admitted that his language and his culture were German, but that intellectually, since the rise of antisemitism, he considered himself no longer German and preferred to call himself a Jew. When Freud now traces his origins to Palestine, he repeats his renunciation, as if to underscore Jewish origins as the only relevant ones. Three months later he tells Zweig, "I can relieve you of the delusion that one must be a German. Should one not leave this God-forsaken people to itself?"[148]

Freud's view may be based in part on a disgust for the political situation in Austria, in which national decline was accompanied by a rise in antisemitism. Close to financial and economic disaster in 1931, Austria's parliamentary government had been steadily disintegrating, and considerable support was being given to the National Socialists in Austria as they continued their rise to power in Germany. A Christian Socialist government with E. Dollfuss as chancellor came to power with a majority of one vote in May 1932. In March of 1933, parliamentary government in Austria broke down completely, and by this time too the Nazis, with Hitler at their head, were in power in Germany, their party being declared the only legal one in July. In May 1933 the Nazis burned Freud's works, with those of other authors they didn't like, in a massive bonfire in Berlin, where it was declaimed, "Against the soul-destroying glorification of the instinctual life, for the nobility of the human soul! I consign to the flames the writings of the school of Sigmund Freud."[149] In July, Freud's grandson was called up in his Berlin classroom as *Jud Freud.* [150] There was a new order forbidding Jews from serving on any scientific council, which of course affected psychoanalysts. Clearly antisemitism was on the rise, and Freud had good reason to say to Pfister in May, "My judgement of human nature, above all the Christian-Aryan variety, has had little reason to change."[151]

Already in 1927, after reading Zweig's study of antisemitism dedicated to him (*Caliban*),[152] Freud had surrendered to his "affective" response to antisemitism, saying that "on the average and taken by and large, mankind are trash."[153] As time goes on, he will need to articulate a deeper, more rational understanding of antisemitism in order to define his Jewish identity more precisely. As Yerushalmi says, "The shock of anti-Jewish barbarism brought the question of what it means to be a Jew to a new pitch of existential urgency." It was this internal urgency that "provided the immediate impulse to the actual writing of *Moses and Monotheism*,"[154] and not just external political events.

Freud analyzes Zweig's ambivalence towards his own Jewishness in a letter Schur reports, dated 18 August 1933. According to Freud, some of Zweig's conflicts over his German-Jewish allegiances relate to his ambivalence towards being Jewish. "One defends oneself in every way against castration," he tells him. That is, presumably, one defends against the limitations imposed by Judaism, whose symbol of allegiance is circumcision. Rather than suggesting that Zweig's ambivalence relates to doubts over his German humanist or Enlightenment allegiance, Freud suggests that "here a piece of opposition to one's own Jewishness may still be hiding cunningly." The implication may be that Freud opposes Judaism insofar as it prevents one's participation in the larger enterprise of *Humanität.* Therefore, in order to identify himself more fully with "Judaism" later, Freud will come to locate the ultimate source of *Humanität* in *Judentum.*

But at this point in 1933 he says,

> Our great master Moses was, after all, a strong antisemite and made no secret of it. Perhaps he was really an Egyptian. And surely he was right.[155]

Schur and Yerushalmi relate Freud's "Mosaic antisemitism" to Moses' attack on the Jewish people for their apostasy at the Golden Calf.[156] If they are correct, then "antisemitism" in Freud's mind can be a way of calling (or driving) the Jewish people back to their higher selves, forcing them to transcend themselves. That antisemitism stimulated Freud to write his own search for a "higher" Judaism with which to identify conforms with this function and prepares the way for Freud's formulation in *Moses and Monotheism.* Ironically, it almost seems like the Nazis deserve a kind of unintended credit.

Freud's proposed Egyptian origin for Moses implies that this recalling of the Jews must be initiated by an "outsider." In the Bible, the Outsider is of course God; in *Moses and Monotheism* the role will be played by an Egyptian Moses. Yerushalmi notes other similarities that imply that Freud writes as a kind of biblical historian: the compression of evolutionary time, the importance of remembering, and the "true pulse of history" beating far beneath its manifest surfaces. Freud's story presents the reader with "a countertheology of history in which the Chain of Tradition is replaced by the chain of unconscious repetition."[157] As a result, "*Moses and Monotheism* is a direct alternative, a new Torah in which Moses is, in effect, apotheosized and takes the place of God." Freud does more than return to the Bible, as his father Jakob bid him do; he rewrites it, composing his own kind of midrash. If Mortimer Ostow is correct in his analysis of Jakob's "birthday inscription," the father's original midrash (exegetical homily), in which the fountain is a metaphor for Torah,[158] anticipated and paved the way for Freud's license with the Bible.

In any event, this letter indicates, as we saw also in the early period,[159] that Freud does feel some hostility towards Jews (being typically Jewish in this respect, too). Linking that hostility to Moses makes it seem almost inherent in being Jewish. Yet Freud is indignant about and disgusted by Jewish self-hatred,[160] as we shall see below.

Nor is this the first time Freud has suggested that Moses was an Egyptian. In 1910 he published "A Special Type of Object-Choice Made by Men," in which this sentence appears:

> A woman rescuing someone else (a child) from the water acknowledges herself in this way as the mother who bore him, like Pharoah's daughter in the legend of Moses (Rank, 1909).[161]

In addition, Reik recalls Freud telling him a joke in connection with this psychoanalytic insight, whose punch line insists that Pharoah's daughter is really the mother of Moses:

> The boy Itzig is asked in grammar school: "Who was Moses?" and answers: "Moses was the son of an Egyptian princess." "That's not true," says the teacher, "Moses was the son of a Hebrew mother. The Egyptian princess found the baby in a casket." But Itzig answers: "Says she!"[162]

Freud's humor anticipates an insight that he will try to "unpack" later in "scientific" (that is, psychoanalytic) terms in *Moses and Monotheism*.

Two months later he writes to Zweig and describes himself by a Jewish joke:

> I am still alive and as I do not smoke anymore I am hardly likely to write anything again—except letters. It reminds me of that *Chasen* [cantor in the synagogue] of whom it was said: "Live he will, sing he will not."[163]

But Freud will not only live; he will sing too.

Freud and Hebrew University

Around this same time, the Hebrew University in Jerusalem was considering the question of whether psychoanalysis ought to be represented on the faculty at the university and "integrated" into its activities. In response to an inquiry from the chancellor, Judah Magnes, Freud writes to support the introduction of psychoanalysis into "our university." It would be significant for the humanities, he says (and he mentions specifically, "the science of religion"), as well as for the medical faculty, from whose curriculum psychoanalysis "must not be absent."[164] Freud refers to Hebrew University as "our university in Jerusalem" again when writing to Israel Wechsler, an American neurologist, in 1929 (i.e., before Wechsler became a member of the board of governors of Hebrew University in 1930), so it seems likely that Rosenbaum is correct in saying that Freud's phrase in his letter to Magnes "reflects his personal identification as a Jew, with Hebrew University, rather than his previous official connection"[165] (Freud was on the board of trustees in 1925 and 1926).

When Magnes writes Freud that the prevailing opinion is that it would be "premature to introduce psychoanalysis before a Chair of Psychology has been established,"[166] Freud withdraws his identification, referring now to "the University of Jerusalem," angry at its "barely disguised rejection of psychoanalysis."[167] Hebrew University bears his identification as a Jew only as long as it accepts psychoanalysis. Freud-the-Jew and Freud-the-psychoanalyst are inseparable in the late period, strengthening Yerushalmi's suggestion that Freud saw psychoanalysis as a replacement for (or the future of) Judaism. So it makes sense that he will soon use "applied psychoanalysis" to define the infrastructure of Jewish character. In any event, Freud will overcome his anger, and in 1936, thanking Hebrew University for its greetings to him on his eightieth birthday, he will once again confess himself "one of yours."[168] Freud's Jewish identification is deeper than an intellectual commitment, as important as that commitment is to him.

Origins of Moses and Monotheism

Freud's last book deeply expresses his sense of himself as a Jew and is in fact its mature culmination, developing a Jewish identity that he can choose to affirm even while describing its involuntary basis. To illustrate this claim, I will focus on Freud's correspondence as it relates to this work. Chapter 5 will then discuss the model of voluntary dual allegiance that *Moses and Monotheism* presents us with as moderns and as modern Jews.

In January 1934, Freud writes Arnold Zweig (who by now has emigrated to Palestine) that he is eager to read his new book, *Bilanz der deutschen Judenheit*[169] now that he knows that Zweig is cured of his "unhappy love" for his "so-called Fatherland."[170] As Freud says, "Such revelling is not for the likes of us." At the end of this letter Freud complains of not being able to write. Accepting his decline by saying "One must not go on working indefinitely," Freud drops a hint nevertheless that something has begun to develop in the deeper layers:

> Not long ago something began to take shape, but it slipped away again. Had you been here, we could have chatted about it.[171]

Freud's rejection of German identification due to German antisemitic barbarism, along with this tantalizing hint of something forming in the depths of Freud's mind, indicates the beginning of *Moses and Monotheism* in relation to 1) an awareness of approaching death; 2) the rise of antisemitism; and 3) a sense of Jewish cultural superiority to such "barbarism." The following letters support this suggestion.

The first four months of 1934 brought a heightening of political tensions in Austria and Germany. In February, civil war broke out in Austria between the Social Democrats and the Dollfuss government. After four days of fighting, the Social Democrats were defeated and driven underground. Freud noted in a letter to Zweig that "our little bit of civil war was not at all nice."[172] Freud is aware that things are likely to get worse, and he admits that were a "Hitlerian viceroy" to rule in Vienna, he would have to go, "no matter where." The situation of the Jews in Austria declined rapidly after this point. In April 1934, the rump of the parliament that Dollfuss had disbanded a year before came together and accepted an authoritarian government. The "rights of man" guaranteed under the democratic constitution were swept away, and even the word "Republic" was removed from the official name of the state.

At the beginning of May, Freud moved for the summer into the more rural setting of Döbling, a suburb of Vienna, describing his surroundings as being "beautiful as a fairy land."[173] On the other hand, he also took along with him Zweig's *Bilanz*, which reminded him in detail of the brutal persecution of Jews taking place in Germany and their gradual exclusion from its cultural life since the Reichstag fire of February 1933. The book describes the substantial contributions made by German Jews to the construction of Western civilization—German Jews in fact being particularly representative of the European humanism that Zweig says is the essence of true German culture. It also describes the tragic dismantling of that civilization and the destruction of its humanistic values by the Nazis. Thus it is no wonder that after reading the book, Freud wrote to its author in Haifa on 12 May 1934:

> I found it painful to read. I hope it has done you good to write it and that it has enabled you to let off steam, for I am almost choking with rancour and fury [*Groll und Wut*].

Zweig says himself in the book's preface that he wrote the work in a "paroxysm of wrath."[174] His *Bilanz* is clearly intended to defend the Jews and humanistic German Jewry against the slander and violence that is being perpetrated by the Nazis. Freud's anger stems from the indignation he shares with Zweig at the injustice of the attack and from the helplessness they both feel at not being able to prevent the "certain" destruction of the civilized culture they have helped to build. Zweig's portrait leaves no doubt about its tremendous worth and the vital role Jews played in helping to bring it to life. Now in scarcely two decades the Nazis will stamp it to death in a tantrum of jealous violence.

Freud has written only one other letter to Zweig the whole summer (on 15 July) when he writes on 30 September about his new work on Moses. So we are right to locate the genesis of *Moses and Monotheism* in this summer of 1934. The first page of the manuscript of *Moses and Monotheism* in the Library of Congress is dated 9 August 1934, in Freud's hand.[175] Jones tells us that Freud mentioned it to him and to Eitingon in August, but that the letter in September to Zweig is "the first full account."[176] The letter in July is taken up with discussion of Zweig's play about Napoleon, continuing remarks about the latter's planned novel about Nietzsche, and Freud's reaction to the "Roehm purge" of June, when the Nazis murdered a number of their own leaders. The "hors-d'oeuvres" left Freud hungry for still more, he joked grimly. With these images as background, let us turn to Freud's letter of 30 September 1934, in which he describes his own "historical novel."

Freud is aware that his summer in the 19th District is almost over, because he adds to his location, "nicht mehr lange." So his letter is written at the end of the period in which he did the bulk of his work. He writes now, he says, from a fear that a copy of Zweig's play about Napoleon has been lost in the mail. But he goes on in a strangely indirect way to explain the reason for his not having written in so long (two-and-a-half months). Five sentences into the letter Freud writes,

> That is to say, I have in a time of comparative leisure, at a loss about what to start with the surplus of spare time, written something myself and this, contrary to my original intention, took up so much of my time that everything else was left undone.[177]

This neglect is rather unusual for Freud, who usually found time to answer his mail even in his busiest times. Furthermore, the casual way in which Freud introduces his topic belies the deep meaning it held for him. For it is clear that he became completely engrossed by the project from its very inception, so captivated that he neglected "everything else."

Freud goes on to describe the origin of the work and its structure. "The starting point of my work is familiar to you," Freud tells Zweig,

> It was the same as that of your *Bilanz*. Faced with the new persecutions, one asks oneself again how the Jew has come to be what he is [*wie der Jude geworden ist*] and why he has attracted this undying hatred [*diesen unsterblichen Haß*].[178]

One can ask initially, Why, when faced with renewed persecutions, should one ask about the nature of Jewish character? Why not ask again what is wrong with the persecutors? Zweig's book in fact implies that this is the real question. Freud instead turns inward, and Ernst Simon points out that Freud's response

> was not greatly different from [that of] many other Jews, who had been more or less isolated from Jewish sources and influences, and [who] with the increase of hatred against their people and religion sought to discover why they were so hated and what they were forced to defend. Formal community or national Judaism did not offer enough to afford them satisfaction, and thus they felt a spiritual need to seek the essential nature of Jewish life and values.[179]

The second of Freud's two questions—namely, Why the Jews?—is shared by both him and Zweig, and the latter's efforts to answer it in his *Bilanz* may indeed have pushed Freud to try his hand. For Zweig's answer centers on the psychotic needs of the Nazis,[180] whereas Freud's effort is related to his approach in answering the first question; that is, he seeks to understand Jewish character.

But the first question, Who is a Jew? is not a major focus for Zweig in his *Bilanz*. For Zweig is not just interested in the Jews; he also addresses his fellow Germans: "The aim of this book is to make the Germans understand what they are doing. For Germans are still what they are."[181] That is, Germans in their true nature are still fellow carriers of pan-European humanism, and Zweig is writing in part to make them return to their senses. "We and they," Zweig wrote, meaning Jews and Germans, "are still soldiers in the same army of human spirituality and European civilization."[182] Faced with the new persecutions that stimulate both him and Freud to write, Zweig does not ask who the Jew is, because he knows. The Jew is the sustainer of the European humanistic mentality, whose special province of mental life has been nourished by the Jews' "descent and by their religious history. It gave them the proud consciousness of being a chosen people dispersed throughout the world, sharers in a common promise."[183]

It is Freud, rather, finding the pan-European humanistic synthesis to which he has wedded his Jewish life threatened by the Nazi onslaught, who asks the question, Who is a Jew? Freud will answer the second question in the same way, namely, by locating antisemitism in Jewish character and culture. So we see that the central focus of Freud's work is the question of Jewish identity. The question has become intensely personal at the end of Freud's life, with so much that he has built in such danger—as Zweig's *Bilanz* makes clear. Freud is asking, Who am *I* as a Jew? and What has it meant?

He soon discovered "the formula," he says.

> Moses created the Jew, and my work received the title: The Man Moses, a historical Novel (with more justification than your Nietzsche-novel).

Freud's choice of genre and his later shift away from it raise questions about the nature of Freud's work. By examining Freud's original 1934 manuscript of *Moses and Monotheism*, Yerushalmi has shown that Freud used this subtitle "merely to indicate his own awareness that he had not found sufficient independent historical data to fully corroborate his reconstruction" in parts 1 and 2. Freud knows that "given the extreme paucity of reliable historical facts concerning Moses, his reconstruction must be based to such an unusual extent on psychoanalytic probability."[184] Therefore the subtitle is not evidence that Freud considered *Moses and Monotheism* a species of literary fiction, much less covert autobiography. He intended his book to uncover objective, scientific truth, not subjective, autobiographical truth.

In any event, given Freud's lifelong identification with Moses, we could have predicted this "formula" as the endpoint to Freud's starting point to attack antisemitism and to define Jewish identity. The first sproutings of the work were hinted to Zweig in January, but it seems it took Freud's rage at the antisemitic destruction of Jewish contributions to European civilization described by Zweig in his *Bilanz* to catalyze Freud's *Groll und Wut* into a defiant protest: Moses created the Jew. That is, as the answer to his questions *Freud* creates a new Jew, "Moses," the projection of his own identity as a "Psychological Jew," in Yerushalmi's felicitous phrase. But this answer takes the same form as his responses to attacks on psychoanalysis. He ignores his critics and publishes his "findings," making another contribution to the "upbuilding of Western civilization" through the discovery of "truth." Freud remains committed to this process as a scientist and as a humanist, believing that this approach will most effectively overcome the barbarism of the Nazis.

But if Zweig's *Bilanz* is the starting point for Freud's work, then it is clear that we are justified in reading *Moses and Monotheism* as a *defense* of the Jewish people rather than as an attack, despite its form and the way it was received by most of Freud's contemporaries in 1939. Freud responds here to antisemitism just as he did in the past. The "fighting Jew" prepares to defend both himself and his people in one blow.

As mentioned above, Ernst Simon pointed out that Freud's response in seeking the nature of Jewish character (in order to discover what it was he was called upon to defend) was a spiritual need that he shared with many of his contemporaries. But this need was also a psychological one, namely, the need for wholeness, for an integrated self. At the collapse of liberalism and the death of his father in the early period, Freud sought out the B'nai B'rith to help him integrate his Jewish identity; now in the late period, when it is clear that the B'nai B'rith can offer no shelter against the Nazis and as Freud himself is about to die, the "old Jew" turns to his deepest Jewish identification, his old hero Moses, first encountered when he studied the Bible with his father, to help him disclose a new Jewish self. This identity develops a reaffirmation (as in the early period) of the dual allegiance—which he depicts as a dual origin—of his Jewish-humanist identity.

In this letter to Zweig, Freud turns to his reasons for holding back the finished work from publication. He writes a long paragraph about the danger to psychoanalytic practice and publications in Vienna should his book (which he says extends the theory of religion developed in *Totem and Taboo*) arouse the wrath of the Catholic hierarchy.[185] In this way, Freud keeps the work suspended in the same matrix that stimulated its birth, namely, antisemitism. He also felt the book needed more work:

> And in addition, there is the fact that the work does not seem to me sufficiently substantiated, nor does it altogether please me. It is therefore not the proper time for a martyrdom. Enough of this for the time being!

Both Freud's frustration and his investment are clear.

For the next four-and-a-half years Freud will labor over his *Moses*, obsessed with it, "fixated" upon it, as he says. He was aware from the very beginning in August 1934 that "it would offend the Jews to be told that their great Moses was really an Egyptian, but for some reason this consideration did not seem to have weighed heavily with him."[186] If Freud's *Moses* is in large part an exercise in self-definition, then the reaction of other Jews is not particularly relevant. And if the work is an attempt to defend Jewry by identifying the spiritual and historical kernel of their religious truth, then there is not much he can do if that truth contradicts their wishes.

Yet to Eitingon he justifies not publishing the work by saying, "Experts would find it easy to discredit me as an outsider."[187] Freud is aware of the amateurish quality of his work. "More important," he tells Zweig in November, "is the fact that this historical novel won't stand up to my own criticism. I need more certainty."[188] This is the real crux: Freud needs to be sure of the solution himself. He tries to give up on it now in November ("So let us leave it aside"),[189] even saying to Eitingon, "I am no good at historical romances. Let us leave them to Thomas Mann."[190] But Freud cannot be free of the matter: "The man and what I wanted to make of him pursue me unrelentingly."[191] Freud has no "inner uncertainty" about the solution, "for that is as good as settled," but he is distressed at the fact that, as he says,

> I was obliged to construct so imposing a statue [N.B.] upon feet of clay, so that any fool could topple it.[192]

This fact restrains Freud from feeling that the work is successful (or finished). "Don't say any more about the Moses book," he pleads with Zweig in December 1934.

Yet three weeks later Freud writes in a different mood to Lou Andreas-Salome. The historical foundations of his Moses story are not solid enough to serve as a basis for his conclusions and so he must remain silent, he says, but adds,

> It suffices me that I myself can believe in the solution of the problem. It has pursued me throughout the whole of my life.[193]

This extraordinary confession supports our reading of the role that Freud's *Moses* is playing in his own development. The "problem" here is the problem of his Jewish identity, and the figure of Moses, the giver of the Law, is at the center of that struggle. For the Law, the *halacha*, is the central defining and enabling feature of traditional Jewish identity, the inheritance of the fathers passed to the sons. In renouncing the Law, that is, in renouncing what Moses gave, Freud, like the modern Jew, loses touch with a primary resource for renewing his knowledge of what makes him Jewish. All that is left is ethnicity or psychology (character traits) or biology (therefore Freud's phylogenetics). The guilt attendant upon this rejection is unavoidable, even if one's own father (like Freud's father, to some extent) joins the son in his "killing" of Moses by refusing the Law and so gives the son a kind of "permission."[194] Because the guilt follows Freud throughout his life (note his following words to Andreas-Salome, "Forgive me"), so too does the problem of Jewish identity in the absence of the Law, the problem of the Psychological Jew, and this problem becomes more acute, more present at the surface, when its humanist amalgam is undermined by antisemitism. For then it seems that no matter what, "the Jew must be burned."

Significantly, when Freud describes the origins of his work to the Gentile Andreas-Salome, he does not mention the question of antisemitism—why the Jew has attracted this undying hated—but only the question of "what has created the particular character of the Jew." By eliminating the question of antisemitism, Freud preserves his humanist-Jewish identity, and so can be satisfied with his solution of the well-born Egyptian Moses as the deepest root for his own self. The answer in *Moses and Monotheism* to the question of antisemitism will be that Christians resent the renunciations of instinct required by the identity that this Moses transmitted to them through the Jew Jesus.[195]

But in suppressing the mention of Christian antisemitism in his letter to Andreas-Salome, Freud seems to open the door to his own kind of antisemitism. The original "Jews" he describes are primitive and violent murderers of their Egyptian deliverer, and they worship a "volcano God." He goes on to deprive them of circumcision, their divinely "chosen" status, the passing through the Red Sea, and any presence at Mt. Sinai. So what is left to them that is Jewish? The main thing, Freud would answer, the historical truth, namely, parricide. The killing of the father, actually indicative in Freud's thought of a subtle but powerful identification,[196] sets in motion the return of the repressed, the father's demands for the instinctual renunciations that are the basis of spiritual progress—that is, the return of the Law. Freud can now embrace what is for him the essence of being Jewish, namely, the instinctual renunciation demanded by the *idea* of the Law, since he has gotten rid of its form, the practical details of the Law's actual observance. The practice of such renunciation of drive has shaped the character of the Jew for refinement and *Geistigheit,* in opposition to the savage "God of the wilderness."

As Freud will say to Zweig in February, complaining about the latter's poem, "Die Schöpfungsromanze,"

> It seems to me to pay too much attention to the barbarous god of volcanoes and wilderness whom I grew to dislike very much in the course of my studies in Moses and who was quite alien to my Jewish consciousness.[197]

This god of volcanoes and deserts is the god of the id, the one that wishes to kill the father; the god of Freud's Jewish consciousness is that of his Egyptian Moses, who, as Schur puts it, stood for the "supremacy of the ego over raw instinctual drives,"[198] making possible the rule of conscious reason and the ego where before there reigned only the unconscious compulsive drives of the id.

Furthermore, Freud continues, "In my text I maintain that the hero Moses had never heard the name [the Tetragrammaton], that the Jewish people never were on Sinai-Horeb and that they never passed through the Red Sea, etc."[199] Declaring its independence from inherited Jewish tradition, Freud's own "creation-romance" "discovers" a new and improved Jewish people to reflect Freud's sense of what a Jew—a Psychological Jew—is. In so doing, he may cut himself off from the resources of the rabbinic tradition that Jews need to formulate an authentic Jewish response to modernity.

Freud will say in May, "Moses will not let go of my imagination [*Moses gibt meine Phantasie nicht frei*]."[200] To Eitingon he wrote, "The 'Moses' has become a fixation for me. I can't get away from it and I can't get on with it. If no new finds at Tel-El Amarna come to my aid I will hide it away forever."[201] Note Freud's concern for objective historical corroboration. The last time he was fixated on Moses was when he wrote (or created) his "*Moses* of Michelangelo." Now Freud will find his "Michelangelo-Moses" in the guise of his new Egyptian "statue," transferring the product of his conscious imagination to the realm of "history" (and biology/genetics), so that he can believe that the image is the legitimate root of his Jewish identity.

The 1935 "Postscript"

By the end of May 1935, Freud had written a "Postscript" to his autobiography of ten years earlier, the *Selbstdarstellung*. Among other things, the addition seems to express a sense of plateau with regard to the *Moses*. In early May, Freud is excited about the excavations at Tel el Amarna, where references to a "Prince Thothmes" make him think that "this Thothmes could be my Moses and I would be able to boast that I had guessed right."[202] But by June he says that the Moses "has been laid aside" and that he can do no more on it.[203] References to the *Moses* subside in Freud's correspondence after this point, until 1937, when he will take up the work again in connection with the publishing of the first two parts of the book,[204] and again in April 1938, as he prepares to leave Vienna for England. There, safe from the Nazis, he will finally be able to complete the revision of the third and most substantial part. Therefore, a look at Freud's 1935 "Postscript" to his autobiography presents us with a glimpse of Freud's self-understanding just before the final push to complete and publish his *Moses.*

Freud reports that a significant change has come about in the ten years since he first published the study, when it seemed as though his life "would soon be brought to an end." His words support my thesis about the character of the final period:

> Threads which in the course of my development had become intermingled [e.g., Jewishness and humanism?] have now begun to separate; interests which I had acquired in the later part of my life have receded, while the older and original ones became prominent once more.[205]

Freud speaks of having made "no further decisive contributions to psychoanalysis" since that time. "This circumstance," he goes on to explain, "is connected with an alteration in myself, with what might be described as a phase of regressive development." His interests have returned to "the cultural problems which had fascinated me long before, when I was a youth scarcely old enough for thinking."[206] These *kulturellen Problemen* concern "the origins of religion and morality," and Freud traces a genealogical line from *Totem and Taboo* (1912) [*sic*] through *The Future of an Illusion* (1927) and *Civilization and Its Discontents* (1930).

Moses and Monotheism clearly completes this series, as we see from how Freud describes his developing ideas about the import of religion. He views the events of human cultural history, and especially religion, as the result of the same psychological processes that go on in the individual, "repeated on a wider stage." At first, Freud expressed a negative valuation of these cultural products, labeling them "illusions." "Later," Freud says, he found a formula which did better "justice" to religion:

> . . . while granting that its power lies in the truth [N.B.] which it contains, I showed that that truth was not a material [*reale*] but a historical truth.[207]

This formula is identical to the one Freud gives Lou Andreas-Salome in January 1935:

> Religions own their compulsive power to the *return of the repressed;* they are reawakened memories of very ancient, forgotten, highly emotional episodes of human history. I have already said this in *Totem and Taboo;*

> I express it now in the formula: the strength of religion lies not in its material [*reale*] but in its *historical* truth.[208]

From the letter to Andreas-Salome, we see that the formula for this insight is new, though its essence is found in *Totem and Taboo.* Furthermore, its development is connected with Freud's work on *Moses and Monotheism.* Thus his last book is really the culmination of a long process of thinking on Freud's part about religion and his own cultural and psychological Jewishness. His words to Andreas-Salome about the problem of his Moses/Jewish identity having pursued him all this life, and his words in the *Selbstdarstellung* about "the origins of religion and morality," are perhaps references to the same developmental circumstance, namely, the renewal of Freud's interest in his own Jewishness now that he is near death. The final resolution of his father's humiliation in the hat-in-the-gutter episode is at hand. Jakob's self-control becomes the Jewish expression of the basis of all spiritual progress.

The "Postscript" indicates that Freud has reached a resting place with his *Moses*, having found a formula that does "justice"[209] to the nature of religion's truth (and specifically that of Judaism). He has found a formula that reflects the form of Judaism's (and his father's) claim on his own self-understanding: it contains a historical truth to which we are all deeply bound. The final "text" is vindicated.

Though Freud is seventy-nine years old in 1935, his defiant Jewish pride is strong. During that summer there was an ironic Jewish joke going around about a parade of Jews in Berlin carrying banners that read "Throw us out." For some reason Freud thought the story was literally true, and he

> wrote a bitter letter about it to Arnold Zweig in which he said he had never heard anything so revolting, but that the lack of dignity it displayed was a characteristic feature of Jews. The only consolation he could find was that the people in question were half German.[210]

Jones connects Freud's indignation with his reaction to his father's humiliation over his fur cap in the gutter. But if we look carefully at the two incidents, we realize that they are different. Jakob Freud in fact displayed great dignity in his self-restraint, and the mature Freud recognized this fact. The Jews in the joke, by contrast, show no self- restraint in their masochistic indulgence in self-hatred. They are cooperating with their oppressors. They have not "struggled against an inward passion for the sake of a higher cause," as did Jakob (and Freud). Freud's anger relates instead to the *contrast* between his father's dignity and the image of these Jews' "characteristic" lack of self-respect. The basis of Freud's capacity for defiance is his knowledge of self-worth and the dignity of his father's example. If my thesis about Freud's mature identification with his father is correct, then his anger may be related to a sense of violence done to this new identification. In any event, Freud is "revolted." The feeling of connection is strong, and his only consolation is that those Jews are not "fully" Jewish. Freud feels less responsible for them if they are only half kin.

It is at this point too, in June 1935, that Freud writes his letter to Leib Jaffe, the president of Keren HaYesod, the agency dedicated to the building of a Jewish National Home in Palestine. "Keren Hajessod," Freud says, is

> a sign of our invincible will to live which has so far successfully braved two thousand years of burdensome oppression! Our youth will continue to carry on the fight.[211]

Freud's Jewish pride is fierce. Knowing he wrote this letter after he finished the first draft of *Moses and Monotheism* makes it difficult to believe that Freud intended his book as an attack on the Jewish people in whose "invincible will to live" he takes such pride. Rather he intended to provide them with the means to continue that fight, namely, by identifying the source of their strength. Psychoanalysis is to become the modern tool (replacing Judaism) for exchanging illusion for reality (or idolatry for truth), for the national transcendence of narcissism, and so for the education of mankind, with the Jews leading the way.

Yet at the same time, Freud regrets the need for Zionism. He writes Zweig in October of how sad it is that "we even judge world events from the Jewish point of view, but how could we do it any other way!"[212] In other words, given the existence of antisemitic persecution, Jews must view the world from a Jewish perspective, if only for self-protection. But Freud regards this negatively, for it represents a diminishing of his humanist ideals. He expresses a similar sentiment nine months later when he replies to a second letter from Erich Leyens, the young Jew who had written him thirteen years earlier about antisemitism in Germany. Leyens writes again now, reminding Freud of his earlier letter and telling him how much he had erred in not following "his prophetic advice."[213] Freud answers,

> You surely do not believe that I am proud of having been right? I was right as the pessimist against the enthusiast, as the old man against the youngster. It would have been better to have been wrong.[214]

Freud's response makes his humanist preference clear. This letter suggests that in this polarized environment, Freud was a "nationalist" (Freud's own word) or Zionist Jew mainly when he was driven from a humanist position by antisemitism. Ideally, Freud would like to reach a humanist position *through* a Jewish one, as in B'nai B'rith. He will do so in *Moses and Monotheism*.

Freud, the Galitzianer

Freud's pride in his Jewish origins becomes even stronger at the end of his life. In November 1935, when the Nuremberg Laws are being promulgated in Hitler's Germany, Freud writes to a Dr. Sigfried Fehl:

> I hope it is not unknown to you that I have always held faithfully to our people, and never pretended to be anything but what I am: a Jew from Moravia whose parents come from Austrian Galicia.[215]

This open pride in his provincial origins contrasts sharply with Freud's "worldly" disdain for the Moravian Jews on his train ride from Freiberg in 1872.[216] Freud has accepted his Jewish roots now and is defiantly proud, in an atmosphere of rising Nazism, to say that he is a "Galitzianer" from the "old country." In defying antisemitism, Freud has come also to a positive identification with the authenticity of his parents' provincial origins. At the end of 1939, Martin Freud began a talk he gave to the Zionist Society in an internment camp in Huyton, England, with the words, "The Freuds came from Galicia and we are 'Galicianer'. . . ."[217] The pride with which Martin spoke of his family's East European roots before an assembly of assimilated West European Jewish professors, doctors, and scholars contained some of his father's defiant spirit as well.

In November–December 1935, Freud made another statement to the B'nai B'rith about his relation to the lodge. He mentions having taken refuge in the sympathy of sure friendship there, surrounded as he was in 1897 by "extreme hostility." He claimed that he had "never lost the feeling of belonging" to the brotherhood, and that

> the total agreement of our cultural and humanitarian ideals, as well as the same joyful acknowledgement of Jewish descent and Jewish existence, have vividly sustained this feeling.[218]

Freud is "joyful" at his Jewish descent, and he identifies intellectually with the humanitarian ideals of the society. Again, Freud's national and

Jewish identifications ideally serve humanistic ends, those of *Humanität*, as an expression of his Jewish identity.

By contrast, Freud reacts to "Jewish self-hate" with disgust. We recall his reaction when he misunderstood the joke about Jews asking to be thrown out of Berlin. Jones mentions that in the summer of 1931 Freud had in his leisure time compiled a "hate list" of seven or eight people. One of the people on that list was a certain "Theodor Lessing," who had dedicated his book, *Jewish Self-Hatred* (which Freud thought "repulsive"), to Freud with the words, "In Devotion from an Opponent." In February 1936, Freud replied to Kurt Hiller, who had written a biographical essay on Lessing and had sent it to Freud, by sending him an account of an exchange of letters he had had with Lessing "long before the War" over the latter's opposition to psychoanalysis. Lessing had ridiculed psychoanalysis "in the most hateful manner as a lucubration of the Jewish spirit." Freud had responded by recalling to him the memory of his namesake, of whom Freud assumed he was a descendent.

Freud was astonished when Lessing replied that he was in fact a Jew himself, and he had even named his daughter from the Old Testament. This Jew's family had adopted the name of Lessing (as many Jewish families had at the time, Freud noted), out of respect for and (liberal Jewish) identification with the author of *Nathan the Wise* (though perhaps with an inadequate degree of respect for themselves as Jews). "I turned away from him in disgust," Freud told Hiller. Yet he went on to say that he thought such self-hatred as Lessing's was "an exquisitely Jewish phenomenon," reminding us that Freud knew that being Jewish in his time was not easy. Many Jews fell into this kind of neurosis, which Freud thought was caused by a combination of intense hatred for and yet identification with one's father.[219] That Freud does not fall prey to such self-hate himself is evidence, by contrast, of his *love* for his father. Some interpreters have argued that Freud himself suffered from this splitting of the personality that results in self-hate, and they point to *Moses and Monotheism* as its manifestation. The broader base of evidence presented here supports a different conclusion.[220]

One such piece of evidence for Freud's true Jewish pride is found in a letter he writes in English to the sister-in-law of the Zionist leader and psychoanalytic physician, David Eder, on the latter's death in 1936. Eder's death, Freud writes, had concerned him "in a quite special way" because of his own closeness to death, and he refers to the "speedy destruction" of the world due to its own evil—the only palliative for him. Freud continues,

> I can imagine how he, too, must have suffered under the bitterness of these times. We were both Jews and knew of each other that we carried in us that miraculous thing in common which—inaccessible to any analysis so far—makes the Jew.[221]

Though the Jewish essence has remained inaccessible to scientific analysis, Freud knows it to be "miraculous," and Jews know that they carry it in common. It was to Eder that Freud had addressed his message in reply to the Hebrew University Zionists when they congratulated him in 1926 on his seventieth birthday, so he and Eder were bound as well by the common interest in that group. In a foreword Freud wrote a few months before his own death, Freud mentions Eder's "love of truth and undaunted courage, together with toleration and a great capacity for love," and he says he believes it was these qualities that aroused Eder's interest in psychoanalysis.[222] Thus it may be too that Freud associated these qualities of character with the "miraculous thing which makes the Jew." Freud's argument for the origins of Jewish character in *Moses and Monotheism* supports this suggestion.

Also in April 1936, Freud writes a "letter in place of a preface" for Max Weinreich's Yiddish translation of Freud's *Introductory Lectures*. Addressing his letter to the Executive Department of YIVO, Freud expresses his pleasure at hearing of the coming publication of this Yiddish translation of his work, and he takes the first sheet they sent him into his hand "with great respect." "Unfortunately," he says,

> I could not do more with it than that. At the time when I was a student, no attention was paid to cultivating the national tradition. I therefore learned to read neither Hebrew nor Yiddish, a fact which makes me now very sorry. Nonetheless I still became a good Jew, though as you probably know not a believing one.[223]

This combination of identification, atheism, and regret has become familiar by now. As noted, Freud's teachers paid more attention to cultivating the particularity of the Jewish "national" tradition than he acknowledges in such statements as this, and Freud's words probably describe his early response to this teaching. His projection reveals both his rejection in the early period and his wish in the late period to reclaim what he has lost. Note that language carries national implications for Freud; it is the voice of his people. The connection established by this translation between his work and his "national tradition" through the language spoken by his parents, and in particular by his mother,[224] inspires Freud with "great respect." And again, Freud's atheism does not preclude his becoming a *guter yid* as far as he is concerned. In May, Freud will again tell Hebrew University that he is "one of yours."[225] Freud's Jewish identification spans the Yiddish of the *shtetl* and the *Wissenschaft* of the university.

In June, Freud is so conscious of his Jewishness and he identifies with it so strongly that even his dog becomes Jewish. Taking mock umbrage at Zweig's mistaken spelling of his chow's (possibly Hebrew) name, Freud writes,

> My Jofie is a stickler for accuracy and does not like being called Zofie by you; Jo as in Jew.[226]

Again we see Freud's Jewish projection. He colors his most personal ties with Jewishness. On the one hand, it is an attempt to create a "Jewish" environment for himself (N.B., using humor); on the other hand, it is a thrust towards self-knowledge.

Freud and the Student Zionist Society, Kadimah

One of the congratulatory greetings Freud received on his eightieth birthday in May 1936 was from the Viennese student Zionist society, Kadimah, to which his son Martin belonged. Freud replied, signing himself

> Yours, Freud, who would have liked to belong to your *Alte Herren* ["Old Boys," i.e., alumni][227]

Picking up on Freud's hint, Kadimah decided to elect him as an *Ehrenbursch* or honorary member, and Freud conveyed through Martin that he would be pleased to accept the honor.

Kadimah was the first and oldest Jewish national students' association, having been established at the University of Vienna in 1882, originally as a dueling fraternity. In 1892 a group of its alumni *(Alte Herren)* formed a Zionist group,[228] and when Herzl published *The Jewish State* in 1896, Kadimah members became his closest collaborators. The Zionist society was founded upon a credo of three points: (1) the struggle against Jewish assimilation; (2) Jewish nationhood; and (3) the settlement of Palestine as a means towards Jewish independence. They bravely proclaimed the message of Jewish nationhood at a time when the leaders of Jewry around the world, and in Vienna in particular, rejected the concept.[229] Martin had become a member in 1909, after he had witnessed a brawl at the University of Vienna between antisemites and Jews, the latter fighting back fiercely in a way that seemed to Martin at that time "out of character." He immediately joined the society,[230] identifying naturally with "fighting Jews." When Martin got home and told his father about his decision, Freud was "plainly delighted,"[231] and is reported to have said, "Your decision was right. That is fine and I am pleased about it."[232] Ernst Freud too was "an active Zionist and was well known as a leader in 'Blau-Weiss'," the Zionist-oriented Jewish youth movement.[233] So Freud's wish to identify publicly with Kadimah was anticipated by his sons' involvement in Zionism, acting with his approval. Freud's request on his eightieth birthday to become one of their "alumni" was perhaps a retrojection of his Jewish identification to his student days at the University of Vienna. As he wrote to Yehuda Devosis in December 1930, "I had already felt the influence of German antisemitism, of which a renewed outbreak took place during my university days."[234]

Freud's wish was fulfilled in a ceremony in his summer house in Döbling on 6 September 1936, when a delegation from Kadimah called upon Freud to present him with the honorary "sash" of the society. A speech was made, and Freud replied with his characteristic blend of proud affirmations and firm denials. He was not politically active, he said, but he had followed the Jewish-national and Zionist endeavors of Kadimah with interest and goodwill. He was not religious, but had always felt a strong sense of belonging to the Jewish people and had encouraged this feeling in his children. All the family had remained Jewish, a matter of pride in a Viennese context. Then,

> as one of the "Kadimah" delegates handed him the red-purple-and-gold sash, he asked: "May I put it on?" —"We did not dare to ask you to do so, Herr Professor," answered one of the "Kadimah." He, thereupon, with the help of Dr. H. Lifczis, put the honorary sash across his chest.[235]

Freud must have looked like a military hero, and felt like one of Hannibal's soldiers.

Up to this time, there had been only five other men elected to be *Ehrenburschen* of Kadimah: Herzl; Zionist leader Max Nordau; Ruben Bierer, the co-founder of Kadimah; Karpel Lippe, early member of Hovevei Zion and senior delegate to the First Zionist Congress in 1897; and Perez Smolensky, the Hebrew author and co-founder of Kadimah.[236] So Freud, as the sixth, was a member of an elite Jewish group. In Fraenkel's opinion, Freud's was not just a "gallant gesture," but rather "an open declaration to the world at large, at a time of danger and of Nazism, that he was a Jew who endorsed the Zionist aims for the Jewish people."[237] Freud's own earlier statements on Zionism (e.g., to Einstein,

Koffler, and Devosis in 1930) sounded a more cautious note. But Freud's Zionist act here at the end of his life may indicate a shift toward more wholehearted support. In any event, it is a vivid symbol of his defiant sense of himself in his eightieth year as a Jew fighting for the national survival of his people. *Moses and Monotheism* must be seen in this context, for it is Freud's hieroglyphic defense of his people.

Moses and Monotheism *Revisited*

By 1937 Freud is back at work on his "Moses"; he is also reading Thomas Mann's *Joseph and His Brothers* at the time.[238] At the beginning of the year, the first essay of what would become *Moses and Monotheism* was published in *Imago* under the title, "Moses ein Ägypter."[239] As he wrote to Eitingon on 5 February 1937, "A fragment which I could free from the Moses work (known to you and A. Zweig) is finished. But the most essential things about it must remain unsaid."[240]

Interestingly enough, the Freuds may have celebrated a Passover seder this year, 1937. The first night of the Jewish holiday fell on Friday, 26 March, and Easter Sunday was 28 March. Martha wrote to Ernst on 4 April (the last day of Passover week had been 3 April) that "not even the *Pessach* festivities [*Pessach Feiertage*] which occurred at the same time [as cold and rain] could save the weather."[241] What kind of festivities were these that could have been expected to cheer things up? Even if the family didn't make a formal seder, Martha's words imply an attachment to or participation in the Jewish festival in some way. This year Freud failed to note in his *Kronik* the fifty-first Easter anniversary of his setting up in medical practice. Had he found some rest from his need for defiance?

Freud finished the second "Moses" essay later in the year, on 11 August;[242] it was published in the December issue of *Imago*, under the title, "Wenn Moses ein Ägypter war . . ."[243] At the end of August, Freud tells Marie Bonaparte that he has begun rewriting Moses III, "but only very slowly." Jones reports that "he found it too difficult, would probably not finish it and in any event would not publish it."[244] Two weeks later we hear again both of his difficulties and of his continuing engagement with the struggle:

> The grandiose nature of the perception that religion contains an *historical* truth continues to fascinate me, but the impetus to present it to others is paralyzed.[245]

He says that he cannot get over the conflict between the drive to express his own ideas and "political" considerations, that is, the threat to psychoanalytic practice in Vienna. The lack of historical evidence in support of his thesis also hinders him.[246]

Knowing that Freud has been at work on the third part of his "Moses," in which the Lamarckian phylogenetic quality of the inheritance that is Jewishness in Freud's mind is made most clear, Freud's response to a letter from the Vienna B'nai B'rith saluting him on the fortieth anniversary of his membership takes on added meaning. Saying that he is touched that the lodge remembers him and wishes him well, Freud thanks his "dear brothers" and assures them, "That which has united us will surely not perish with the changing times."[247] Given the antisemitic character of the "changing times," we may detect here evidence of Freud's conviction that the essence of what he shares with his Jewish brethren will outlast any destruction the Nazis might inflict in their brief reign of hate. That is, *die Heimlichkeit der gleichen seelischen Konstruktion,* whose secret Freud has penetrated in his *Moses* (as far as he is concerned), will endure, because it is a phylogenetic inheritance, a special case of the inheritance of acquired characteristics.[248]

Freud expresses this phylogenetic idea in ontogenetic terms to Hans Ehrenwald in December, when he acknowledges a copy of Ehrenwald's book, *Über den sogenannten jüdischen Geist.*[249] Having begun to ask himself "several years ago" how the Jews had acquired "their particular character," and following his usual practice of going back to the earliest beginnings, Freud had found that

> the first so to speak embryonic experience of the people, the influence of the man Moses and the exodus from Egypt, conditioned the entire further development up to the present day—just like a regular history of a neurotic individual.[250]

Note that again Freud does not mention antisemitism as a catalyst for writing his book when describing it to this Gentile author, nor does he mention the question of the origins of antisemitism as one of his concerns. In any event, Freud goes on to list the spiritual consequences of the Mosaic conditioning he has discovered:

> In the first place there is the this-worldliness of the view of life and the overcoming of magical thinking, and the rejection of mysticism, both of which can be traced back to Moses himself . . .

Jewish thinking, for Freud, is focused on "this side," rather than on "the beyond" that magic and the mystical occult concern themselves with. Remember Freud's Jewish "sobriety." This view of Jewish character is not new for Freud, as we have seen; what is new is his attributing it to Moses. Interestingly enough, Freud does not mention that his Moses is an Egyptian (though he asks Ehrenwald to look at his *Imago* essays). In December 1934 Freud tells Zweig that "Moses being an Egyptian is not the essential point, though it is the starting point."[251] The essential point is what Freud does with it.[252]

Freud adds another "Mosaically derived" Jewish trait to this list the following month in a letter to his son Ernst:

> It is typically Jewish [*echt jüdisch*] not to renounce anything and to replace what has been lost. Indeed Moses, who in my opinion left a lasting imprint on the Jewish character, created the prototype for that.[253]

Freud seems to be referring to his argument in *Moses and Monotheism* that Moses responded to the loss of the political support for the monotheism of the Egyptian Aton religion when Akhnaton died by choosing the Jewish people to serve as its new vehicle, replacing the Egyptian people, who had rejected it. The Jews became the material for the religion's imprint, and by means of a refined form of his master Akhnaton's sun religion, Moses stamped the Jewish people with character traits that are a consequence of its spirituality. In this way Moses create the "Psychological Jew," where Jewish "content is replaced by character."[254] This Jew survives through the centuries, even in the absence of Jewish observance (so Yerushalmi's subtitle, "Judaism Terminable and Interminable"). In this refusal to give up, Freud sees the "tenacity of Jewry," and evidence for the presence of the interminable Jew.

In his letter to Ernst, Freud is thinking of his son's recent acquisition of a new house on the coast of England, which was a replacement for one Ernst had owned on the German island of Hiddensee,[255] presumably property that was confiscated by the Nazis or made inhospitable by them. But the Jew will not give up so easily. Freud sees the Jewish character that he believes Moses created expressed in his son's act, confirming his theory of the transmission of Jewish identity. That is, he sees his own Jewishness passed on—genetically perhaps—to his son Ernst, and he responds with pleasure: "My best wishes for the opening of Hidden House!" Freud also confirms his conviction of the essential *historicity* of his "solution" to the problem of Jewish identity in this letter, when he says of his essay on Moses, "It is my first appearance as a historian, late enough!"

But Moses is not the only famous Jewish figure in whose image Freud sees himself in 1938. On 13 March 1938, at a board meeting of the Vienna Psychoanalytic Society convened just after Hitler invaded and annexed Austria, "it was decided that everyone should flee the country if possible, and that the seat of the society should be wherever Freud would settle."[256] Freud's comment at the time appears, significantly, also in *Moses and Monotheism*. At the meeting he said,

> After the destruction of the Temple in Jerusalem by Titus, Rabbi Jochanan ben Sakkai asked for permission to open a school at Jabneh for the study of the Torah. We are going to do the same. We are, after all, used to persecution by our history, tradition, and some of us by personal experience . . .[257]

Freud will refer to this tradition (a well-known one) again in a letter of recommendation for Jacob Meitlis seven months later, with a significant introduction (see below), at which time the full meaning of Freud's identification with R. Yochanan ben Zakkai will become clear. At this point, it is worth noting again the metaphor of the Jerusalem Temple for the edifice of psychoanalysis and the parallel drawn between Torah study and psychoanalytic research. Furthermore, there is his identification with the Jewish historical "tradition" of persecution fueling this image of Jewish strength and tenacious perseverance in a cause.

Rabbi Yochanan ensured the spiritual (and so physical) survival of the Jewish people by opening a school; *mutatis mutandis*, Freud says, "we are going to do the same." How closely does Freud understand the analogy? We recall his dream about Theodor Herzl at the end of the early period, in which Freud dreamed that "something must be done to save the Jewish people." But there is a significant addition here that follows what is quoted above. Freud qualified the "us" in his last sentence by laughing and pointing at Richard Sterba, the one Gentile present at the time, adding, "with one exception."[258] The psychoanalytic "tribe" is at base humanist, and so its allegiances transcend the Jewish people. Though Freud at this point uses an image from Jewish history to characterize the psychoanalytic movement as a whole, shaping the group image using one of the Jewish people, nevertheless he does not relinquish his dual allegiance, which the psychoanalytic movement reflects.

At the end of April, Freud writes Jones that he is working an hour each day at the third part of his "Moses," which he says, torments him like an "unlaid ghost."[259] The image is psychologically apt, especially if the "Moses" is linked to Freud's relationship with his father. Jakob's "ghost" calls out for justice, namely, a positive link to Jews and Judaism, through a return to the Bible that began their journey together as Jews.

Two weeks later Freud in fact compares himself "with the old Jacob who, when a very old man, was taken by his children to Egypt."[260]

The biblical patriarch of course is the progenitor of the twelve tribes of the Jewish people, a potent Jewish identification. Schur reports that Freud used the metaphor of Jacob struggling with the "angel" (Gen. 32:24-32) "to describe the force of his drive toward making new discoveries."[261] The wish preceding the biblical image in Freud's letter to his son Ernst is Freud's desire "to die in freedom." Juxtaposed to the image of Jacob, these words point to the role *Moses and Monotheism* will play by means of its new ideas in freeing Freud (who also identified with Joseph,[262] the biblical interpreter of dreams), from the guilts associated with his failures to fulfill his Jewish allegiances. His Egyptian Moses will fulfill Freud's Jewish responsibilities to his father and to his people, just as the biblical Joseph did, who also assumed an Egyptian identity in order to become his family's provider. Thus Freud will come to play both father and son in this projected Jewish familial metaphor.

Freud continues the metaphor in his letter to identify himself with another figure from the Jewish "tradition" of antisemitism, namely, the Wandering Jew. Once Freud imagines himself safe in "Egypt" (and he mentions Thomas Mann's novel, *Joseph the Provider*), he says,

> Let us hope that there won't follow in days to come an exodus from Egypt. It is high time that Ahasuerus come to rest somewhere.[263]

Ahasuerus, the "Wandering Jew," or in the German version of the legend, *Der ewige Jude*, the "Eternal Jew," is the central figure of an antisemitic Christian legend that concerns in its most common form a shoemaker in Jerusalem who taunted Jesus on his way to crucifixion, and was therefore condemned by the latter to wander forever without a resting place, that is, without dying, until Jesus' Second Coming. Freud was familiar with this legend at least from 1928, for he wrote then to George Viereck, who had written a psychoanalytically conducted autobiography of the Eternal Jew, that "the memoirs of your 'Eternal Jew' are assured of my greatest interest."[264]

Freud's identification now ten years later may indicate that he feels that the persecution he has endured over the years is related to his "taunting" of Christianity with his views of religion (e.g., *The Future of an Illusion*, in 1927). In any event, the ideas embedded in the legend point us indirectly to themes in Freud's "unlaid ghost," *Moses and Monotheism*. The eternally Wandering Jew, Ahasver, is a Christian personification of the Jewish people as a whole,

> incorporating the themes of the participation in the crucifixion, condemnation to eternal suffering until Jesus' second coming, and the bearing of witness to the truth of the Christian tradition.[265]

Freud's last book intersects with these themes, being very much concerned with the "eternality" of the Jewish people, that is, its uncanny survival over the centuries in spite of dispersion and persecution. But Freud also finds a new twist for Jewish "participation" in the crucifixion, namely, the killing of Moses as its prefiguration. In addition, the crucifixion represents, Freud says, the "return of the repressed" in its repetition of the killing of the father of the primal horde. Psychoanalysis here discloses the content of revelation. And so thirdly, Freud bears witness in *Moses and Monotheism* to the "historical truth" at the heart of the Christian tradition, namely, parricide. Christianity mediates in Freud's conception the consoling atonement for the inherited memory traces of this deed and its attending guilt, while at the same time satisfying the urge to repeat the deed. Christianity is the "fulfillment" of Judaism in this sense, though not a cultural advance over it,[266] for the basis of cultural progress is not the satisfaction of a drive, but rather its renunciation.[267]

It is in this sense that psychoanalysis is a real advance over both Christianity and Judaism, in delivering to the Jews the "fourth humiliation" with which *Moses and Monotheism* opens, namely, the denial of the Jewish creation of monotheism. As Yerushalmi points out, in Freud's view this renunciation of narcissism is only the last in a series of painful humiliations which human beings have had to endure in order to exchange illusion for reality:

> the "cosmological" blow delivered by Copernicus to the idea of the centrality of our planet in the universe; Darwin's "biological" blow to Man's supposedly privileged place in the hierarchy of creation; and—most devastating of all—Freud's own "psychological" blow to Man's last imagined refuge ("the ego is not master in its own house").[268]

In so far as Jews suffer this humiliation for the spiritual gain it offers, they will grow into a greater people, and psychoanalysis, godless though it be, will have functioned as the "last of the prophets," impelling the Jews to fulfill their destiny as a "light unto the nations." No wonder Freud considers his last book "quite a worthy exit."

On 4 June 1938 Freud was finally permitted by the Nazis to leave Vienna. When they insisted that he sign a statement that he had been well treated by the authorities, he added a sentence after his signature that shows the strength of his defiance, even at the age of eighty-two: "I can recommend the Gestapo most highly to everyone."[269] Martin Freud notes that the style is that of a commercial advertisement, and he reports that its irony was missed by the Nazis as they passed the certificate from man to man, shrugged their shoulders, and marched off.[270] Gay is puzzled by the risk that Freud takes at this moment. But Freud's act is consistent with his Jewish identity. For example, once Anna had obtained permission from the Nazis for the Freuds to leave Vienna, she was ordered by the Gestapo to report daily to the police. When Freud heard of the demand, he said, "You, Anna, have of course refused to obey so humiliating an order."[271] That this same sense of dignity finds expression at such a dangerous final moment in the form of a *joke* in response to the absurd Nazi request, in defiance of the danger, shows the indomitable strength of Freud's Jewishness, especially when confronted by antisemitism, and it shows how connected *Witz* was to Freud's sense of himself as a Jew.

As he was arriving in England on 6 June, Freud dreamed he was landing at Pevensey, the spot where William the Conqueror had landed in 1066.[272] In his first letter written on the day he arrived, Freud told Eitingon that the enchantment of his new surroundings made him want to shout, "Heil Hitler!"[273] Freud comes in and goes out with the same indomitable, fighting spirit of a "conquistador" (as he adventurously described himself to Fliess in 1900).[274]

Freud's arrival brought forth welcomes and appeals from Jewish groups anxious to attach themselves to their famous fellow Jew. Freud responded to YIVO, for example, having been a member of YIVO's honorary presidium for a long time, with a repetition of his characteristic combination of solidarity and denial:

> I was very glad to receive your greeting. You no doubt know that I gladly and proudly acknowledge my Jewishness though my attitude toward religion, including ours, is critically negative.[275]

By this time we know how to qualify Freud's negative attitude with his "Mosaic" participation.

Two weeks after he arrived in England, Freud began the final rewriting of his "Moses III" (noted on 21 June in his *Kronik*). On 28 June, he writes to Zweig, saying, "I am enjoying [*mit Lust*] writing the third part of *Moses*." The obstacles seemed to have been cleared from his path, for less than a month after he took up the task, Freud noted in his *Kürzeste Kronik*, on 17 July 1938, what he wrote on the same day to his brother, Alexander: "Have just written down the last sentence of my Moses III."[276] That Alexander was his correspondent perhaps points to the familial context for the original formation of Freud's Jewish identity. Recall that it was Freud who named his brother. Is he now complementing by means of his *Moses* the implied commitment to classical humanism that the name "Alexander" represented?

In any event, it seems that Freud was eager to communicate a kernel of his new work to his fellow psychoanalysts, because he had Anna read "Der Fortschritt in der Geistigkeit" ("The Progress in Spirituality")[277] at the International Psychoanalytical Congress in Paris on 2 August.[278] It is noteworthy that Freud chose to release a section that makes the hero Moses and his chosen people, the Jews, responsible for the triumph of *Geistigkeit* over *Sinnlichkeit*, of spirituality over sensuality, which, he originally wrote, is "the alternative that was more significant culturally."[279] Freud makes the Jews ultimately responsible for the most culturally valuable and significant advances in Western civilization. Furthermore, the story about Rabbi Yochanan ben Zakkai and his Torah school at Yavneh appears in this section, described as a political misfortune that taught the Jews to value at its true worth their religious literature, the Torah. "From that time on," Freud writes, "Holy Scripture and the spiritual endeavor with it were what held the dispersed people together."[280]

It may be, as Freud told Jones in 1936, that his "historical novel" contains "a refutation of the Jewish national mythology"[281] and that "its contents are suitable to wound Jewish feelings, insofar as they do not want to submit themselves to science," as he told Devosis in December 1938, when the latter inquired about a Hebrew translation of *Moses and Monotheism*.[282] But in the context of Freud's values and allegiances, to attribute "progress in *Geistigkeit*" (intellectuality, spirituality) to the Jewish people is high praise, perhaps the highest he can give. Nor is it insignificant in this context that Freud contrasts this intellectual character of the Jewish people, which he says has had the effect of checking "the brutality and the tendency to violence which are apt to appear where the development of muscular strength is the popular ideal,"[283] with that obvious reference to Nazi Germany. The Jews, not the Germans, are responsible for what is worthwhile in civilization. Jakob Freud's response to the antisemitic violence done to him looks now like "the worthier alternative." And "this characteristic development of the Jewish nature [i.e., valuing intellectuality over muscular strength] was initiated by the Mosaic prohibition against worshipping God in a visible form."[284] Freud speaks here indeed as a Jewish spiritual patriot, as Simon says, though in a humanist form. In any event, he is hardly denigrating or attacking his people.

As news spread that *Moses and Monotheism* was about to be published, Jews began to petition Freud in an attempt to dissuade him from publishing it. Freud's letter to Zweig of 28 June 1938 speaks of "a young American Jew imploring me not to deprive our poor unhappy people of the one consolation remaining to them in their misery." "What an overestimation!" Freud exclaims. "Can one really believe that my arid treatise would destroy the belief of a single person brought up by heredity and training in the faith, even if it were to come his way?"[285] Apparently Freud knows that Judaism is stronger than psychoanalytic reason.

In mid-October, Charles Singer, an eminent British-Jewish historian of science and medicine, conveyed to Freud through his son Ernst a pamphlet (probably on Jewish affairs) and "the message that he would be wise to keep *Moses and Monotheism* in his desk, particularly since the English churches, bulwarks against anti-Semitism, would take the book as an attack on religion."[286] This was probably not the best tack to take with Freud, since the Catholic church, which was supposed to protect him from the Nazis, had proven to be such a "broken reed." Freud responded on 31 October, describing his *Moses* as an extension of *Totem and Taboo,* and insisting that "it can be called an attack on religion only insofar as any scientific investigation of religious belief presupposes disbelief." Repeating his commitment to atheism, Freud goes on to say that really only Jewry will have reason to feel offended by the book. This shortsightedness on Freud's part shows how closely *Moses and Monotheism* was tied to Jewry in his mind, for there is certainly enough in it to offend Christendom too.

However, his belief that Jewry will be offended places him in a dilemma:

> Needless to say, I do not gladly hurt my fellow people either. But what can I do about it? I have spent my whole long life standing up for what I held to be the scientific truth, even when it was uncomfortable and disagreeable to my fellow human beings. I cannot conclude it with an act of denial.

Freud of course opens *Moses and Monotheism* with this very issue, namely, the tension between truth and national Jewish solidarity (or "interests"), to both of which, as we have seen, Freud feels an allegiance.[287]

Yerushalmi shows how deliberately Freud names himself as a Jew in the very first sentence of his book:

> To deny a people the man whom it praises as the greatest of its sons is not a deed to be undertaken lightly—especially when one belongs oneself to that people.[288]

The original sentence in Freud's 1934 manuscript read merely, "One will not easily decide to deny a nation its greatest man because of the meaning of a name."[289] Note too the change from "nation" to "people" in the published version.[290] Freud will suffer this ascesis in solidarity with his people. Though he does not gladly or lightly force his people (and himself) into this renunciation (Yerushalmi's "fourth humiliation"), he must do so, he says, in the name of truth, the hope of knowledge, and the exchange of illusion for reality, which take precedence over personal comfort, including his own. Recalling Freud's conclusions about the basis of civilization's development in "The Progress in *Geistigkeit*," we are not surprised to see Freud practicing a similar renunciation upon himself first. As at the beginning of his research on dreams, Freud submits himself to the first analysis. As the "starting point," such renunciation, the transcendence of narcissism, led him to the "essential point" of Jewish identity.

In any event, Freud has another reason for going ahead with publication of his *Moses:*

> At present, we Jews are reproached with the charge that we have in the course of the centuries become cowardly (we were once a valiant nation). In this transformation I have had no part. So I must risk it.

As a Jew Freud identifies with the brave nation that fought valiantly for its Temple and its religious/spiritual survival. The *means* by which Freud sees this battle being fought after the physical destruction of the Temple (the "visible Temple" of the Nathan letter) is the *geistig* endeavor for *wissenschaftliche Wahrheit* (cf. the "invisible edifice of Judaism").

Freud makes this point forcibly in a letter he writes on 30 November 1938 as part of a recommendation for Jacob Meitlis to go to South Africa "to revive among our fellow-people there interest in our scientific institute in Vilno" [i.e., YIVO]. Freud says that he has no doubt that Meitlis will be successful, and he continues,

> We, Jews, have always known how to respect spiritual values. We preserved our unity through ideas, and because of them we have survived to this day. The fact that Rabbi Jochanan ben Zakkai immediately after the destruction of the Temple obtained from the conqueror permission to establish the first academy for Jewish knowledge in Jabneh was for me always one of the most significant manifestations in our history.[291]

Here at the very end of his life, Freud uses the Yochanan ben Zakkai story in an entirely Jewish social context, and with Freud's view of the role of the Jews in the progress of civilization, it bears the full weight of his pride. It is through *ideas* that Jews have been able to preserve their unity and survive, and for that reason they know how to respect "spiritual values." At the end of his life, Freud affirms a link with traditional Jewish learning, another link with his father,[292] and he sees the survival of the Jews bound up with it., Freud comes by his own route to affirm a position closer to tradition than he may realize. He adds,

> Once again our people is faced with dark times requiring us to gather all our strength in order to preserve unharmed all culture and science during the present harsh storms.[293]

Jews are to be the guardians of enlightened civilization while the Nazis plunge Europe back into the Dark Ages. Here Zweig and Freud seem to agree on the Jewish role.

In a meeting on 7 November with Meitlis and other members of YIVO, Freud spoke of the "community of interests and emotions" he shared with Jews. "We are all of the same blood," he said according to Meitlis, "not without a note of pride."[294] "Freud's Jewishness was an integral part of his universalism," Meitlis observes.[295] On the other hand, Freud affirms his commitment to the "scientific truth" independently of any "national interests," and in this meeting, when he spoke at length of his theory of monotheism, "He had no preference for any religion," Meitlis reports. Furthermore, Freud told them that

> all religions were human matters created by human beings and he could discern no trace of sanctity in any of them. It was the function of science to reveal this truth and to liberate spiritual movement from all later additions and extraneous elements.[296]

In other words, "science" (i.e., psychoanalysis) carries on the Jewish tradition of investment in and dependence upon ideas, for scientific ideas liberate *Geistigkeit* hidden in religious traditions.[297] We are reminded of Lessing's, "Education of the Human Race." This is what Freud thinks he is doing in *Moses and Monotheism*, in spite of the anger of his fellow human beings, the Jews.

Given these commitments and values embedded in the nature of *Moses and Monotheism*, we can perhaps echo the author's sentiments more easily than did most of his contemporaries, when Freud writes to Hanns Sachs in March 1939 and says,

> The Moses, printed in German at Albert de Lange, made its appearance here today in two copies. Quite a worthy exit, I believe.[298]

Summary

Before turning in chapter 5 to the implications of my study for the development of a model of dual allegiance for modern Jewish identity, let me summarize the picture of Freud's Jewish identity that has emerged from his correspondence and psychoanalytic writings in the late period.

Freud's Jewish identity in the late period is a more mature recapitulation of his Jewish identity in the early period, having gone through the "incubation" of the middle period. As noted, it was in the middle period, when Freud suppressed his Jewishness in the interests of the advance of psychoanalysis, that he interpreted the *Moses* of Michelangelo in such a way so as to create an unconscious identification with his father and the virtue of self-restraint that Jakob displayed in the face of antisemitism. The fruits of this creation emerge in the late period. In the early period, Freud responded to his father's example by adopting a martial ideal; he became a "fighting Jew." In the late period, though still a fighter, Freud's fighting Jewish spirit is channeled by his identification with his father into an idealization of the latter's virtue: Moses bequeathed to the Jews the psychological pattern of drive renunciation embodied in Jakob Freud's self-restraint. This habit of the constant suppression of natural desires and impulses led to the ethical and intellectual refinement of Jewish (and Western) civilization at its best. Thus, though Freud is "almost choking with rancor and fury," he turns to matters that can raise the Jews (and humanity) out of the insane frenzies of Nazi irrationality and hatred, namely, *Moses and Monotheism.*

In the early period, on the other hand, "red with rage," Freud acts in the opposite way. He gives in to his anger and verbally attacks those who have provoked it. In 1934, by renouncing the satisfaction to be gained from satisfying the direct expression of his anger, Freud produces a spiritual defense of his people's character, hoping to contribute to their survival and further development by a dependence on ideas, the "invisible edifice" of Jewish tradition. Characteristically, Freud does this within a humanist framework, the *Wissenschaft* of "applied psychoanalysis."

What is the picture of Freud's Jewish identity in the late period, and how is it related to the early period? The late period begins with Freud's encounter with death, first that of close friends and family, and then his own. The reality of death throws life into relief, and it forces Freud to reconsider himself and return to his deepest roots. Therefore, we see a renewed Jewish identification in the late period, an identification with Eastern European origins, ethnic traditions (even numerological superstitions), and Jewish languages (Yiddish and Hebrew). He asserts proudly (or defiantly) in 1935 that he is "a Jew from Moravia whose parents come from Austrian Galicia."[299] He repeatedly expresses his pain at not knowing Hebrew or Yiddish and so feeling cut off in that way. As a formal expression of this identification, Freud affiliates with YIVO, the Jewish research institute dedicated to the study and preservation of Yiddish/Jewish culture. This commitment seems a far cry from Freud's disdain of the early period or his denials to Roback in the middle period.

The continuing importance of jokes and wit to Freud's sense of himself as a Jew is underscored by his defiant irony added to the statement the Gestapo require him to sign in 1938, confirming that he had been "well treated." That Freud could defy the threat of death with a witticism reveals the deep courage of this Jew's stance toward life, expressed in the joke. It is a secular tradition, but profoundly Jewish in Freud's mind, brought out by the confluence of antisemitism and the threat of death. When events work to deny Freud's Jewishness its value, he responds with an affirmation—the fighting Jew. But the bravado from the early period has matured, and he can temper it with self-restraint, or sublimate it.

Freud can do this because he is deeply rooted in Jewish traditions. While remaining an atheist, Freud returns to the Bible as a historical source of Jewish identity, a link with his father, and a recapitulation of the early period. He does so through psychoanalytic and humanist reinterpretation, but it is a return nonetheless. This return to Jewish tradition is reflected also in his identification with a rabbinic figure, Rabbi Yochanan ben Zakkai. The only other rabbi to whom Freud refers is "Rabbi don Akiva," from Gutzkow's play, whom Freud mocked in the early period. Akiva saw into the depth of things, but ben Zakkai founded a school. Freud will do both, besting the former and imitating the latter. In the early period, Freud made fun of a rabbi; in the late period, he admires one. And so, in spite of his rejection of Jewish religion, Freud can take pleasure in his old age in being popularly acclaimed as though he were a "great, God-fearing Rabbi." As he says, *Judentum* is still very important to him "emotionally."

In his selective return to biblical and rabbinic traditions, Freud reaffirms the importance of *ideas* to the survival of the Jewish people, repeating an insight preserved from the Nathan letter in the early period, now given broader scope. The importance of Jewish survival to Freud strengthens his feeling of Jewish belonging. He is proud to have remained a Jew and to have nurtured his children in the solidarity he feels. The Jews are his people, as it were, one family. Freud shares their historical fate, and as a result, he comes to affirm an allegiance to Zionism more publicly in the late period, in spite of his self-restraint over "nationalist ideals." As a public expression of this personal development, he affiliates formally with the student Zionist society, Kadimah, becoming an honorary member. He is a "nationalist Jew." In 1886, he told a conversation partner at a cocktail party that he was neither German nor Austrian, but a Jew. In 1926, he states the same thing in an interview intended for publication. What was private in the early period with respect to Freud's Jewishness becomes public in the late period. It is the "return of the suppressed," in a higher key. Freud uses his public, psychoanalytic work to help him define his private sense of his own Jewishness, creating his own wholeness.

Freud associates formally, too, with Hebrew University in Jerusalem, serving on the board of trustees and taking an active interest in the founding of an academic chair in psychoanalysis. He sees the university, in its dependence on ideas, ultimately as an extension of the *Geistigkeit* that has its origins in Jewish tradition. That is, the *Humanität* of the university is rooted in Jewish culture, and in this way, Freud brings together the humanist and Jewish allegiances that were first joined in the early period in B'nai B'rith. The humanist tradition is an expression of prophetic ideals, so Freud can include Georg Brandes as a descendent of "our prophets."

In his 1926 address to B'nai B'rith, Freud makes a public attempt to define his Jewish identity, fruit born in the late period from seeds planted in the early one. He confesses an awareness of Jewish intimacy, a kind of common Jewish "home" *(Heimlichkeit)*, a shared "soul-structure," and he specifies the character traits of intellectual courage and independence of judgment as being due to his Jewishness. With these traits, Freud's "psychological" Jewish identity becomes a heroic stance towards the world, the Jew standing alone against popular opposition in the name of the truth, and this paves the way for his identification with the greatest of the Hebrew prophets, Moses. The martial ideal of the early period becomes the heroic ideal of truth in the late period. This truth must be revealed, furthermore, by "spiritual" means, namely, the renunciation of the satisfaction of an urge derived from a drive, a capacity transmitted to Western civilization by the Jews, and originating, according to Freud, with an Egyptian Moses.

The identification with Moses as a vehicle for the expression of Freud's Jewish identity is actually common to all three periods of Freud's development, underscoring its importance. It remains characteristically hidden and private in the early period, discernible only by inference. In the middle period, it becomes the means by which Freud tries to universalize psychoanalysis, seeking to transfer his "Mosaic" authority to the

Gentile Joshua-Jung. The failure of this effort sends Freud back to a Moses who embodies his father's (Jewish) self-control.

And though Freud will overturn the Jewish tradition's story of Moses' identity, he will use the Hebrew prophet to express a trait that is authentically related to Jewish religion, namely, the renunciation of impulse in the name of something higher. This self-discipline is a basic foundation of Jewish religious life, and is the psychological foundation of the Law. As Ben Zoma says in *Mishna Pirkei Avot* 4:1, "Who is strong [or "a mighty hero"]? The one who conquers his impulse [or "temperament"]."

In making Moses an Egyptian in the late period, Freud strikes a balance between his humanism and his "fanatical" Jewish nature, renouncing Jewish narcissism, yet using something non-Jewish to show the ultimate superiority of Jewish culture and the greatness of Jews. This may be his best revenge. The provocation of antisemitism in the late period is the same provocation that produced the "fighting Jew" in the early period, but the fighter has matured. Freud is disgusted by Jewish self-hate because he is aware of essential Jewish worth, believing that the Jewish pattern of the renunciation of drive is responsible for civilization's spiritual progress. Rooted in his father Jakob's example of dignity and self-control, Freud makes an essential peace with the tradition of his fathers. In this sense, *Moses and Monotheism* is Freud's return to self-analysis that resolves, in the late period, conflicts over his Jewish identity that were set up in the early period. Again, it is with some justification that Freud can feel he has made "quite a worthy exit."

5

Dual Allegiance and Modern Identity

From this survey, it is obvious that Freud's attitude toward his Jewishness over the course of his life was a critical, and not incidental or peripheral, element of his identity. Freud's Jewishness mattered to him, and he credited it with some basic elements of his character, including independence of mind, courage to stand firm in his convictions when alone and opposed, and particularly the capacity for self-restraint and self-transcendence. By the end of his life, he comes to understand why it matters so much: it is an inalienable, almost physical, phylogenetic link to the dawn of human and Jewish history.

To some extent, as Yerushalmi points out, Freud's story in *Moses and Monotheism* is a way of explaining "the enormous weight, the gravitational pull, of the Jewish past, whether it be felt as an anchor or a burden." In Jewish terms,

> what is Lamarckism if not the powerful feeling that, for better or worse, one cannot really cease being Jewish, and this not merely because of current antisemitism or discrimination, and certainly not because of the Chain of Tradition, but because one's fate in being Jewish was determined long ago by the Fathers, and that often what one feels most deeply and obscurely is a trilling wire in the blood.[1]

Like Heinrich Heine, Freud felt the inherited and indelible "longevity and irremediability of being Jewish."[2] The high assimilation and intermarriage rates in recent surveys[3] indicate that for many this psychological root has not taken hold, or is no longer felt. The truth is that "Psychological *Judentum*" *is* terminable—it is not biologically transmitted—especially in the absence of an ideology that gives Jews a reason to *choose* the tradition, as opposed to being chosen *by* it.

David Stern makes this point powerfully in his review of Yerushalmi's book, where he argues that Freud's Jewish identity cannot serve as a model for modern Jews in part because of "the strange passivity of his prescription for Jewishness,"[4] namely, its phylogenetic nature, "a notion of Jewish identity that excluded the individual will altogether."[5] Since, as Stern rightly says, voluntarism is the most salient feature of modern Jewish identity, and furthermore since Freud "sincerely took psychoanalysis for the future of Judaism" (a belief that today appears "fatuous and tragically mistaken"), Freud disqualified himself as a progenitor of modern Jewish identity: "In the case of Jewish identity, heroism eluded him."[6]

It is likely that Stern overstates his case. Freud's example may convey a *form* while leaving us free to choose a Jewish content that will serve us better. For it is not true that Freud's Judaism was purely a passive inheritance of status. In choosing psychoanalysis as the content of his godless Judaism,[7] Freud was in fact not passive. As a humanistic discipline, psychoanalysis *qua* Judaism functioned for Freud in the same way that his involvement in B'nai B'rith did, namely, as a Jewish vehicle for the expression of liberal and humanistic values. Contrary to Stern's insistence that Freud could not overcome the false opposition between the parochial and the universal, so that he "succumbed to the belief that being a Jew and being a modern secular Western intellectual are mutually exclusive,"[8] in fact Freud's Jewish identity was modern precisely in its Jewishness of dual allegiance—the combined commitment to Jewish particularity (even if genetically imposed) and human universality, mediated by Jewish tradition and the universal horizon of biblical particularism. Freud's Jewish identity in his understanding is not confined to his physically inherited Jewishness; it is also expressed by his Mosaically linked humanism.

And contrary to Stern's claim that Freud's "*Moses and Monotheism* Judaism" excludes voluntarism, it in fact embodies Freud's chosen embrace of his Jewishness, namely, the status of being chosen. It is a Jewishness of chthonic commitment, choosing to accept a fanatical belonging to one's people independently of and even in opposition to rational assent. That is, Freud chooses to be chosen. It is doubtful whether this feeling of belonging can continue over many generations without rational Jewish content (defined in terms of Jewish literature, life, and practice), though there are many spectacular stories of return after several generations of assimilation to make us wonder. On the other hand, Jewish content without the feeling of belonging is equally sterile, as is evident from the many knowledgeable yet disaffected Jews in both Israel and America today. Furthermore, in making the renunciation of drive *the* Jewish contribution to civilization and its spiritual progress that makes him proud to be a Jew, Freud was in fact choosing a central feature of Jewish religious life within the *halacha,* namely, the decentering of the ego in the presence of a divine demand for self-transcendence in obedience to the Law: *na 'aseh ve nishma'*, "we will obey and then understand."

Freud invents a new, mythic basis for a shared kinship across lines of (now genetic) difference, namely, the heritage of parricide. This heritage is held in common between Jews and non-Jews, providing Freud with a basis for a shared community. We are all—both Jews and Gentiles—in some sense bound by (Christian theologians would say, with Freud, "guilty of") the same past, and can therefore work toward building a common future based on this kinship, in addition to our tribal allegiances. The similarity to the Christian doctrine of original sin is accepted by Freud, who claims to have identified its prototype.[9] Through the story in his *Moses,* Freud provides everyone with a tribal kinship based on guilt. As in the Nathan letter, and as in Jewish tradition, the Jew becomes the paradigm for the human and shows the way towards a higher and deeper humanity *(Humanität).*

However, in Freud's "counter-theology," it is only by acknowledging this past, by admitting that we have inherited the memory (and so the guilt, even if only by unconscious transference) of parricide, that we discover this kinship with our brethren across lines of difference. By disclosing the deepest root of (his) Jewish identity, "how the Jew has come to acquire the character he has," Freud forges also his deepest human link with non-Jews. He finds that the access to a shared universal human community is achieved in the discovery and acceptance of the particular, irrational roots of his own Jewishness, that is, a Jewish (particular) form of the universal human trait of phylogenetic parricide. In the face of the racist and tribal Nazi destruction of any human civilization capable of transcending lines of difference, taking place at the time of Freud's writing and whose racialism is "uncomfortably reminiscent" of Freud's,[10] it does not seem inappropriate at all to call Freud's chosen vision for Jewish-humanist identity heroic.

Clearly, Freud has written a *myth* in *Moses and Monotheism.* That is, as Yerushalmi demonstrates and Stern articulates, the primal parricidal murder of Moses never took place in historical terms. If it had, Jewish tradition, true to its own disclosive nature, would not have concealed the deed, but would have trumpeted it as further proof of the perversity of the "stiff-necked" people. But this misses the point, as moderns have so often done when reading the texts of the ancient past. Just as we all participate in the events described in the Garden of Eden story—they describe not what "happened" but what happens—and rebel against the limits God places on our own autonomy, so we "kill" God/the Father, and take his authority into ourselves ("eating his body"). As moderns we can avoid stumbling over the literal myth (so what that it didn't "happen"?), while seeing through to its truth. Our historicity should not become a new fundamentalism.

In the recognition of the aggression inherent in our humanity, we can create a more knowing sense of self. We can more easily transcend our impulse to cling to immediate gratifications and satisfactions, knowing that they are in part illusions, that they cannot therefore nourish our deeper needs for community and wholeness. The truth is that we must "kill the Father" in order to leave the Garden; but we must also learn to love the "Mother" (tradition, our spiritual matrix) in order to return to "the Garden" as an adult: "A tree of life is she to those who grab hold of her." In this love of the tradition lies the hope for Jewish renewal today. We can recognize that "parricide" and "mother-loving" are modes-of-being-in-the-world that must be given content by particular experience within particular traditions, for example, Judaism.

In any event, Freud's dual allegiance is much more connected to the structure of Jewish tradition than has been recognized, as the following analysis of a crucial traditional text illustrates.[11]

As is well-known, the first mishna of tractate Rosh HaShanah from the Mishna (order "Holidays") outlines four "New Years" that structure the Jewish liturgical year. But these are four which are really two, because the other two "Rosh HaShanot" ("New Years"), in the months of Elul and Shevat, are linked subordinately to the two "main" New Years, in Nisan and Tishrei. The newborn animals tithed after the first of Elul were conceived in the spring of the previous Nisan, the first month, and the climatological cycle that produced the fruits that will be tithed from the first (or fifteenth) of Shevat onwards began with the rains of Tishrei, the seventh month. This prominence of Nisan and Tishrei is even greater in the experience of the Jewish people in the Diaspora, for whom Passover and Rosh HaShanah mark major turning points in the Jewish year, but for whom tithing the fruit of the land and the newborn of domestic animals did not hold.

Now Nisan, both in the Mishna and in the liturgical year, can be said to represent the "Rosh HaShanah" of Jewish history, the month that celebrates the birth of the Jewish people, the pole of the particular, whereas Tishrei represents the "Rosh HaShanah" of nature/Creation, the month that celebrates the creation of the world and during which the whole world is judged, the pole of the universal. Anyone familiar with the details of this first mishna and the themes of the major holidays associated with these months will recognize the cogency of this interpretation. In effect, traditional Jewish identity is defined by an experience of dual allegiance to these two poles. To be a Jew in the context of lived traditional observance is to live with a dual commitment to realizing one's humanity in coordination with one's Jewishness, and one's Jewishness in coordination with one's humanity. They are the deep foci of the year. To be a Jew is to know that God relates to me both as a Jew created out of Jewish history and as a human creature dependent on the produce or gifts of the land, its livestock, and its sky (sun, rain). It is by fully responding to Jewish history that I most fully realize my humanity; but it is also by fully recognizing and responding to my natural humanity that I most fully realize my Jewishness. This dual possibility is the deep fruit of dual allegiance, the basis of a human community that transcends lines of difference.

Although Freud was not an observant Jew, nor did he study mishna or gemara, his parents hailed from the Pale of Settlement in Galicia and grew up with traditional backgrounds. The depth of Jakob Freud's learning, in particular, is only now beginning to be appreciated, as we saw in chapter 2. On the basis of the Jewish life that Freud experienced and the Jewish people that he knew most intimately, who raised and taught him, Freud's own dual allegiance, to his Jewishness and to *Humanität*, is psychologically rooted in the traditional structure of dual allegiance that defines Jewish identity from the Mishna, even if unconsciously. It has been transmitted to him in the structure of the Jewish soul, *der Heimlichkeit der gleichen seelischen Konstruction.*

What can we learn from Freud's version of Jewish history and Jewish identity, including his dual allegiance, for the question of *modern* identity, and of modern Jewish identity in particular? Can Freud's example indeed serve as a model? I would say yes and no (a Jewish answer). Its content cannot serve us, but its form can. With regard to the former, Freud's understanding of "Judaism" is as idiosyncratic as it is partial. Judaism is much more than nineteenth-century Protestant Bible critics thought it was, namely, rational prophetic ethics (as profound as they are). In that sense, Freud's view simply reflects the prejudice of his age and its anti-Jewish culture (one that dispensed with "the Law" in order to free "the Spirit"), and is therefore thoroughly inadequate to sustain Jewish life. Though Freud's own children married Jews (at least in their first marriages), the next generation married out and effectively left the Jewish community. Freud's family is in fact another casualty of assimilation, and his psychological Judaism bears some responsibility. The loss bears witness to the risk of dual allegiance in the absence of Jewish content.

On the other hand, with regard to the form of Freud's compromise-formation, the very fact that Freud needed to forge such a deep attachment to *Judentum*—in both senses, people and religion—by writing *Moses and Monotheism*, demonstrates that his humanistic *Gymnasium* education was insufficient to define him as a human being, especially in the presence of antisemitism. He needed a dual allegiance to be fully himself. In spite of all Freud's attempts to be a humanist, "unprejudiced and impartial," he discovers at the end of his life that he is a "fanatical Jew." His particular roots cannot be abandoned without losing dignity and self-respect, and must therefore be defended, even developed, in order that he can feel that he has vindicated finally the last text remaining from the early period, namely, Jewish religion. Freud finds a measure of peace with this achievement, and so proclaims his last book "a worthy exit." His example can serve as a reminder that we need our tribalism, even as humanistic moderns.[12]

Freud's discovery of the inalienable depth of his Jewishness—deeper than reason can say—is evidence too for the philosophically necessary relationship between the particular and the universal. A generic, universal human being (or community) does not exist, any more than a generic human language does. Freud needed to confront his own radical particularity in order to have something universal to say (even if we judge it mistaken), and it is in this sense that he discovers the *value* of his particularity (and not just its tenacity). As human beings, we come only in particular forms, and our access therefore to the humanity we share in common—*Humanität*—is through our particular cultural and biological forms. Freud finds again at the end of his life what he found at the end of the early period in the Vienna B'nai B'rith, namely, that his liberal, humanist ideals can be expressed *through* his Jewishness.

On this basis I suggest that particularity and difference are a *resource* rather than a liability for community in common with others—including others of different cultural traditions—and so such particularity should be affirmed and nourished by both those who share that particular tradition, as well as by those who are outside of it. Such particularity is one more access to an understanding of what it is to be human, a wisdom all can share and all need to hear. Modern community must be based on such support for multicultural particularity.

This perception means a new model for the interaction of the larger society of which we are a part. Rather than the "melting pot," we need to think of the "tossed salad," with each element retaining its distinctive taste. Or, to vary the metaphor, at any point in time we must imagine that we are like many gears, parts of a larger machine we do not control. Each gear turns on its own axis and each depends on the other to revolve on its axis. Furthermore, the boundaries of each must be clearly defined and communicated (therefore the need for multicultural education) in order for the teeth to mesh; otherwise they cut and tear one another.

The college campus is one environment in which to explore and experiment with this new perception as a way of living, and not only as a way of thinking. Nowhere else are so many different cultures and ethnicities thrown together in such ignorance of one another, yet with such eagerness to learn and grow (sometimes). If we can create a multicultural community there, perhaps there may be some hope for it in the America outside the campus. For it is clear to all who live and work on college campuses that they are reflections of the society from which they are drawn, with all of the narrowness, ignorance, and fear that unfortunately pervades so much of an American society raised with television as its primary educational medium. If the humanities are to retain their civilizing role in the liberal arts curriculum, they must begin to utilize multicultural philosophical assumptions that can overcome the fear of difference. Such a goal is consonant with the humanizing purposes of liberal arts education.

Freud's experience suggests that dual allegiance cannot be avoided; it is simply in the nature of human existence. We are all unavoidably particular, rooted in a particular family, race, gender, and cultural tradition. But we are also all bound by larger structures of allegiance in the modern world, such as national allegiance and global or humanitarian allegiance. The duality of the Jew is only a particularly sharply defined example of common human experience. The Jew *can* be a paradigm for the human; but so can every particularity. Admittedly, acknowledging this depth raises the issue of a conflict of allegiances. But isn't it better to have such conflicts out in the open, especially if they are a shared element of human existence? In fact, we must all learn to negotiate dual allegiance; it is a maturational task. It is also necessary to the maintenance of the kind of multicultural community mentioned above, for one must learn how to journey back and forth between "home-cultures" and "other-cultures" in order to learn about and support both—in order to live together, side by side. The exercise broadens one's humanity even as it develops one's social skills. It teaches by particular (for example, Jewish) experience that "nothing human is alien to me" (or to any of us). Freud's exploration of his Jewishness teaches us that a similar motto grounds the affirmation of both Jewish particularity and humanism: *Judaeus sum, nihil humani a me alienum puto.* We need—as Freud needed—both affirmations to build a modern world that is better than the one that destroyed Freud's.

Notes

Preface

1. "I am Jewish, [therefore] I consider nothing human alien to me." Yosef Hayim Yerushalmi, *Freud's Moses: Judaism Terminable and Interminable* (New Haven: Yale University Press, 1991), 97.

2. The conventional English spelling of Wilhelm Marr's coinage, "anti-Semitism," blurs the object of its hatred, for "Semites" could logically refer also to Arabs as well as to Jews. Marr intended to replace *Judenhaß* ("Jew-hatred") with a less vulgar and even scientific-sounding word, making Jew-hatred seem more acceptable. The conventional spelling, even contained in Webster's ninth version of the dictionary, contributes to this uncivilized goal.

Chapter 1. Introduction

1. Samuel Jaffe, University of Chicago, personal communication. Cf. Harry Trosman, *Freud and the Imaginative World* (Hillsdale, N.J.: Analytic Press, 1985), 103.

2. Personal communication.

3. Maryse Choisy, *Sigmund Freud: A New Appraisal* (New York: Philosophical Library, 1963), 108.

4. Sigmund Freud, *Notes upon a Case of Obsessional Neuroses*, in *The Standard Edition of the Complete Psychological Works of Sigmund Freud*, 24 vols., ed. and trans. James Strachey (London: Hogarth Press and the Institute of Psychoanalysis, 1953–74), 10:67–110. Henceforth, "Stnd. Ed."

5. Sigmund Freud, *Analysis of a Phobia in a Five-Year-Old Boy,* Stnd. Ed., 10:152–204.

6. Sigmund Freud, *From the History of an Infantile Neurosis,* Stnd. Ed., 17:3–145.

7. Sigmund Freud, *Psycho-Analytic Notes on an Autobiographical Account of a Case of Paranoia (Schreber),* Stnd. Ed., 12:178–307.

8. Sigmund Freud, *Autobiography,* trans. James Strachey (New York: Norton, 1935), 147.

9. Ibid., 148.

10. Ibid., 148–49.

11. Ibid., 149–50.

12. Sigmund Freud, "Obsessive Actions and Religious Practices," Stnd. Ed., 9:115–27.

13. Cf. Earl A. Grollman, *Judaism in Sigmund Freud's World* (New York: Bloch, 1965).

14. Robert S. Wistrich, *The Jews of Vienna in the Age of Franz Joseph* (Oxford: Oxford University Press, 1989), 539–40.

15. Ibid., 543.

16. In his speech to B'nai B'rith in May 1926; Ernst Freud, ed., *Letters of Sigmund Freud,* trans. Tania Stern and James Stern (New York: Basic Books, 1960), 366–67. Henceforth, *Letters.*

17. Martin Freud, "Who was Freud?" in Joseph Fraenkel, ed., *The Jews of Austria: Essays on their Life, History, and Destruction* (London: Vallentine, Mitchell, and Co., 1967), 202.

18. Martin Freud, *Sigmund Freud: Man and Father* (New York: Vanguard, 1958), 11. Martin reports that Aunt Dolphi once took Amalia, over ninety at the time, to buy a new hat. "Studying carefully her image crowned by the hat she had agreed to try on, Amalia . . . finally shouted, 'I won't take this one; it makes me look old'" (ibid.).

19. Cf. Freud's words about Goethe, one of his heroes: "He who has been the undisputed darling of his mother [as Freud was] retains throughout life that victorious feeling, that confidence in ultimate success, which not seldom brings actual success with it" (S. Freud, "A Childhood Recollection from *Dichtung und Wahrheit*" (1917), in S. Freud, *Character and Culture,* ed. P. Rieff [New York: Collier Books, 1963], 201).

20. Monica McGoldrick and Randy Gerson, *Genograms in Family Assessment* (New York: Norton, 1985), 22.

21. Michael Molnar, ed. and trans., *The Diary of Sigmund Freud, 1929–1939. A Record of the Final Decade,* the Freud Museum, London (New York: Charles Scribner's Sons, 1992), 278n. Henceforth, *Diary.*

22. Franz Kobler, "Die Mutter Sigmund Freuds," *Bulletin des Leo Baeck Instituts* 5 (1962): 152.

23. Martin Freud, *Sigmund Freud: Man and Father,* 11.

24. Peter Gay, *Freud: A Life for Our Time* (New York: Norton, 1988), 6.

25. Emanuel Rice, *Freud and Moses: The Long Journey Home* (New York: SUNY Press, 1990), 57.

26. Ibid., 65.

27. Paul Mendes-Flohr, "History and *Kultur:* The German-Jewish Perspective," in *A Land of Two Rivers. The German-Jewish Vision of a New Babylon.* Forthcoming from Yale University Press.

28. Ibid.
29. Ibid.
30. Ibid.
31. Cf. George L. Mosse, *German Jews Beyond Judaism* (Bloomington: Indiana University Press, 1985), 3–5; and Mendes-Flohr, *A Land of Two Rivers,* chap. 1.
32. Sigmund Freud, *The Interpretation of Dreams,* trans. James Strachey (New York: Avon, 1965), 225–26.
33. Ibid.
34. Cited in John E. Gedo and Ernest Wolf, "The 'Ich.' Letter," *Psychological Issues* 9, nos. 2–3 (1976): 75.
35. Freud, *The Interpretation of Dreams,* 230; cf. Ernst Simon, "Sigmund Freud, the Jew," *Leo Baeck Institute of Jews from Germany Yearbook* 2 (1957): 271.
36. Ibid.
37. Martin Freud, "Who was Freud?"201.
38. Gay, *Freud: A Life,* 595.
39. Wistrich, *The Jews of Vienna,* 558 n. 86.
40. Freud, *The Interpretation of Dreams,* 230.
41. Ibid., 460.
42. Ibid., 229–30.
43. Ibid., 229.
44. Ibid., 224.
45. On 11 March 1902, in Jeffrey M. Masson, *The Complete Letters of Sigmund Freud to William Fliess, 1887–1904,* trans. and ed. J. Masson (Cambridge: Harvard University Press, 1985), 456. Henceforth, *Complete Fliess Letters.*
46. Paul C. Vitz, *Sigmund Freud's Christian Unconscious* (New York: Guilford Press, 1988).
47. Freud, *The Interpretation of Dreams,* 226.
48. Ibid., 230.
49. Both Drucker and Sulloway dispute the historical reality of this discrimination, but for our purposes, Freud's perception is what matters. Cf. Peter F. Drucker, "What Freud Forgot," *Human Nature* 2, no. 3 (March 1979): 40–47; Frank J. Sulloway, *Freud, Biologist of the Mind: Beyond the Psychoanalytic Legend* (New York: Basic Books, 1979).
50. Cf. Sander S. Gilman, *Jewish Self-Hatred. Anti-Semitism and the Hidden Language of the Jews* (Baltimore: Johns Hopkins University Press, 1986).
51. Leo Goldhammer, "Theodor Herzl and Sigmund Freud: Träume," in *Theodor Herzl-Jahrbuch,* ed. Tulo Nussenblatt (Wien: Victor Glanz, 1937), 268.
52. Cf. Dennis Klein, *Jewish Origins of the Psychoanalytic Movement,* 2d ed. (Chicago: University of Chicago Press, 1985, xiii–xiv.
53. Wistrich, *The Jews of Vienna,* 548.
54. Sigmund Freud, *An Autobiographical Study,* trans. James Strachey (New York: Norton, 1952), 14–15.
55. Wistrich, *The Jews of Vienna,* 558.
56. Freud, *An Autobiographical Study,* 14–15.
57. "*deutsch-kleinstädtisch*"*;* 3 December 1885, in E. Freud, *Letters,* 188.
58. To Martha Bernays, 2 February 1886; E. Freud, *Letters,* 203.

59. Stanley Rothman and Phillip Isenberg, "Sigmund Freud and the Politics of Marginality," *Central European History* 7 (1974): 58–78. See also Rothman and Isenberg, "Freud and Jewish Marginality," *Encounter* 43, no. 6 (1974): 46–54.

60. Rothman and Isenberg, "Sigmund Freud and the Politics of Marginality," 68.

61. William J. McGrath, *Freud's Discovery of Psychoanalysis: The Politics of Hysteria* (Ithaca: Cornell University Press, 1986), 295.

62. Martin S. Bergmann, "Science and Art in Freud's Life and Work," in Lynn Gamwell and Richard Wells, eds., *Freud and Art: His Personal Collection of Antiquities* (London: Freud Museum, 1989), 176.

63. Cf. Marianne Krüll, *Freud and His Father,* trans. Arnold J. Pomerans (New York: Norton, 1986).

64. Klein, *Jewish Origins,* xi.

65. On the "Rome dreams," cf. McGrath, *Freud's Discovery,* and Alexander Grinstein, *On Sigmund Freud's Dreams* (Detroit: Wayne State University Press, 1968).

66. Klein, *Jewish Origins,* 71.

67. On 26 December 1908. Hilda C. Abraham and Ernst L. Freud, eds., *A Psychoanalytic Dialogue: The Letters of Sigmund Freud and Karl Abraham, 1907–1926,* trans. Bernard Marsh and Hilda C. Abraham (London: Hogarth Press and the Institute of Psychoanalysis, 1965).

68. Klein, *Jewish Origins,* 71. Sharing Jewish jokes with fellow Jews is of course itself an expression of this solidarity.

69. Ibid., 86.

70. Freud, *The Interpretation of Dreams,* 228.

71. Theodor Reik, "Sigmund Freud," in *Jewish Heritage Reader,* ed. Lily Edelman (New York: Taplinger [1965]), 222.

72. Sigmund Freud, *Jokes and their Relation to the Unconscious,* trans. James Strachey (New York: Norton, 1963).

73. Simon, "Sigmund Freud, the Jew," 282.

74. Martin S. Bergmann, "Moses and the Evolution of Freud's Jewish Identity," in *Judaism and Psychoanalysis,* ed. M. Ostow (New York: Ktav, 1982), 117.

75. Ibid., 118.

76. To Fliess, 22 June 1897; Masson, *Complete Fliess Letters*, 254.

77. Reik, "Sigmund Freud," 222.

78. Freud, *The Interpretation of Dreams,* 227.

79. Klein, *Jewish Origins,* 94.

80. McGrath, *Freud's Discovery,* 294–95; cf., too, Leonard Shengold, "Freud and Joseph," in *Freud and His Self-Analysis,* ed. Mark Kanzer and Jules Glenn, Downstate Psychoanalytic Institute Series (New York: Jason Aronson, 1979), 1:67–86.

81. To Carl Jung, 17 January 1909; William McGuire, ed., *The Freud/Jung Letters: The Correspondence between Sigmund Freud and C. G. Jung,* trans. Ralph Manheim and R. F. C. Hull (London: Hogarth Press and Routledge and Kegan Paul, 1974), 196–97.

82. "The events at the beginning of time engender similarly those at the end."

83. Freud, *The Interpretation of Dreams,* 251 n. 3.

84. Ibid., 249–50.

85. David S. Blatt, "The Development of the Hero: Sigmund Freud and the Reformation of Jewish Tradition," *Psychoanalysis and Contemporary Thought* 11, no. 4 (1988): 656.

86. Ernest Jones, *The Life and Work of Sigmund Freud,* 3 vols. (London: Hogarth Press, 1953, 1955, 1957), 1:51.

87. To Martha Bernays, 28 April 1885; E. Freud, *Letters,* 140–41.

88. To Karl Abraham in 1908, in H. Abraham and E. Freud, *A Psychoanalytic Dialogue.*

89. Fritz Wittels, *Sigmund Freud: His Personality, His Teaching, and His School* (New York, 1924), 140.

90. As Freud says in a letter to Ludwig Binswanger in 1912; in Simon, "Sigmund Freud, the Jew," 290n.

91. In S. Freud, *Character and Culture,* 80–106.

92. Ibid., 103.

93. Bergmann, "Moses and the Evolution of Freud's Jewish Identity," 131.

94. Ibid., 124. Cf. *Pirkei Avot* 4:1: "Who is a hero? The one who conquers his impulse, as it is said, 'Better is forbearance than physical prowess, and one who masters his temperament than one who captures a city'" (my translation).

95. Mortimer Ostow, "Discussion of Martin S. Bergmann's Paper," *Judaism and Psychoanalysis,* 147.

96. Yerushalmi, *Freud's Moses,* 70. But did Freud name the chow?

97. To A. Zweig, 17 June 1936, in Ernst Freud, ed., *The Letters of Sigmund Freud and Arnold Zweig,* trans. Elaine Robson-Scott and William D. Robson-Scott (London: Hogarth Press and the Institute of Psychoanalysis, 1970). Henceforth, *Freud/Zweig Letters.*

98. To A. Zweig, 30 September 1934; in *Freud/Zweig Letters.*

Chapter 2. The Early Period

1. Anna Bernays, *Erlebt* (privately printed, 1930), 7; cited in Marianne Krüll, *Freud and His Father* (see chap. 1, n. 63), 263.

2. Anna Bernays, "My Brother, Sigmund Freud," *The American Mercury* 51 (November 1940): 336.

3. Ernst Freud, Lucie Freud, and Ilse Grubrich-Simitis, eds., *Sigmund Freud: His Life in Pictures and Words,* trans. Christine Trollope (London: André Deutsch, 1978), 327 n. 79. Henceforth cited as *Pictures and Words.*

4. To Wilhelm Fliess, 3, 4, and 15 October 1897; in Masson, *Complete Fliess Letters* (see chap. 1, n. 45), 268–271.

5. Jones, *Life and Work* (see chap. 1, n. 86), 1:19.

6. E.g., Puner, Velikovsky, Oehschlegel, Vitz.

7. Paul C. Vitz, *Sigmund Freud's Christian Unconscious* (New York: Guilford Press, 1988).

8. Ibid., 96.

9. Jones, *Life and Work,* 1:143. The importance for Freud of the fact that it was Easter is confirmed by his annual observance of the date in relation to Easter itself, no matter what date in the calendar it fell, thus constituting "a moveable feast." Cf. Molnar, *Diary* (see chap. 1, n. 21), 123.

10. "You owe Nature a death." Sigmund Freud, *The Interpretation of Dreams,* Stnd. Ed. (see chap. 1, n. 4), 4:205.

11. Harry Trosman, *Freud and the Imaginative World* (see chap. 1, n. 1), 5.

12. E.g., to Fliess, 6 February 1899; in Masson, *Complete Fliess Letters,* 343.

13. Sigmund Freud, *An Autobiographical Study,* Stnd. Ed., 20:8.

14. The number 35 was considered a lucky number in Eastern European Jewish folklore: 5 x 7. Seven is a number often used in the Bible to symbolize the completion or fulfillment of something. Freud took a special interest in the number 7 (cf. to Abraham 22 August 1924 and 12 August 1924), reflecting even if unconsciously biblical and rabbinic tradition, and perhaps too a link with his father.

15. Reuben M. Rainey, "Freud as a Student of Religion: Perspectives on the Background and Development of his Thought," *AAR Dissertation Series,* no. 7 (Missoula, Mont.: Scholars Press, 1975), 13. Rice reports that Menahem Schmelzer of the Jewish Theological Seminary of America has identified the Freud family's Philippsohn Bible as the 1839 edition (Emmanuel Rice, *Freud and Moses: The Long Journey Home* (see chap. 1, n. 25), 212 n. 3.

16. Yerushalmi, *Freud's Moses* (see Preface, n. 1), 71–72 .

17. The original spelling of the family name was "Freide," after "a highly respected woman in whose honour the family adopted the name." Reuben Klingsberg, ed., *Freudiana: From the Collections of the Jewish National and University Library* (Jerusalem: Jewish National and University Library, 1973), v.

18. Yerushalmi, *Freud's Moses,* 71, 104–5. Cf. Mortimer Ostow, "Sigmund and Jakob Freud and the Phillipsohn Bible (With an Analysis of the Birthday Inscription)," *International Review of Psycho-Analysis* 16 (1989): 483–92; and Rice, *Freud and Moses,* 36–37, 73–84.

19. Yerushalmi, *Freud's Moses,* 74.

20. Ostow, "Freud and the Phillipsohn Bible," 490.

21. Ibid., 72.

22. Ibid., 488.

23. Robert Alter, *The Invention of Hebrew Prose, Modern Fiction and the Language of Realism* (Seattle and London: University of Washington Press, 1988), 23.

24. *lekh kera'* may recall by assonance *lekh lekha,* "Go yourself," commanded to Abraham at both the beginning and high point of his career (Gen. 12 and 22).

25. Jakob's use of the Sephardic *nusakh* for the *Shemonah Esreh* may indicate that at one time he *davened* in a *schul* that followed this rite.

26. Ostow, "Freud and the Phillipsohn Bible," 487.

27. Jacob Milgrom, ed., *The JPS Torah Commentary: Numbers* (Philadelphia and New York: Jewish Publication Society, 1990), 461.

28. Perhaps alluding to the language in Num. 24:4, preceding Bilaam's prophecy, "How goodly are thy tents, O Jacob."

29. Yerushalmi, *Freud's Moses,* 73–74 n. 48.

30. Ostow, "Freud and the Phillipsohn Bible," 488.

31. Simon, "Sigmund Freud, the Jew," 305.

32. Torah Temimah on Exod. 32:19.

33. Yerushalmi, *Freud's Moses,* 104–6.

34. Ibid., 74; cf. Ostow, "Freud and the Phillipsohn Bible," 490.

35. Ostow, "Freud and the Phillipsohn Bible," 488.

36. Ibid.

37. Ibid., 486.

38. Sigmund Freud, *Totem and Taboo,* Stnd. Ed., 13:xv.

39. "Tell it not in Gath, herald it not in the streets of Ashkelon, lest the daughters of the Philistines rejoice, lest the daughters of the uncircumcised exult."

40. To Wm. Fliess, 21 September 1897; in Masson, *Complete Fliess Letters,* 265. Two days later, Freud will join the Vienna B'nai B'rith.

41. Simon, "Sigmund Freud, the Jew," 280.

42. Yerushalmi, *Freud's Moses,*" 66–67, 73.

43. Rice, *Freud and Moses,* 48–54.

44. This would have been the *Erste Öffentliche Israelistische Haupt- und Unterreal- (Volks- und Bürger-) Schule;* Rainey, "Freud as a Student of Religion," 39.

45. Ibid., 40; 9–33.

46. Rice, *Freud and Moses,* 65.

47. Ibid.

48. For example in the 1930 preface to the Hebrew edition of *Totem and Taboo,* Stnd. Ed., 13:xv; and his "Letter in Place of a Preface" in the Yiddish edition of the *Introductory Lectures:* "I . . . learned to read neither Hebrew nor Yiddish, a fact which makes me now very sorry."

49. Rainey, "Freud as a Student of Religion," 41.

50. Simon, "Sigmund Freud, the Jew," 284 n. 52.

51. Rice, *Freud and Moses,* 48–53.

52. Rainey, "Freud as a Student of Religion," 39.

53. Hugo Knöpfmacher, "Sigmund Freud in High School," *American Imago* 36 (1979): 288.

54. Rainey, "Freud as a Student of Religion," 10, based on Freud's letter of 18 September 1874 to Eduard Silberstein. Cf. Walter Böhlich, ed., *Sigmund Freud: Jugendbriefe an Eduard Silberstein, 1871–1881* (Frankfurt am Main: S. Fischer, 1989); and *The Letters of Sigmund Freud to Eduard Silberstein, 1871–1881,* ed. Walter Böhlich, trans. Arnold J. Pomerans (Cambridge: Harvard University Press, 1990).

55. Judith Bernays Heller, "Freud's Mother and Father, A Memoir," *Commentary* 21, no. 5 (May 1956): 419.

56. Edmund Engelman, *Berggasse 19: Sigmund Freud's Home and Offices, Vienna 1938* (New York: Basic Books, 1976), 90, 92 (plates 15 and 17).

57. Bernays, "My Brother, Sigmund Freud," 337.

58. Willy Aron, "Notes on Sigmund Freud's Ancestry and Jewish Contacts," *YIVO Annual of Jewish Social Sciences* 11 (1956–57): 288.

59. Yerushalmi notices that in the German of Jakob's "Gedenkblatt" Freud's name is written as "Sigmund," implying a possible paternal warrant for Freud's change as an adolescent (*Freud's Moses,* 132 n. 19). His act might therefore have implied an identification with his father, rather than just a defense against antisemitism.

60. Cf. Richard Sterba, "The Humanistic Wellsprings of Psychoanalysis," *Psychoanalytic Quarterly* 43 (April 1974): 167–76.

61. Rice, *Freud and Moses,* 48.

62. Jones, *Life and Work,* 1:163; no date given, German unpublished.

63. Ibid., 175; letter to Martha Bernays, 10 January 1884.

64. Ibid., 179; letter to Martha Bernays, n.d.

65. Rainey, "Freud as a Student of Religion," 37.

66. Ibid., 38.

67. Jon Levenson has identified the Jewish root of this humanist position in his *Universal Horizon of Biblical Particularism* (New York: American Jewish Committee, Institute of Human Relations, 1985).

68. Klein, *Jewish Origins* (see chap. 1, n. 52), 43 n. 12.

69. Ibid., 45–46.

70. Rainey, "Freud as a Student of Religion," 59 n. 74.

71. *Humanität* in the original German is translated misleadingly in the Standard Edition (9:255) as "a love of the humanities," giving the impression that Hammerschlag is talking about academic disciplines instead of a value (Samuel Jaffe, personal communication). *Menschlichkeit* is perhaps the Yiddish/Jewish approximation of Freud's meaning.

72. Sigmund Freud, *Five Lectures on Psychoanalysis,* Stnd. Ed., 11:53.

73. Sterba, "The Humanistic Wellsprings of Psychoanalysis," 175.

74. Rainey, "Freud as a Student of Religion," 38.

75. Ibid., 36.

76. To B'nai B'rith, 6 May 1926; "Address to the Society of B'nai B'rith," Stnd. Ed., 20:273.

77. Reportedly, Jakob Freud's motto was "Think ethically and act morally." Peter Gay, *Freud: A Life* (see chap. 1, n. 24), 645.

78. Rainey, "Freud as a Student of Religion," 43.

79. Ibid.

80. Wistrich, *The Jews of Vienna* (see chap. 1, n. 14), 555.

81. Rainey, "Freud as a Student of Religion," 45.

82. Ibid., 46.

83. Ibid., 26, 51.

84. Forty out of sixty-five pages are devoted to a discussion of the moral laws. Cf. Freud's acknowledgment of the "ethical demands of human civilization."

85. Rainey, "Freud as a Student of Religion," 51.

86. As in Sigmund Freud, *The Future of an Illusion,* Stnd. Ed., 21:53; Rainey, "Freud as a Student of Religion," 51.

87. As he tells Emil Fluss in a letter dated 16 June 1873; E. Freud, *Letters* (see chap. 1, n. 16), 3–4.

88. Sigmund Freud, "Some Reflections on Schoolboy Psychology," Stnd. Ed., 13:241.

89. Sterba, "The Humanistic Wellsprings of Psychoanalysis," 169.

90. Sigmund Freud, *Autobiography* (see chap. 1, n. 8), 13.

91. Bernays, "My Brother, Sigmund Freud," 336.

92. Harry Trosman, "Freud's Cultural Background," *Psychological Issues* 9, nos. 2–3 (1976): 67–68.

93. Ibid., 67.

94. Sterba, "The Humanistic Wellsprings of Psychoanalysis," 173.

95. Alexander Grinstein, *Sigmund Freud's Writings: A Comprehensive Bibliography* (New York: International Universities Press, 1977), 129–57.

96. Ronald C. Clark, *Freud: The Man and the Cause* (New York: Random House, 1980), 23–26.

97. Ibid., 23; letter to Silberstein, 4 September 1872.

98. Sigmund Freud, "Screen Memories," Stnd. Ed., 3:313.

99. In Ernst Freud, "Some Early Unpublished Letters of Freud," *International Journal of Psycho-Analysis* 59 (1969): 420.

100. There may be a pun here, "relatives in the Faith" [*Verwandten im Glauben*] meaning "fellow Jews."

101. Klein, *Jewish Origins*, 12, 17.

102. Cf. Bernays, "My Brother, Sigmund Freud," 336–37.

103. To Martha Bernays, 10 January 1884; E. Freud, *Letters*, 86–87.

104. On 29 August 1883; ibid., 50.

105. To Emil Fluss, 28 September 1872; in E. Freud, "Some Early Unpublished Letters."

106. Note the classical grammatical structure, like *mirabile dictu!*

107. On 7 February 1873; in E. Freud, "Some Early Unpublished Letters."

108. On 1 May 1873; Rainey, "Freud as a Student of Religion," 20.

109. Freud, *Autobiographical Study*, Stnd. Ed., 20:8.

110. George Christoph Tobler's essay, "The Fragment," afterward known as "Die Natur," first published anonymously in the *Tiefurter Journal* in 1782 and sometimes attributed to Goethe; printed in T. H. Huxley, "Nature: Aphorisms by Goethe," *Nature* 1 (4 November 1869): 9.

111. Clark, *Freud*, 28.

112. On 1 May 1873; Rainey, "Freud as a Student of Religion," 20.

113. Letter to Fluss, 17 March 1873; ibid., 22.

114. Ibid.

115. Ibid., 60 n. 77.

116. Gedo and Wolf, "The 'Ich.' Letters" (see chap. 1, n. 33), 79–80.

117. Ibid., 80.

118. Theo Pfrimmer, *Freud Lecteur de la Bible* (Paris: Presses Universitaires de France, 1982), 379–80; cited in Vitz, *Sigmund Freud's Christian Unconscious* (see chap. 2, n. 7), 34.

119. On 22 April 1928; in Böhlich, *Jugendbriefe*. Cf. idem, *Letters to Silberstein*, 186. Translations from Böhlich's German edition are my own.

120. On 7 February 1884; E. Freud, *Letters*, 96–97.

121. On 11 July 1873; in Böhlich, *Letters to Silberstein*.

122. Cf. Ps. 78:24.

123. Böhlich, *Jugendbriefe*, 239.

124. Ibid., 240.

125. Freud did not transmit this understanding to his children, as is clear from Martin's report of his own behavior at his wedding, when he tried, out of respect, to remove his hat before entering the synagogue.

126. According to Rozenblit, there were a "few thousand Jews of Sephardic extraction in Vienna"; Marsha L. Rozenblit, *The Jews of Vienna, 1867–1914: Assimilation and Identity* (Albany: SUNY Press, 1983), 148.

127. Ernst Freud and Lucie Freud, *Sigmund Freud, Briefe 1873–1939*, 3d ed. (Frankfurt am Main: S. Fischer Verlag, 1980), 15; cited in Yerushalmi, *Freud's Moses*, 68.

128. Yerushalmi, *Freud's Moses*, 68.

129. Ibid., 132 n. 33.

130. Standard Edition, 18:264f. Cf. Ernst Simon, "Freud and Moses," in *Entscheidung zum Judentum, Essays and Vorträge* (Frankfurt am Main: Suhrkamp, 1980), 200f.

131. Yerushalmi, *Freud's Moses*, 132 n. 33.

132. My translation, in Böhlich, *Jugendbriefe*. English edition, Böhlich, *Letters to Silberstein* (see chap. 2, n. 54), 62–63.

133. Gay, *Freud: A Life*, 526.

134. Heinrich Heine, *Heine's Prose and Poetry*, trans. Margaret Armour (London: J. M. Dent and Sons, 1934), 61.

135. To Oskar Pfister, 24 February 1928, in Ernst Freud and Heinrich Meng, eds., *Psychoanalysis and Faith: The Letters of Sigmund Freud and Oskar Pfister*, trans. Eric Mosbacher (London: Hogarth Press and the Institute of Psychoanalysis, 1963).

136. Böhlich notes the reference to Goethe's *Sprichwörtlich:* "Alles in der Welt läßt sich ertragen / Nur nicht eine Reihe von schönen Tagen" (Everything in the world can be borne / Save a round of holidays); in English edition, p. 64.

137. Böhlich, *Jugendbriefe*, 75 n. 7.

138. Ludwig Feuerbach (1804–72), "Der Mensch ist, was er ißt," in Jacob Moleschott, *Lehre der Nahrungsmittel: Für das Volk* (1850) 'Advertisement'; Angela Partington, ed. *The Oxford Dictionary of Quotations*, 4th ed. (Oxford: Oxford University Press, 1992), 281.

139. Perhaps Freud's family did not eat *Hamentaschen*, triangular-shaped cookies customarily eaten on Purim.

140. To Silberstein, 13 August 1874; Böhlich, *Jugendbriefe*.

141. On 22 April 1928; in ibid.

142. Cf. Rainy, "Freud as a Student of Religion," 20.

143. To Silberstein, 6 August 1873; in ibid., 23.

144. Ibid., 22.

145. Theodor Reik, *Jewish Wit* (New York: Gamut Press, 1962), 155; cited in Estelle Roith, *The Riddle of Freud: Jewish Influences on his Theory of Female Sexuality* (London and New York: Tavistock, 1978), 65.

146. Cf. his letter to Ludwig Binswanger, 8 October 1936; E. Freud, *Letters,* 431.

147. To Silberstein, 8 November 1874.

148. On 7 March 1875; Böhlich, *Jugendbriefe.*

149. Preface to the Hebrew translation of *Totem and Taboo,* December 1930, Stnd. Ed., 13:xv.

150. On 13 August 1874; Böhlich, *Jugendbriefe.*

151. According to Böhlich's note 8 in ibid., 137.

152. On 28 June 1875; Böhlich, *Jugendbriefe.*

153. To Silberstein, 14 August 1878; Böhlich, *Letters to Silberstein,* 169.

154. On 15 March 1875; Böhlich, *Jugendbriefe.*

155. My translation from the German; Böhlich, *Jugendbriefe.* Cf. Böhlich, *Letters to Silberstein,* 53.

156. On 8 November 1874; Böhlich, *Letters to Silberstein,* 70–71.

157. Freud, *Autobiography* (see chap. 1, n. 8), 15.

158. On 6 August 1878; in Rainey, "Freud as a Student of Religion," 20.

159. On 21 February 1875; Böhlich, *Letters to Silberstein,* 89.

160. Sterba mentions the moral self-restraint characteristic of humanistic studies, quoting the Latin motto *Quidquid agis prudenter agas et respice finem* (Whatever you do, do carefully and consider the consequences); idem, "The Humanistic Wellsprings of Psychoanalysis" (see chap. 2, n. 60), 173.

161. On 26 March 1880, my translation; cf. Böhlich, *Letters to Silberstein,* 177–78.

162. Freud's use of the Spanish *Don,* a title of lordship, underscores his irony. He is perhaps influenced by Heine in "The Rabbi of Bacherach," where the apostate is named "Don Isaak."

163. Based on the life of Uriel da Costa (1590–1647), of Amsterdam.

164. Karl Gutzkow, *Uriel Acosta: A Tragedy in Five Acts,* trans. M. M. (New York: M. Ellinger and Co., 1860), act 4, scene 1.

165. Jones, *Life and Work,* 1:99.

166. To Martha Bernays, 23 July 1882; E. Freud, *Letters,* 22.

167. To the editor of the *Jewish Observer and Middle East Review,* published in the 4 June 1954 issue, p. 10.

168. E. Freud et al., *Pictures and Words* (see chap. 2, n. 3), 326, has 2 September as the date of Martha's return, as does E. Freud, *Letters,* 7n. Since Ernst Freud edited both of these works, we may assume that 2 September is his testimony. But Ernest Jones gives the date as 11 September in his biography, 1:115.

169. Jones, *Life and Work,* 1:106.

170. Ibid.

171. As Martha writes to her granddaughter at the end of her life, "Do you

remember the prediction the family made for my future?" (Esti Freud, "Mrs. Sigmund Freud," *The Jewish Spectator,* Spring 1980, 29). Since Esti was not alive at the time, the story must have become part of the family lore.

172. Cited by Yerushalmi, *Freud's Moses,* 11.

173. Freud commented to his daughter Mathilde in 1908 that the decisive factor in making his choice in a wife was "to find an honorable name and a warm atmosphere at home" (26 March 1908; Molnar, *Diary,* 299n).

174. Presentation by Samuel Jaffe entitled "Freud's 'Nathan' Letter" given at a meeting of the Psychoanalytic Workshop, the University of Chicago, 4 April 2988.

175. Jones, *Life and Work,* 1:111.

176. Ibid., 104.

177. Ibid., 111.

178. Ibid., 113.

179. Gotthold Ephraim Lessing, *Nathan the Wise. A Dramatic Poem in Five Acts,* trans. Bayard Quincy Morgan (New York: Frederick Ungar, 1955). All quotes are from this edition. Originally published in 1779.

180. On 12 July 1883; in E. Freud et al., *Pictures and Words,* 96.

181. Ibid.

182. Martin Freud, "Who was Freud?" (see chap. 1, n. 17), 203–4.

183. Mosse, *German Jews Beyond Judaism* (see chap. 1, n. 31), 9.

184. Cited in Mendes-Flohr, *A Land of Two Rivers.*

185. Ibid.

186. Michael A. Meyer, *Response to Modernity: A History of the Reform Movement in Judaism* (New York: Oxford, 1988), 65.

187. Ibid.

188. Ibid.

189. Jaffe, "Freud's 'Nathan' Letter" (see n. 174 *supra*).

190. Ibid.

191. Simon, "Sigmund Freud, the Jew" (see chap. 1, n. 34), 303. Jaffe suggests in "Freud's 'Nathan' Letter" that maneuvering Martha to pick up the stationery and so show the merchant the "treasure" his former master has produced functions as Freud's substitutive atonement for his oedipal aggression.

192. Paul Roazen, *Freud and His Followers* (New York: Knopf, 1975), 48 n. 2. Cf. Gay's report also: On a Friday afternoon in London in 1938, Martha Freud joined her husband and his guest, "a young Oxford philosopher," in their home. "You must know," she told their visitor, "that on Friday evenings good Jewish women light candles for the approach of the Sabbath. But this monster—*Unmensch*—will not allow this, because he says that religion is a superstition." "Freud gravely nodded and agreed," Gay reports. "'Yes,' he said, 'it *is* a superstition,' to which the Frau Professor, addressing her visitor, rejoined: 'You see?' In retrospect, their guest, perceptive but generous, thought the indignation humorous, mingled with obvious affection, a standing joke, repeated for half a century for the benefit of sympathetic visitors" (Peter Gay, *A Godless Jew: Freud, Atheism, and the Making of Psychoanalysis* [New Haven: Yale University Press, 1987], 152–

53). Yet, as Gay notes, this vignette indicates that Martha had retained a trace of indignation and perhaps sadness over the forfeiting of her religious practice that her husband had required of her.

193. Letter from E. Philipp to Jones, 28 October 1953, in Gay, *Freud: A Life,* 54.

194. Gay, *A Godless Jew,* 152–54.

195. Freud and Martha were first married in a civil wedding in Wandsbek on 13 September 1886, but followed it on the next day, in conformity with Austrian law, with a religious Jewish ceremony. The latter took place on a weekday, with few guests, at Martha's mother's home, to avoid formal evening dress. Martha's uncle Elias Philipp coached Freud with the Hebrew. Molnar, *Diary,* 206.

196. On 2 November 1896; in Masson, *Complete Fliess Letters,* 202.

197. Martin Freud, *Sigmund Freud: Man and Father* (see chap 1, n. 18), 10.

198. On 22 June 1897; in Masson, *Complete Fliess Letters,* 254.

199. Cf. Freud's preface to the second edition of *The Interpretation of Dreams* (see chap. 1, n. 32), xxvi.

200. Martin Freud, *Sigmund Freud: Man and Father,* 27.

201. Cf. Freud's letter to Fliess, 12 February 1929, in Max Schur, *Freud: Living and Dying* (New York: International Universities Press, 1972), 62, 535.

202. E.g., to Stefan Zweig, 7 February 1931, Freud says that he "owed to cigars the greater part of his self-discipline and steadfastness at work"; Molnar, *Diary,* 53.

203. Jer. 3:12 has the 10th of Av, whereas 2 Kings 25:8–9 gives the 7th of Av as the date of the first destruction; Josephus gives the 10th of Av as the date for the destruction of the Second Temple (Josephus, *The Jewish War,* Book 6:249–50, trans. H. St. J. Thackeray [New York: G. P. Putnam's Sons, 1928], 446–49). The observance is a rabbinic compromise, lest the community be forced to fast twice. Yet this is not exactly "false calculation," so Freud's meanng is not entirely clear.

204. Abraham Geiger, *Judaism and Its History* (Lanham, Md.: University Press of America, 1985), 175–76. First edition, 1864.

205. Rainey, "Freud as a Student of Religion," 58–59.

206. Harry Trosman and Roger Simmons, "The Freud Library," *American Psychoanalytic Journal* 21 (1973): 684.

207. Geiger, *Judaism and Its History,* 80.

208. Ibid., 80–81.

209. Ibid., 81.

210. Ibid., 382.

211. W. Gunther Plaut, *The Rise of Reform Judaism: A Sourcebook of its European Origins* (New York: World Union for Progressive Judaism, 1963), 201.

212. *Olat Tamid,* prayer book, 100; cited in *The Encyclopaedia Judaica,* s.v. "Einhorn, David," by Sefton D. Temkin.

213. Geiger, *Judaism and Its History,* 93.

214. Ibid., 65.

215. Max Wiener, ed., *Abraham Geiger and Liberal Judaism: The Challenge of the*

19th Century, trans. E. J. Schlochauer (Philadelphia: Jewish Publication Society, 1962), 262.

216. Plaut, *The Rise of Reform Judaism,* 202.

217. Sigmund Freud, "On the Occasion of the Opening of the Hebrew University," Stnd. Ed., 19:292.

218. Meyer, *Response to Modernity* (see chap. 2, n. 186), 60.

219. Aron, "Notes on Sigmund Freud's Ancestry," 295.

220. Willy Aron, "Hacham Isaac Bernays (1792–1849): A Biographical Essay," *The Jewish Forum,* March 1949, 44.

221. *The Encyclopaedia Judaica,* s.v. "Bernays, Michael," by George Schwab.

222. Cf. Yeshayahu Leibowitz, "Commandments," in *Contemporary Jewish Religious Thought: Original Essays on Critical Concepts, Movements, and Beliefs,* ed. Arthur Cohen and Paul Mendes-Flohr (New York: Scribner, 1987), 67–80.

223. Recall Freud's own discussion of the importance of food in relation to the Jewish holidays in his letter to Eduard Silberstein, above.

224. Rainey, "Freud as a Student of Religion," 39, 43.

225. Ibid., 43.

226. Ibid., 39.

227. Cf. his letter to Silberstein, 22 August 1874, in Böhlich, *Jugendbriefe.*

228. Gotthold Ephraim Lessing, "The Education of the Human Race," in *Lessing's Theological Writings,* trans. Henry Chadwick (Stanford, Calif.: Stanford University Press, 1957), 82. Originally published in 1780, the year following *Nathan der Weise.*

229. Ibid., 95.

230. Ibid., 96–97.

231. Cf. Klein, *Jewish Origins,* xiv–xvi.

232. Lessing, "The Education of the Human Race," 96.

233. Cited in Rainey, "Freud as a Student of Religion," 47.

234. Ibid., 65.

235. Jones, *Life and Work,* 1:163.

236. Aldo Carotenuto, *A Secret Symmetry: Sabina Spielrein between Jung and Freud,* trans. A. Pomerans et al. (New York: Pantheon, 1984), 117.

237. Talmud Yerushalmi 48b [4.12].

238. Terence, *Heautontimorumenos* ("Self-Tormentor"), act 1, scene 1, v. 25; cf. Pierre Villey, *Les essais de Michel de Montaigne* (Paris: SFELT, 1946), lxix.

239. Samuel Jaffe, University of Chicago, personal communication.

240. Engelman, *Freud's Home and Office,* 90, 92 (plates 15 and 17), 52.

241. Heinrich Heine, "Der Rabbi von Bacherach. Ein Fragment," in *Werke,* Band 2 (Wiesbaden: R. Lowit, n.d.), 185.

242. Mendes-Flohr, *A Land of Two Rivers.*

243. Ibid.

244. "The Jew is for joy and joy is for the Jew."

245. Cf. Gilman, *Jewish Self-Hatred* (see chap. 1, n. 50); and Kurt Schlesinger, "Jewish Humor as Jewish Identity," *International Review of Psychoanalysis* 6 (1979): 317–29.

246. E.g., letters to Silberstein, 18 September 1874, in Böhlich, *Letters to Silberstein,* 62–64 and to Fluss, 17 March 1873, in E. Freud, "Some Early Unpublished Letters."

247. Sukkot is considered in the midrashic tradition to be a particularly intimate time between God and the people of Israel. On Shemini Atzeret, the climax of the Sukkot season, the other nations are said to be away and God is alone with his beloved, Israel. So it is a time of special Jewish joy.

248. James Kugel, "Two Interpretations of Midrash," *Prooftexts* 3 (1983): 147.

249. Esti Freud, "Mrs. Sigmund Freud," 29.

250. Jaffe, "Freud's 'Nathan' Letter."

251. Rainey, "Freud as a Student of Religion," 65.

252. Plaut, *The Rise of Reform Judaism,* 11.

253. Ibid., 41. Fraenkel however criticized Reform Judaism for rejecting ritual forms, holding that they had acquired a holiness independent of their origins.

254. Sigmund Freud, *Moses and Monotheism,* trans. Katherine Jones (New York: Vintage, 1955), 166.

255. Martin Freud, *Sigmund Freud: Man and Father* (see chap. 1, n. 18), 10.

256. Ernst Freud et al., *Pictures and Words,* 261.

257. To Fliess, 2 November 1896; Masson, *Complete Fliess Letters,* 202.

258. Martin Freud, "Who was Freud?" 207–8.

259. Ibid., 204; cf. Rozenblit, *The Jews of Vienna.*

260. Martin Freud, "Who was Freud?" 204.

261. Letter to Freud, 30 December 1923, in E. Freud and H. Meng, *Psychoanalysis and Faith.*

262. He in fact fathers six children, following his father's example.

263. August 1882; Jones, *Life and Work,* 1:102.

264. Simon, "Sigmund Freud, the Jew," 281.

265. On 26 August 1882; Jones, *Life and Work,* 1:174.

266. David R. Mesher, "Rabbinical References in *Daniel Deronda,*" *Notes and Queries* 222 (October 1977): 407.

267. George Eliot, *Daniel Deronda,* ed. Graham Handley (Oxford: Clarendon Press, 1984), 366.

268. Ibid., 367.

269. Ibid., 499.

270. On 6 June 1883; Jones, *Life and Work,* 1:167.

271. Ibid.

272. Ibid., 255–56.

273. Elliot Oring, *The Jokes of Sigmund Freud: A Study in Humor and Jewish Identity* (Philadelphia: University of Pennsylvania Press, 1984), 18.

274. Jones, *Life and Work,* 1:168.

275. Ibid., 167.

276. On 10 January 1884, to Martha Bernays; E. Freud, *Letters,* 87.

277. Cf. letters to Martha Bernays of 15 November 1883 and 19 March 1884; E. Freud, *Letters,* 75, 100.

278. Oring, *The Jokes of Sigmund Freud,* 13–15.

279. Martin Freud, "Who was Freud?" 208.

280. Max Graf, "Reminiscences of Professor Sigmund Freud," *Psychoanalytic Quarterly* 11 (1942): 474.

281. Jones, *Life and Work,* 1:2; to Martha Bernays, 1 January 1884.

282. E. Freud, *Letters,* 86.

283. Cf. Oring, *The Jokes of Sigmund Freud,* 17.

284. On 19 July 1883; Jones, *Life and Work,* 1:2.

285. Gay, *Freud: A Life,* 645.

286. Jones, *Life and Work,* 1:167.

287. Wittels, *Sigmund Freud* (see chap. 1, n. 89), 60.

288. Jones, *Life and Work,* 1:167. The brevity of this argument may imply that Freud's idea was more of an expression of frustration and anger at Judaism than the result of an attraction to Christianity, *contra* Vitz.

289. Wistrich, *The Jews of Vienna* (see chap. 1, n. 14), 53.

290. To Fliess, 15 September 1895; in Masson, *Complete Fliess Letters.*

291. Ibid.

292. Sigmund Freud, *Jokes and their Relation to the Unconscious,* Stnd. Ed., 8:80–81.

293. Self-restraint is of course a value in classical humanism too, as Sterba makes clear above.

294. On 29 August 1883; in E. Freud, *Letters.* Freud's words are reminiscent of the attitude of halakhic Jews toward the Law: "*na'aseh ve-nishma'*," we will do first, not knowing beforehand why; then we will understand.

295. On 4 September 1883; E. Freud, *Letters,* 54.

296. Yerushalmi, *Freud's Moses,* 39.

297. Ibid.

298. "Die Massen sind träge und einsichtlos, sie lieben den Triebverzicht nicht." Sigmund Freud, *Gesammelte Werke, Chronologisch Geordnet,* 18 vols., ed. Anna Freud et al., in collaboration with Marie Bonaparte (London: Imago, 1940–52; Frankfurt am Main: S. Fischer Verlag, 1968), 14:328; S. Freud, *The Future of an Illusion,* Stnd. Ed., 21:7.

299. On 23 October 1883; E. Freud, *Letters,* 71.

300. Cf. Freud's reference in the letter of 29 August to Heinrich Heine's Asra, the people who love only once and then perish, in choosing a Romantic literary image to characterize the kind of passionate people he and Martha are.

301. John E. Gedo and Ernest S. Wolf, "Freud's *Novelas Ejemplares,*" *Psychological Issues* 9, nos. 2–3 (1976): 88.

302. Cf. Krüll, *Freud and His Father,* 176–79.

303. Jones, *Life and Work,* 1:140. Jones cannot always be trusted to make accurate assessments of things Jewish, but it seems likely that his report conveys the general sense.

304. Ibid., 161.

305. Ibid., to Martha Bernays, 15 April 1884.

306. On 10 January 1884; E. Freud, *Letters,* 87.

307. Nevertheless, Freud will later name his second daughter after Sophie Schwab.

308. Wistrich, *The Jews of Vienna,* 557.

309. On 16 September 1883; E. Freud, *Letters,* 65.

310. Babylonian Talmud, Bava Metzia 58b.

311. E.g., Öhlschlegel, Wittels, Oring, Puner, Robert, Rosmarin, etc.

312. Gilman, *Jewish Self-Hatred,* 250–51.

313. Ibid., 289–92.

314. This word is lacking in the German edition, E. Freud, *Sigmund Freud, Briefe.* A *Schammes,* which Freud mentions earlier in the letter, is Yiddish for the man in charge of the daily cares of the synagogue, including worship services and maintenance.

315. Including, in the English edition of Freud's letters, the name of Marthe for the man's wife. E. Freud, *Letters,* 165.

316. Ibid., to Martha Bernays, 4 November 1885.

317. Wistrich, *The Jews of Vienna,* 558.

318. For example: "Two Jews are sitting outside a bath-house. One sighs, 'So, another year has passed.' Or, 'Taken a bath?' 'No,' his friend says, 'is one missing?'"

319. Christopher Hutton, "Freud and the Family Drama of Yiddish," in *Studies in Yiddish Linguistics,* ed. Paul Wexler (Tübingen: Max Niemayer, 1990), 12.

320. Freud, *Autobiographical Study,* Stnd. Ed., 20:9.

321. On 6 January 1885; E. Freud, *Sigmund Freud, Briefe;* lacking in E. Freud, *Letters* (1960).

322. Gay, *Freud: A Life,* 242.

323. Martin Freud, "Who was Freud?" 208.

324. Cf. Franz Rosenzweig's interpretation of Abraham's origins in *Aram Naharaim,* literally "a land of two rivers" (Gen. 24:10). As Paul Mendes-Flohr explains, "The Jew resides on the banks of two cultures, that of the world and that of Judaism. This dual allegiance is the ground of an authentic pluralism, a pluralism that preserves one's integrity *both* as a Jew *and* as a citizen of the world" (Mendes-Flohr, *A Land of Two Rivers*).

325. Clark, *Freud* (see chap. 2, n. 96), 32; cf. Klein, *Jewish Origins,* 54.

326. Sulloway, *Freud, Biologist of the Mind* (see chap. 1, n. 50), 135–237.

327. 1) Mathilde, born 16 October 1897, named after the wife of Josef Breuer; 2) Jean Martin, born 7 December 1889, named after Jean-Martin Charcot, with whom Freud had worked closely in the winter of 1885; 3) Oliver, born 19 February 1891, named after Oliver Cromwell, the regicide, but also the man who invited the Jews back to England; 4) Ernst, born 6 April 1892, named after Ernst Brücke, in whose physiological laboratory Freud had spent six happy and productive years; 5) Sophie, born 12 April 1893, named for Samuel Hammerschlag's niece, Sophie Schwab, who married Freud's friend Joseph Paneth; and 6) Anna, born 3 December 1895, named for Hammerschlag's daughter, Anna Hammerschlag. Cf. Peter Gay, "Six Names in Search of an Interpretation," *Hebrew Union College Annual* 53 (1982): 296–97.

328. Ibid., 301.

329. Ibid., 307.

330. To Fliess, 3 December 1895; Masson, *Complete Fliess Letters,* 153.

331. Anna Freud, "Inaugural Lecture for the Sigmund Freud Chair at the Hebrew University, Jerusalem," *International Journal for Psycho-Analysis* 59 (1978): 148. Cited in Yerushalmi, *Freud's Moses,* 100.

332. Masson, *Complete Fliess Letters,* 20 n. 3.

333. Ibid.

334. Rozenblit, *The Jews of Vienna,* 76.

335. I.e., Alsergrund, the ninth, where 10 percent of Vienna's Jews lived; ibid.

336. To Fliess, 8 November 1895; Masson, *Complete Fliess Letters,* 150.

337. Simon, "Sigmund Freud, the Jew," 273.

338. To whom Dreyfus was falsely accused of selling military secrets.

339. Graf, "Reminiscences of Professor Sigmund Freud," 473.

340. Freud, *The Interpretation of Dreams,* Stnd. Ed., 4:xxvi.

341. On 30 June 1896; Masson, *Complete Fliess Letters,* 193.

342. Ibid., 15 July 1896.

343. Ibid., 26 October 1896.

344. Literally, "he had made much in my life."

345. On 2 November 1896; Masson, *Complete Fliess Letters,* 202.

346. On 6 February 1899; ibid., 344.

347. Cf. Gay, *Freud: A Life,* 648–51.

348. Klein, *Jewish Origins,* 72.

349. Previously dated incorrectly, according to Masson, as 12 June.

350. Masson, *Complete Fliess Letters,* 232.

351. Klein, *Jewish Origins,* 70; Freud, *The Interpretation of Dreams,* 226–30.

352. Klein, *Jewish Origins,* 70–71.

353. Cf. William Novak and Moshe Waldoks, *The Big Book of Jewish Humor* (New York: Basic Books, 1985).

354. Cf. Klein, *Jewish Origins,* 97 n. 6; Oring, *The Jokes of Sigmund Freud,* 61. Freud will use the proverb himself in a letter to Sandor Ferenczi on 28 May 1924.

355. Klein, *Jewish Origins,* 71, 97 n. 6.

356. On 24 March 1930; in A. A. Roback, *Freudiana* (Cambridge, Mass.: Sci-Art Publishers, 1957), 34.

357. Yerushalmi, *Freud's Moses,* 69.

358. Erika Freeman, *Insights: Conversations with Theodor Reik* (Englewood Cliffs, N.J.: Prentice-Hall, 1971), 80.

359. Yerushalmi, *Freud's Moses,* 69.

360. Ibid.

361. Peter Gay, *Freud, Jews, and Other Germans. Masters and Victims in Modernist Culture* (New York: Oxford University Press, 1978), 110.

362. Hutton, "Freud and the Family Drama of Yiddish," 13–14.

363. Ibid., 16.

364. Sigmund Freud, *Jokes and their Relation to the Unconscious* (see chap. 1, n. 72), 49.

365. Hutton, "Freud and the Family Drama of Yiddish," 17.

366. Jones, *Life and Work,* 1:22.

367. Masson, *Complete Fliess Letters,* 267 n. 3.
368. "verständiger Mensch"; 8 February 1897; Masson, *Complete Fliess Letters,* 229.
369. Sigmund Freud, *The Interpretation of Dreams,* 170–71.
370. Klein, *Jewish Origins,* 71.
371. On 3 December 1897; Masson, *Complete Fliess Letters,* 285.
372. Robert Gordis, "The Two Faces of Freud," *Judaism* 24 (1977): 199.
373. Cf. Gilman, *Jewish Self-Hatred.*
374. Klein, *Jewish Origins,* 72.
375. Samuel Jaffe, University of Chicago, personal communication.
376. Klein, *Jewish Origins,* 72.
377. On 12 December 1897; Masson, *Complete Fliess Letters,* 286.
378. Klein, *Jewish Origins,* 155–156.
379. Ibid.
380. Ibid., 87.
381. Ibid.
382. Freud, quoting Fliess back to him in a letter of 7 August 1901.
383. Cf. letters from Freud to Fliess of 7 August 1901 and 19 September 1901.
384. Rozenblit, *The Jews of Vienna,* 150.
385. Ibid.
386. E.g., to Enrico Morselli, 18 February 1926: "I am not sure opinion, which looks upon psychoanalysis as a direct product of the Jewish spirit, is correct, but if it is, I wouldn't be ashamed." In E. Freud, *Letters,* 365.
387. Klein, *Jewish Origins,* 71.
388. Stnd. Ed., 3:289–97.
389. Cf. to George Viereck, 20 July 1928; E. Freud, *Letters,* 382.
390. Heller, "Freud's Mother and Father," 419.
391. Molnar, *Diary,* 123.
392. He may have resented a compulsory attendance at the seder as a youth, as many youngsters do when they cannot understand the Hebrew language or deep ideas embedded in the liturgical game of the ritual meal.
393. The name "Israel," according to the biblical gloss (Gen. 32:29), asserts that Jacob "wrestled with God and with men and prevailed." Israel is the "Godwrestler."
394. Meyer, *Response to Modernity,* 30.
395. Yerushalmi, *Freud's Moses,* 12.
396. Sigmund Freud, *The Interpretation of Dreams,* 478; Stnd. Ed., 4:442.
397. In Freud's letter to Fliess about the trial of Alfred Dreyfus (7–23 February 1898), written on 9 Febrary 1898, Freud mentions Zola with admiration but does not mention Herzl, the *Neue Freie Presse*'s correspondent, neither here nor on 11 September 1899.
398. Wistrich, *The Jews of Vienna,* 578.
399. Peter Löwenberg, "A Hidden Zionist Theme in Freud's 'My Son the Myops . . .' Dream," *Journal of the History of Ideas* 31 (1970): 130ff., cited in Yerushalmi, *Freud's Moses,* 12.

400. Steven Beller, *Vienna and the Jews, 1867–1938. A Cultural History* (Cambridge: Cambridge University Press, 1989), 133.

401. German text in Yerushalmi, *Freud's Moses*, 107; full English text in Ernst Pawel, *The Labyrinth of Exile. A Life of Theodor Herzl* (New York: Farrar, Straus, and Giroux, 1989), 456.

402. Leo Goldhammer, "Herzl and Freud," *Herzl Yearbook* (New York), 1958, 1:194–96; cf. idem, "Herzl and Freud: Träume," 266–68.

403. Jacob Meitlis, "The Last Days of Sigmund Freud," *The Jewish Frontier*, September 1951, 21.

404. Martin Freud, *Sigmund Freud: Man and Father*, 68–71.

405. Reported in Josef Fraenkel, "Professor Freud and the Student Society 'Kadimah'," *The Gates of Zion* (London), April 1964, 16.

406. Sigmund Freud, "Obituary of Hammerschlag," Stnd. Ed., 9:255–56; German original: *Die Neue Freie Presse* (Vienna), Morgenblatt, 11 November 1904.

407. Freud, *Jokes*, Stnd. Ed., 8:111–15.

408. Simon, "Sigmund Freud, the Jew," 281–82.

409. Freud, *Jokes*, Stnd. Ed., 8:112.

410. Ibid., 111.

411. Ibid., 112.

412. Simon, "Sigmund Freud, the Jew," 281.

413. Freud, *Jokes*, Stnd. Ed., 8:113.

414. Simon, "Sigmund Freud, the Jew," 281.

415. Freud, *Jokes*, Stnd. Ed., 8:113.

416. Ibid.

417. Cf. to Martha Bernays, 5 August 1885, in Ernst Freud, *Letters*, 164: "a man as poor as only a Jew can be."

418. Freud, *Jokes*, Stnd. Ed., 8:114.

419. "Of course He'll forgive me; that's His job." Ibid.

420. Ibid., 114–115.

421. Ibid., 115.

422. In this respect, Jewish jokes are like the wisdom literature in the Hebrew Bible.

423. As he describes himself to Fliess, 1 February 1900, in Masson, *Complete Fliess Letters*, 398.

424. Steven E. Aschheim, "The East European Jew and German Jewish Identity," *Studies in Contemporary History* (1984): 3–22.

Chapter 3. The Middle Period

1. Cf. S. Freud, "A Difficulty in the Path of Psychoanalysis," (1917), Stnd. Ed., vol. 17.

2. Jones, *Life and Work*, 2:365.

3. Cf. Masson, *Complete Fliess Letters*, 455–57; letters to Fliess of 8 March and 11 March 1902.

4. Klein, *Jewish Origins,* 2:32.

5. Jones, *Life and Work,* 2:32.

6. Though Steven Beller's research into the socioeconomic, educational, and cultural background of the cultural elite in Vienna shows that the exclusively Jewish composition of Freud's early circle was "no accident," but was a function of a typically Jewish career plan, a product of the Jewish assimilation, Peter Drucker suggests that Freud, consciously or unconsciously, barred non-Jewish figures such as Wagner-Jauregg from attending the initially informal private meetings of the Psychological Wednesday Society (Beller, *Vienna and the Jews,* 14 n. 1). If so, then Freud's conscious choice to include Jung and Binswanger in 1907 seems all the more pointedly to indicate a shift in self-definition.

7. Jones, *Life and Work,* 2:9–10.

8. Wittels, *Sigmund Freud,* 140.

9. Klein, *Jewish Origins,* 94. Its similarity to Christian supersessionism and the natural Jewish resentment it would arouse, however much in harmony with the cultural context, is noted below.

10. Yerushalmi, *Freud's Moses,* p. 111; photo after p. 80.

11. To Martha Bernays, 2 February 1886; E. Freud, *Letters,* 202.

12. Sigmund Freud, "Obsessive Acts and Religious Practices," Stnd. Ed., 9:115–27.

13. On 18 July 1908; McGuire, *Freud/Jung Letters* (see chap. 1, n. 81), 165.

14. Marthe Robert, *From Oedipus to Moses: Freud's Jewish Identity,* trans. Ralph Manheim (New York: Doubleday, 1976), 41.

15. Paul L. Rosen, "Freud on Jewish Identity, Ethnicity, and Politics," *Jerusalem Quarterly* 40 (1986): 128.

16. On 14 January 1908; McGuire, *Freud/Jung Letters,* 109.

17. Jones, *Life and Work,* 2:42–47.

18. These phrases appear in a second letter from Freud about the issue, which he sent on 9 May, six days after the first, having not heard from Abraham.

19. H. Abraham and E. Freud, *A Psychoanalytic Dialogue* (see chap. 1, n. 67), 3 May 1908.

20. Yerushalmi, *Freud's Moses,* 31.

21. Ibid., 30.

22. Like Mary Baker Eddy's "Christian Science," founded in 1866, Freud's "Jewish Science" would be cast as a new kind of religion.

23. Letter to Ferenczi, 8 June 1913; in Jones, *Life and Work,* 2:149.

24. Klein, *Jewish Origins,* 103–5; cf. Rank's "The Essence of Judaism," in Klein, *Jewish Origins,* 170–73.

25. See below; cf. Gay, *Freud: A Life,* 448.

26. On 7 March 1926; ibid., 445.

27. Yerushalmi, *Freud's Moses,* 99.

28. Gay, *Freud: A Life,* 180.

29. H. Abraham and E. Freud, *A Psychoanalytic Dialogue,* 11 May 1908.

30. Sigmund Freud, *Moses and Monotheism* (see chap. 2, n. 254), 17: "It is not attractive to be classed with the scholastics and Talmudists who are satisfied to

exercise their ingenuity, unconcerned how far removed their conclusions may be from the truth."

31. Susan Handelman, *The Slayers of Moses. The Emergence of Rabbinic Interpretation in Modern Literary Theory* (Albany: SUNY Press, 1982), 129–52.

32. Ibid., 147.

33. Ibid., 149.

34. Sigmund Freud, *Jokes* (see chap. 1, n. 72), 74.

35. Ibid., 75.

36. Babylonian Talmud, Shabbat 49b; cited in Handelman, *The Slayers of Moses*, 24, 74.

37. Another example is Rashi's comment (based on Babylonian Talmud, Baba Kamma 92) on Gen. 21:1, where "The Lord had visited Sarah" follows immediately after Gen. 20:17–18, where Abraham prayed on behalf of Abimelech, "to teach you that whoever prays for mercy on behalf of his fellow when he himself is also in need of that very thing [for which he prays on the other's behalf] will himself receive a favorable answer [from God] first." Again, in assuming that juxtaposition intends to teach an inference that must be drawn by the interpreter, rabbinic hermeneutics reminds us of Freud's method of interpreting psychical products, like the dream or wit.

38. Cf. Mendes-Flohr, *A Land of Two Rivers;* Beller, *Vienna and the Jews*, 93–95.

39. Or the Jewish perception of it, unqualified by the self-subordination to its source, namely, God—an option not available to the atheist Freud.

40. On 18 April 1915; Gay, *Freud: A Life*, 368, German unpublished.

41. H. Abraham and E. Freud, *A Psychoanalytic Dialogue*, 20 July 1908. In a letter to A. A. Roback on 24 March 1930, Freud will accept "speculative leanings" in place of "mystical" ones, to which he objected. "The two are by no means the same," Freud says, "and psychoanalysis is a teaching based on the empirical" (Roback, *Freudiana*, 34, 229).

42. Cf. C. G. Jung, *Memories, Dreams, Reflections*, ed. Aniela Jaffe, trans. Richard Winston and Clara Winston (New York: Vintage, 1965), 155–56.

43. Cf. McGuire, *Freud/Jung Letters*, 216n.

44. Rainey's dissertation contains a concise chapter on Freud's superstitions and his interest in the occult (Rainey, "Freud as a Subject of Religion," 89–105). Cf. also Jones, *Life and Work*, 3:375–407.

45. Cf. Sigmund Freud, *Delusions and Dreams in Jensen's Gradiva*, Stnd. Ed., 9:71–72.

46. On 16 April 1909; McGuire, *Freud/Jung Letters*, 218.

47. Cf. S. Freud, "The Uncanny" (1955), Stnd. Ed., 17:247–48.

48. Fliess told Freud that "the reader of thoughts merely reads his own thoughts into other people" (Freud's letter to Fliess, 7 August 1901; Masson, *Complete Fliess Letters*, 447).

49. Cf. too Freud's slip of the pen in a letter to A. A. Roback on 20 February 1930, in which he at first writes "mythical" for "mystical," when he reacts negatively to Roback's suggestion (which he sees as a "reproach") that he has "mystical leanings" (Roback, *Freudiana*, 27).

50. Rainey, "Freud as a Student of Religion," 98.

51. Jung, *Memories,* 147–48.
52. Ibid., 152.
53. H. Abraham and E. Freud, *A Psychoanalytic Dialogue,* 13 May 1913.
54. On 13 August 1908; McGuire, *Freud/Jung Letters,* 168.
55. On 17 January 1909; ibid., 196–97.
56. Ibid.
57. Sigmund Freud, "The *Moses* of Michelangelo" (1955), Stnd. Ed., 13:233.
58. On 14 November 1911; McGuire, *Freud/Jung Letters,* 464.
59. H. Abraham and E. Freud, *A Psychoanalytic Dialogue,* 26 December 1908.
60. To Sandor Ferenczi, 4 February 1915; Jones, *Life and Work,* 2:119.
61. Freud, *The Interpretation of Dreams* (see chap. 1, n. 32), 229.
62. E. Freud and H. Meng, *Psychoanalysis and Faith* (see chap. 2, n. 135), 2 February 1909.
63. On 17 January 1909; McGuire, *Freud/Jung Letters,* 196.
64. E. Freud and H. Meng, *Psychoanalysis and Faith,* 9 February 1909; cf. too, 16 October 1927, "*heillosen Ketzer.*"
65. Ibid., to Pfister, 19 October 1918.
66. On 8 June 1913; in Gay, *Freud: A Life,* 239.
67. Beller, *Vienna and the Jews,* 118.
68. "[May you be inscribed in the Book of Life] for a good year." Letter to Freud from Max Eitingon, 1 October 1913; Gay, *A Godless Jew* (see chap. 2, n. 192), 123.
69. Anna Freud, Preface III, in E. Freud and H. Meng, *Psychoanalysis and Faith,* 11.
70. The holiday in 1909 fell on 16 September; Clark, *Freud,* 274.
71. On 9 March 1909; McGuire, *Freud/Jung Letters,* 211.
72. Lessing, *Nathan the Wise,* 4.2.88–90.
73. Gay, *A Godless Jew,* 72–73.
74. To A. Drujanow, 3 March 1910; ibid., 33.
75. Ken Frieden, *Freud's Dream of Interpretation* (Albany: SUNY Press, 1990), 131.
76. The rabbis however did not see this as "play," but rather, somewhat like Freud (*mutatis mutandis*), as an attempt to discern the divine intention at the heart of reality, that is, of creation. Cf. Howard Eilberg-Schwartz, "Who's Kidding Whom? A Serious Interpretation of Rabbanic Word-Plays," *Journal of the AAR* 55, no. 4 (Winter 1987): 765–88.
77. E. Freud and H. Meng, *Psychoanalysis and Faith,* 16 October 1910.
78. Rosen, "Freud on Jewish Identity, Ethnicity, and Politics," 136.
79. On 9 July 1913; E. Freud, *Letters,* 302.
80. Ibid., 302 n. 7.
81. To Ferenczi, 28 July 1912; Gay, *A Godless Jew,* 120.
82. On 28 August 1913; Gay, *Freud: A Life,* 204.
83. Yerushalmi, *Freud's Moses,* 45.
84. On 29 July 1912; in Simon, "Sigmund Freud, the Jew," 290n, citing L. Binswanger, *Erinnerungen an S[igmund] F[reud]*, (Bern, 1955), 60–61.
85. To Otto Rank, 18 August 1912; Gay, *Freud: A Life,* 231.

86. On 8 June 1913; Jones, *Life and Work,* 2:149.
87. Yerushalmi, *Freud's Moses,* 97.
88. Ibid. "I am a Jew; nothing human is alien to me."
89. To Ferenczi, 11 August 1911; Jones, *Life and Work,* 2:350.
90. On 21 March 1912; McGuire, *Freud/Jung Letters,* 495.
91. On 12 November 1911; ibid., 459.
92. Cf. Jung to Freud, 2 April 1909, "my pregnancy fantasies"; ibid., 217.
93. On 2 November 1911; ibid., 453.
94. On 12 November 1911; ibid., 459.
95. On 14 November 1911; ibid., 460.
96. On 5 November 1911; Nathan G. Hale, ed., *James Jackson Putnam and Psychoanalysis: Letters between Putnam and Sigmund Freud, Ernest Jones, William James, Sandor Ferenczi, and Morton Prince, 1877–1917* (Cambridge: Harvard University Press, 1971), 133.
97. To Jones, 9 August 1911; in Jones, *Life and Work,* 2:350.
98. Ibid., 353.
99. H. Abraham and E. Freud, *A Psychoanalytic Dialogue,* 1 July 1913; cf. too, 1 June 1913.
100. Klein, *Jewish Origins,* 162.
101. Freud, *Totem and Taboo* (1955), Stnd. Ed., 13:133.
102. Ibid., 146.
103. Simon, "Sigmund Freud, the Jew," 284.
104. Wistrich, *The Jews of Vienna* (see chap. 1, n. 14), 569.
105. On 13 January 1910; McGuire, *Freud/Jung Letters,* 288.
106. On 11 February 1910; ibid., 294.
107. On 13 February 1910; ibid., 295.
108. On 12 November 1911; ibid. 459.
109. Theodor Reik, "Freud and Jewish Wit," *Psychoanalysis* 2 (1954): 19.
110. Ibid., 18.
111. See Spielrein's letter to Freud of 11 and 12 June 1909 in Carotenuto, *A Secret Symmetry* (see chap. 2, n. 236), and Bruno Bettelheim's introduction; cf. Gay, *Freud: A Life,* 396n, 752.
112. Cf. Gay's comments in the bibliographic essay of his Freud biography on Jung's claim (and Peter Swales's detective stories) that Freud committed adultery with Minna Bernays. Given that Jung "was himself sexaully quite active during these years, beyond the bounds of marriage," Jung's claim might be projective fantasy (Gay, *Freud: A Life,* 752–53).
113. Hale, *James Jackson Putnam,* 25 December 1911; cf. to Ferenczi, 30 November 1911, in Jones, *Life and Work,* 2:352.
114. Carotenuto, *A Secret Symmetry;* cf. Yerushalmi, *Freud's Moses,* 43–45.
115. Quoted in Duane Schultz, *Intimate Friends, Dangerous Rivals: The Turbulent Relationship between Freud and Jung* (Los Angeles: Jeremy P. Tarcher, 1990), 124.
116. Ibid.
117. Ibid.

118. Yerushalmi, *Freud's Moses,* 44.
119. Quoted in Schultz, *Intimate Friends,* 129.
120. On 21 June 1909; McGuire, *Freud/Jung Letters,* 236–37.
121. On 20 August 1912; in Carotenuto, *A Secret Symmetry,* 116.
122. On 28 August 1913; in ibid.
123. Cf. Jones, *Life and Work,* 2:366.
124. Cf., for example, S. Freud, "The *Moses* of Michelangelo," 213.
125. On 17 October 1912; Jones, *Life and Work,* 2:367.
126. Meyers Reisebuecher series: *Rom und die Compagna* (Leipzig/Vienna: Bibliographisches Institut, 1912), 7th ed., revised by R. Schoener.
127. Molnar, *Diary* (see chap. 1, n. 21), 289n.
128. Freud, "The *Moses* of Michelangelo" (1914), 213; cited in Yerushalmi, *Freud's Moses,* 76.
129. Yerushalmi refers us here to Freud's theory of the origin of the dramatic hero's "tragic guilt," namely, patricide, in *Moses and Monotheism* (1939), 111.
130. Yerushalmi, *Freud's Moses,* 76.
131. Bergmann, "Moses and the Evolution of Freud's Jewish Identity" (see chap. 1, n. 74), 131.
132. On 16 January 1914; Jones, *Life and Work,* 2:366. German unpublished.
133. H. Abraham and E. Freud, *A Psychoanalytic Dialogue,* 16 April 1914. Does that imply that the disclosure of its author's (Jewish) identity at the beginning of the late period is its "punch line"?
134. Hale, *James Jackson Putnam,* 17 May 1914.
135. On 7 November 1914, to Hermann Struck; E. Freud, *Letters,* 306.
136. Reik, "Freud and Jewish Wit," 17, 20.
137. In Theodor Reik, *The Search Within. The Inner Experience of a Psychoanalyst* (New York: J. Aronson, 1974), 637; idem, *Jewish Wit* (see chap. 2, n. 145), 33.
138. Reik, "Freud and Jewish Wit," 16.
139. Theodor Reik, "Sigmund Freud," in *Jewish Heritage Reader,* ed. Lily Edelman (New York: Taplinger, c. 1965), 226.
140. H. Abraham and E. Freud, *A Psychoanalytic Dialogue,* to Abraham, 26 July 1914.
141. Jones, *Life and Work,* 2:171.
142. Ibid.
143. Ibid., 172.
144. The disputation between the rabbi and the monk involves the question again of which religion is superior. Cf. Hal Draper, ed., *The Complete Poems of Heinrich Heine. A Modern English Version by Hal Draper* (Cambridge, Mass.: Suhrkamp/Insel Publishers Boston, 1982), 667–88.
145. Rosen, "Freud on Jewish Identity, Ethnicity, and Politics," 138.
146. H. Abraham and E. Freud, *A Psychoanalytic Dialogue,* 10 December 1917.
147. On 30 March 1922; Jones, *Life and Work,* 3:84.
148. Freud, *Moses and Monotheism,* 125.
149. Oskar Pfister, *Psychoanalysis in the Service of Education* (London: Henry Kimpton, 1922).

150. E. Freud and H. Meng, *Psychoanalysis and Faith,* 9 October 1918.
151. Cf. Lessing, *Nathan the Wise,* 4.7.145.
152. Gay, *A Godless Jew,* 82.
153. E. Freud and H. Meng, *Psychoanalysis and Faith,* 16 February 1929.
154. Lessing's Nathan replies to the Friar, "What makes me for you / A Christian, makes yourself for me a Jew!" (4.7.146f.).
155. Oskar Pfister, "Die Entwicklung des Apostel Paulus. Eine religionsgeschichtliche und psychologische Skizze," *Imago* 6 (1920): 243–90.
156. E. Freud and H. Meng, *Psychoanalysis and Faith,* 9 May 1920.
157. E.g., to Arnold Zweig, 30 September 1934, in E. Freud, *Freud/Zweig Letters;* also cf. Yerushalmi, *Freud's Moses,* 17–18.
158. Yerushalmi, *Freud's Moses,* 18.
159. On 18 August 1910. The last phrase is in English in the original. In Hale, *James Jackson Putnam,* 105.
160. On 25 January 1920; E. Freud, *Briefe,* 343–44.
161. To Silberstein, 6 August 1873; Böhlich, *Letters to Silberstein* (see chap. 2, n. 54), 33.
162. To Eitingon, 3 February 1920, in Jones, *Life and Work,* 3:19.
163. On 4 February 1920; Gay, *Freud: A Life,* 393.
164. To Lajos Levy, 4 February 1920; ibid., 392.
165. E. Freud and H. Meng, *Psychoanalysis and Faith,* 6 April 1922.

Chapter 4. The Encounter with Death

1. On 20 January 1920; Gay, *Freud: A Life,* 391. Original German in Schur, *Freud: Living and Dying* (see chap. 2, n. 201).
2. Gay, *Freud: A Life,* 391.
3. H[ilda] D[oolittle], *Tribute to Freud* (Boston: David R. Godine, 1974), 128.
4. To Ernest Jones, 24 August 1922; in Gay, *Freud: A Life,* 418.
5. To Jones, 25 April, 1923; Jones, *Life and Work,* 3:89. Freud told Ferenczi in 1924 that from the beginning he had been sure the growth was cancerous (6 August 1924; Jones, *Life and Work,* 3:93).
6. Ibid., 3:91.
7. Psychoanalytic "Committee" circular letter, 1 May 1923; ibid., 93.
8. Ibid., 92; Young-Bruehl points to at least one other occasion, in 1938 when Anna returned home from detention by the Gestapo. Freud wept then and declared that "he wanted them all to flee Vienna at once" (Elizabeth Young-Bruehl, *Anna Freud: A Biography* [New York: Summit, 1988], 227).
9. Gay, *Freud: A Life,* 422.
10. On 18 August 1923; ibid.
11. Ibid., 425.
12. Jones, *Life and Work,* 3:93–94.
13. To Eitingon, 26 September 1923; ibid., 94.

14. Ibid.
15. Schur, *Freud: Living and Dying*, 362–63.
16. Molnar, *Diary*, xix.
17. Yerushalmi, *Freud's Moses*, 45.
18. On 4 July 1923; ibid., 46; cf. also William G. Niederland and Jacob Schatzky, "Four Unpublished Letters of Freud," *Psychoanalytic Quarterly* 2 (1956): 148–49.
19. Recall that Freud had been a member of the nationalistic *Leseverein der deutschen Studenten* until it was disbanded by the government in 1878 (Clark, *Freud*, 32; cf. Klein, *Jewish Origins*, 54).
20. H. Abraham and E. Freud, *A Psychoanalytic Dialogue*, 4 May 1924; Jones, *Life and Work*, 3:102.
21. On 28 May 1924; Jones, *Life and Work*, 3:102.
22. Freud, *The Interpretation of Dreams*, 226.
23. Schlesinger, "Jewish Humor as Jewish Identity," 319.
24. Abraham to Freud, 3 December 1924; in H. Abraham and E. Freud, *A Psychoanalytic Dialogue*.
25. To Abraham; ibid., 22 August 1924.
26. Jones, *Life and Work*, 3:116.
27. Freud, *Autobiographical Study*, Stnd. Ed., 20:71.
28. Sigmund Freud, *On the History of the Psycho-Analytical Movement*, Stnd. Ed., 14:7–66.
29. Freud, *Autobiographical Study*, Stnd. Ed., 20:7.
30. Freud, *The Psycho-Analytical Movement*, Stnd. Ed., 14:40.
31. Gay, *Freud: A Life*, 27n.
32. Ibid.
33. Freud, *Autobiographical Study*, Stnd. Ed., 20:8–9.
34. Ibid., 8.
35. Ibid., 8 n. 3.
36. As mentioned, both Rice and Yerushalmi argue that the Freud family Bible profoundly influences the shape of Freud's interest, character and life. Cf. Rice, *Freud and Moses* (see chap. 1, n. 25), and Yerushalmi, *Freud's Moses* (see Preface, n. 1).
37. Published on 26 February 1925; Sigmund Freud, "Letter to the Editor of the *Jewish Press Centre in Zurich*," Stnd. Ed., 19:291.
38. Letter to Arthur Schnitzler, 24 May 1926; Henry Schnitzler, "Freuds Briefe an Arthur Schnitzler," *Die Neue Rundschau* 66 (1955): 100.
39. Ibid.; cf. too Freud's "Letter in Place of a Preface" to his *Introductory Lectures*, in Sigmund Freud, *Araynfir in Psikhoanaliz*, trans. Max Weinreich, Heft 1 (Vilna: YIVO, 1936).
40. Rainey, "Freud as a Student of Religion" (see chap. 2, n. 15), 50.
41. Samuel Hammerschlag, "Das Program der israel Religionsschule in Wien," in *Bericht der Religionsschule der israelitischen Cultusgemeinde in Wien über die Schuljahre 1868 und 1869* (Vienna: Druck von Jacob Schlossberg, 1969), 11; cited ibid., 38.

42. Meitlis, "The Last Days of Sigmund Freud" (see chap. 2, n. 403), 21.

43. The Standard Edition (19:292) claims that only the "original English" is extant. But the German text appears in *The Hebrew University, Jerusalem. Inauguration. April 1, 1925* (Hebrew University, 1925), 110–111. Thanks to Dan Sharon of the Asher Library, Spertus Museum of Judaica, Chicago, for calling my attention to this text.

44. *Encyclopaedia Judaica,* s.v. "Chajes, Zvi Hirsch," by Eliahu Hirschbein. Cf. too Rabbi Dr. Alfred Willman, "Famous Rabbis of Vienna," in Fraenkel, *The Jews of Austria* (see chap. 1, n. 17), 319–26.

45. Willman, "Famous Rabbis," 366.

46. Letter to Jacob Meitlis, 30 November 1938; in Meitlis, "Last Days of Sigmund Freud," 21.

47. On 19 December 1925, to Samuel Freud; in Gay, *Freud: A Life,* 455.

48. Klingsberg, *Freudiana* (see chap. 2, n. 17), vi.

49. Gay, *Freud: A Life,* 482.

50. On 28 January 1926; Jones, *Life and Work,* 3:120.

51. On 25 April 1926; Simon, "Sigmund Freud, the Jew," 275.

52. On 18 February 1926; E. Freud, *Letters,* 365.

53. Klein, *Jewish Origins,* 82.

54. Gay, *Freud: A Life,* 445.

55. Considering Fliess's attempts in the early period to prevent Freud from smoking (to protect his health), it is significant that Freud writes to his former friend and father figure on this topic at this time in his life. It is as though he were resolving old conflicts, severing one last link with Fliess in order to return fully to his real father. Fliess's birthday (24 October) fell on the day after Jakob Freud died (23 October 1896), facilitating the replacement of his father by Fliess in Freud's psyche.

56. On 12 February 1928; in Schur, *Freud: Living and Dying,* 62, 535.

57. Molnar, *Diary,* 69.

58. Ibid., 276; cf. Freud's letter to Stefan Zweig, 7 February 1931, in which he says that he "owed to cigars the greater part of his self-discpline and steadfastness at work" (ibid., 53).

59. On 16 April 1909; McGuire, *Freud/Jung Letters,* 220.

60. As in his letter to Ferenczi, 11 May 1911; Jones, *Life and Work,* 3:387.

61. Justin Miller, "Interpretations of Freud's Jewishness, 1924–1974," *Journal of the History of Behavioral Sciences* 17 (1981): 374 n. 89.

62. Jones, *Life and Work,* 3:381.

63. Cf. Rainey, "Freud as a Student of Religion," 89.

64. Ibid., 98.

65. *B'nai B'rith Mitteilungen für Österreich* 26 (May 1926).

66. To Marie Bonaparte, 26 April 1926; Jones, *Life and Work,* 3:124.

67. Ibid.

68. On 28 January 1926; in Simon, "Sigmund Freud, the Jew," 276. Cf. too the same sentence in Freud's letter in the *B'nai B'rith Monatsblätter* of 1926, written a week earlier; in Molnar, *Diary,* 189.

69. George Sylvester Viereck, *Glimpses of the Great* (London: Duckworth, 1930), 34. Also published separately in 1927 (Gay, *Freud: A Life,* 711).

70. Klein, *Jewish Origins,* 80–81.

71. Ibid., 73.

72. Joseph Wortis, *Fragments of an Analysis with Freud* (New York: McGraw-Hill, 1975), 144.

73. Klein, *Jewish Origins,* 72.

74. Ibid.

75. Ibid.

76. Aron, "Notes on Sigmund Freud's Ancestry" (see chap. 2, n. 58), 290–91.

77. Klein, *Jewish Origins,* 86.

78. Strachey translates *schuldig* as "ashamed" (Sigmund Freud, "Address to the Society of B'nai B'rith," Stnd. Ed., 20:273), giving a different sense.

79. Rainey, "Freud as a Student of Religion," 51.

80. Ibid., 45ff.

81. Still, Freud's first words to Oscar Nemon, when the sculptor began his bust of the founder of psychoanalysis in 1931, were "I am sure you know your profession is the oldest in the world. . . . Did not God create man from clay?" H. Meng, "Freud and the Sculptor," in H. M. Ruitenbeek, *Freud As We Knew Him* (Detroit: Wayne State University Press, 1973), 351.

82. Eicha Rabbah 2:13. However, the saying continues, "but if you hear that there is Torah [i.e., divine teaching that could serve as an alternative to Jewish teaching], do not believe it."

83. Simon, "Sigmund Freud, the Jew," 281–82.

84. Freud, "Address," Stnd. Ed., 20:273–74; idem, "Ansprache an die Mitglieder des Vereins B'nai B'rith," *Gesammelte Werke,* 17:51–53.

85. Freud, quoting Breasted, in *Moses and Monotheism,* 21 n. 1.

86. Sigmund Freud, "The Uncanny," in *On Creativity and the Unconscious: Papers on the Psychology of Art, Literature, Love, and Religion,* ed. Benjamin Nelson (New York: Harper and Row, 1979), 122–61.

87. To Martha Bernays, 26 August 1882; Jones, *Life and Work,* 1:174.

88. David Bakan, *Sigmund Freud and the Jewish Mystical Tradition* (Princeton, N.J.: Van Nostrand, 1958), 305–19.

89. Ibid., 306; Freud, "The Uncanny," 131.

90. Bakan, *Sigmund Freud and the Jewish Mystical Tradition,* 314–15.

91. Ibid., 316; Bakan's italics. Cf. also Rice, *Freud and Moses.*

92. E. Freud, *Letters,* 10 May 1926.

93. Klein, *Jewish Origins,* 81–82.

94. On 24 May 1926; Schnitzler, "Freuds Briefe an Arthur Schnitzler," 100.

95. E. Freud and H. Meng, *Psychoanalysis and Faith,* 11 April 1926.

96. On 16 February 1929.

97. On 4 March 1923; Gay, *A Godless Jew,* 56.

98. E. Freud and H. Meng, *Psychoanalysis and Faith,* 22 October 1927.

99. Freud's self-description to an American physician in "A Religious Experience," Stnd. Ed., 21:170.

100. *Encyclopaedia Judaica,* s.v. "Brandes, Georg," by Frederick Julius Billeskov-Jansen and Leni Yahil.

101. Ibid., s.v. "YIVO" by Sol Liptzin.

102. Aron, "Notes on Sigmund Freud's Ancestry," 293.

103. Meitlis, "The Last Days of Sigmund Freud," 20.

104. On 5 December 1927; David James Fisher, "Sigmund Freud and Romain Rolland: The Terrestrial Animal and His Great Oceanic Friend," *American Imago* 33 (1976): 20. Freud took over a year-and-a-half to answer this implied challenge, and when he did so it was to ask Rolland's permission to allow him to use a brief analysis of the "oceanic feeling" as a jumping-off point for his *Civilization and Its Discontents* (1930).

105. I.e., Ramakrishna and Vivekenanda. Cf. Romain Rolland, *Prophets of the New India* (New York: Boni, 1930).

106. Henry George Liddell and Robert Scott, *A Greek-English Lexicon,* rev. ed. (Oxford: Clarendon Press, 1925–40), 1751.

107. Wortis, *Fragments,* 158.

108. Cf. Fisher, "Sigmund Freud and Romain Rolland," 39–42.

109. Ibid., 7.

110. Ibid., 4.

111. *Seinem grossen, ozeanischen Freund, das Landtier,* 18.3.1931. Ibid., 40.

112. A. A. Roback, *Jewish Influence in Modern Thought* (Cambridge, Mass.: Sci-Art Publishers, 1929), 160.

113. Ibid., 166.

114. Ibid., 160.

115. On 20 September 1928, to Yehuda Devosis; in Gay, *Freud: A Life,* 600; again to Devosis, 11 September 1938; ibid., 732n.

116. On 24 March 1930; Roback, *Freudiana,* 33; the letter in German, 228.

117. Ibid., 25–28, 226–27.

118. Ibid., 33, 228.

119. Roback, *Jewish Influence,* 198.

120. On 24 March 1930; Roback, *Freudiana,* 33; the letter in German, 228.

121. Ibid., 30–31.

122. Ibid., 35.

123. Conor Cruise O'Brien, *The Siege: The Saga of Israel and Zionism* (New York: Simon and Schuster, 1986), 186.

124. Ibid., 178–88.

125. Cf. Shmuel Etinger, "The Zionist Movement and the 'National Home' Between the World Wars," in H. H. Ben-Sasson, *History of the Jewish People* (Cambridge: Harvard University Press, 1976), esp. 1006–8.

126. Klingsberg, *Freudiana,* viii.

127. O'Brien, *The Siege,* 180.

128. Klingsberg, *Freudiana,* xviii.

129. Yerushalmi, *Freud's Moses,* 118 n. 49.

130. On 15 December 1930; Gay, *Freud: A Life,* 598n.

131. Wortis, *Fragments,* 144.

132. On 20 June 1935; in Klingsberg, *Freudiana,* ix.

133. Gay, *Freud: A Life,* 600.

134. On 20 September 1928; ibid.

135. To Isaac Landman, 1 August 1929; Gay, *A Godless Jew,* 126.

136. Sifrei, Eikev 46.

137. Molnar, *Diary,* 280.

138. To Thieberger, 28 January 1926; Simon, "Sigmund Freud, the Jew," 276.

139. To Einstein, 26 February 1930; Gay, *Freud: A Life,* 598n; to Koffler, same date, Klingsberg, *Freudiana,* viii.

140. Freud says he "makes no exceptions in favor of Jewry (*Judentum*)" but Simon has pointed out his avoidance of Jewish themes in *Totem and Taboo* (Simon, "Sigmund Freud, the Jew," 283f.).

141. Freud, *Totem and Taboo,* Stnd. Ed., 13:xv; idem, *Totem and Tabu,* in *Gesammelte Werke,* 14:569.

142. On 7 April 1931; Gay, *Freud: A Life,* 575. Oscar Philipp, an Orthodox Jewish relative on Martha's side of the family, read *Future of an Illusion* and said it in fact strengthened his Orthodox Jewish faith (Molnar, *Diary,* 292n), so Rabbi Feuchtwang's sentiment may have been shared by other Jews.

143. 6 May 1931; Joseph Philip Hes, "A Note on an as yet Unpublished Letter by Sigmund Freud," *Jewish Social Studies* 48 (1986): 322. Thanks to Dr. Zanvel Klein, *z"l,* for bringing this letter to my attention.

144. Ibid., 324.

145. On 13 June 1935; E. Freud, *Freud/Zweig Letters,* 107.

146. Samuel Jaffe, University of Chicago, personal communication. We are reminded of the dialectic of *ausleben* and *entbehren* in Freud's letter in the early period (29 August 1883) about the difference between him and Martha on the one hand, and *das Gesindel* on the other.

147. Freud, *The Future of an Illusion,* Stnd. Ed., 21:54.

148. On 18 August 1932. Recall Freud's letter to Erich Leyens in July 1923, at the beginning of the late period.

149. Ernst Freud et al., *Pictures and Words,* 282.

150. Hugo Knöpfmacher, "Sigmund Freud in High School," *American Imago* 36 (1979): 299.

151. On 28 May 1933; i.e., they are *Gesindel.*

152. Arnold Zweig, *Caliban oder Politik und Leidenschaft, Versuch über die menschlichen Gruppenaffekte, dargestellt am Antisemitismus* (Potsdam: Gustav Kiepenheuer Verlag, 1927).

153. On 2 December 1927; in E. Freud, *Freud/Zweig Letters,* 3.

154. Yerushalmi, *Freud's Moses,* 15.

155. On 18 August 1933; Gay, *Freud: A Life,* 605; cf. Schur, *Freud: Living and Dying,* 468, 563, who does not publish the last sentence.

156. Yerushalmi, *Freud's Moses,* 117; Schur, *Freud: Living and Dying,* 468.

157. Cf. Yerushalmi, *Freud's Moses,* 34–35.

158. Ostow, "Freud and the Philippson Bible" (see chap. 2, n. 18), 487.

159. E.g., to Martha Bernays, 16 September 1883; E. Freud, *Letters,* 58–66.

160. Cf. letter to Kurt Hiller, 9 February 1936; Jones, *Life and Work,* 3:159–60.

161. Sigmund Freud, "A Special Type of Object-Choice Made by Men," Stnd. Ed., 11:174; cf. Otto Rank, *Der Mythus von der Geburt des Helden* (Wien: Victor Glanz, 1909).

162. Reik, "Freud and Jewish Wit," 18.

163. On 25 October 1933; in E. Freud, *Freud/Zweig Letters.*

164. On 17 November 1933; Milton Rosenbaum, "Freud-Eitingon-Magnes Correspondence. Psychoanalysis of the Hebrew University," *Journal of the American Psychoanalytic Association* 2, no. 2 (1954): 314.

165. Ibid., 312.

166. Ibid., 315.

167. Ibid., 316.

168. Gay, *A Godless Jew,* 122.

169. Arnold Zweig, *Bilanz der deutschen Judenheit, 1933. Die Wahrheit über die deutschen Juden* (Amsterdam: Querido Verlag, 1934); idem, *Insulted and Exiled: The Truth about the German Jews* (London: John Miles, 1937).

170. Zweig had said as much in a letter of 21 January, referring to "this terrible return to barbarism" on the part of Germany.

171. On 28 January 1934; E. Freud, *Freud/Zweig Letters.*

172. On 25 February 1934; E. Freud, *Letters,* 65.

173. To Marie Bonaparte, 2 May 1934; Jones, *Life and Work,* 3:189.

174. Zweig, *Insulted and Exiled,* ix.

175. Yosef Hayim Yerushalmi, "Freud on the 'Historical Novel': From the Manuscript Draft (1934) of *Moses and Monotheism,*" *International Journal of Psycho-Analysis* 70 (1989): 376.

176. Jones, *Life and Work,* 3:192. Freud writes his first full account of the *Moses* (and writes so many later letters about it) to Arnold Zweig in Palestine, where the Jewish people are struggling to found a new home. Perhaps Freud is "drawing strength" from an "indestructible national feeling."

177. On 30 September 1934; E. Freud, *Freud/Zweig Letters,* 91.

178. Ibid.

179. Simon, "Sigmund Freud, the Jew," 285.

180. Zweig, *Insulted and Exiled,* 67.

181. Ibid., 90.

182. Ibid.

183. Ibid., 83.

184. Yerushalmi, "Freud on the 'Historical Novel'," 294; Yerushalmi, *Freud's Moses,* 18.

185. Yerushalmi has shown that Freud's fears were not paranoid, but rather indicate an awareness of Pater Wilhelm Schmidt's extreme hostility to psychoanalysis (he associated Freud with Bolshevism) and his influence in putting an end to the Italian psychoanalytic movement (Yerushalmi, *Freud's Moses,* 27–29).

186. Jones, *Life and Work,* 3:194.

187. On 27 October 1934; ibid.

188. On 6 November 1934; E. Freud, *Freud/Zweig Letters,* 97.

189. Ibid.

190. On 13 November 1934 (Jones, *Life and Work,* 3:194), probably thinking of Mann's *Joseph and His Brothers,* which Mann was working on at this time.

191. On 16 December 1934; E. Freud, *Freud/Zweig Letters,* 98.

192. Ibid.; cf. also 6 November 1934, "I should not like to endanger the final formula of the whole book, which I regard as valuable, by founding it on a base of clay."

193. On 6 January 1935; Ernst Pfeiffer, ed., *Sigmund Freud and Lou Andreas-Salome Letters,* trans. William Robson-Scott and Elaine Robson-Scott (New York: Norton, 1985), 205.

194. Or, as Krüll would say, a "mandate" for such rejection; cf. her *Freud and His Father.*

195. In his *Bilanz* (222–23), Zweig attributes this point to Freud "in a lecture," so it may have preceded *Moses and Monotheism.*

196. Simon, "Sigmund Freud, the Jew," 303.

197. On 13 February 1935; E. Freud, *Freud/Zweig Letters,* 102.

198. Schur, *Freud: Living and Dying,* 462.

199. On 13 February 1935, *Freud/Zweig Letters,* 102.

200. On 2 May 1935; ibid., 106.

201. To Eitingon, 12 May 1935; in Gay, *Freud: A Life,* 608. Cf. 13 June 1935; E. Freud, *Freud/Zweig Letters,* 107.

202. On 2 May 1935; ibid., 106.

203. On 13 June 1935; ibid., 107.

204. Sigmund Freud, "Moses ein Ägypter," *Imago* 23 (I) (1937): 5–13; and idem, "Wenn Moses ein Ägypter war . . . ," *Imago* (IV) (1937): 387–419.

205. Sigmund Freud, *An Autobiographical Study* (see chap. 1, n. 54), 136–37. Subsequent references are to this Norton edition.

206. Ibid., 137. Cf. too, as discussed above, Freud's sentence about the early influence of his Bible reading that he added at this time.

207. Ibid., 138.

208. On 6 January 1935; Pfeiffer, *Freud/Andreas-Salome Letters,* 205.

209. Perhaps a particularly "Jewish" sensitivity in Freud's mind, knowing the esteem in which he holds the biblical prophets.

210. On 13 June 1935; Jones, *Life and Work,* 3:198.

211. On June 20, 1935; Gay, *A Godless Jew,* 123.

212. On 14 October 1935; ibid., 610.

213. Niederland and Schatzky, "Four Unpublished Letters," 150.

214. On 25 July 1936; ibid.

215. On 12 November 1935; Gay, *Freud: A Life,* 597.

216. To Emil Fluss, 18 September 1872.

217. Josef Fraenkel, "Professor Freud and Kadimah" (see chap. 2, n. 405), 16.

218. In *B'nai B'rith Mitteilungen für Österreich* 35 (November and December 1935): 193; cited by Klein, *Jewish Origins,* 72, 86.

219. On 9 February 1936; Jones, *Life and Work,* 3:160.

220. Jones reports Freud's negative response to A. Zweig's sadness over Alfred Adler's sudden death in 1937, translating Freud's word for Adler, *Judenbub,* as "Jew boy." Gay points out that there is no satisfactory translation for the

German (he suggests "Jewish boy"), "but Jones's solution has the wrong weight to it. Freud's reference to Adler is callous and snide, but not quite so disdainful or bigoted [or antisemitic] as 'Jew boy' would imply" (Gay, *Freud: A Life*, 615n). In other words, what seems like Freud's Jewish antisemitism in his letter to Zweig is probably Jones's.

221. To Barbara Low, 19 April 1936; E. Freud, *Letters*, 428.

222. J. B. Hobman, ed., *David Eder. Memoirs of a Modern Pioneer* (London: Victor Gollancz, 1945).

223. On 30 April 1936; Sigmund Freud, *Araynfir in Psikoanaliz* (see chap. 4, n. 39). I am indebted to Dr. Zanvel Klein, z"l, for this translation from the Yiddish translation of Freud's published German.

224. Freeman, *Insights* (see chap. 2, n. 358), 26: "his mother 'did not speak in High German, but Galician Yiddish.'"

225. Gay, *A Godless Jew*, 122.

226. On 17 June 1936; E. Freud, *Freud/Zweig Letters*, 131. As Yerushalmi points out, in German the dog's name sounds like the Hebrew word for beauty. However, the first time Freud enters the chow's name in his "Shortest Chronicle," it appears as "Jo-Fi," perhaps as though Freud thought it was a Chinese name (Molnar, *Diary*, 61). In Palestine at the time, Zweig of course may have appreciated the connection to Hebrew even more than Freud.

227. Quoted in Fraenkel, "Professor Freud and Kadimah," 17. Martin Freud confirms Freud's honorary membership in Kadimah in his book *Sigmund Freud: Man and Father*, 165.

228. Molnar, *Diary*, 206. Cf. Fraenkel, "Professor Freud and Kadimah," 15.

229. *Encyclopaedia Judaica*, s.v. "Kadimah," by Getzel Kressel.

230. Martin Freud, *Sigmund Freud: Man and Father*, 163.

231. Ibid., 165.

232. Fraenkel, "Professor Freud and Kadimah," 15.

233. Ibid.

234. Molnar, *Diary*, 46.

235. Fraenkel, "Professor Freud and Kadimah," 17.

236. Ibid.

237. Ibid.

238. Molnar, *Diary*, 214.

239. Freud, "Moses ein Ägypter," 5–13.

240. Molnar, *Diary*, 215.

241. Ibid., 217.

242. To Marie Bonaparte, 13 August 1937; E. Freud, *Letters*, 436.

243. Freud, "Wenn Moses ein Ägypter war . . .," 387–419.

244. On 28 August 1937; Jones, *Life and Work*, 3:216.

245. Marie Bonaparte, 10 September 1937; ibid.

246. Yerushalmi, *Freud's Moses*, 21.

247. October 1937; in Hugo Knöpfmacher, "Sigmund Freud and B'nai B'rith," 447–48.

248. Cf. Gay, *A Godless Jew*, 133–35; idem, *Freud: A Life*, 601–2; cf. Rosen, "Freud on Jewish Identity, Ethnicity, and Politics," 134–35.

249. Gay, *A Godless Jew,* 131–32.
250. On 14 December 1937; listed as "Anonymous" in E. Freud, *Letters,* 439.
251. On 16 December 1934; E. Freud, *Freud/Zweig Letters.*
252. Cf. Freud's remark when he thanks Zweig for a list of writers who thought that Moses was Egyptian: "But not one of them made anything of it"; 17 June 1936; E. Freud, *Freud/Zweig Letters,* 131.
253. On 17 January 1938; E. Freud, *Letters,* 440.
254. Yerushalmi, *Freud's Moses,* 10.
255. E. Freud, *Letters,* 440 n. 1.
256. Jones, *Life and Work,* 3:221.
257. Ibid.; cf. Freud, *Moses and Monotheism,* 147.
258. Jones, *Life and Work,* 3:221. Sterba nullified this exception, deciding to share the fate of his Jewish colleagues by fleeing to Switzerland and later refusing the blandishments of the Nazis to cooperate with them.
259. On 28 April 1938; Jones, *Life and Work,* 3:225.
260. ". . . as Thomas Mann is to describe in his next novel," Freud continued to Ernst Freud, 12 May 1938; E. Freud, *Letters,* 442.
261. Cited in Molnar, *Diary,* 216.
262. Freud, *The Interpretation of Dreams,* Stnd. Ed., 5:484 n. 2. Cf. also Rice, *Freud and Moses,* and Leonard Shegold, "Freud and Joseph," in Mark Kanzer and Jules Glenn, eds., *Freud and his Self-Analysis* (New York: Jason Aronson, 1979), 67–86.
263. On 12 May 1938; E. Freud, *Letters,* 442–43.
264. On 20 July 1928; ibid., 382. Cf. George S. Viereck and Paul Eldridge, *My First Two Thousand Years: The Autobiography of the Wandering Jew* (New York: Macaulay, 1928).
265. *Encyclopaedia Judaica,* s.v. "Wandering Jew," by Yvonne Glikson.
266. Samuel Jaffe, University of Chicago, personal communication; cf. Yerushalmi, *Freud's Moses,* 50–51.
267. Freud, *Moses and Monotheism,* 142–56.
268. Yerushalmi, *Freud's Moses,* 4; cf. S. Freud, "A Difficulty in the Path of Psycho-Analysis" (1917), Stnd. Ed., 17:139–43.
269. "Ich kann die Gestapo jedermann auf das beste empfehlen."
270. M. Freud, *Sigmund Freud: Man and Father,* 217.
271. Ibid.
272. Jones, *Life and Work,* 3:288.
273. On 6 June 1938; ibid.
274. On 1 February 1900; Masson, *Complete Fliess Letters,* 398.
275. On 8 June 1938; Meitlis, "The Last Days of Sigmund Freud," 20. Cf. also Freud's letter in 1938 to the secretary of the *Jewish Observer and Middle East Review* (4 June 1954): 10, where Freud echoes the same sentiments.
276. Gay, *Freud: A Life,* 633, 736.
277. Freud, *Moses and Monotheism,* part 3, section 2C (Stnd Ed., 23:111–15; idem, *Der Mann Moses and die monotheistische Religion,* in *Gesammelte Werke,* 16:219–23).
278. Published separately in *Int. Zeit. Psych. Imago* 24 (1/2) (1939): 6–9.

279. Later altered to read "the worthier alternative"; Freud, *Moses and Monotheism,* Stnd. Ed., 23:115.

280. Ibid.

281. On 3 March 1936; Jones, *Life and Work,* 3:207.

282. Yehudah Devosis, 11 December 1938; Gay, *Freud: A Life,* 638.

283. Freud, *Moses and Monotheism,* Stnd. Ed., 23:115.

284. Ibid.

285. E. Freud, *Freud/Zweig Letters,* 163.

286. Gay, *Freud: A Life,* 637.

287. The conflict is reminiscent of one Freud discusses between truth and love, in reference to the question of whether a man should in the name of truth relate his previous sexual experiences to his wife. Interestingly, Freud argues in the name of love that he should not.

288. Freud, *Moses and Monotheism,* 3.

289. Yerushalmi, *Freud's Moses,* 6–7.

290. Ibid., 117 n. 28.

291. Meitlis, "The Last Days of Sigmund Freud," 21.

292. Cf. Rice's claim that Jakob Freud must have studied in a yeshiva as a youth; *Freud and Moses,* 93–94.

293. Meitlis, "Last Days," 21.

294. Ibid., 20.

295. Ibid., 22.

296. Ibid., 21.

297. As Freud tells Jung with regard to biblical texts: "I hold that the surface versions of myths cannot be used uncritically for comparison with our psychoanalytical findings. We must find our way back to their latent, original forms by a comparative method that eliminates the distortions they have undergone in the course of their history" (17 December 1911; McGuire, *Freud/Jung Letters,* 473).

298. On 12 March 1939; Hanns Sachs, *Freud: Master and Friend* (Cambridge: Harvard University Press, 1946), 184.

299. To Dr. Sigfried Fehl, 12 November 1935; Gay, *Freud: A Life,* 597.

Chapter 5. Dual Allegiance and Modern Identity

1. Yerushalmi, *Freud's Moses,* 31.
2. Ibid., 31–32.
3. Cf. for example the 1990 American Jewish Population Survey.
4. David Stern, "The Ego and the Yid," *The New Republic,* 21 September 1992, 49.
5. Ibid., 48.
6. Ibid., 49.
7. Cf. Yerushalmi, *Freud's Moses,* 99.
8. Stern, "The Ego and the Yid," 49.

9. Sigmund Freud, *Moses and Monotheism* (see chap. 2, n. 254), 109f., 175.

10. Stern, "The Ego and the Yid," 48.

11. I am indebted to the teaching of Dov Berkovits, at the Pardes Institute of Jewish Studies, in Jerusalem, for the content of this analysis. Its application is my own responsibility, an attempt to provide an example of the love of the tradition in the service of the renewal of Jewish identity.

12. Cf. Jonathan Sarna (guest columnist), untitled article in *Moment* 17, no. 5 (October 1992): 18.

Selected Bibliography

Abraham, Hilda C., and Ernst L. Freud, eds. *Briefe 1907–1926, Sigmund Freud, Karl Abraham.* Frankfurt am Main: S. Fischer, 1965.

Abraham, Hilda C., and Ernst L. Freud, eds. *A Psychoanalytic Dialgue: The Letters of Sigmund Freud and Karl Abraham, 1907–1926.* Translated by Bernard Marsh and Hilda C. Abraham. London: Hogarth Press and the Institute of Psychoanalysis, 1965.

Alter, Robert. *the Invention of Hebrew Prose. Modern Fiction and the Language of Realism.* Seattle and London: University of Washington Press, 1988.

Aron, Willy. "Hakham Isaac Bernays (1792–1849): A Biographical Essay." *The Jewish Forum*, March 1949, 41–44.

——. "Notes on Sigmund Freud's Ancestry and Jewish Contacts." *YIVO Annual of Jewish Social Sciences* 11 (1955–57): 286–95.

Aschheim, Stephen E. "The East European Jew and German Jewish Identity." *Studies in Contemporary History* , 1984, 3–22.

Bach, Hans I. *The German Jew. A Synthesis of Judaism and Western Civilization.* Oxford and New York: Oxford University Prfess, 1984.

Bakan, David. "Freud and The Zohar." *Commentary* 29, no. 1 (January 1960): 65–66.

——. "Moses in the Thought of Freud: An Ambivalent Interpretation." *Commentary* 26 (October 1958): 322–31.

——. *Sigmund Freud and the Jewish Mystical Tradition.* Princeton, N.J.: Van Nostrand, 1958.

Beller, Steven. *Vienna and the Jews, 1867–1938. A Cultural History.* Cambridge: Cambridge University Press, 1989.

Bergmann, Martin S. "Moses and the Evolution of Freud's Jewish Identity." In *Judaism and Psychoanalysis,* ed. Mortimer Ostow, 111–115. New York: Ktav, 1982.

Berkower, Larry. "The Enduring Effect of the Jewish Tradition upon Freud." *American Journal of Psychiatry* 125 (February 1969): 103–9.

Bernays, Anna Freud. "My Brother, Sigmund Freud." *The American Mercury* 51 (November 1940): 335–42.

Bernfeld, Suzanne C. "Freud and Archaeology." *American Imago* 8 (1951): 107–28.

Binswanger, Ludwig. *Sigmund Freud: Reminiscences of a Friendship.* New York and London: Grune and Stratton, 1957.

Blatt, David S. "The Development of the Hero. Sigmund Freud and the Reformation of the Jewish Tradition." *Psychoanalysis and Contemporary Thought* 11, no. 4 (1988): 639–703.

Böhlich, Walter, ed. *The Letters of Sigmund Freud to Eduard Siberstein, 1871–1881.* Translated by Arnold J. Pomerans. Cambridge: Harvard University Press, 1990.

——, ed. *Sigmund Freud: Jugendbriefe an Eduard Silberstein, 1871–1881.* Frankfurt am Main: S. Fischer, 1989.

Bonaparte, Marie, Anna Freud, and Ernst Kris, eds. *Aus den Anfängen der Psychoanalyse; Briefe an Wilhelm Fliess, Abhandlungen und Notizen aus den Jahren 1887–1902.* Frankfurt am Main: S. Fischer Verlag, 1954.

——. *The Origins of Psycho-Analysis: Letters to Wilhelm Fliess, Drafts and Notes, 1887–1902.* Translated by Eric Mosbacher and James Strachey. New York: Basic Books, 1954.

Brandell, Gunnar. *Freud: A Man of His Century.* Translated by Iain White. Sussex, G.B.: Harvester Press, 1979.

Brome, Vincent. *Freud and His Early Circle.* New York: William Morrow, 1967.

Carotenuto, Aldo. *A Secret Symmetry: Sabina Spielrein between Jung and Freud.* Translated by Arno Pomerans, John Shepley, and Krishna Winston. 2d ed. New York: Pantheon, 1984.

Choisy, Maryse. *Sigmund Freud: A New Appraisal.* New York: Philosophical Library, 1963.

Clare, George. *Last Waltz in Vienna—The Rise and Destruction of a Family—1842–1942.* New York: Holt, Rinehart, and Winston, 1982.

Clark, Ronald C. *Freud: The Man and the Cause.* New York: Random House, 1980.

Cuddihy, John Murray. *The Ordeal of Civility: Freud, Marx, Levi-Strauss, and the Jewish Struggle with Modernity.* New York: Delta, 1974.

Diller, Jerry Victory. *Freud's Jewish Identity. A Case Study in the Impact of Ethnicity.* Rutherford, Madison, Teaneck, N.J.: Fairleigh Dickinson University Press, 1991.

Doolittle, Hilda. *Tribute to Freud.* Boston: David R. Godine, 1974.

Draper, Hal, ed. *The Complete Poems of Heinrich Heine. A Modern English Version by Hal Draper.* Cambridge, Mass.: Suhrkamp/Insel Publishers Boston, 1982.

Drucker, Peter F. "What Freud Forgot." *Human Nature* 2, no. 3 (March 1979): 40–47.

Eilberg-Schwartz, Howard. "Who's Kidding Whom? A Serious Interpretion of Rabbinic Word-Plays." *Journal of the AAR* 55, no. 4 (Winter 1987): 765–88.

Eissler, Kurt R. *Sigmund Freud and Die Wiener Universität.* Stuttgart: Hans Huber Bern, 1966.

Eliot, George. *Daniel Deronda.* Edited by Graham Handley. Oxford: Clarendon Press, 1984.

Engelman, Edmund. *Berggasse 19: Sigmund Freud's Home and Offices, Vienna 1938.* Introduction by Peter Gay. New York: Basic Books, 1976.

Erikson, Erik. *Identity: Youth and Crisis.* New York: Norton, 1968.

Etinger, Shmuel. "The Zionist Movement and the 'National Home' between the World Wars." In H. H. Ben-Sasson, *History of the Jewish People.* Cambridge: Harvard University Press, 1976.

Falk, Avner. "Freud and Herzl." *Contemporary Psychoanalysis* 14 (1978): 357–87.

Fisher, David James. "Sigmund Freud and Romain Rolland: The Terrestrial Animal and His Great Oceanic Friend." *American Imago* 33 (1976): 1–59.

Fraenkel, Josef. ed. *The Jews of Austria: Essays on their Life, History, and Destruction.* London: Vallentine, Mitchell, and Co., 1967.

——. "Professor Freud and the Student Society 'Kadimah'." *The Gates of Zion,* April 1964, 15–17.

Freeman, Erika. *Insights: Conversations with Theodor Reik.* Englewood Cliffs, N.J.: Prentice-Hall, 1971.

Freud, Ernst, ed. *Brautbriefe: Briefe an Martha Bernays aus den Jahren 1882 bis 1886.* Frankfurt am Main: Fischer Taschenbuch Verlag, 1988.

——. *Briefwechsel: Von Sigmund Freud, Arnold Zweig.* Frankfurt am Main: S. Fischeer Verlag, 1968.

——. *Letters of Sigmund Freud.* Translated by Tania Stern and James Stern. New York: Basic Books, 1960.

——. *The Letters of Sigmund Freud and Arnold Zweig.* Translated by Elaine Robson-Scott and William D. Robson-Scott. London: Hogarth Press and the Institute of Psychoanalysis, 1970.

——. *Sigmund Freud, Lou Andreas-Salome, Briefwechsel.* Frankfurt am Main: S. Fischer Verlag, 1966.

——"Some Early Unpublished Letters of Freud." *International Journal of Psychoanalysis* 50 (1969): 419–27.

Freud, Ernst, and Lucie Freud, eds. *Sigmund Freud. Briefe 1873–1939.* 3d ed. Frankfurt am Main: S. Fischer Verlag, 1980.

Freud, Ernst, Lucie Freud, and Ilse Grubrich-Simitis, eds. *Sigmund Freud: His Life in Pictures and Words.* Translated by Christine Trollope. London: André Deutsch, 1978.

Freud, Ernst, and Heinrich Meng. *Briefe 1909–1939, Sigmund Freud, Oskar Pfister*. Frankfurt am Main: S. Fischer Verlag, 1968.

Freud, Ernst, and Heinrich Meng. *Psycho-Analysis and Faith: The Letters of Sigmund Freud and Oscar Pfister*. Translated by Eric Mosbacher. London: Hogarth Press and the Institute of Psychoanalysis, 1963.

Freud, Esti D. "Mrs. Sigmund Freud." *The Jewish Spectator*, Spring 1980: 2931.

Freud, Martin. *Sigmund Freud: Man and Father*. New York: Vanguard, 1958.

——. "Who was Freud?" In *The Jews of Austria: Essays of their Life, History, and Destruction*, ed. Josef Fraenkel, 197–211. London: Vallentine, Mitchell, and Co., 1967.

Freud, Sigmund. *Araynfir in Psykhoanalyz*. Heft 1. Translated by Max Weinreich. Vilna: YIVO, 1936.

——. *An Autobiographical Study*. Translated by James Strachey. New York: Norton, 1952.

——. *Autobiography*. Translated by James Strachey. New York: Norton, 1935.

——. *Character and Culture*. Edited by Philip Rieff. New York: Collier, 1963.

——. German original of 1926 speech to members of the B'nai B'rith Lodge. *B'nai B'rith Mitteilungen für Österreich* 26 (May 1926): 103–5.

——. *Gesammelte Werke, Chronologisch Geordnet*. Edited by Anna Freud, Edward Bibring, Willie Hoffer, Ernst Kris, and Otto Isakower, in collaboration with Marie Bonaparte. Vols. 1–17. London: Imago, 1940–52; vol. 18, Frankfurt am Main: S. Fischer Verlag, 1968.

——. *The Interpretation of Dreams*. Translated by James Strachey. New York: Avon, 1965.

——. *Jokes and their Relation to the Unconscious*. Translated and edited by James Strachey. New York: Norton, 1963.

——. *Der Mann Moses und die monotheistische Religion. Schriften über die Religion*. Frankfurt am Main: Fischer Taschenbuch Verlag, 1975.

——. *Moses and Monotheism*. Translated by Katherine Jones. New York: Vintage, 1955.

——. "Moses ein Ägypter." *Imago* 23, no. 1 (1937): 5–13.

——. "The *Moses* of Michelangelo." In *Character and Culture*, ed. Philip Rieff, 80–106. New York: Collier, 1963.

——. Statement to the B'nai B'rith Wien. *B'nai B'rith Mitteilungen für Österreich* 35 (November-December 1935): 193.

——. "The Uncanny." In *On Creativity and the Unconscious: Papers on the Psychology of Art, Literature, Love, and Religion*. Edited by Benjamin Nelson. New York: Harper and Row, 1979.

——. "Wenn Moses ein Ägypter war . . ." *Imago* 23, no. 4 (1937): 387–419.

Frieden, Ken. *Freud's Dream of Interpretation*. Albany: SUNY Press, 1990.

Fromm, Erich. *Sigmund Freud's Mission*. New York: Grove Press, 1959.

Gamwell, Lynn, and Richard Wells, eds. *Freud and Art: His Personal Collection of Antiquities.* London: The Freud Museum, 1989.

Gay, Peter. *Freud, Jews, and Other Germans. Masters and Victims in Modernist Culture.* New York: Oxford University Press, 1978.

——. *Freud: A Life for Our Time.* New York: Norton, 1988.

——. *A Godless Jew. Freud, Atheism, and the Making of Psychoanalysis.* New Haven: Yale University Press, 1987.

——. "Six Names in Search of an Interpretation." *Hebrew Union College Annual* 53 (1982): 295–307.

Gedo, John E., and Ernest Wolf. "Freud's *Novelas Exemplares*," *Psychological Issues* 9, nos. 2–3 (1976): 88.

Gedo, John E., and Ernest Wolf. "The 'Ich.' Letters." *Psychological Issues* 9, nos. 2–3 (1976): 75.

Geiger, Abraham. *Judaism and Its History.* Lanham, Md.: University Press of America, 1985.

Gilman, Sander L. *Jewish Self-Hatred. Anti-Semitism and the Hidden Language of the Jews.* Baltimore: Johns Hopkins University Press, 1986.

Goldhammer, Leo. "Herzl and Freud." In *Herzl Yearbook,* 194–96. New York, 1958.

——. "Theodor Herzl and Sigmund Freud: Traume." In *Theodor Herzl Jahrbuch,* ed. Tulo Nussenblatt, 266–68. Wien: Victor Glanz, 1937.

Gordis, Robert. "The Two Faces of Freud." *Judaism* 24 (1977): 192–200.

Graf, Max. "Reminiscences of Professor Sigmund Freud." *Psychoanalytic Quarterly* 11 (1942): 465–76.

Graupe, Heinz Moshe. *The Rise of Modern Judaism: An Intellectual History of German Jewry 1650–1942.* Translated by John Robinson. Huntington, N.Y.: R. E. Krieger, 1978.

Grinstein, Alexander. *On Sigmund Freud's Dreams.* Detroit: Wayne State University Press, 1968.

——. *Sigmund Freud's Writings: A Comprehensive Bibliography.* New York: International Universities Press, 1977.

Grollman, E. A. *Judaism in Sigmund Freud's World.* New York: Bloch, 1965.

Grunfeld, Fredric V. *Prophets without Honor. A Background to Freud, Kafka, Einstein, and their World.* New York: McGraw-Hill, 1980.

Grusd, Edward E. *B'nai B'rith. The Story of a Covenant.* New York: Appleton-Century, 1966.

Gutzkow, Karl. *Uriel Acosta: A Tragedy in Five Acts.* Translated by M. M. New York: M. Ellinger, 1860.

Hale, Nathan G., ed. *James Jackson Putnam and Psychoanalysis: Letters between Putnam and Sigmund Freud, Ernest Jones, William James, Sandor Ferenczi, and Morton Prince, 1877–1917.* Cambridge: Harvard University Press, 1971.

Handelman, Susan A. *The Slayers of Moses: The Emergence of Rabbinic Interpretation in Modern Literary Theory*. Albany: SUNY Press, 1982.

Hartman, Geoffrey H., and Sanford Budick, eds. *Midrash and Literature*. New Haven: Yale University Press, 1986.

The Hebrew University, Jerusalem, Inauguration. April 1, 1925. Hebrew University, 1925.

Heine, Heinrich. "Der Rabbi von Bacherach. Ein Fragment." In *Werke*, Band 2. Wiesbaden: R. Lowit, n.d.

——. *Heine's Prose and Poetry*. Translated by Margaret Armour. London: J. M. Dent, 1934.

Heller, Judith Bernays. "Freud's Mother and Father: A Memoir." *Commentary* 21, no. 5 (May 1956): 418–21.

Hes, Josef Philip. "A Note on an As Yet Unpublished Letter by Sigmund Freud." *Jewish Social Studies* 48 (1986): 321–24.

Hobman, J. B., ed. *David Eder. Memoirs of a Modern Pioneer*. London: Victor Gollancz, 1945.

Hutton, Christopher. "Freud and the Family Drama of Yiddish." In *Studies in Yiddish Linguistics*, ed. Paul Wexler, 9–22. Tübingen: Max Niemayer, 1990.

Huxley, T. H. "Nature: Aphorisms by Goethe." In *Nature* 1 (4 November 1869).

Ibsen, Henrik. *An Enemy of the People*. In *Six Plays by Henrik Ibsen*, trans. Eva Le Gallienne, 67–94. New York: Modern Library, 1957.

Jaffe, Samuel. "Freud as Rhetorician: *Elocutio* and the Dream-Work." *Rhetorik. Ein internationales Jahrbuch* 1 (1980): 42–69.

——. "Freud's Nathan Letter." Unpublished paper presented at the Psychoanalytic Workshop, The University of Chicago, 4 April 1988.

Janik, A., and S. Toulmin. *Wittgenstein's Vienna*. London: Weidenfeld and Nicholson, 1973.

Jones, Ernest. *The Life and Work of Sigmund Freud*. 3 vols. London: Hogarth Press, 1953, 1955, 1957.

Josephus. *The Jewish War*. Translated by H. St. J. Thackeray. New York: Putnam's Sons, 1928.

Jung, Carl Gustav. *Memories, Dreams, and Reflections*. Edited by Aniela Jaffe. Translated by Richard Winston and Clara Winston. New York: Vintage, 1965.

Kepnes, Steven D. "Freud and Judaism: The Path to Rapprochement." *Listening: Journal of Religion and Culture* 20, no. 3 (Fall 1985): 230–43.

Kiell, Norman. *Freud without Hindsight: Reviews of His Work (1893–1939)*. Translated by Vladimir Rus and Denise Boneau. Madison, Conn.: International Universities Press, 1988.

Klein, Dennis. *Jewish Origins of the Psychoanalytic Movement*. 2d ed. Chicago: University of Chicago Press, 1985.

Klingsberg, Reuben, ed. *Freudiana. From the Collections of the Jewish National and University Library*. Jerusalem, 1973.

Knöpfmacher, Hugo. "Sigmund Freud and B'nai B'rith." *Journal of the American Psychoanalytic Association* 27 (1979): 441–49.

——. "Sigmund Freud in High School." *American Imago* 36 (1979): 287–99.

Koret, Reuven. "The Pious Fraud: Freud and Joseph, Mann and Moses." *Response* 15, no. 1 (Winter-Spring, 1986): 3–14.

Krüll, Marianne. *Freud and his Father*. Translated by Arnold J. Pomerans. New York: Norton, 1986.

Kugel, James. "Two Interpretations of Midrash." *Prooftexts* 3 (1983): 131–55.

Kushner, Martin D. *Freud—A Man Obsessed*. Philadelphia: Dorrance and Co., 1967.

Leibowitz, Yeshayahu. "Commandments." In *Contemporary Jewish Religious Thought: Original Essays on Critical Concepts, Movements, and Beliefs*. Arthur Cohen and Paul Mendes-Flohr, eds. New York: Scribner, 1987.

Lessing, Gotthold Ephraim. "The Education of the Human Race." In *Lessing's Theological Writings*, trans. Henry Chadwick, 82–98. Stanford, Calif.: Stanford University Press, 1957.

——. *Nathan the Wise. A Dramatic Poem in Five Acts*. Translated by Bayard Quincy Morgan. New York: Frederick Ungar Press, 1955.

Levenson, Jon. *The Universal Horizon of Biblical Particularism*. New York: American Jewish Committee, Institute of Human Relations, 1985.

Lifton, Robert J. "Discussion of Martin S. Bergmann's Paper." In *Judaism and Psychoanalysis*, ed. Martimer Ostow, 152–55. New York: Ktav, 1982.

Liddell, Henry George, and Robert Scott. *A Greek-English Lexicon*. Rev. ed. Oxford: Clarendon Presss, 1925–40.

Lowenberg, Peter. "A Hidden Zionist Theme in Freud's 'My Son the Myops . . . Dream." *Journal of the History of Ideas* 31 (1970): 129–132.

Lowenstein, R. M. "Sigmund Freud as a Jew: A Study in Ambivalence and Courage." *Journal of the History of the Behavioral Sciences* 7 (1971): 36369.

Masson, Jeffrey M. *The Complete Letters of Sigmund Freud to Wilhelm Fliess, 1887–1904*. Translated and edited by Jeffrey M. Masson. Cambridge: Harvard University Press, 1985.

McGoldrick, Monica, and Randy Gerson. *Genograms in Family Assessment*. New York: Norton, 1985.

McGrath, William J. *Freud's Discovery of Psychoanalysis: The Politics of Hysteria*. Ithaca: Cornell University Press, 1986.

McGuire, William, ed. *The Freud/Jung Letters: The Correspondence between Sigmund Freud and C. G. Jung*. Translated by Ralph Manheim and R. F. C. Hull. London: Hogarth Press and Routledge and Kegan Paul, 1974.

McGuire, William, and Wolfgang Sauerländer, eds. *Briefwechsel: Sigmund Freud, C. G. Jung*. Frankfurt am Main: S. Fischer Verlag, 1974.

Meitlis, Jacob. 'The Last Days of Sigmund Freud." *The Jewish Frontier*, September 1951, 20–22.

Mendelssohn, Moses. *Jerusalem, or on Religious Power and Judaism.* Translated by Allan Arkush. Introduction and commentary by Alexander Altmann. Hanover and London: University Press of New England, 1983.

Mendes-Flohr, Paul, *A Land of Two Rivers. The German Jewish Vision of a New Babylon.* New Haven: Yale University Press. Forthcoming.

Mesher, David R. "Rabbinical References in *Daniel Deronda*.." *Notes and Queries* 222 (October 1977): 407–9.

Meyer, Michael A. *Response to Modernity. A History of the Reform Movement in Judaism.*

Milgrom, Jacob, ed. *The JPS Torah Commentary. Numbers.* Philadelpha and New York: Jewish Publication Society, 1990.

Miller, Jonathan, ed. *Freud: The Man, His World, His Influence.* London: Weidenfeld and Nicolson, 1972.

Miller, Justin. "Interpretations of Freud's Jewishness, 1924–1974." *Journal of the History of Behavioral Sciences* 17 (1981): 357–74.

Molnar, Michael, ed. and trans. *The Diary of Sigmund Freud, 1929–1939. A Record of the Final Decade.* London: The Freud Museum. New York: Charles Scribner's Sons, 1992.

Mosse, George. *German Jews Beyond Judaism.* Bloomington: Indiana University Press, 1985.

Nelson, Benjamin, ed. *Freud and the Twentieth Century.* London: Allen and Unwin, 1958.

Niederland, William G., and Jacob Shatzky. "Four Unpublished Letters of Freud." *Psychoanalytic Quarterly* 2 (1956): 147–54.

Novak, William, and Moshe Waldoks. *The Big Book of Jewish Humor.* New York: Basic Books, 1985.

O'Brien, Conor Cruise. *The Siege: The Saga of Israel and Zionism.* New York: Simon and Schuster, 1986.

Öhlschlegel, Lydia. "Regarding Freud's Book on 'Moses'." *The Psychoanalytic Review* 30 (1943): 67–77.

Oring, Elliott. *The Jokes of Sigmund Frreud. A Study in Humor and Jewish Identity.* Philadelphia: University of Pennsylvania Press, 1984.

Ostow, Mortimer, ed. "Discussion of Martin S. Bergmann's Paper." In *Judaism and Psychoanalysis*, ed. Mortimer Ostow, 143–51. New York: Ktav, 1982.

——, ed. *Judaism and Psychoanalysis.* New York: Ktav, 1982.

——. "Sigmund and Jakob Freud and the Philippsohn Bible (With an Analysis of the Birthday Inscription)." *International Review of Psychoanalysis* 16 (1989): 483–92.

Partington, Angela, ed. *The Oxford Dictionary of Quotations.* 4th ed. Oxford: Oxford University Press, 1992.

Pawel, Ernst. *The Labyrinth of Exile. A Life of Theodor Herzl.* New York: Farrar, Straus, and Giroux, 1989.

Pfeiffer, Ernst, ed. *Sigmund Freud and Lou Andreas-Salome Letters.* Translated by Elaine Robson-Scott and William Robson-Scott. New York: Norton, 1985.

Pfister, Oskar. "Die Entwicklung des Apostel Paulus. Ein religionsgeschichtliche und psychologische Skizze." *Imago* 6 (1920): 243–90.

——. *Psychoanalysis in the Service of Education.* London: Henry Kimpton, 1922.

Pfrimmer, Theo. *Freud, Lecteur de la Bible.* Paris: Presses Universitaires de France, 1982.

Plaut, W. Gunther. *The Rise of Reform Judaism: A Sourcebook of its European Origins.* New York: World Union for Progressive Judaism, 1963.

Puner, Helen. *Freud: His Life and Mind.* New York: Grosset and Dunlap, 1947.

Rainey, Reuben M. "Freud as a Student of Religion: Perspectives on the Background and Development of his Thought." *AAR Dissertation Series,* no. 7. Missoula, Mont.: Scholars Press, 1975.

Rank, Otto. *Der Mythus von der Geburt des Helden.* Wien: Victor Glanz, 1909.

——. *The Myth of the Birth of the Hero.* Translated by F. Robbins and S. E. Jelliffe. New York: Robert Brunner, 1952.

Reik, Theodor. "Freud and Jewish Wit." *Psychoanalysis* 2 (1954): 12–20.

——. *From Thirty Years with Freud.* Translated by Richard Winston. New York: International Universities Press, 1940.

——. *Jewish Wit.* New York: Gamut Press, 1962.

——. *The Search Within. The Inner Experience of a Psychoanalyst.* New York: J. Aronson, 1974.

——. "Sigmund Freud." In *Jewish Heritage Reader.* Edited by Lily Edelman. New York: Taplinger, 1965.

Rieff, Philip. *Freud. The Mind of the Moralist.* New York: Viking, 1959.

Rice, Emanuel. *Freud and Moses: The Long Journey Home.* Albany: SUNY Press, 1990.

Ricoeur, Paul. *Freud and Philosophy: An Essay on Interpretation.* Translated by Denis Savage. New Haven and London: Yale University Press, 1970.

Roazen, Paul. *Brother Animal: The Story of Freud and Tausk.* New York: Alfred A. Knopf, 1969.

——. *Freud and his Followers.* New York: Knopf, 1975.

Roback, A. A. *Freudiana.* Cambridge, Mass.: Sci-Art Publishers, 1957.

——. *Jewish Influence in Modern Thought.* Cambridge, Mass.: Sci-Art Publishers, 1929.

Robert, Marthe. *From Oedipus to Moses: Freud's Jewish Identity.* Translated by Ralph Manheim. New York: Doubleday, 1976.

——. *The Psychoanalytic Revolution: Sigmund Freud's Life and Achievement.*

Translated by Kenneth Morgan. New York: Harcourt, Brace, and World, 1966.

Roith, Estelle. *The Riddle of Freud. Jewish Influence on his Theory of Female Sexuality.* London and New York: Tavistock Publications, 1987.

Rolland, Romain. *Prophets of the New India.* New York: Boni, 1930.

Rosen, Paul L. "Freud on Jewish Identity, Ethnicity, and Politics." *Jerusalem Quarterly* 40 (1986): 119–44.

Rosenbaum, Milton, and A. M. Silbermann. *Chumash with Targum Onkelos, Haphtaroth and Rashi' Commentary: Shemoth.* Jerusalem: The Silbermann Family, 1985.

Rosenbaum, Milton. "Freud-Eitingon-Magnes Correspondence. Psychoanalysis at the Hebrew University." *Journal of the American Psychoanalytic Association* 2, no. 2 (1954): 311–17.

Rosmarin, Trude Weiss. *The Hebrew Moses: An Answer to Sigmund Freud.* New York: The Jewish Book Club, 1939.

Rothman, Stanley, and Phillip Isenberg. "Freud and Jewish Marginality." *Encounter* 43, no. 6 (1974): 46–54.

Rothman, Stanley, and Phillip Isenberg. "Sigmund Freud and the Politics of Marginality." *Central European History* 7 (1974): 58–78.

Rozenblit, Marsha L. *The Jews of Vienna, 1867–1914: Assimilation and Identity.* Albany: State University of New York Press, 1983.

Ruitenbeek, Henrik., ed. *Freud as We Knew Him.* Detroit: Wayne State University Press, 1973.

Sachs, Hanns. *Freud: Master and Friend.* Cambridge: Harvard University Press, 1946.

Sarna, Jonathan. Untitled article in *Moment* 17, no. 5 (October 1992): 18.

Schlesinger, Kurt. "Jewish Humor as Jewish Identity." *International Review of Psychoanalysis* 6 (1979): 317–29.

Schnitzler, Henry. "Sigmund Freud: Briefe an Arthur Schnitzler." *Die Neue Rundschau* 66 (1955): 95–106.

Schönwald, Richard L. *Freud: The Man and His Mind 1856–1956.* New York: Alfred A. Knopf, 1956.

Schorske, Carl E. *Fin-de-Siècle Vienna: Politics and Culture.* New York: Alfred A. Knopf, 1980.

——. "Politics and Patricide in Freud's *Interpretation of Dreams.*" *American Historical Review* 78:328–47. Reprinted in *Fin-de-Siècle Vienna,* ed. Carl E. Schorske, 181–207. New York: Vintage, 1981.

Schultz, Duane. *Intimate Friends, Dangerous Rivals. The Turbulent Relationship between Freud and Jung.* Los Angeles: Jeremy P. Tarcher, 1990.

Schur, Max. *Freud: Living and Dying.* New York: International Universities Press, 1972.

Shengold, Leonard. "Freud and Joseph." In *Freud and His Self-Analysis,* ed. Mark Kanzer and Jules Glenn, 67–86. New York: Jason Aronson, 1979.

——. "A Parapraxis of Freud's in Relation to Karl Abraham." *American Imago* 29, no. 2 (1972): 123–59.

Simon, Ernst. "Freud and Moses." *Entscheidung zum Judentum. Essays and Vorträge.* Frankfurt am Main: Suhrkamp, 1980.

——. "Sigmund Freud, the Jew." *Leo Baeck Institute of Jews from Germany Yearbook* 2 (1957): 270–305.

Stanescu, Heinz. "Young Freud's Letters to his Rumanian Friend, Silberstein." *The Israel Annals of Psychiatry and Related Disciplines* 9, no. 3 (December 1971): 195–207.

——. "Unbekannte Briefe des jungen Sigmund Freud an einen rumänischen Freund." *Neue Literatur, Zeitschrift des Schriftstellerverbandes der RFD* 16, no. 3 (June 1965): 123–29.

Sterba, Richard. "The Humanistic Wellsprings of Psychoanalysis." *Psychoanalytic Quarterly* 43 (April 1974): 167–76.

Stern, David. "The Ego and the Yid." *The New Republic,* 21 September 1992, 43–49.

Sulloway, Frank J. *Freud, Biologist of the Mind: Beyond the Psychoanalytic Legend.* New York: Basic Books, 1979.

Terence. *The Self-Tormentor.* Translated by John Sargeaunt. New York: G. P. Putnam's Sons, 1926.

Trosman, Harry. "Freud's Cultural Background." *The Annual of Psychoanalysis* 1 (1973): 318–35.

——. *Freud and the Imaginative World.* Hillsdale, N.J.: Analytic Press, 1985.

Trosman, Harry, and Roger Dennis Simmons. "The Freud Library." *American Psychoanalytic Journal* 21 (1973): 646–87.

Van Herik, Judith. *Freud on Femininity and Faith.* Berkeley: University of California Press, 1982.

Velikovsky, Immanuel. "The Dreams Freud Dreamed." *Psychoanalytic Review* 30 (1941): 487–511.

Viereck, George Sylvester. *Glimpses of the Great.* London: Duckworth, 1930.

Viereck, George S., and Paul Eldridge. *My First Two Thousand Years: The Autobiography of the Wandering Jew.* New York: Macaulay Co., 1928.

Vitz, Paul C. *Sigmund Freud's Christian Unconscious.* New York: Guilford Press, 1988.

Vogel, Leon. "Freud and Judaism: An Analysis in the Light of his Correspondence." *Judaism* 24 (1977): 181–93.

Wallace, Edwin R. "Freud and Anthropology: A History and Reappraisal." *Psychological Issues.* Monograph 55. New York: International Universities Press, 1983.

——. "The Psychodynamic Determinants of *Moses and Monotheism.*" *Psychiatry* 40 (1977): 79–87.

Weiner, Max, ed. *Abraham Geiger and Liberal Judaism: The Challenge of the 19th Century.* Translated by E. J. Schlochauer. Philadelphia: Jewish Publication Society, 1962.

Wistrich, Robert S. "The Jewish Identity of Sigmund Freud." *Jewish Quarterly* 34, no. 3 (1987): 47–55.

——. *The Jews of Vienna in the Age of Franz Joseph.* Oxford: Oxford University Press, 1989.

Wittels, Fritz. *Freud and His Time.* New York: Liveright, 1931.

——. *Sigmund Freud: His Personality, His Teaching, His School.* New York, 1924.

Wollheim, Richard. *Sigmund Freud.* New York: Viking, 1971.

Wortis, Joseph. *Fragments of an Analysis with Freud.* New York: McGraw-Hill, 1975.

Yahuda, A. S. "Sigmund Freud on Moses and his Torah." *Bitzaron* 1 (1946): 455–68; 2, 6–17, 121–34.

Yerushalmi, Yosef Hayim. "Freud on the 'Historical Novel': From the Manuscript Draft (1934) of *Moses and Monotheism,*" *Interntional Journal of Psycho-Analysis* 70 (1989): 375–95.

——. *Freud's Moses: Judaism Terminable and Interminable.* New Haven: Yale University Press, 1991.

Young-Bruehl, Elisabeth. *Anna Freud: A Biography.* New York: Summit, 1988.

Zilboorg, Gregory. *Sigmund Freud: His Exploration of the Mind of Man.* New York: Scribner, 1951.

Zweig, Arnold. *Bilanz der deutschen Judenheit, 1933: Die Wahrheit über die deutschen Juden.* Amsterdam: Querido Verlag, 1934.

——. *Caliban oder Politik und Leidenschaft, Versuch über die menschlichen Gruppenaffekte, dargestellt am Antisemitismus.* Potsdam: Gustav Kiepenheurer Verlag, 1927.

——. *Insulted and Exiled: The Truth about the German Jews.* London: John Miles Publishers, 1937.

ADDENDUM
Freud's Kiddush Cups

As I was preparing the index for this book, Freud's letter to Marie Bonaparte, written from his London exile and containing a discussion of his kiddush cups, came to my attention (Lawrence Douglas and Alexander George, "Freud's Phonographic Memory and the Case of the Missing Kiddush Cups," *Tikkun* 9, no. 1 [January/February 1994]: 74–76, 90–91). In the letter, Freud says that he received the kiddush cups as a gift in 1917 from the wife of the rabbi of Vienna's largest Temple, at a reception held in his honor following the conclusion of his introductory lectures to psychoanalysis delivered at the University of Vienna. Thus, they were not the family kiddush cups, as I had assumed in this book.

Freud's discussion concerns his analysis of his motivations for removing the kiddush cups from the table and putting them out of sight in a drawer, when Edmund Engelman was photographing the apartment. Freud conjectures at first that he was "struck by the fact that the Jewish artifacts looked out of place surrounded by the relics of their biblical oppressors." At the time, Freud was just putting the finishing touches on *Moses and Monotheism,* and he considers the possibility that he might have been sensitive to Jewish displeasure at the conjunction in Engelman's photographs. Freud rejects this interpretation, however, preferring an oedipal explanation, in which the cups—"rounded, stemmed vessels from which blessed nourishment is drunk"—represent his mother's breasts. Freud thinks he hid the cups to protect his possessing the mother from the punitive father.

From Freud's description of the kiddush cups, it seems likely, combined with the evidence presented in this book, that even if these cups were not those with which Jakob Freud "made kiddush," nevertheless, Freud had tasted his father's kiddush in his youth, mingled with his mother's festive food. I suggest that in hiding the kiddush cups in a drawer, preventing them from being photographed for posterity, Freud was protecting not only his oedipal desire for his mother, but also his renewed attachment to *Judentum*, forged in the work lying on his desk at the time, *Moses and Monotheism*. As he told Jones in 1926, Jewishness (like, too, I suggest, his unanalyzed relationship with his mother) is his "private affair" and "inessential for psychoanalysis." Freud wanted to be remembered for posterity with a humanist face, but he has left us enough clues to enable us to disclose his Jewish heart hidden from view.

General Index

Index of Sigmund Freud's Letters